THE
LADY OF
FASHION

THE LIFE AND THE THEATRE
OF ANNA CORA MOWATT

BY

Eric Wollencott Barnes

Charles Scribner's Sons,
New York

For Peggy

Acknowledgments

I should like to express my thanks to all those who have so generously given their time, their expert knowledge and their good will to assist me in writing this book. The credit due my wife is incalculable for without her assistance in my research, her work in preparing the manuscript, and her never-failing encouragement this story would still be a project for the future. I am also under obligation of a special sort to my friend Charles Coleman Sellers who has given me valuable data, technical advice, and detailed and painstaking criticism all along the way. Particular thanks go to the Mount Vernon Ladies Association of the Union for allowing me access to its archives, and to Miss Irene Warren, librarian of the Association, for much helpful advice; to Dr. Marius Blesi and the Graduate Faculty of the University of Virginia for permission to quote from Dr. Blesi's unpublished dissertation, *The Life and Letters of Anna Cora Mowatt;* and to Mrs. Frederick J. McCarthy for generously allowing me to use material from the notes for her master's thesis (University of Maryland), *Anna Cora Mowatt and Her American Audience.* For professional assistance and many friendly services I am grateful to Dr. Henry W. Wells, of the Brander Matthews Dramatic Museum, Columbia University; Miss Mary Reardon, of the Theatre Collection, Houghton Library, Harvard University; Miss May Davenport Seymour, of the Theatre Section, Museum of the City of New York; Mrs. Ralph Catterall, of the Valentine Museum, Richmond, Virginia; Mr. Zoltan Hraszti, Rare Book Section, the Boston Public Library; Mr. George N. Williams II, the Historical Society of Pennsylvania; Mr. Pat Carroll, librarian of The Players Club; and to staff members of the British Museum, the Library of Congress, the New York Public Library, the Historical Society of Pennsylvania, the New-York Historical Society, the Missouri Historical Society, the New York State Library, the library of Russell Sage College, and the library of Dickinson College.

I am indebted to my mother, Mrs. William G. Barnes, for special information on Anna Cora's appearance in Memphis; to Mrs. Laurence McKinney for many apt suggestions on the handling of certain material in the text; and to Mrs. Marian H. Mowatt for turning over to me the memorandum of Professor Williston mentioned in the notes to Chapter Twenty. To Mr. and Mrs. Dwight Marvin is due my special gratitude, not only for helpful criticism but for having provided the happy surroundings in which a good deal of the book was written.

Permission to quote letters and other manuscript material has been kindly granted by: the Library of Congress; the Theatre Collection, Houghton Library, Harvard University; the Boston Public Library; the Historical Society of Pennsylvania; the New York Public Library; the Brander Matthews Dramatic Museum, Columbia University; and Miss May Davenport Seymour.

As much as possible I have tried to let Anna Cora Mowatt tell her own story. Passages in quotation marks, unless otherwise indicated, are taken from THE AUTOBIOGRAPHY OF AN ACTRESS, Anna Cora's record of her life through May, 1853. Dialogue is given as reported either by Anna Cora or by other witnesses of the events and situations in which it figures. A detailed account of the materials on which this narrative is based will be found at the back of the book.

For kind and expert assistance in seeing the book through the final phase of preparation, I wish to thank Mr. J. G. E. Hopkins of Charles Scribner's Sons, New York, and Mr. B. D. Farrer of Secker and Warburg, London.

E. W. B.

Table of Contents

CONTENTS

List of Illustrations

Prologue

The Park Theatre on the evening of June 6, 1845, presented a spectacle unparalleled in the history of that venerable institution. From pit to dome the house was packed—not with the raucous miscellany that usually composed a New York theatre audience in those days, but with the beauty and fashion and wealth of highest society. Ladies in full décolletage, in diamonds and plumes, and gentlemen in frilled shirts and brocaded waistcoats filled pit, boxes and galleries to overflowing. Such a glittering assemblage had never before been seen in a New York theatre.

The evening was memorable also for the heat. It still rises in faint waves from yellowed newspaper clippings and the faded pages of diaries describing the occasion. Even on the Battery not a breath of air stirred, while within the theatre the frantic agitation of lace and mother-of-pearl fans merely sent the temperature higher. Only the cupids on Manager Simpson's newly decorated ceiling were oblivious to the torrid atmosphere, and more than one upward glance from the auditorium showed envy of their happy position in the empyrean, and their sensible garb of clouds. But there was nothing anyone could do about it. Long before the curtain rose, curls were coming out and collars wilting as perspiration poured from the faces of stately dowagers, elegant maidens, beaux, merchant princes and statesmen.

Yet neither heat nor the discomfort of the Park's hard moreen-covered seats diminished in any way the enthusiasm of the audience as it waited with mounting excitement for the performance to begin. For everyone in the theatre, as well as hundreds who had failed to get in, knew that what was about to take place was of historic importance.

The attraction which had brought together this dazzling throng was the debut of a new actress—Mrs. Anna Cora Mowatt. As a rule such occurrences created no great stir in the city, though some deluded managers still believed that the announcement "first time on any stage" could stimulate flagging box-office receipts. But this particular first appearance had a special significance because of the lady involved. Mrs. Mowatt had already attracted wide attention. She was known as the writer of lively articles for *Godey's* and *Graham's* and other magazines; as the composer of touching verses for the annuals; as an author with two entertaining novels to her credit; and most recently as the creator of *Fashion*, an epoch-making play. But this was not all. Mrs. Mowatt's talents had carried her in other directions. Four years ago she had achieved success—and notoriety—by appearing alone on a public platform as a reader of poetry, something no woman, at least in America, had ever done before. The venture had caused considerable lifting of eyebrows at the time. But this reaction was as nothing compared to the effect created by the announcement that Mrs. Mowatt was about to become an actress. For the public and for her extensive circle of acquaintances, the fact that a respectable married woman of mature years —Mrs. Mowatt was twenty-six—should elect to go on the stage professionally was something the imagination could scarcely grasp. Yet the truly sensational aspect of this present instance of her hardihood has not been mentioned. Mrs. Mowatt was not only a woman venturing into ways at which most tenderly bred females of the period shuddered. She was a lady. Furthermore she was a lady of position. She came in fact from the best and oldest New York society. As the daughter of Samuel Ogden she had been nourished in the very bosom of the Knickerbocracy, as N. P. Willis termed it. Her antecedents were of the highest Revolutionary and Federalist respectability. Now she was about to ally herself with a world in which social position was meaningless, where (so one heard) even the elemental proprieties were non-existent. Small wonder that the sudden announcement in the papers that Mrs. Mowatt would appear at the Park Theatre in the stellar role of Bulwer's *Lady of Lyons* should have sent a shock through New York's Upper-Tendom. Yet this was almost at once replaced by a feeling of delightful titillation. Though Anna Mowatt's newest exploit threatened to shake the order of things to the very foundations, the spectacle would be well worth seeing. With this idea Society stampeded the box-office of the Park.

Five minutes after the curtain had risen on the first act of *The Lady of Lyons,* all these things were forgotten. Even those members of the audience who had witnessed half a dozen performances of the already-hackneyed play were lost in the enchantment of the new actress as she recreated Bulwer's heroine. By the end of the act there was no mistaking the audience's reaction. The applause was not for a plucky beginner struggling against great odds; it was the tumultuous expression of thrilled delight. By the middle of the third act, where the climactic emotional scene of the play occurs, it was evident that the débutante was an artist of high order. Without experience save for a few amateur performances, without training so far as anyone knew, and with only two rehearsals, Anna Cora Mowatt had demonstrated the powers of a veteran. In a part which the finest actresses of the time regarded as a supreme test of ability, this newcomer suddenly appeared as a rival to them all.

At the final curtain the demonstration was overwhelming. A few of the more conservative judges compared it with the ovation which had greeted Fanny Kemble's first appearance on the New York stage, or with the welcome given Forrest upon his return from England. But in the minds of the majority of those present at the Park that evening, Anna Mowatt's triumph was the most complete which the American stage had ever witnessed. Old men recalling the occasion forty or fifty years later could still hear the shouts thundering in their ears.

Thus began one of the most extraordinary careers in the annals of the American theatre. Indeed, in the entire history of the stage there is perhaps no other instance of an actress starting at the top and maintaining that position throughout her professional life. In Anna Mowatt's case this life was brief. After eight years of unqualified success she turned her back to that public upon which she had (in the words of Edgar Allen Poe) "undoubtedly wrought a deeper impression . . . than any one of her sex in America." In a generation she was all but forgotten, except as the author of the one durable American play written before the middle of the nineteenth century. Yet her effects on the theatre were permanent and far-reaching. After 1850 the actor ceased to be regarded as a social and moral vagabond, and the drama as one of the arts of the devil. By that time the American theatre was well on the way to becoming respectable. This was largely the doing of Anna Cora Mowatt, who in addition to genius possessed boundless courage, an uncompromising moral sense, and—superlatively—what the modern world calls glamor.

Such a personality, in such an age, must have had a "history." In the attempt to reconstruct that history, some light may be thrown on odd facets of our great-grandfathers' times, particularly on the little-known theatre of their day. But this is of secondary importance. The real motive for the story is the lady herself.

CHAPTER ONE

The Exiles' Return

Anna Cora Ogden's life by the time she was sixteen had already assumed the outlines of one of those melodramatic romances in which she was later to achieve fame. All major elements were there: reversal of fortune, exile in a remote land, disaster at sea, clandestine marriage, lingering illness. And the events were strung together with the same careless disregard for plausibility as in a plot by Bulwer-Lytton or Sheridan Knowles.

Farther in the background there was also action and color. Samuel Gouverneur Ogden, Anna's father, belonged to a family which had figured in Colonial and Revolutionary history and was allied, by blood or marriage, with half a dozen of the great patrician names of New York and New Jersey. Samuel's father was that renowned cleric the Reverend Doctor Uzal Ogden, whose career very nearly disrupted the early organization of the Protestant Episcopal Church in America. Early in his ministry the Reverend Uzal developed heretical views in the matter of the sacraments which almost resulted in dismissal from his parish. Yet his popularity was so great that he was elected the first

I

Episcopal Bishop of New Jersey—an election which the General Convention of the Church in its wisdom did not see fit to ratify. Eventually, the highly independent Dr. Ogden left the Episcopal Church to become a Presbyterian, and by the end of his life had become so tolerant as to show sympathy for the Methodists. Anna Cora never saw the Reverend Uzal, but his tendencies toward heterodoxy were transmitted to his granddaughter. She inherited other traits from him, including a compelling manner in argument, a highly critical spirit, a sense of humor, a profound need for faith and a susceptibility to throat infections.

Samuel Gouverneur Ogden, the Reverend Uzal's eldest son, showed some of the latter's revolutionary tendencies, but his chief talent was for making money—and occasionally losing it. At fourteen, he was articled as a clerk to the New York mercantile establishment of Gouverneur and Kemble. By the time he was twenty he had set up for himself, and when he was married in 1803 he was the proprietor of a flourishing import-export business and owner of four of the finest ships in the American-European trade. Each of these vessels mounted fifteen guns—a precautionary measure against the Barbary pirates—and when Samuel's eldest son was born (all four ships being then in New York harbor), the new arrival was greeted with a sixty-gun salute.

Eliza Lewis, Samuel's first wife and the mother of Anna Cora, was the granddaughter of Francis Lewis, a signer of the Declaration of Independence; so on this side, too, Anna Cora was well-rooted in American history. The first Mrs. Ogden was a gentle creature whose rôle in life was that of most nineteenth-century women. Once married, she devoted herself to the producing and care of children. She was the mother of fourteen, of whom Anna Cora was the ninth. Despite evidences of proper submissiveness to her husband, Mrs. Ogden seems to have exercised some determination as regards her personal affairs. At a fairly early point in her married life she decided that she would live to the age of fifty. For eight years after the birth of her last child she lingered with her family—who adored her—and then, a few days from her fiftieth birthday, she quietly died.

Although the domestic affairs of Samuel Ogden were marked by regular expansion, his business career had its ups and downs. In 1806 he fell in with the South American adventurer-hero, Francisco de Miranda. This romantic character had played a spectacular if unimportant rôle in the French Revolution, and was now in America seeking new outlets for his energy. His specific scheme was to liberate his native Venezuela from Spain. In this project he received some encouragement (or at least he interpreted it as such) from President Jefferson and other high American officials, and accordingly he set about organizing a filibustering expedition into the Spanish Main. Through Colonel William Smith, the son-in-law of John Adams, he met Samuel Ogden. The latter, fired by the idea of liberating an oppressed people from the yoke of a decadent European monarch—and at the same time aware of the possibilities for extending his trade operations to Latin America—joined enthusiastically in Miranda's plan. He turned over to Miranda his finest ship, the *Leander*, and the sum of 40,000 pounds, which represented his entire personal fortune and all that he could borrow on his name.

The expedition consisted of the *Leander* and two smaller ships, with a complement of about 200 men. The assumption that this force would be a match for the Spanish power indicates the low esteem in which Spain was generally held at the time. But the assumption proved rash. The Spanish authorities, supposedly forewarned by Aaron Burr, who had his own designs in Latin America, were waiting for Miranda when he arrived at Caracas. The liberator was defeated; and though he managed to escape with his own life, he lost most of his men and all of Samuel Ogden's investment, including the ship *Leander*.

The affair created a big international noise. Since America was technically at peace with Spain, the activities of two American citizens in sponsoring an expedition against that nation's sovereign power could not be sanctioned without belying our peaceful intentions. Spain demanded that the culprits be punished.

3

Smith and Ogden were therefore brought to trial, an event which raised the feelings of republican and liberty-loving Americans to a high pitch. This undoubtedly had its effects on the final verdict; the defendants were acquitted. Smith and Ogden emerged from the ordeal not only with honor but with something of the aura of heroes. Their effort had been the first spark to the fuse which set off the series of revolutions leading to the independence of the Spanish-American colonies. Bolivar himself recognized the psychological value of the incident and later offered to reimburse Ogden for his losses. The record does not show that this offer was ever fulfilled.

If the Venezuelan fiasco left Samuel Ogden a ruined man, it did not impair his credit. Within a short time his ships were again unloading at New York docks and he had established important business connections abroad. He was the American agent for several large French exporters, and his firm had become the principal channel for the flow of Bordeaux wine into the United States. In fact his interests in France soon assumed such proportions that they could only be handled on the spot. Accordingly, in 1818 Ogden embarked with his family—which had increased without interruption—for Bordeaux. On September 12, 1819, nearly a year after the Ogdens had arrived in France, the brood of eight was augmented by a daughter, Anna Cora. This brought the balance to five boys and four girls— a most convenient division for the casting of plays when, a little later, the family began to indulge its passion for amateur theatricals.

When Anna Cora was a year old, Samuel Ogden, finding the house he had rented in Bordeaux somewhat cramped, purchased a beautiful little estate just outside the gates of the city. La Castagne was a self-contained property, with a small but elegant late Renaissance château of twenty-two rooms, vineyards, gardens, orchards, an aviary, livestock of every variety, and an assortment of picturesque peasant cottages complete with peasants. The whole establishment had great charm. For the young Ogdens it was paradise.

Here the family lived in quiet self-sufficiency. The children

4

spent most of their time out-of-doors in the gardens or meadows, or in the farmyard, which they found endlessly diverting. In the warm evenings they gathered on the long terrace which stretched before the château, on one side of which there was a drop of some twenty feet to the gardens below. Here the family would stroll up and down or sit on the marble benches talking over the events of the day, watching the distant landscape of vineyards and villages fade into the blue-green shadows of the twilight.

Behind the house a meadow sloped down to a grove of trees. In the center of this little wood, a carefully preserved *bosquet au naturel,* there was a clearing known as Calypso's Grotto. Here moss-covered marble benches arranged in a semi-circle formed a kind of Druid temple. In this secluded spot, from which one had only an occasional glimpse of blue sky through the interlaced branches above, the children gathered to tell stories and act in impromptu plays.

This early enthusiasm for the drama resulted naturally from the fact that the Ogden children, despite the range in ages, were a closely-knit group happiest when doing things together. Since they had to depend for amusement mainly on their own resources, play-acting formed a logical outlet for their energies. The pastime was enhanced by the taste for literature which all the children shared. They had all begun to read early, and in the well-stocked library of the château was food for the most insatiable literary appetite. In addition to the masterpieces of French literature, there was at hand a splendid collection of the English poets. As so often happened with our ancestors, because of the dearth of juvenile literature the tender mind was brought at once into contact with the classics. At an age when the modern child finds delight in the doings of animated trains and taxicabs, the little Ogdens were thrilling to *Phèdre* and *Macbeth,* with a liberal dash of Montaigne to quiet the nerves and develop principles. By the time she was ten, according to her own assertion, Anna Cora had read Shakespeare "many times over"—a statement which, in view of her precocious literary accomplishment, is easily credible.

The children's fondness for the drama was encouraged by their father, a great admirer of Talma who was then at the height of his fame, and a devotee of the Théâtre Français. In the *grande salle* of the Château de la Castagne Mr. Ogden had a small stage constructed, and throughout the winter this was the center of the children's life. Plays were constantly in process of preparation or performance. The senior Ogdens entertained frequently, and the parties invariably included a play by the children. We have no record of the guests' reactions to these exhibitions. For the children themselves they were an endless source of excitement.

In later life Anna Cora could recall only one of these occasions: that on which she made her début. "The play represented was Othello translated into French. My eldest sister enacted Desdemona; my eldest brother Othello; the second sister Emilia; the second brother Cassio, doubling the part with that of the uncle; the third brother Iago, doubling the part with that of the judge. The other brothers and sisters filled in the remaining characters. . . . A difficulty occurred about the judges in the trial scene. Our dramatic corps proved insufficient to furnish judges. To supply this vacancy, the four younger children were summoned, dressed in red gowns and white wigs, made to sit on high benches, and instructed to pay great attention and not to laugh. Of these children I was the youngest; and at four years old in the sedate and solemn character of a judge, upon a mimic stage, I made my first appearance in that profession of which it was the permission of divine Providence that I should one day in reality become a member."

When Anna Cora was six, the family returned to America. Samuel Ogden's affairs had prospered greatly, and he had gained a practical monopoly as representative of the great Bordeaux wine firms. He now felt that he must make America the center of his operations, a motive strengthened by his desire to bring up his children in his native country, to which he was ardently attached. However, most of the children looked forward to the return with misgivings; for even those who had not been born in France had become thoroughly Gallicized. As for Anna

Cora and her two younger sisters May and Emma (the latest additions to the throng), America was regarded as a foreign country. They did not even speak English, and the idea of exchanging their beautiful La Castagne for a wilderness infested by savage Indians—a notion acquired from their French neighbors —reduced them to tears.

For a few months after leaving La Castagne the family stayed in Bordeaux while final arrangements for the journey were completed. On September 17, 1826, they sailed for New York. Their ship, the *Brandt*, was a solid German craft and her master, Captain Steinauer, an experienced seaman. But in those days the Bay of Biscay was still a match for both ships and men. The vessel had scarcely moved out of the Gironde when she ran into nasty weather. Violent, contrary winds and high seas slowed her progress, so that at the end of two weeks she was still in the treacherous Bay. Suddenly, on September 30th, a violent gale descended on her. What happened was later set down by Charles, Anna Cora's eldest brother:

"At about half past six there was a terrible, deafening crash; the sound of which, breaking upon drowsy ears, still reverberates in my mind. The vessel had been struck on the larboard bow by a tremendous wave, which, crossing her from stem to stern, rent up everything, and completely swept our decks, whilst it threw the ship with her beam ends in the sea. The caboose, longboat, and water casks, cables and everything amidships, her bulwarks, and every particle of the saloon, were violently shattered and washed away, and the deck around the companionway and forecastle hatch completely torn up, making the whole ship a wreck indeed. The masts alone were uninjured. Fortunately she soon righted.

"My first thought was, of course, for my brothers, knowing that they had gone on deck; and as soon as possible, I rushed, half clad, up the companionway. Here a scene of desolation presented itself that I should in vain attempt to describe. The naked decks, with nothing but the masts standing, the rigging flying in every direction, the bulwarks destroyed, and presenting no barrier to the sea, which, with every roll of the vessel, washed over the deck and down into the cabin; then the waves, mountain high, and foaming with fury, that seemed every moment to threaten destruction; whilst the gusty blasts, howling through the rigging, were a fit dirge for the impending fate."

Reaching the top of the companionway, Charles looked about for some sign of the two younger boys. He dared not step on deck, for the wind would have swept him into the sea. Presently he saw, clinging with one hand to the rigging amidships and with the other drawing a line from the sea, the second mate of the vessel. In a moment he saw his brother Thomas, the younger of the missing boys, being hauled over the side of the ship. Seizing the youngster, the mate struggled with him across the deck towards Charles. As the latter grasped the almost lifeless form of the child, the mate pointed astern and shouted, "The other one is lost!" And indeed as Charles looked, he saw a faint speck on the crest of a receding billow, and a small hand clutching at the air. In a moment it was gone. That was the last glimpse of Gabriel.

It was clear what had happened. The two boys who were on deck at the instant when the ship had nearly capsized had been hurled into the water. When the vessel righted herself Gabriel was seen holding to a fragment of the jolly boat. The mate then tossed him a rope. The boy had let go of the boat to swim toward the line, which sank before he could seize it. When he turned back to the bit of wreckage, this too had been carried beyond his reach, while the ship herself, driven by the furious gale, was already far away.

Thomas, fortunately, had managed to seize a piece of the torn rigging as he was swept overboard. To this he had clung with a frantic grip and was eventually pulled back on deck by the mate. When he was placed in his older brother's arms, the boy's fingers were still cramped in a paroxysm of terror about the bit of line that had saved his life.

Staggering down the companionway with his burden, Charles at last reached the saloon where the rest of the family had collected. Anna Cora and her younger sister were clinging to their

mother who held the youngest of all, four-year-old May, in her
arms. Thrusting her at one of the older girls, the horrified
mother seized the dripping form of the half-drowned Thomas.
Then Charles told what had happened. Though every wave
sent a stream of water into the cabin, and the violent pitching
of the ship made it seem that the others would at any moment
join little Gabriel, Mrs. Ogden gave one loud cry, and then subsided into speechless grief. The children's reaction was the same.
The blow of their loss numbed the family to the sense of their
own danger, which was steadily increasing.

At nightfall the ship was struck astern by another gigantic
wave which stove in the deadlights and again deluged the cabin.
Several men were injured and the helmsman nearly killed at
the wheel. There seemed no likelihood that the ship could survive. Yet miraculously she did. Forty-eight hours later the
storm had abated and the sun shone again. The *Brandt* was a
shambles, but somehow temporary repairs were made and she put
about for the nearest European port.

On October 9th the *Brandt* limped into Le Havre. There
the Ogdens were met by the oldest boy, Samuel, who was at
the time located in Havre where he had a position in the office
of one of Mr. Ogden's business associates. Samuel came anxiously
on board, eager to learn what had happened. When he saw
further the state of the ship, his mother's grief-stricken expression, and noted the gap in the family group—no explanation
was necessary.

Six days later they embarked once more, this time on the
Queen Mab. Again it seemed as though the sea had some special
grudge against the family of Americans. The ship encountered
violent weather the whole voyage across, and it was forty days
before she made New York harbor.

At La Castagne the Ogden children had had unbounded
freedom and an endless variety of amusements. During the last
months when the family had lived again in Bordeaux itself,
there had been the *jardins publiques* where they had romped
with other children who spoke their own language, and boule-

vards lined with fascinating shops to provide diversion on long walks in the winter sunshine. But New York, with its straight streets and monotonous rows of low red-brick or frame houses— where carriages jolted over rough pavement, or splashed through deep mud where there was no paving at all—offered only the most dismal prospect. The children had no friends outside the family circle and only the older ones could even speak the language. Besides, there was so much crudeness and confusion everywhere. People jostled one on the street without so much as a *"pardon,"* and everyone was wrapped up in his own personal affairs. There were few trees at best: almost none in the lower part of the town, except a row of scraggly elms along the Battery. Now, of course, it was the dead of winter and not a sprig of green was visible anywhere. With faces pressed against cold window-panes, the children looked out at the snow and endlessly asked: "Shall we never return?"—"Must we stay here always?"

Presently they were all in school. Matilda and Anna Cora were sent to Mrs. Okill's select academy for young ladies. For Anna Cora the curriculum was a mixture of misery and delight. In grammar, arithmetic and algebra she stood always near the foot of the class. She never mastered the multiplication table; and though French was her native language, when it came to conjugating verbs it might as well have been Greek. But in "reading, recitation of poetry, mythology, history, mental philosophy [sic]" she took top honors. In general, though, her schooling was irregular. The terrible voyage, during hours of which the children had been in damp cabins—sometimes soaked to the skin—had started a bronchial condition which was to remain throughout life. For days at a time Anna Cora was confined to bed with no resources except books; and she read anything and everything she could find. Poetry was her favorite reading, and besides her old friends Shakespeare and Racine, anything else that came her way she soaked up like a sponge. When she was not reading she was scribbling verses of her own. Any occasion—a marriage, a birth, a death—supplied a subject. For hours at a time she would string together lines of doggerel, and then dream that somebody would find and proclaim them masterpieces. She would even invent strategies to insure that they would be found. Copies were dropped on the floor of her brothers' rooms; they appeared propped up on the nursery mantelpiece. When the weather was fair and she could go out-of-doors, she scribbled verses on the garden walls. One day she was rewarded by seeing one of her brothers with one of the familiar sheets of paper in his hand. Anna Cora followed him downstairs and watched him enter the drawing-room where she knew her father at that moment to be. Cautiously she crept to the door to listen.

"Just read this, Papa," she heard her brother say. "It's some of Anna's nonsense."

There was a silence which meant that her father was reading the manuscript. Then her heart skipped a beat when she heard Mr. Ogden say, "I wish you would call her."

Anna Cora's impulse was to flee; but before she could get to the stairs the door opened and her brother seized her. She was led back into the drawing-room, feeling like "a culprit who had been guilty of some heavier crime than that of mutilating English and writing bad poetry."

But her father's face was kindly. "Did you write these lines yourself?" he asked.

"Yes," was the faltering reply.

"Are you sure that nobody helped you? Are you sure that you did not get them out of some book?"

Anna Cora was indignant; not at the imputation of plagiarism but at the idea that her unique creation could possibly be attributed to anyone else. At the same time a feeling of elation came over her. She had given tangible form to something which had been inside her, and through the little poem this vague something had been shared by someone else! For the first time she experienced the thrill of communication, and it was like nothing she had ever known before.

"They are not very good grammar," continued Mr. Ogden glancing down at the small sheet of paper. "But they are quite pretty for all that. Who knows what my little chicken may turn out one of these days?"

It was slight praise, but coming from her father it was enough. From that moment she was satisfied that she could do something, she was not quite sure what. Perhaps write poetry; perhaps something else. There was only one thing she was suddenly quite aware of, as her father began to point out the flaws in her masterpiece. She must work very hard. If she wished others to share all the wonderful excitements which she was beginning to feel inside her, she must strive endlessly to perfect the means which would enable others to see, hear, feel as she did. And from this moment on, Anna Cora became a worker. Except for a brief and wholly normal period of juvenile egotism, she never had more than a modest regard for her own talents. But somewhere along the way she had picked up the old French saying, *"le génie est une longue patience,"* and she knew that when patience was combined with effort something was bound to happen. Her consistent formula for rebuffing Fate was simply to work a little harder at whatever task was uppermost.

After two years at Mrs. Okill's, the girls went to another boarding-establishment at New Rochelle. Here the régime was harsh and inflexible, with no opportunity to develop one's personal thoughts on any subject. The school considered itself an efficient mold, into which the fluid personalities of little girls might be poured with the expectation that they would emerge in the one and only form proper to their station in life. Anna was thoroughly miserable. Her own nature refused to set in the mold, and the price of her rebellion was a long series of punishments. Her one source of consolation was a tiny garden which she was permitted to plant and care for as her own. By the 1830's, the return to Nature which had caught the fancy of philosophers in the eighteenth century had assumed the form of a popular movement. Gardening, which former ages had regarded as the pursuit of peasants, had now acquired the status of a social grace. Little girls were instructed in not only embroidery, dancing, and sketching in water-colors, but the rudiments of horticulture. One could now exhibit a perfect tea-rose of one's own cultivation with as much propriety as one's mother had displayed her samplers. To quote one guide in such matters, "The exchange of rose-cuttings, particularly in rural districts, is a suitable adjunct to morning calls and may, in the absence of more elevated themes, form an acceptable topic of polite conversation."

Aside from this one accomplishment, which she was always to pursue with delight when circumstances permitted, Anna Cora got little from the New Rochelle school except a deep sense of the meaning of Freedom. When at last the girls were summoned home—Anna Cora was now twelve—their father's house was indeed like heaven. They once more became day scholars in good schools and "were as merry as uncaged linnets."

Home meant among other things unlimited opportunity to indulge once more the favorite Ogden pastime of theatricals. Anna Cora soon became the impresario (as well as stage manager and director) of these productions. Furthermore, she now had to exercise her ingenuity to provide suitable works for performance. Due to alterations in the *corps dramatique* (some of the older children were now married, others away at school), the standard pieces of the family repertory had to be tailored to fit the changes in personnel. Old characters—particularly if they were *too* old—sometimes had to be eliminated, new characters had to be added. Often plots had to be changed, and this meant writing new scenes or altering dénouements. From play-doctoring to play-writing was a natural transition. Presently Anna Cora was dramatizing episodes from history, especially American history; for the little Ogdens—surrounded by their multitude of connections, with constant reminders of the family's past, and living in the rabidly republican atmosphere of the Jacksonian era—had abandoned their allegiance to France and were now ardently American.

Sometimes the children merely took the framework of a plot and improvised scenes and dialogue as they went along. "We did not care particularly for audiences," Anna Cora recorded later; "they generally consisted of our schoolmates or

13

any accidental visitors, and very often we had no audience at all. These plays merely took the place of other childish games, and afforded an intellectual excitement as well as amusement."

When she was fourteen, Anna Cora decided that the time was ripe for a first-class production. The occasion was her father's birthday and the piece selected was Voltaire's *Alzire* translated into English. There would be a large audience, mainly adults, friends of their parents and older sisters. This meant that there must be no improvisation, but absolute finish in every detail. Voltaire's play had been chosen because it involved a minimum of scenery and only such characters as the children, with the aid of a few friends, could fill. All the male characters were taken by young girls, for by this time the brothers had passed beyond the stage when they could take part in such frivolity. To have invited other boys of their own age, but outside the family, would have so violated their parents' sense of propriety as to be unthinkable.

"A great difficulty arose in procuring costumes for the Spanish and Moorish heroes—a difficulty which came near ruining our project. Mr. Simpson, the excellent and gentleman-like manager of the Park Theatre, with his delightful family, lived opposite. We had no acquaintance with them beyond bowing to the children when we met in the street. It was proposed, however, that three or four of the most confident of our number should pay a visit to Mrs. Simpson, and beg her to use her influence with her husband to lend us certain costumes from the wardrobe of the theatre. Mrs. Simpson received us very kindly. I was made spokesman on the occasion, and, but for her sweet face and gentle manners, should have found some difficulty in making known the wishes of our youthful committee. Evidently much amused at our enthusiasm, she promised that we should have the dresses. In return, we invited her children to be present at the performance."

Alzire was a grand success. A special feature was a prologue written for the occasion by a friend, Miss Anna L. Putnam (sister of the publisher), and recited by little Julia, aged four. Julia had joined the family after its arrival in America, preceded by another Gabriel who had lived only a year. She was the fourteenth and last child of Eliza Lewis Ogden, who in another four years passed to her well-earned rest.

Alzire not only won general acclaim for its artistic merits; in it, Anna Cora demonstrated as never before her own talents as an actress. As Alzire, the heroine of the piece, she succeeded in completely losing her "own identity in that of the heroine." And the connection with the Simpsons, who had so generously supplied the costumes for the play, was to have consequences in her later life. Whether Mr. Simpson was one of the Ogden's invited guests we do not know. But he may well have been; for though he did not move in the same circle as they—the circle of Astors and Fishes, of Stuyvesants and Duyckincks—he was after all a neighbor and "gentlemanlike," although as the term implies not actually a gentleman. At any rate it was from this moment that his acquaintanceship with Anna Cora began: an acquaintanceship that was to lead Samuel Ogden's fifth daughter in time to the stage of the Park Theatre itself. But that was all in the future, and destiny would provide many stops along the way.

Up to this time Anna Cora, though constantly engaged in acting or writing or managing plays, had never been inside a real theatre. This was not because of any parental restriction; indeed the Ogdens and their older daughters, like other cultivated New Yorkers, were frequent attendants at the Park or the National. But with Anna Cora it was otherwise. The Ogdens were parishioners at Grace Church, whose rector at the time was the Reverend Doctor Manton Eastburn. Anna, who seems not to have been an unduly religious child, had nevertheless developed a passion for Dr. Eastburn which readily extended itself to a complete acceptance of all his views. Dr. Eastburn disapproved of theatres. In fact he preached long sermons against them, describing them with sulphurous flourishes as "abodes of sin and wickedness." His words apparently had little effect on his congregation in general. It was composed in the main of prosperous and fashionable New Yorkers, who even by the 1830's had moved far from the simple unworldly ways of their fathers. But to little Anna Ogden, the exhortations of the distinguished cleric, whose very glance sent strange thrills up and down her spine, were at least a temporary deterrent to theatregoing.

But now her passion for the Rev. Dr. Eastburn was to be put to the test. Fanny Kemble, whose name—for a number of reasons apart from her talents as an actress—was on everybody's lips, was about to make her farewell appearance on the stage. Anna Cora had followed her career avidly (Dr. Eastburn had said nothing against reading dramatic criticism); and the rumors of her charms, of her spell-binding beauty and histrionic gifts had worked themselves insidiously into Anna Cora's consciousness. Besides, was it not said that Miss Kemble was exemplary in her private life, a model of filial devotion and a scrupulous observer of the proprieties? And would she not take her place soon in the best society of Philadelphia, when she married Mr. Pierce Butler to whom she was engaged and for whom she was abandoning the stage? The more Anna Cora reasoned along these lines, the more she listened to her sisters' rapturous reports of Miss Kemble's acting—for they had seen her again and again in this last engagement—the more she weakened.

Yet she could not easily withdraw from a position she had stated to one and all. She was becoming quite desperate. On the last morning of Miss Kemble's engagement, as she and her sister Matilda were walking to school, they were overtaken by Mr. Ogden.

"I am going to take seats to see Fanny Kemble tonight in the *Hunchback*. Would you like to go?" The remark was pointedly addressed to Matilda who immediately accepted the invitation with delight. Then Mr. Ogden turned to Anna Cora and said casually, "And so you, Anna, are *never* going?"

The direct question was the last straw to her weakening resistance. In a faltering voice she replied, "I *should* like to see Fanny Kemble just *once*."

Her father smiled and promised to see what he could do about getting an extra seat.

That day Anna Cora was more than ever distracted from

algebra and French verbs. She could do nothing but think of the theatre and long for evening to come. When at last the day came to an end and the girls, in their most elegant frocks, were ushered into the box which their father had taken, Anna was trembling with expectancy. Then suddenly she was bewildered. The crowd, the dazzling gas-lights from the great chandelier overhead, the music, the sea of waiting faces down in the pit, rising in waves in balcony and galleries about them, was like nothing in her experience. And then she became fearful. It was all so overpowering. She remembered again the Rev. Dr. Eastburn's warning about "sin and wickedness". Yet she could not quite see where the harm lay in this great hall with all these hundreds of people whose eyes were now focused on the brilliant painted curtain. Shyly she took her father's arm and asked him to point out what it was that made it so wrong. Before Mr. Ogden could reply the curtain began to rise, and Anna Cora's misgivings vanished in the spell of the lighted stage.

Fanny Kemble did not appear until the second scene of the play; but the moment she stepped onto the stage Anna Cora was completely hypnotized. "I thought I had never beheld any creature so perfectly bewitching. The tones of her voice were richest music, and her dark, flashing eyes seemed to penetrate my very soul. Her 'Clifford, why don't you speak to me?' made me start from my very seat; and her 'Do it!' to Master Walter, electrified me, as indeed it did the whole audience."

Fourteen years later in this same theatre, in this very scene, little Anna Ogden—in the dignity of her married name, Mrs. Mowatt—was to electrify many in this same audience, and in a way to defy comparison even with the great Fanny Kemble. But there was nothing in the circumstances of this present evening to suggest this moment in the future. All Anna Cora knew as she sat on the edge of her chair, clutching the velvet rail of the box, was that no one, not even the Rev. Dr. Eastburn, could weave a spell like this.

CHAPTER TWO

The Mourning Bride

Anna Cora was fourteen and still to outward appearances a child. Her chestnut hair fell in long ringlets loose about her shoulders. Her deep blue eyes, set wide apart, were serenely innocent. Because of her slenderness and the way she carried her head, slightly uptilted, and because of the fine texture of her pale skin, she reminded people of a delicate but hardy flower. In the family and to her intimates she was generally known now as "Lily."

Her parents and sisters continued to regard her as a little girl, but Anna Cora was beginning to feel differently about herself. She could still burst into peals of laughter over nothing at all; and on occasion she was not above a game of hop-scotch or a boisterous run in the garden with younger sisters. But more and more she was beginning to act like a young lady and to feel like one. She was rereading Shakespeare and finding him very different now. Romeo and Juliet were no longer figures in a story made entrancing by duels and rope ladders, potions and horrible tombs. They were two young people to whom something very special had happened, and Anna Cora began to grasp what it was. Then, practically without warning, the same thing happened to her.

It had begun two years before, when Anna Cora was thirteen. Her sister Charlotte, who was Mrs. Lewis Yates and the mother of two small children, had been summering at Rockaway, a new and fashionable resort on the south coast of Long Island. Her husband, an Englishman, was at the moment in his native land on business. Among the guests at Rockaway Hall where Mrs. Yates and her children were staying was Mr. James Mowatt, a young New York lawyer of position and fortune. Mr. Mowatt was a bachelor and not overly shy, though in every way a gentleman. One day on the hotel veranda an opportunity had presented itself for him to speak to the charming Mrs. Yates. The chance remark was prolonged to polite conversation. This was followed by other conversations into which was presently injected a certain ardor. Whereupon Mrs. Yates, with perfect good humor—for it was obvious that Mr. Mowatt's intentions were to the highest degree honorable—informed the young lawyer that she was not a widow, as he evidently supposed, but a happily-married woman—although her husband was momentarily not available. Mr. Mowatt may not have been crushed by this intelligence, but he was very disappointed: so much so that Mrs. Yates, who was not only sympathetic but practical-minded, suggested that since he could not have *her* he might be interested in one of her sisters, There were plenty of them, she said, and then added, "One of them very much resembles me. Call upon me in New York, and I will make you acquainted with her."

Mr. Mowatt, surprisingly enough, was heartened by this suggestion of a substitute and gratefully accepted Mrs. Yates's invitation. When he was informed a few weeks later that she had returned to the city and was at her father's house in Warren Street, he hastened to pay his respects.

Anna Cora and Matilda, her next older sister, happened to be at school (which was not far away) when a servant arrived with the message that Miss Matilda was wanted at home. When the girls asked anxiously if anything was wrong, the girl replied no, but that there was a gentleman in the drawing-room who entreated that Miss Matilda might be sent for. When the gentleman was identified as Mr. Mowatt, about whom there had been a good deal of talk in the family, Lily's curiosity got the better of her and she determined to go along with Matilda. The girls ran all the way home and dashed immediately upstairs to Matilda's room. There Lily watched yearningly while her sister's hair was recurled and her school frock exchanged for more becoming attire. All this was done with great care, for Matilda was approaching marriageable age; and in a family with eight daughters it was a matter of principle, if not of expediency, to regard any eligible male as a prospective husband.

At last Matilda was ready to make her entrance into the drawing-room. Lily accompanied her to the foot of the stairs and looked longingly as her sister, with ribbons flying, disappeared in a billow of India muslin through the high walnut doors.

Not till then did Lily recall that she had left school without permission; and visions of black marks rose before her eyes. But it was too late to do anything about that now. Besides, she was determined to have one look at Mr. Mowatt, *coûte que coûte*! With this thought she seized her satchel of books which was lying nearby, threw open the drawing-room doors, raced the length of the room, deposited the books on the center-table (as if that were their proper place) and rushed out again, having taken a quick look at the trousered figure on the sofa.

As the door banged behind her she heard a deep voice ask: "Who is that?"

"Only one of the children from the nursery," answered Mrs. Yates, who was of course chaperoning the interview.

"Do call her back," urged Mr. Mowatt.

Charlotte came to the door and called to the figure flying up the stairs. "Anna, Anna, come back and speak to Mr. Mowatt!"

"I don't care for Mr. Mowatt," replied Anna Cora in a tone calculated to reach the drawing-room. Then she flounced up to the nursery which she shared with Julia. A servant was sent after her; but she was deaf to the summons. Finally, when she heard the caller taking his leave, she hurried downstairs to return to school. But there had been a mistake in her timing. At the foot of the steps of the front stoop, Mr. Mowatt was waiting— and she rushed headlong into his outstretched arms. There, as she struggled to free herself, he began pelting her with questions. How old was she? Did she go to school? Did she like it? What did she like to study best? Anna Cora answered his questions breathlessly, imploring to be released. When he asked what she liked best to read and she cried, "Shakespeare!" he was so astonished that he loosened his grasp, and Anna was away like a flash. On the other side of the street she looked back and burst into laughter at the sight of Mr. Mowatt, transfixed at the foot of the steps with arms still outstretched and a look of complete bafflement on his face.

Some hours later one of Mr. Mowatt's intimates who was on the threshold of matrimony asked him how long *he* intended to remain a bachelor.

"Not long," he answered, "if a little girl whom I saw today would only grow up." And then, according to report, he quoted Moore's lines:

> O, *there are looks and tones that dart*
> *An instant sunshine through the heart,*
> *As though the soul that moment caught*
> *Some treasure it through life had sought.*

Mr. Mowatt had a taste for poetry and (under proper stimulus) was not above airing it even on a busy New York street-corner.

Matilda herself seems not to have languished from having been so promptly abandoned by Mr. Mowatt in favor of Anna Cora. She was after all not quite sixteen and her mind was not irrevocably fixed on marriage. Romance came her way in due time, and she was happily married to a Mr. Wellman of Cincinnati.

Mr. Mowatt was now a frequent and regular visitor at the Ogden mansion, and invariably asked for Lily (he had straightway adopted the family's pet name for Anna Cora). Usually his desire to see her was frustrated by the fact that she was in

21

school, or studying her lessons, or in bed. But this only made him more persistent. The girls had again changed schools and were finishing their education at Madame Chegaray's at 15th Street and Union Square, about half a mile from the house. Mr. Mowatt now adopted the habit of meeting them on the way home. He would walk beside Lily carrying her books and slate, catechizing her about her studies. It soon developed that Mr. Mowatt had remarkable gifts for making things clear—and interesting. Soon, Anna Cora tells us, "under the stimulus of his suggestions, my ambition to become an accomplished scholar was aroused." Soon also she discovered the pleasure of tyranny and began to enjoy ordering Mr. Mowatt about and inflicting little pains which she might have the delight of assuaging. Now and then she made her sisters take a different way home, in order to avoid the assiduous lover. But after a few days Mr. Mowatt saw through this strategy and stationed one of his clerks to watch which street they took.

None of these vagaries disturbed the tenor of Mr. Mowatt's devotion, or interfered with his intention to have a wife in whose education he would have a hand. Under his encouragement and instruction Anna Cora made rapid progress in school. He directed her reading, furnished her with books, corrected her compositions, and (what she thought most delightful of all) supplied her with an endless quantity of flowers as a reward for her industry.

If her parents were aware of what was going on, they did not seem unduly concerned. It was obvious Mr. Mowatt's intentions were serious; but it was unlikely that a man of his position or age—he was twenty-eight—would do anything foolish. Also with seven girls at home, all of lively disposition and socially inclined, it was impossible to follow closely the details of all their activities. As for Lily herself, she was still hardly more than a child. At least that is what they thought—and continued to think until she had passed her fifteenth birthday, when events caused them to revise their notions.

Mr. Mowatt was present at the performance of *Alzire*, and was naturally the most enthusiastic spectator of all. Indeed it must have been the spectacle of little Lily so convincingly expressing the mature passions of Voltaire's heroine that acted as a spur to his well-controlled ardor.

The morning after the performance he called. It was Saturday and there was no school. Mr. Mowatt arrived very early and asked particularly for Lily. The older girls were engaged in the intricate process of making themselves presentable for the day, but Lily rushed into the drawing-room "in morning dress." She could not wait to hear Mr. Mowatt repeat his praises of her performance; and she was quite astonished (and not a little disappointed) when he immediately plunged into a somewhat different matter. Lily scarcely realized what he was talking about, but she understood enough to become thoroughly alarmed. When he put the question point-blank, instead of replying she jumped up and ran to the door, calling loudly for Charlotte. Mrs. Yates came quickly downstairs to inquire what on earth was the matter—a query which Lily found herself suddenly unable to answer.

When Mr. Mowatt had gone, she confided to Charlotte what had taken place. Charlotte was greatly amused, and said that of course he was only making fun of her because she was such a forward child. But Lily could not be sure; and when on the following day a letter came from Mr. Mowatt, she had no doubts at all. This time she went to Louisa. Swearing the older girl to secrecy, Lily put the note in her hands.

"Well, and what are you going to do?" she asked, not very helpfully, when she had read the document.

"Get you to help me write an answer, and tell him I am too young to marry anybody, and say something about *friendships*, and all that sort of thing—because," added Lily as an afterthought, "I *do* like him very much."

Louisa refused to write the letter, but she agreed to correct it. Lily went up to the nursery where she still slept, and after several painful attempts finally got the reply on paper. Louisa said that it would do, privately believing that it contained such childish nonsense, it could not help but bring Mr. Mowatt to his senses. Its effect, however, was quite the reverse. Mr. Mowatt merely laughed at what he considered girlish shyness and increased his visits, assuming the attitude of an accepted rather than a rejected lover. In the end, this singular behavior had its reward. Within a few weeks of her fifteenth birthday, Lily's oft-repeated "no" became "yes".

Mr. Ogden was now approached. He received the news with equanimity, but dismissed the idea of an immediate wedding. Although fifteen was by no means an unusual age for girls to be married, in Lily's case it would be premature. In his eyes she was still a little girl, the liveliest and most diverting of all his daughters, and he was not quite ready to part with her. As for her suitor, he could find no objection to Mr. Mowatt personally; and if the lovers remained of the same mind until Lily was seventeen, he would give his consent.

So Mr. Mowatt, though not dismissed, was put off. He became uneasy. After Lily's fifteenth birthday she was removed from Madame Chegaray's and received private instruction in music and drawing at home. This eliminated the chance for daily meetings on the homeward walk. Furthermore, the next winter she was due to make her bow to society. This meant exposure to possible rivals; so far, Mr. Mowatt had had the field to himself. He began to urge a runaway marriage; but Lily was faithful to her filial obligation. Once she almost yielded—indeed, she let matters progress so far as arrangements for the wedding—but when the friend who was to act as bridesmaid came to fetch her, she backed down.

Her coming-out was scheduled for October 17th, which was her father's birthday. There was to be a grand ball, and the girls, as was their custom at such times, would present a play. The work chosen was Congreve's *The Mourning Bride*. As usual the play had to be rewritten to meet the family requirements. This time the problem was gifted little Julia, for whom there was no part in Congreve's text. Lily met this need by giving Queen Zara, the heroine, a child—a rather precocious and talkative child.

The critical day was approaching and preparations were moving at a frantic pace. Mr. Mowatt came to the house daily; but in the midst of all the activity of rehearsing and sewing and scene-building, he was an outsider. Also, his popularity with the family had declined since the announcement of the engagement. Though the wedding was theoretically still two years away, he represented a threat to family solidarity. The sisters knew that when the time came, Lily's departure would deprive them of a mistress of the revels. Then there would be no *Alzires*, no *Mourning Brides*—a prospect too dismal to contemplate! So there was a coolness toward Mr. Mowatt. Sometimes he was even slighted and subjected to petty annoyances; and this was something, as Anna Cora later pointed out, "to which a man of spirit could ill submit."

Morose and frustrated, her fiancé now redoubled his entreaties. Lily felt sorry for him and suggested that he again try to obtain Mr. Ogden's consent. That, Mr. Mowatt said with gloomy conviction, was useless. He continued to urge that they run away, but Lily resisted. Then, when he had quite ceased trying to persuade her, she became so grieved at the sight of his deepening melancholy that of her own free will she agreed to marry him within a week.

Now the problems really began. "What was I to do, and who was to aid me? I could not leave my father's house alone. I could not be married without a *bridal wardrobe*. These were huge barriers to be surmounted; but I went resolutely to work, determined to overcome them."

Lily's first step was to engage the alliance of a young nursery-maid, who was very much attached to her. Next she took her sister Matilda—to whom she was closest—into her confidence. Matilda was startled and fearful. She argued, she entreated, she prayed Lily to give up her mad plan. When she saw that it was all useless, she concluded that the wisest course would be to do whatever she could to help. The question of wardrobe was most vexing. Even though they would do the sewing themselves, yards of materials had to be purchased. This presented a real difficulty since neither girl had any money. Here Lily's dramatic inventiveness came to the rescue. Time and again in plays of her own and of others, people used jewels instead of cash. They were not only more picturesque, they were handier. Did not heroines often buy off dastards or reward the faithful—as the case might be—with the very pearls about their necks? Anna Cora had no pearls, but she had a gold watch, and a few pieces of quite valuable jewelry—heirloom diamonds and emeralds—which she would dispose of!

The girls had heard of places where such transactions were made, and were even familiar with the universal symbol of the three golden balls. Early the morning after the momentous decision had been made, they hunted out a pawnshop. The proprietor, a somewhat frightening individual with a large nose and sharp eyes, studied the young ladies for some time through narrowed lids, and then began to ask questions which Lily thought were impertinent. She finally managed to persuade him that the jewels were her own; and the business was concluded. Then she was asked to sign her name on a slip of paper. Lily was somewhat taken aback. Then summoning all her dignity she seated herself at the grimy counter and wrote, very carefully, "Mrs. James".

The diamonds and emeralds brought about a tenth of their value; even so, this represented a sum larger than either of the girls had ever seen before. They felt very rich, and as soon as they were out of the shop they engaged a carriage. It was raining torrents, but they were undismayed. For hours they splashed about the city, going from shop to shop, until the carriage was filled with parcels and their pockets were empty. Among other purchases were a large wax doll and a huge basket of sugarplums. The doll was a farewell present to little Julia, while the sweets were to be consolatory offerings for the other younger children.

Since the parcels could not be carried into the house without exciting suspicion, they were deposited at a corner confectioner's. Later that evening they were smuggled up to Matilda's room. Here for the next five or six nights the three girls—Matilda, Lily, and the nursery-maid—sewed madly on the trousseau. As a precaution against discovery by their mother when she paid her nightly visit to the nursery, a figure of rags was placed beneath the covers of Lily's bed.

Finally the 6th of October arrived. Mr. Mowatt had been busy with his part in the preparations. There was some difficulty in finding a clergyman to perform the ceremony. To each one approached, it had been necessary to explain the circumstances; and since Samuel Ogden was a person to be reckoned with, the gentlemen of the cloth were reluctant to officiate at a wedding of which he did not approve, although the bride, now fifteen, was of legal age to be married. Dr. Eastburn, the object of Lily's earlier passion and the rector of Samuel Ogden's church, showed understandable prudence in declining. Bishop Onderdonk, also approached, refused on the ground that he had daughters of his own and his sanction of such an example would be bad for them. A third clergyman likewise refused. In desperation James Mowatt turned to the pastor of New York's French church, l'Eglise du Saint Esprit. This gentleman, the Reverend Mr. Antoine Verren, was a native of Marseilles, with the proverbial temperament of the *méridional*. Moreover he himself had eloped with his wife, so he scarcely could do otherwise than to agree to perform the ceremony. The wedding was conducted—not inappropriately for Lily's case—in French. The date was October 6, 1834.

The ceremony took place in the morning, which made getting out of the house a problem, especially since Lily was wearing a white embroidered muslin frock which to an observant mother might seem slightly strange on a brisk October day. Nevertheless Lily managed to kiss her father and mother without exciting undue suspicion (neither even noticed the white rose and sprig of geranium in her hair), and to slip through the front door. Matilda had gone on ahead, carrying the bridal veil and white gloves rolled up in a handkerchief. At the corner Lily shook out the veil and put on the gloves. At St. John's Park they were met by Mr. Mowatt and his two groomsmen, and the party proceeded on its way.

The vows had been spoken and the registry book opened when the Rev. Mr. Verren became worried. Twice he asked Anna Cora her age, and although each time she promptly answered "fifteen", which was all quite right and legal, the good *pasteur* seemed very dubious. And no wonder; for the little figure bent over the registry, with six inches of pantalette showing beneath the froth of petticoats, and the long dark curls hanging down her back, seemed more like a child ready for her first Communion than a woman about to assume the responsibilities of marriage. Even to Lily herself it was all like some wonderfully exciting game, or a scene from an impromptu play.

"What could a girl of fifteen know of the sacred duties of a wife?" she afterwards wrote. "With what eyes could she contemplate the new and important life into which she was entering? She had known nothing but her childhood—had scarcely commenced her girlhood. What could she comprehend of the trials, the cares, the hopes, the responsibilities of womanhood? I thought of none of these things . . . I only remembered that I was keeping a promise. I had perfect faith in the tenderness of him to whom I confided myself. I did not in the least realize the novelty of my own situation."

Lily removed the veil and tucked it in her reticule. Outside the rectory the groomsmen took their departure, and Mr. Mowatt and the two girls started back for the Ogden mansion. As they turned into their own street, they almost ran headlong into Mr. Ogden, on his way to his counting-house. He walked back a few paces with them, exchanging civilities with Mr. Mowatt. He had hardly noticed the girls. As he turned to leave, however, his eye took in Anna Cora's white gown. "Why, how like a bride you look!" he exclaimed. "One of these days, Mowatt, she will grow up to be quite a fine girl!" At the mention of "bride", Lily began to tremble violently from head to foot. Fortunately Mr. Ogden was in a hurry and did not notice her agitation.

The girls now returned to the house, as though they had simply been out for an hour or two on some inconsequential errand, and passed the rest of the day in their normal pursuits. It was planned that on the morrow Mr. Mowatt would come for Lily and take her away to the country where they would pass a few weeks until the inevitable upheaval in the family should have a chance to subside. That evening Mr. Mowatt called as usual, and the family chatted together in the drawing-room. As usual the topic uppermost was the forthcoming ball and the production of *The Mourning Bride*; and though Mr. Mowatt was largely ignored, it might have been noted that this made him less melancholy than usual.

When at last the gathering broke up and Mr. Mowatt had taken his departure, Lily went up to the nursery to bed. When she looked at little Julia, sleeping peacefully, she saw that the child's cheeks were wet. Suddenly a wave of desolation swept over her. She had earlier confided in Julia, so that the shock of her departure might not be too severe on the little sister who had been her special charge. Julia, though only five, had kept the secret well; but the bedtime tears showed how miserable the news had made her. As Lily bent over the little figure, the full realization of what she had done came over her. She would have given anything, at that instant, to find that it was all a dream and that she might wake up to know herself still a little girl, sharing the nursery with her baby sister.

At breakfast the next morning, Lily found some excuse to kiss everyone present. She had already greeted her father at his bedside earlier in the morning. The second embrace caused Samuel Ogden to look up anxiously and ask if anything were wrong. She could only make a little choking sound and rush out of the room. Hastily she gathered up her bonnet and shawl. The nursery-maid, who was to accompany her on her honeymoon, had already left the house with her portmanteau. Lily slipped through the door and into the street, where Matilda was waiting for her. Together the two girls set off. Halfway up the block Lily turned back for a farewell glimpse of the house. As she looked, she saw the door open and Julia appear on the stoop. Presently Mrs. Ogden also came out and took Julia by the hand to bring her back into the house. At sight of the two figures Lily's eyes filled with tears. When she saw Julia draw closer to her mother and bend down and kiss the latter's hand, it was more than she could bear. She clutched Matilda's arm and cried, "Let us run! O, let us run!"

Mr. Mowatt and the nursery-maid were waiting for them at the steamboat landing. Great clouds of smoke were billowing from the vessel's gilded smokestacks. The whistle was blowing as Mr. Mowatt led Lily up the gangplank. In another moment they were pushing out into the Hudson. Lily stood at the rail waving her handkerchief to Matilda standing on the bank. When the edge of a warehouse interposed itself between them and Matilda had disappeared, Lily knew that the first chapter of her life was over. But she was not afraid. The hand that held hers was firm but gentle, and when she looked into her husband's eyes she no longer felt that it was all a terrible dream. Or if it was a dream, it was one from which she hoped never to awaken.

CHAPTER THREE

"A Household Harp"

The young couple were to spend their honeymoon in Nyack, at the home of James's married sister. They had scarcely been greeted by their hostess and installed in their room when Anna Cora set herself to write a long letter to Samuel Ogden. She was in anguish at the thought of his feelings when he learned of the marriage. Her action not only defied convention; it constituted the first breach in the perfect trust that had always existed between her father and herself. But most painful of all to set down was the admission of her deceit, which seemed to her a violation of the fundamental principle of her nature.

Somehow the letter did get written, and in due course a reply was received. Lily's fears had not been unjustified. Mr. Ogden had been offended almost beyond words, and his indignation against Mr. Mowatt knew no bounds. There were further letters;

but nothing, it seemed, would avail to pacify Lily's irate parent. Never, never would he forgive her. Between letters the time stretched endlessly. "Those days seemed like a 'never' indeed to me. . . . I was almost heart-broken at the idea of losing my father's love, upon which I had drawn too largely. My thoughts 'through all the faithful past, went sorrowing', and I could not bear to dwell upon a future of which he did not form the principal feature." Such thoughts Anna Cora probably kept to herself; else they might have made Mr. Mowatt somewhat doubtful of his own position. Although there is no mention of the fact in the record, he seems to have behaved admirably through it all. But he might well have pondered the irony of having interrupted production of a play entitled *The Mourning Bride*, when he found himself with the real thing on his hands.

The period of suspense, which seemed eternal to Lily, and probably to James Mowatt, who had hoped for a somewhat different atmosphere on his honeymoon, lasted in fact three days. In view of the number of letters exchanged, and the variety of emotions aroused and subdued during this time, one must assume that every steamer between Nyack and New York was utilized for the correspondence. When the letter of forgiveness finally arrived, accompanied by an invitation to return home, Lily begged that the honeymoon might be curtailed. No matter what his personal feelings may have been, in the interests of prudence this seemed to James Mowatt the better course. Within a week the couple was back in the mansion on Warren Street, where father, mother, all welcomed them with open arms, and without one chiding word. Lily was overwhelmed by what she felt to be such completely undeserved tenderness. As for Mr. Mowatt, she informs us he was received less cordially, but "still with kindness."

Samuel Ogden's feelings must have been mixed. While genuinely upset at the loss of his favorite child and shaken by this first challenge to his authority, he was after all a practical man. By every standard James Mowatt was an excellent match. He was of good family, well-off, professionally respected, kindly, and of unblemished personal reputation. And though to Ogden's systematic mind it would have been more suitable to marry off his daughters in the order of their ages, it was on the whole wiser not to be too much of a stickler in these matters.

As for Mrs. Ogden, her reaction was completely a mother's. When she heard of the elopement, her main concern was for Lily's health. When Matilda described to the family the wedding and the departure for Nyack, Mrs. Ogden remembered having seen Lily walking up the street in a flimsy summer dress. She was thoroughly alarmed, and went immediately to the nursery, where her worst fears were confirmed. Lying in a drawer of the great mahogany bureau, among the pantalettes and cambric nightgowns, were Lily's flannel petticoats—left behind! The child would catch her death of cold. Her joy at having her delicate Lily home from Nyack without even a sniffle dominated all other feelings.

It was some time later that Lily learned another detail in connection with her flight. When Mrs. Ogden had gone to the nursery that morning, she had found a white geranium lying on the table. She knew that Lily must have worn it the day before: a bridal adornment. . . . She took the sprig and tenderly planted it. It grew and flourished as long as she lived—the favorite among the little collection of house plants in which she took such delight.

After a brief stay under the parental roof, the Mowatts moved to Flatbush. This was only four miles from New York, yet it was really open country; and for Lily, who suffered from a chronic bronchial trouble dating back to that terrible crossing of the Atlantic in 1825, fresh air and exercise were desirable. Since Lily was too young and inexperienced to be burdened with household cares, the couple found quarters in an old mansion which had been converted into a boarding-house.

This dwelling, located on what had once been part of the original Vanderbilt farm, had been built before the Revolution. Designed as the country seat of a wealthy Englishman, it had been requisitioned as a military headquarters during the war, and had later passed into the hands of General Giles. In the 1830's it was regarded as the most handsome residence in the environs of New York. The mansion was approached by an

33

avenue bordered with great dark pines. This parted directly in front of the portico to form a circle, in the center of which was a fountain. Behind the house were gardens and orchards, as well as a farmyard and stables.

The mansion itself, of Georgian design, was a splendid example of eighteenth-century elegance. The wide halls were beautifully paneled. A broad, gracefully-curved stairway led to the upper floor. There was a spacious ballroom with gilded cornices and ceiling ornamented with intricate plaster arabesques. The establishment boasted one of the rarities of the age, a greenhouse filled with exotic plants.

Under the kitchens there were dark vaults where it was said English prisoners had been confined during the war; and there was a secret chamber above the ballroom, accessible only by a small window. Here, according to local legend, a young girl had been imprisoned and starved to death; now her ghost wandered at night through the house. A romantic atmosphere hung over the whole place, as though it had been made to order for an imaginative girl with a head full of plots and a disposition to Byronic emotions.

James Mowatt regarded it as a perfect setting for the Lily he had plucked in Warren Street; and when he saw that his bride had become greatly attached to Melrose, as the place was called, he decided to purchase it. As for Lily herself, she was delighted at the prospect of living permanently in such picturesque surroundings. When a little later her sister May, four years her junior, was invited to come and stay with them so that Anna Cora might have companionship during the long days while James was at his office in the city, her happiness was complete.

At Melrose something of the old atmosphere of La Castagne was re-created. The spacious house with its handsome furniture, its orchards and arbors and flower gardens, the stables, and all sorts of pets—horses, dogs, rabbits, pigeons—even a goat—furnished the girls with constant amusements. And though Lily was now sixteen, a married woman with a position in society and mistress of a large country establishment, she occasionally forgot this fact. More than once, a visitor in white

gloves and lace and feathers, driving up to the house for a
formal call, found Mrs. Mowatt and her little sister gleefully
rolling hoops in the graveled driveway.

Under her husband's tutelage Anna Cora learned to shoot; in
his company she would roam the countryside for hours. On these
excursions she wore a garment of her own design, described as
"half-Turkish costume", by which she seems to have anticipated
Mrs. Bloomer's invention. She became so expert with her light
single-barreled gun that she could bring down swallows on the
wing. Later, when her passion for life and all things living became a veritable religion, she found it inconceivable that she
should ever have indulged in such a pastime. But in those days,
as she tells us, "I seldom saw with my own eyes or judged with
my own judgment."

Mr. Mowatt's major concern continued to be his wife's intellectual development. Out of his own broad background and
keen appreciation for literature, he saw to it that his young bride
read not only widely but well. She wrote critiques of everything
she read, and made copious extracts which she set down in the
form of a journal. For several years, as this journal witnessed,
she read and commented upon between ninety and a hundred
volumes yearly. With James she also read French and did exer-
cises in English composition.

This constant supervision of Lily's activities, and the discipline
upon which he insisted, might indicate that James Mowatt was
something of a tyrant—or at least of a dictatorial nature. But
there is nothing in the picture of him, as given by his wife and
supported by the few remaining letters from his hand, to show
that this was so. His was a deeply sensitive and intuitive nature.
He had perceived extraordinary qualities in Anna Ogden when
he had first met her; and he felt a kind of moral compulsion to
do all in his power to bring her talents to fulfillment. If, like
most husbands of the time, he seemed to have a distinctly
proprietary attitude toward his wife, there is no recorded instance
of his failing to yield to her wishes on any important issue. He
was conscious always of her individuality and her compelling
personal charm. Later, when their rôles were reversed and it was

Lily who became the mainstay of the family, whose talents and beauty made her the object of adoration to thousands, he was content to slip quietly and gracefully into the background. If he did so with a considerable sense of self-satisfaction, no one could blame him. No matter how great were Anna Cora's personal triumphs later, it was James Mowatt who had provided her with the means to make something of herself.

Three things above all James Mowatt taught his wife. These were self-confidence, self-discipline, and the habit of sustained effort. He was quick to praise, thoughtful and intelligent in his criticism of her work, and always encouraging.

In the second year of her marriage Anna Cora experienced a greater sorrow than the temporary loss of her father's affection when she eloped. In the winter of 1836, Eliza Lewis Ogden died. Although her personality had always been eclipsed by that of her masterful husband and exuberant children, her presence had been a powerful influence in the family. If Lily's concern at the time of her elopement was mainly for her father's forgiveness, it was because she was sure of her mother's. She knew that her mother would understand, and she knew that her mother was incapable of harboring resentment. It was Eliza Ogden who by her own candor and scrupulous regard for truth established the atmosphere of mutual trust which kept the family so tightly bound together. Like Samuel Ogden, she had a profound respect for the conventions. But this never interfered with the flow of sympathy when an appeal was made to her generous nature. She had a large capacity for tolerating human weakness in others, though not in herself. This trait she passed on to all her children, but in richest measure to Anna Cora.

Her death coincided with, and may even have contributed to, a change in Samuel Ogden's affairs. In the general fever of expansion which infected most Americans during the 1830's, he found he had overreached himself. It was not, of course, a repetition of the Miranda affair; but there were reverses, particularly abroad, and at home he became embroiled in an endless series of litigations. It was these which led some wag of the time to say that Samuel Ogden had the widest circle of relations of any man in New York, for he was connected by blood or lawsuit to practically everybody in town. To add to his other cares, his eldest daughter Charlotte had just become a widow; and though she did not remain long in this state, at the moment she and her children were dependent on him.

But Samuel Ogden was not a man to languish under either financial inconvenience or bereavement. Within a year he married again. His second wife, Miss Julia Fairlie, came also of a well-established New York family. She was a most lovable woman who soon won the complete affection of all her stepchildren. By this second marriage four daughters were added to the family. The youngest of these, Virginia, was born in 1850 when Samuel Ogden was seventy-one. For a man who so loved children, life could offer no greater reward than that enjoyed by Lily's father. For nearly half a century (Charlotte was born in 1804) he had at least one child about the house, small enough to dandle upon his knee! In the later years there was a happy blending of children and grandchildren, all more or less of an age.

Meanwhile, at Melrose life went its pleasant way. Day after day, the hours of reading and lessons continued. Three times a week Anna Cora was visited by her singing-teacher, for James Mowatt thought that something ought to be done with her voice—which from her childhod had attracted attention by its extraordinary purity and silvery timbre. She worked hard at drawing, too, until it was discovered that it was not good for her lungs to spend long hours bent over a drawing-table.

Lily took delight in all these pursuits. But her greatest pleasure came with the evening hours. After May had been tucked into bed, Lily and James would settle down in the library to read. Side by side at the book-laden table, in the soft glow of the whale-oil lamp, they pored over volumes of philosophy. The particular interest at present was esthetics, which Lily found marvelously stimulating. She had never stopped writing verses; but now as she explored the philosophical theories of poetry in Aristotle and Sidney and Boileau, her effort took on a scientific interest. She was fascinated by Aristotle's analysis of tragedy and the theory of catharsis, by Longinus's exposition of the sublime, by Wordsworth's ideas on poetic diction. Of the last she was suspicious: Wordsworth made poetry sound so *ordinary*. She was greatly relieved when Coleridge set everything to rights by pointing out that since ordinary people did not speak poetry, why should poetry employ the diction of ordinary people? Irrefutable logic!

Coleridge led inevitably to Schlegel. From the *Lectures on Literature* Lily learned that the original and highest form of poetry was to be found in the epic. That was enough for her. All her previous scribblings faded into insignificance before the prospect which now opened up. She would write an epic! Something grand, something with sweep—something immortal, no doubt!

The first thing was to find a subject. Having just finished Trueba's *Romance of Spain*, she plunged into Spanish history for a theme. The daily routine was now altered to make room for epic-writing, to which Lily devoted herself with the same methodical application as to singing or drawing lessons. Each day she did a regular stint; and each night in the library she read the results to James.

"Mr. Mowatt listened, of course, with partial ears, and I believe I had a way of making versification sound more musical than it was—of creating a sense through certain modulations of voice which did not exist in the words themselves!"

Though she did not realize it, Lily had already developed the essential quality of the actress. It was not only her beautiful voice but her innate sense of poetic values that later enabled her to impart a charm and sometimes even grandeur to the most unmitigated trash. The new masterpiece, *Pelayo or the Cavern of Cavadonga*, was not quite that bad, even though Lily herself in time could not look at a page of it without shuddering. *A Poetical Romance in Five Cantos* (that is the subtitle) moves relentlessly through a hundred-and-thirty stanzas of varying pattern. The rhymes, which sometimes strained the authoress's ingenuity, are on the whole correct. The lines are not absolutely regular, but this is readily explained:

> *'Twas nature taught me first to Rhyme,*
> *And my impatient restless muse*

To pen my thoughts scarce gives me time,
And pruning wholly doth refuse
And when I count—takes wing!

Like most writers' early works, even when they deal with
the far-away and long ago, *Pelayo* has a certain autobiographical
coloring. We learn of the heroine Ormesinda, a Gothic maid,

Scarce sixteen summers bloom had shed
O'er her young brow its richn'ing glory,
And yet her heart was fondly wed
With one whose locks would soon prove hoary—

The story of Ormesinda and her warrior lover is handled with
Byronic dash. There is much action and, of course, feeling. The
hero's sword play is alternated with fits of weeping. The heroine
is chastely delicate and spends most of her time in situations
which give emphasis to the fact. Like all epics *Pelayo* ranges
freely, in both the horizontal and the vertical sense, through
geography and time. At one point the American flag is unfurled,
at least symbolically, by reference to the future national anthem.
The authorship of this, incidentally, is attributed to Joseph Rod-
man Drake, who did write a poem called "The American Flag".
However, Anna Cora caught this slip herself and appended a
foot-note: "Since this was in type we have heard it [The Star
Spangled Banner] ascribed to Mr. McKey."

With the reading of each day's accomplishment James's enthusiasm mounted. As a purely quantitative effort—as evidence
of sustained application—*Pelayo* was indeed remarkable. So impressed was James that upon the poem's completion he immediately proposed that it be published. Lily was startled. "I
was not ambitious," she informs us. "I had thought more of
feeding birds and taming pigeons than of winning fame. I loved
to think that I possessed a household harp that would make
pleasant music for the ears of kindred and friends; but I shrank
from playing my part of imperfect musician before the world.
Yet I was easily persuaded. The authorship of *Pelayo* was to be
kept a profound secret. I assumed the name of 'Isabel' and the
book was published by the Harpers."

Surprisingly, *Pelayo* attracted a good deal of attention—

mostly unfavorable. Critics, languishing with little opportunity to exercise their talents (for epics by native writers were few and far between) descended on *Pelayo* with energy and delight. A typical opinion was that of Willis Gaylord Clark, writing in the *Knickerbocker Magazine* for September 1836:

> The subject of Pelayo is not without its capabilities: but the execution of the poem, we are compelled to say, is indifferent enough. Perhaps little else ought to be expected from a writer who takes frequent occasion to advise the reader that she is not yet seventeen, and who makes it a matter of boasting that her restless, impatient muse eschews all pruning or revision. . . . If it were not rather ungallant to dissect the first "unpruned" effort of a lady of sixteen, and moreover, if it were not dangerous withal—for our fair authoress threatens to give two words for one in reply to the hapless critic who shall dare to incur her resentment by adverse comment—we should be induced to point out and serve up numerous blemishes and not a few glaring faults which judicious revision might have amended, if not obviated altogether. Among the rank shoots, however, that demand the extirpating hoe of criticism, it must be confessed there are a few robust flowers, but who would voluntarily labor in an unweeded garden where every stroke he aims at a useless or noxious plant is to be followed by a blow or two on the ear by a female hand? . . .

Clark's reference to "two words for one" regarding adverse criticism, concerns a somewhat unusual precaution Anna Cora took in publishing her maiden effort. Having read Byron's *English Bards and Scotch Reviewers,* 'she hit upon the idea of warning critics, in the preface to *Pelayo*, that if they attacked the poem, she would deal with *them* later. Before the last notice of the work had appeared, she was busy with her retaliation. The result was another slender volume entitled *Reviewers Reviewed*. This, so the subtitle indicates, is a *satire*. In it "Isabel" makes good her threat and systematically lampoons (lambastes would more accurately describe the style of her attack) the prominent critics of the day: James Watson Webb of the *Courier and Enquirer*, George P. Morris of the *Mirror*, Col. Stone of the *Commercial Advertiser*—and with special vigor, Lewis Gaylord Clark, editor of the *Knickerbocker Magazine*, whom she had confused with his brother, Willis, author of the offending review which we have noted.

Reviewers Reviewed also has a preface—in which Anna Cora defends her earlier effort:

> Pelayo, the first rude effusion of a warm, though untutored heart, was presented to the public with all the rainbow hope, that unmingled buoyancy which ever attends the joyous visions of expectant youth. I studied not the science of poetry [a slight inaccuracy, committed doubtless in the interests of rhetoric]—I heeded not its rules; in the enthusiasm of the moment, I only felt that Nature formed her poets before Nature's scorners shackled them with modern trammels.

Anna Cora then explains that her allusion to unfriendly critics in the preface to *Pelayo* was merely the result of a "playful exuberance of spirit" which might have amused a circle of her friends. She marvels at the misapprehension of her motives. Yet this she can overlook. What she cannot forgive is the implied derogation of the poetic genius of her native land, noted in some of the criticisms of *Pelayo*. One critic had pointed out the folly of writing poetry when poetry itself was on the wane. Anna Cora is outraged at this idea:

> In the old world, where the muse's glory had reached its meridian height, her power may well decline. But are not we of the new world? and shines she here, or has she ever shone, in full maturity and splendor, arrayed in laurels from which time has plucked no leaf? How revolting to our national pride, how humiliating, to believe that America should only produce a sickly poetic fire, expiring at its birth! Can poetry be on the wane while such men as Halleck and Bryant are in their prime? Though its infant pinions are yet weak, may they not one day soar beyond even proud Albion's constellated host of bards?

The main idea of *Reviewers Reviewed* (which runs to 1600 lines without missing a beat) is that before critics begin to pick flaws in other people's poetry, they had better try to write some themselves.

If the attention bestowed on *Pelayo* was surprising, the reception of *Reviewers Reviewed* was more so. The book had an even wider sale than *Pelayo* and actually received several favorable notices—probably, reflected Anna Cora, "through the sympathy of some critic who had himself been lashed by his contemporaries." As for the fate of the epic, in later years she could only think of that with a smile. "Its existence was as ephemeral as it deserved to be. As readily crushed by the critics as a butterfly could be crushed, it died an easy death. I alone suffered in its expiring agonies."

After this splash in the literary pond, during which Lily was in some trepidation for fear the identity of "Isabel" would be discovered, domestic life was a welcome relief. There was a great deal of entertaining at Melrose, for Anna Cora had now taken her place as a young matron in New York society. However, these entertainments were never wholly frivolous. Although there were occasional balls, these were never mere dancing-parties. Usually there was special music, or poetry-reading (by Anna Cora), or plays. There were also community responsibilities in the village of Flatbush. The Mowatts regularly attended the Episcopal Church, and Lily was in great demand at bazaars, where she sold flowers or operated the fortune-teller's booth. Sometimes they went into New York to the theatre; but there is no proof that the excitement created by her first visit when she saw Fanny Kemble built up any overwhelming desire for the drama which could not be satisfied at home. In fact, she did not develop a passion for the professional theatre until she herself went on the stage.

Yet some form of dramatic activity was constantly in progress at Melrose. There were regular weekly "concerts" performed by Lily and May and any other of the sisters who chanced to be visiting just then. The word "concert" was a designation used to justify the time the girls spent in studying music, though it seems that none of them had any musical talent. Anna Cora herself, whose actual voice was unusually fine, had difficulty keeping on key—a distinct advantage in speaking the lines of a play, but a handicap when singing. So the "concerts" generally involved burlesques of Italian opera (to which Lily's singing was ideally suited), scenes from tragedies, and *tableaux vivants*. For most of these exhibitions, Mr. Mowatt made up the entire audience.

One original dramatic creation of this period was a work entitled "The Gypsy Wanderer, or The Stolen Child", with a cast of three, little Julia being the temporary addition. This was described as an operetta; and its plot was refreshingly simple. It involved a noble lady whose child had been stolen by the gypsies —and who, in consequence of this deed, had had an aversion for gypsies ever since! She would not even allow them in the house; and when a gypsy child sang one day under her window she ordered her niece Lucille (played by May) to send the child away. But Lucille, tender-hearted, persuaded her to let the waif in. Whereupon it was discovered (several songs and two or three scenes later), through the interesting device of a birth-mark, that the gypsy waif was none other than Lady Ivon's own little lost Florette. The representation of this work, notes Lily, "occupied an hour and a half."

These idyllic occupations might have continued indefinitely had not Anna Cora suddenly been taken ill. The chronic bron-chitis was diagnosed as consumption, already so far advanced that drastic action was imperative. The classic remedy of the time was a sea-voyage, and Lily was ordered immediately to Europe.

So in the spring of 1837, accompanied by one of her father's sisters, she sailed for Liverpool. Was it chance or some prophetic instinct that led the ladies to travel on one of the packets of the Collins Company—known as the Dramatic Line because the ships all bore the names of famous stage figures? There were the *Siddons*, the *Garrick*, the *Talma*, and so on. Lily and her aunt traveled on the *Roscius*, named for the great Roman actor. Among their fellow-passengers was the celebrated comedian Tyrone Power (whose choice of this ship undoubtedly *had* been dictated by a sense of appropriateness.) The great Irish actor was returning to his native land after a triumphant American tour, with fresh laurels on his brow and 20,000 Yankee dollars in his pockets.

CHAPTER FOUR

Second Exile

The separation from James and her beloved May were a cruel wrench for Lily. But when she boarded the *Roscius* she was too weak and ill for grief. She was also terrified at the prospect of the long Atlantic crossing, remembering that earlier voyage and its tragic consequences. Yet this time the sea was on its best behavior. A steady wind sent the ship at a lively clip and acted as a tonic for the invalid who spent most of the days on deck wrapped in heavy shawls. The bracing salt air and bright sunshine worked wonders. By the time the *Roscius* reached Liverpool Lily was no longer coughing, and a faint tinge of color had come into her pale cheeks.

The two ladies went immediately to London where they passed a week shopping, sightseeing, and going to the theatre. Though Anna Cora devoted less time than most girls of the period to clothes—unless they were costumes for a play—she loved pretty things. She had to admit, with some reluctance, that there was a refinement and smartness about English mantuas and slippers that made the American product seem just a little crude.

Shopping gave an excuse for constantly moving about the city. London was full of reminders of home, yet it was foreign too and daily presented something new and strange to stimulate Lily's lively curiosity. Although this was not her first experience of Europe—she had memories still of Bordeaux—London was so different. It was no gay little provincial city; it was a great metropolis of the world, where every square and street-corner offered evidence of the range and power of the British Empire. As the ladies drove through Regent Street or swept down Buckingham Palace Road, they could scarcely keep their heads inside the carriage. There was so much to see; if something attracted their attention on one side they were bound to miss something utterly fascinating on the other. A company of horse-guards, resplendent in glittering cuirasses and streaming black plumes, would gallop past with a clatter of hooves and a jingle of swords—more thrilling than any spectacle behind the footlights of the Bowery. As they rolled through Hyde Park they would pass handsome equipages painted blue or pale rose or shiny black, with liveried coachmen up before, and haughty footmen, arms folded, perched precariously up behind. There would be gilded crests on the doors, and if they looked hard they might glimpse the profile of some august personage within. But it was not only the magnificence and splendor that Lily found picturesque. She was just as captivated by the ragamuffins who were always appearing to open the door when the carriage stopped, and the crossing sweeps vociferously offering their services to anybody affluent enough to hire them.

Lily marveled at the efficiency and skill of the London milliners and mantuamakers. The ladies planned to visit the Italian Opera, and needed suitable gowns to mingle with the *haut monde* that frequented Her Majesty's Theatre. Accordingly, they sought out a court dressmaker who had been highly recommended; and at five o'clock of the evening before the performance they were to attend, their measurements were taken. "Within eight minutes (three of which were passed in astonish-

45

ment at my giving my name as a married woman) I was fitted
and in the carriage again! The dress came home the next
morning, and became me à merveille." When one reflects on the
complexities of even the simplest toilette of the time, not to
mention a ballgown, one might marvel with Lily at such speed.
And yet it was all a matter of organization and an unlimited
labor market. Half a dozen expert seamstresses (at sixpence an
hour each) could easily turn out a handsome creation by simply
working all night.

Covent Garden, Her Majesty's Theatre, which was about three
times the size of the Park in New York, exceeded in magnificence
anything the ladies had yet seen. They went on a Saturday, which
was the most fashionable night, and the audience were all in
costume de bal. Most of the assemblage were of the nobility, and
it was only by a stroke of luck that Lily and her aunt had
managed to secure places. They discovered that even peers were
not completely devoid of the commercial instinct on which the
power of England rested. By paying an exorbitant price, the two
were able to obtain the Duchess of Grosvenor's box for the evening. If the price startled them, they did not hesitate to pay it;
for in addition to the opera, they would be able to see the Queen,
who was scheduled to attend on that evening. In this delightful
expectation, however, they were disappointed. "The queen was
present," Lily wrote to James, "but our republican curiosity was
not gratified, for she sat directly beneath our *loge.*"

The opera itself was splendid. The offering was *Lucia di Lammermoor,* and the singing of Persiani was almost too sublime for
words. "Her mad scene was *painfully* powerful—*terribly* beautiful,"—thus she put it to James. Strangely enough, when she
came herself to play the Bride of Lammermoor, in the stage
version of Scott's novel, the critics would strain the language in
a similar way to describe her performance of Lucy Ashton.
It is not unlikely that something of Persiani's interpretation of
Lucia was incorporated later into Anna Cora's own projection
of the part; and that the lyrical quality with which she lifted
the scene above the crude melodrama of the original was due

to the memory of Donizetti's exquisite aria—which forever haunted her after hearing Persiani.

In London Lily also saw Madame Vestris, the leading actress of the English stage. This lady had toured America a few seasons before, but with little success. Seeing her now in her own theatre with the company which she had selected and trained, Lily thought she understood why this had been. A play, as she now saw for perhaps the first time, was not a mere vehicle for the display of one individual's talents. It was (if the author's intention was to be realized) a group creation in which each player contributed his part—giving his personal art to the whole, and reflecting the equally personal arts of his fellow-actors. Even a great star, if truly an actress and not just a showy personality, could display her art only if properly supported. So it was with Madame Vestris. "She is nothing alone," Lily wrote to May. "This is her sphere—she is the planet round which her satellites move. Drawing light from her they shine themselves, and thus add to her lustre. She is nothing alone—she must have a certain entourage to develop and set forth her powers."

This is astute criticism from an eighteen-year-old girl who had scarcely visited the theatre more than five or six times in her life. One can search the professional reviews of the period in vain for similar understanding of the actor's art. One would wait for more than half a century before the theatre itself showed the same perceptions. But in this as most things Lily was ahead of her time. For a brief season when she herself was a star, she succeeded in abolishing the star-system; but the system itself was too firmly established to give way entirely. In America, where worship of the glittering personality has been one of the negative by-products of the gospel of individualism, the star-system continues to be the backbone of the theatre.

Shopping and theatre-going did not consume all the ladies' time. With that almost maniacal compulsion to see everything which has always made the American tourist the wonder of Europeans, Lily and her aunt systematically did the sights. They were properly impressed by all the usual things: the Tower and the crown jewels; Westminster Abbey; St. Paul's. They gazed with particular admiration at the colossal statue of Achilles opposite the entrance to Hyde Park, erected in honor of the Duke of Wellington by the *English ladies* (underlined by Lily in her report to James).

One memorable morning was spent at Madame Tussaud's, where the two visitors had the gratification of standing only a few feet from the Queen. She was in wax, it is true, but so like life that she practically breathed! As for the figure of Madame de St. Amaranth (she who had rejected the vile solicitations of Robespierre, and thus become the victim of his fury)—it actually *did breathe*. She was stretched upon a couch in a dying attitude, her bosom heaving with expiring agony. (How many transmogrifications has this lady undergone in the course of a century! In one's childhood she was the Sleeping Beauty. For present-day children she is a somnolent blonde with Hollywood contours. But the figure is the same. Only the mechanism—which in Lily's day was clockwork—is now electrified).

The very last day, as they were attempting to squeeze their greatly-augmented wardrobes into recalcitrant trunks and portmanteaus, news was brought that the Queen was momentarily expected to visit the National Gallery. Abandoning their packing, the ladies summoned their carriage and dashed to Trafalgar Square where they joined the eager crowd. They stood for an hour and a half, but the Queen did not arrive. On the basis of a rumor that she had changed her destination, they sped to St. James' Place. Here they passed another hour, only to be disappointed again. Well, no one could say they had not tried!

That night—"the loveliest moonlight night I ever beheld"—they left London. Twenty-four hours later, after a pleasant passage across the North Sea, they were in Hamburg. From Hamburg they proceeded by *Schnellpost* (which one of them thought must mean "snail-post") to Bremen. Here they were awaited by Anna Cora's younger sister Emma, who had married a wealthy young German merchant, Henry Mecke, only a short time before. Lily and her aunt were to spend the winter with them.

Lily's usual delight in all sorts and conditions of people seems not to have operated in the case of the Germans. But if she did not warm to the people themselves, that fact did not lessen her curiosity about them. Their extraordinary tastes, particularly in the matter of food and drink—and funerals—were the object of the most careful observation—and reflection. As usual, when Lily reflected it was with pen in hand. She began to note down what she saw and heard in Bremen. Two years later these notes formed the basis of an article which was published in *The Ladies' Companion.*

Usages and Manners of the Northern Germans begins with a description of German meals—the most remarkable feature of which, for Lily, is their length. She marvels at the devices by which the consumption of food can be prolonged indefinitely. There is not only the food itself, fifteen or twenty courses— but toasts, songs, speeches, and, naturally, conversation. When the foreigner thinks the time at last arrived for the guests to leave their seats (we can imagine Lily as having been long on the edge of *hers*), there is a further ceremony. Each gentleman now takes out a pipe and indulges "in the luxury of sending forth fantastic wreaths of smoke to encircle the fair one by his side, without the remotest fear of a distasteful frown deepening on her brow; and she, if fatigued, or preferring a more poetic garland, may soon disappear, almost unperceived, amid the clouds of smoke which darken the air, and refresh herself with the perfume of the carefully-tended garden. . . ."

From dinner-parties Lily proceeds at once to funerals, there being evidently some association in her mind between the two. She is fascinated by the long flaxen wigs worn by pallbearers in Hamburg. Like Mark Twain later, she notes the institution in Germany of special houses, where the dead are laid out in comfort and allowed to remain for several days with a bell-rope attached to their hands so that help can be instantly summoned in the event of a return to animation: all of which is merely a precaution against faulty diagnosis.

But Anna Cora's finest praise is reserved for German cemeteries and the loving care expended by survivors of the deceased in keeping these hallowed spots neat and pretty. She is lyrically moved by the attitude of those who come to mourn: a father and his children standing with bowed heads beside a mother's grave, or "a young widow bending over a shattered column, and with gentle hands training the ivy at its base to wind round that sculptured emblem, even as her thoughts and affections intwine the memory of the departed." All that is lacking in the description is the weeping-willow, and its absence is a symptom of the author's restraint. Even so, Anna Cora's fond lingering on the theme of death is very typical of the period. Yet in her case, as with our great-grandmothers in general, it is a tendency easy to misjudge. Like so many young women of her time Anna Cora lived in the shadow of incurable disease, and had she not been able to romanticize death, she might have sunk into a helpless pessimism.

Another vignette of her Bremen winter, eventually appeared in *The Ladies' Companion*. It was called *Bridal Customs of the North Germans*. As in the matter of funerals, Anna Cora was struck by the picturesqueness surrounding a ceremony so universal. The "Binding of the Myrtle," a pre-nuptial rite in which only unmarried ladies took part, particularly charmed her. In fact the whole business of Marriage, including the silver and golden weddings—for Lily did not believe in leaving a subject until she had exhausted its possibilities—had an element of drama which she found very satisfying.

Bremen life on the whole was not too exciting. There was not a great deal to see. The charm of the old Hanseatic architecture seems to have been lost on Lily, though she does lavish attention on the cathedral—particularly the burial vaults, where, due to some strange property of the air, bodies had been preserved for centuries without decay. This attraction was apparently popular with *most* tourists, for the coffins were left open to display the bodies in their moldering shrouds. Among other notable personages laid here to rest was the Countess of Stanhope. She was said to have been a great beauty, and her teeth were still perfect. By her side (but evidently not related) was a noble baron who "yet retained his corpulent appearance." There was also the body of a young student, who had been shot

THE ASTOR HOUSE, NEW YORK

from Meyer's Universum, c. 1850

in a duel for his lady love. One could still see the hole in his breast made by the ball; and one of the ladies in Anna Cora's party severed a lock from the head of this long-dead Romeo. The traveler of the period had a catholic taste in souvenirs.

Meanwhile Lily was not idle. On the contrary, the routine of study went on with the same relentless application and method as at Melrose. The two ladies had taken a small furnished house for themselves, so that the program of self-improvement might proceed without interruption. At nine she had a two-hour German lesson. This was followed by a visit from her piano-teacher, who in turn was followed by a singing-master. Although Lily had a keen feeling for the nuances of language and was already bi-lingual, she found German a most obdurate tongue. However, this fact only whetted her determination, and after three months she could report with satisfaction that she was tasting "with exquisite enjoyment" the beauties of Goethe and Schiller.

Mr. Mowatt had planned to join his wife about the first of February. Happily he was able to speed his departure, and arrived in Bremen the middle of January. The letter announcing the changed date had miscarried, so that when he appeared Lily was greatly startled. She was practicing at the piano when he walked into the little salon, and the sudden sight of him so shocked her that she sprang violently to her feet. The brusque movement brought on a hemorrhage of the lungs—an effect to be produced throughout her life whenever she met with too-sudden excitement. The joyful reunion was thus dampened by a temporary relapse. Nevertheless, during the months in Bremen Lily's basic constitution had been noticeably strengthened, and within a few weeks she was again on her feet. To hasten her recovery it was decided that they should move southward through Switzerland, southern France, and on into Italy. The plans for the journey were almost completed, when James fell ill, attacked by a disease of the eyes which threatened to destroy his sight. James was at this time an ardent believer in homeopathy; but the two most eminent practitioners of the art in Bremen were unable to help him. For four months he could only sit in a darkened chamber, suffering excruciating pain. Nothing but the sound of his wife's voice could bring surcease from the agony, and Lily read or talked to him from morning to night.

During this time the Mowatts heard about the celebrated Dr. Hahnemann who was located in Paris. When, toward the end of December, James rallied sufficiently to make the journey, they set out for France. It was bitterly cold, and the trip would have been a trial of endurance even for a well man. They traveled by boat up the Rhine, then overland by diligence, and for brief stretches on newly-constructed railway lines. Despite the discomfort and the constant shifting from one means of locomotion to another, they made the trip in three days.

In Paris they were greeted by the parents-in-law of Anna Cora's oldest sister, Charlotte, who had been widowed at about the time of Lily's elopement, and was now remarried to a Frenchman, M. Joseph Guillet. Though she and her husband were living in America, M. Guillet's mother and sisters received the Mowatts with great kindness and did everything possible to assist the invalid. Above all they urged that he see their own physician, in whom they had the utmost confidence. But James was determined to see Dr. Hahnemann.

Samuel Christian Friedrich Hahnemann, the father of homeopathy, was one of the most distinguished medical figures of the age. A native of Meissen, he had been hounded from city to city in Germany—mainly by the opposition of apothecaries whose business he menaced—until in his old age he was forced to become an exile. He had been settled now in Paris for about five years, had achieved an international reputation, and amassed a fortune. At this time he was about 85 years old.

A consultation presented some difficulty, since James was too ill to visit the great man and the Doctor too old to leave his own house. Indeed by now most of Hahnemann's consultations were carried on by his wife, whom Anna Cora describes as a woman of remarkable gifts. She had been trained in medicine by her husband, acted as his assistant, and actually conducted a considerable part of his practice. When in desperation Anna Cora undertook to see the doctor herself, it was Mrs. Hahnemann

—clad in an elaborate afternoon gown, with long golden curls about her shoulders—who managed the interview, referring occasionally to the wizened figure who sat huddled in an easy-chair in a corner of the room. She was disappointed when Mrs. Hahnemann refused to prescribe without seeing the patient personally; and there was nothing for it but somehow to get James to the great man's house. Finally, this was done; but the results were disappointing. Although James faithfully followed the regimen and took the medicines prescribed, his sufferings merely increased. Homeopathy was then abandoned, and the Guillet family physician called in. All to no avail, and for four months James lay in his darkened room, certain now that he would never see again.

Then relief came from an unexpected quarter. Dr. Valentine Mott, the eminent New York surgeon, happened to be passing through Paris. Although on a pleasure trip, he could not turn a deaf ear to the entreaties of the daughter of Samuel Ogden. He immediately undertook to help, and in two weeks there was a distinct change for the better. In a short while the bandages were removed from James's eyes, and he could sit in the lightly-curtained drawing-room of their apartment. On the day when he could finally walk in the Champs Elysées, there was great jubilation.

With the load of James's threatened blindness removed, Anna Cora's spirits soared. Although James himself seldom ventured under the blaze of ballroom chandeliers—they were far more dazzling than sunlight in the Champs Elysées—he insisted that Anna Cora and her aunt join the social whirl. With their numerous connections, the Mowatts were the constant recipients of invitations to balls and soirées which, after so many months of ill-health and depression, Lily was delighted to accept. The most magnificent of these events, a fancy-dress ball given by an American millionaire, was described for the readers of *The Ladies' Companion*. How the housewives of Hartford and Buffalo must have reveled in this record of refined opulence! The gorgeous mansion of their expatriate countryman was guarded for the occasion by fifty *gendarmes,* and the line of carriages waiting to discharge the guests stretched down the street as far as the eye could see.

> Twelve gorgeous saloons were thrown open. Where the uncouth door once had been, costly drapery was suspended, tastefully gathered in folds or festoons; the carpets of velvet, the divans, ottomans, and couches were all that could be imagined of luxurious and beautiful. The walls were fluted with gold or rich silks, and hung with the works of the first masters; the ceilings painted in a thousand devices. . . . The thousand lights shed a flood of brilliancy which would almost have eclipsed sunshine; and the sparkling of diamonds threw a lustre around almost dazzling.

The costumes were "of every clime, 'of every land where woman smiles or sighs.' " There was a pageant and a ballet, involving shepherdesses, Turks, knights, and Highlanders on horseback. And there were tableaux representing Madame de Pompadour and Louis XV with his court in powdered wigs and jewelled robes, and at their close "the giddy waltz and gay quadrille were merrily joined in by the company in general." Afterwards came a banquet of the most delicate viands in endless tempting variety set out on a gold service. As a final note (for Anna Cora was mindful of the audience for which she wrote):

> The cost of this ball is currently estimated at eight thousand dollars. One lady present wore so many diamonds (said to be valued at two hundred thousand dollars) that she was escorted to her carriage by *gendarmes*, for fear of robbery.

In the brilliant social life of Paris, Anna Cora herself was something of a figure. Her sparkling wit, her complete command of French, which after all was her first language, and her cosmopolitan background enabled her to move with ease through the aristocratic salons of the rue de l'Université and the Faubourg St. Honoré. Her appearance was arresting. She was below medium height, but so slender and so perfectly-proportioned that she gave the impression of being taller. Despite her youth she had great dignity, and in her manner there was none of that arch helplessness that so many small women affect. All descriptions are unanimous as to the extraordinary grace of her movements, and the elfin prettiness which had first attracted James Mowatt's attention had ripened into warm beauty. Her quick responsiveness to people and situations was reflected in the animation of her face; and the radiance of her smile, which once seen was never forgotten, gave her a fascination that men— and women—found irresistible.

Through the American minister, General Cass, and her father's French connections, Anna Cora met a number of distinguished personalities in Paris. She was particularly charmed with Madame de Lasteyrie, the daughter of La Fayette, who lived austerely in a great barn of an apartment in the Faubourg St. Germain and spent her days in good works. She also met Lady Bulwer, in Paris seeking a divorce from Sir Edward (soon to become Lord Lytton). She sympathized with that noble lady who had suffered much at the hands of her frivolous and irresponsible husband. Through Lady Bulwer she made the acquaintance of Mrs. Trollope. Like any proud daughter of Columbia, Anna Cora had been prepared to dislike thoroughly this lady whose treatment of America in her *Domestic Manners of the Americans* had been so merciless. But she found Mrs. Trollope actually the soul of kindness and a delightful companion. Lily herself now knew something of the larger world, and as she viewed America in a new perspective, she was forced to conclude that Mrs. Trollope's reflections on our native habits were in the main well-founded. In the end she felt only sympathy for Mrs. Trollope, who was after all the victim of a dreadful affliction. "Mrs. Trollope! What a name! Surely Juliet was wrong if she thought a rose would smell as sweet were it called a dandelion."

In Paris Anna Cora became a devotée of Rachel, and went again and again to the Théâtre Français to see her. Although she never met the great tragedienne, she became acquainted with Rachel's two younger sisters, and through them Anna Cora learned something of Rachel's private life, which she found wholly admirable. As for Rachel the artist, she could only be described as overwhelming. "From the moment she came upon the stage, I was always under the influence of a spell.

Her eyes had the power of a basilisk's upon me, and flashed with an intense brightness which no basilisk's could have rivalled. I never expect to see that acting equalled—to surpass it in impassioned force and grandeur, appears to me to be impossible."

Despite her busy social life and constant theatre-going, Anna Cora found time to study and to write, keeping to a fixed schedule in which so many hours of the day were allotted to each subject. She went on struggling valiantly with music. She read German literature diligently and plunged into Italian. Somehow she also managed to write long letters to her father and sisters, which later stood her in good stead as sources for articles in *Sargent's* and *Godey's*. Some of her more serious reflections found their way into these letters. Her childhood fondness for France had increased with her new insight into the values of French civilization. In a letter to May she wrote: "Poverty is not here considered to be nearly so much a crime as with us and in England. Talents, education, manners, even *personal attractions,* are placed before riches. Entrance into good society may be commanded by *these*, while with us the entrance is too often purchasable."

There is this telling comment on the American passion for imitating European ways. "The customs and fashions which we imitate as Parisian are not infrequently mere caricatures of those that exist in Paris. For instance, it is the present *mode* not to introduce persons who meet at parties or in visiting, but the custom is intended to obviate the ceremoniousness of formal introductions. Everyone is expected to talk to his neighbor; and if mutual pleasure is received from the intercourse, an acquaintance is formed. The same fashion in vogue with us renders society cold and stiff. We abolish introductions because the Parisians do so; but we only take this first step in our transatlantic imitations. Few persons feel at liberty to address strangers. Little, contracted circles of friends herd in clannish groups together, and mar the true object of society. As yet, we only *follow* the fashions; we do not conceive the spirit which dictated them."

This observation contains the germ of *Fashion,* the first American play of real distinction, and the first important satire of society in the New World. The play itself was still five years off, but the subject was already being studied with absorbed attention. Anna Cora's comedy of manners, based on a comparison of French and American society, is a facet of the International Theme: a theme which Anna Cora Mowatt was to exploit with telling effect a generation before the advent of Henry James.

Not only our drawing-room manners, but our habits of dress, particularly feminine, reflected the mania of the '30's and '40's for aping Europe—and often with ludicrous results. "Expensive materials, worn here only at balls, are imported by American merchants and pronounced to be 'very fashionable in Paris.' They are universally bought by our belles, who, instead of wearing them at proper seasons, parade the streets in what is meant exclusively for evening costume." Ten years before, Fanny Kemble, freshly arrived from England, was completely nonplussed to see that New York ladies often did their morning shopping in evening gowns.

Both James and his Lily were now apparently restored to health and eager to return to America. Even before leaving Paris they made plans for an elaborate homecoming celebration. Anna Cora devoted the last weeks of her stay to composing the pièce de résistance for this grand occasion, a dramatic work in six acts and in blank verse entitled *Gulzara, or the Persian Slave*. To insure that nothing might be lacking in the production, the most ambitious which she had yet undertaken, she commissioned a prominent French scene-painter to do the settings (one for each act!) and ordered sumptuous costumes from a leading couturier.

Late in August, 1840, James and Lily and all their baggage— including the six sets of imported scenery—embarked on the *Ville de Lyons* at Havre and set sail for New York.

CHAPTER FIVE

Gulzara and the Great Step

Anna Cora had been away from America for fifteen months. When she left she was scarcely more than an adolescent, totally inexperienced in practical matters (even house-keeping) and accepting as completely natural the fact that she should be the center of a circle of admiring friends and relatives. When she sailed on the *Roscius* she had been very ill, hardly caring whether she lived or died. But the months abroad had wrought a great change. James's Lily had finally grown up. She had apparently regained her health; and instead of being the pampered invalid, the object of solicitude to all around her, she had been forced to assume the responsibility for both her husband's well-being and her own. During the agonizing months of James's illness she had taken the initiative not only in finding proper medical attention for him, but in managing the details of their living and travels. In addition she had found time to satisfy her restless urge for creative activity, and to enjoy the gay life of Paris. The flower had opened.

Almost the first important event after the return to Melrose was the fête at which *Gulzara* was performed. The occasion, as for so many others in the family, was Samuel Ogden's birthday, the 17th of October. The date had to be set back a few days until the full moon; because of the four-mile drive to Flatbush, it would have been difficult for the guests to find their way on a dark night.

Weeks before the great day the house was in a turmoil of preparation. Since the boys no longer took part in family theatricals, *Gulzara* had been designed for an all-female cast. Lily's inventiveness was thoroughly equal to the problem. The action of the play takes place in the harem of Sultan Suliman (the Sultan being conveniently away from home at the time). Gulzara, the latest addition to the ménage, is the heroine of the piece, whose action centers around the jealousy of Ayesha, the Sultan's former favorite, towards the newcomer. The only male part is that of Amurath, the Sultan's ten-year-old son— which could be credibly performed by a girl and had been specifically written, of course, for the precocious Julia. Lily herself played the rôle of Gulzara.

There are six characters in the play. The cast for the first production, in addition to Lily and Julia, included May, Elizabeth Mowatt (James's younger sister), Ida Yates (Lily's niece), and an old school friend, Anna Battelle. In order to facilitate things the entire cast took up residence at Melrose for the weeks preceding the performance.

Rehearsals were conducted systematically, but not always with professional decorum. There were frequent interruptions due to uncontrollable fits of laughter over efforts to scream musically and faint gracefully. Sometimes in the more touching passages of the play the company would dissolve in tears—not simulated, as Anna Cora informs us, "but genuine outbursts of girlish feeling."

The more violent scenes proved so alarming to the household staff of Melrose, mainly simple maids from the village of Flatbush, unused to such goings-on, that these episodes had to be rehearsed in the barn. Here the girls practiced all the modulations of screaming (a good deal of which is required in *Gulzara*) without attracting undue attention—or so they thought. The convenient mounds of hay enabled them to acquire more confidence and fewer bruises in their swooning. This exercise never failed to send them off into shrieks of laughter—which one day was echoed from the barn loft. Looking up, the girls beheld a circle of grinning faces surrounding the hay-chute. A group of laborers from the estate, who up to this moment had watched the rehearsal with silent respect, had been unable to restrain themselves when the fainting began.

At last the grand day arrived. The weather was perfect and the awaited moon rose in full splendor. At six o'clock, carriages began to roll up to the portico of the mansion; they bore the cream of New York society, which had been looking forward to the Mowatts' homecoming-party as the event of the season. Twittering belles in corkscrew curls and fringed shawls were handed out of the carriages by gentlemen in yellow kid gloves and frock coats with velvet facings. Mr. Mowatt met them at the door (the continental fashion of having guests announced by a servant was just coming in, but it was considered effete by most people), and directed them up the broad staircase to leave their wraps. Everyone understood, of course, that if Anna Cora did not receive with her husband it was because she was up to something; and there was excited whispering and laughing as the guests passed each other on the stairs.

Finally everybody was assembled in the ballroom, at one end of which a stage with a regular proscenium and draw curtain had been erected. In the hall a full band, imported from the city, struck up an overture: perhaps the *Turkish March* from Beethoven's *Ruins of Athens,* which was very popular at the moment and would have made a suitable introduction to a domestic drama involving the household of Sultan Suliman.

Then the main lights were extinguished and the footlights turned up. While there was, of course, no gas in the country, whale-oil lamps in front of specially-constructed reflectors provided ample illumination for the small stage. When the red brocaded curtains parted and the first of the Parisian settings was revealed, the audience gave a gasp of delighted astonishment. They had expected Anna Cora to do something clever—she always did; but they were not prepared for this elegant display. They not only recognized the beautiful set as professional; the hall of the Sultan's palace looked to them, too, strikingly authentic. From the time when the ohs and ahs had died down and little Julia appeared wearing one of the handsome costumes also imported from Paris, the audience was convinced that it was being treated to something very special.

Anna Cora played Gulzara with great feeling and to continued rounds of applause; but the palm of the evening, so she herself insists, went to Julia whose performance of Amurath produced alternately floods of tears and gales of laughter. There were, of course, abundant laurels for all the others, and when the curtain at last closed—with audience and actors exhausted by their enthusiasm—everyone agreed that there had never been anything like it and that Anna Cora was undoubtedly a genius.

Gulzara was followed by a ball and then supper. When the final guest departed the moon had long since disappeared, but by that time the sun was rising and there was no danger of the horses getting off the road.

Gulzara was later published in *The New World,* whose associate editor, Epes Sargent, had heard of the success of the play and had solicited the manuscript. The work attracted much favorable attention from the critics—most of whom, as Anna Cora notes with disarming candor, were guests at the performance. Sargent, however, was not among these; and his introductory critique of the play gave Anna Cora particular pleasure since the writer was not personally acquainted with her:

> The drama of Gulzara, or the Persian Slave, was written by a young lady lovely and accomplished. There is a unity and simplicity in its design and execution which cannot fail to give sincere pleasure. It is pervaded by rare and delicate thought; many passages are strikingly beautiful, and the impartial critic will think, with us, that the drama would do credit to a much more experienced writer.

The ball at Melrose and the production of *Gulzara* with its lavish scenery and costumes was the last large-scale entertainment at which the Mowatts were hosts to New York society. Within a few months of that October dawn when James and Lily had sped the last guest down the long avenue leading to the road, they too would drive down the same avenue—turning back at the gates for a final glimpse of Melrose.

Although James Mowatt had returned from Europe much improved in health, his eyes were still in such condition that he could not resume his law practice. He could read very large print for a few minutes a day, but it was out of the question to attempt to decipher handwritten legal documents. Doomed to professional inactivity, he became restless and rash.

The late 1830's was a time in which many Americans, with less reason than James Mowatt, succumbed to the lure of easy money and plunged into speculation. This is what happened to Lily's husband. He had begun investing heavily in New York real estate in the mid-thirties and had made large profits, at least on paper. However, the financial reforms of the last years of Jackson's administration—which resulted in the banks' suddenly calling in loans in order to meet their obligations to the states—had found him, like countless others, without defenses. The sudden necessity for producing hard cash, where there was only paper, was disastrous. By the fall of 1841 there was almost nothing left.

All this, of course, was completely unknown to Lily. All she understood of her husband's finances was that money had never been lacking. Now, to be informed that there was almost no money at all left her in a state of bewilderment. But she was less bewildered than James himself. The change in his fortunes, combined with his physical affliction, plunged him into deepest melancholy. It was this fact, more than the disappearance of their wealth, that alarmed Lily. Secondly, she thought of Melrose which had meant so much to them both.

"Is there no possible means of saving this house?" she asked. James shook his head in dejection.

"None that I can imagine."

"How long may we remain here?"

James was not certain how soon his creditors would act; but naturally, in view of the general state of things, they would not wait long. "A month perhaps—certainly not longer."

"And where shall we go?"

"Heaven knows!" In all the six years of their married life— even in the depths of his misery in Europe—James had never spoken in such a tone of complete despair.

Lily did what she could to comfort him; and that afternoon while James was resting in his darkened room she walked up and down the long arbor behind the house. It was her favorite spot in the garden, for it had been built especially for her. Now, with the bright early autumn sunlight filtering through the heavy leaves beginning to turn yellow at the edges, and striking full on the great bunches of luscious fruit, it made her think of the Garden of Eden. Melrose had been a sort of Paradise— she realized that now as she looked out over the bright garden with the broad lawns and the woods beyond. And they must leave it, just as Adam and Eve had had to leave Eden; but certainly for different reasons! *They* had done nothing to deserve being thrust out into the cold world.

Lily might now have dissolved in tears at the thought of the injustice of it all, but her mind was far too busy for vain regrets. She had but to recall James's terrible despondency when he broke the news of the disaster to realize that something must be done. She knew enough of the world to be aware that what was happening to them had happened to other people before, even before Mr. Jackson had become President; and that, dire though the circumstance might be, one could survive it.

Lily had not far to look for an example of this. Her sister Charlotte, through whom James had first found his way to the Ogden house, had passed through something similar—even worse. Her marriage to Mr. Yates had not turned out to be very happy; moreover, he had soon died leaving her penniless. She had then married M. Guillet and had gone to live in Paris. Now she was separated from her second husband and again without resources, and with five children to support! But Charlotte had managed. As a girl she had studied painting in France, and when she had gone back with M. Guillet she had continued to work, developing her gift to the point where she had taken prizes at the Paris Salon. At present she was literally supporting herself and her children with miniature-painting.

Lily took stock. What Charlotte had done, could she not also do? Were there no gracious gifts within her nature that might be used to save her husband and her home? She began systematically to review the possibilities. The two main resources for impoverished gentlewomen of the time were sewing and school-teaching. Neither of these could Lily contemplate for long. Her sewing was like her singing: a trifle erratic, and aimed more at general effect than solid durability. And, despite James's efforts, there were gaps in her preparation that would prove a handicap in teaching. Although she knew most of Shakespeare by heart and spoke four languages fluently, she could not parse a sentence or conjugate an irregular verb. She was at home in Greek mythology and knew something of philosophy; but the multiplication table still baffled her.

Then she thought of writing, and for a moment this opened up a real hope. *Gulzara* had appeared in *The New World* and had attracted favorable comment. Mr. Sargent, with whom she and James were now personally acquainted, had been most encouraging. But writing took so much time before it produced results; and there was an urgency in this situation which demanded that whatever she did must net quick returns. Besides, the pecuniary rewards of authorship were poor unless one had a great reputation. Most of the contributors to even such prosperous magazines as *Godey's Lady's Book* received nothing for their work except the honor of having it published. And though at any other time Lily would have been content with that, she did not see how honor would feed and shelter them just now.

Her thoughts moved naturally from *Gulzara* to her success in the title rôle of the play. Suddenly she stopped her pacing of the arbor walk. Here was a possibility! Discounting the fact that her audience had been largely composed of friends, there was no denying that they had been genuinely affected by her performance of the Persian Slave. Dozens of times before that, too, had she proven—always discreetly for friends, of course— her ability to act. *There* was her gift! But the moment she considered it seriously, this idea too had to be rejected. A career of acting, *professional* acting, would mean association with the theatre; and that was unthinkable. Lily had progressed beyond the stage of believing the theatre to be the abode of vice and wickedness that the Rev. Dr. Eastburn had once proclaimed it, and which most clergymen still proclaimed it. But it was not a life which a woman of gentle breeding could conceivably adopt.

The idea that the theatre itself might not welcome her with open arms to an exalted place in its midst did not cross Lily's mind. Doubtless it would have, had she given the matter much thought, for she was already very objective about herself. At the moment she could only regret that the one means she possessed for survival was outlawed by a barrier of opinion which even a mind as ingenious as hers could not surmount.

Yet she could not wholly tear her thoughts from the idea. The longer she reflected, the more certain she felt that her greatest talent, however modest in itself, must be exploited. She had seen often enough that she had power over an audience. And there were other assets. She had a remarkable speaking voice. Her experience as a linguist and her sensitivity to the values of the spoken word had developed unusually fine enunciation. She had imagination: on more than one occasion she had completely identified herself with the character she was portraying. She also had physical charms. People said that she was beautiful, although she had her own ideas on that subject. Her figure lacked the curves prescribed by the highest fashion, and her features, which her friends thought so exquisitely aristocratic, she considered a trifle large. Her own ideal was someone like Julia: all soft roundness with rosebud mouth and a haze of golden hair. However there was no accounting for tastes, and if people enjoyed looking at her so much the better—if they were willing to pay for the pleasure.

But how could she perform as an actress without going into the theatre and hopelessly compromising her reputation? How could one act without company and scenery and—she got no further, for in a flash the solution came to her.

One of the events of that New York winter had been a series of appearances by the elder Vandenhoff, an actor famous in both England and America. Vandenhoff had filled the National Theatre night after night with his readings from Shakespeare and other poets. People had thrilled to the magnetism of his personality and the powers of his imagination as he populated an empty stage with character after character of his own creation.

Lily's heart beat with excitement. What Vandenhoff had done she would do! It did not matter that she was young and unknown. She too had thrilled people with her readings, whole drawing-roomsful. She had seen tears wiped away when she recited "Woodman, Spare that Tree." Even General Morris himself, who had written it, could scarcely contain his emotions when he heard her. As for her rendering of "Edward"—that left people wide-eyed with horror.

Lily jumped up from the bench where she had sunk in the midst of her meditations. Gathering up her skirts she ran with all speed to the house to tell James about her wonderful scheme. James was sitting at the tea-table, sunk in dejection, when she burst into the library. He looked up at her in alarm. She was breathless and her cheeks were flushed. He half-rose to come to her, his dim eyes staring with concern. But she pushed him back into his chair and seated herself beside him. From his solicitous inquiry it was evident that he thought something had happened to her, that their troubles had gone to her head.

Then she poured out her plan. By the time she had outlined it, the poor man was so overwhelmed that he had no strength to argue with her. He made no remark about the propriety or impropriety of what she proposed. He had, of course, no doubts as to her ability to rival Vandenhoff or anyone else who ever sought to charm the public. His only protest was the state of her health. She had always been so delicate. Could she possibly endure the strain involved in such an undertaking?

But Lily brushed this aside. In the last few moments, as the prospect of achieving something herself, of helping *him*, had grown in her mind, she felt an increase of power, of actual physical strength which she had never known before. Of course she could do it!

Her enthusiasm was contagious. To see his little Lily so bright, so excited, so positively happy, caused James himself to rally. He began to discuss with her the practical aspects of the matter. What sort of things would she read? Shakespeare?

Lily shook her head. She did not think Shakespeare would be wholly suitable. She was not really experienced enough for that —at least in public. Too many people would have just heard Mr. Vandenhoff, and there might be a tendency to make comparisons. She would do rather simple, appealing things. She might do selections from Scott: *Marmion*, or *The Lady of the Lake*. Scott was so terribly popular! And then she would do some short pieces (again, for one, "Woodman, Spare that Tree!") —things with feeling. In fact there was so much talk now about American poetry, why wouldn't it be rather a good idea to specialize in that? Most Americans were still smarting under that horrible remark of Sydney Smith's ten years before: "Whoever reads an American book! Whoever sees an American play! . . ." It would please people to have him refuted publicly—by Anna Cora Mowatt.

James approved of this. He thought it might be a good thing to consult their new friend Epes Sargent, who was himself a poet and had very refined literary tastes. James would drive into New York tomorrow and go over the whole question with Mr. Sargent. The discussion lasted until late that night, and when they at last took their candles from the mahogany table under Lily's portrait—where they stood like footlights shining up into the face of a new star—and started up the long stairway, it was with lighter steps than in many a day.

Next morning James went to the city as planned, while Lily broke the news to May. The reaction was stronger than Lily had expected. May was horrified, and burst into a fit of weeping. She was a rather timid girl and the thought of her darling sister exposing herself on a platform before the gaze of hundreds— strangers at that—was more than she could bear.

"You *cannot* go through it. I am sure you cannot!" she sobbed.

"We none know what we *can* do until we are tried," said Lily with a touch of severity—much more to bolster her own courage than to contradict poor May.

"What will our friends say of you if you make a public appearance?" This excruciating vision sent May off into more tears.

"What will our friends *do* for us in case I do not? Will they preserve to us this sweet home? Will they support us? Will they sympathize with us in our adversity?" Lily had not given this matter a thought, but as she spoke the words she realized their truth.

"But you will lose your position in society!" May knew her argument was weak, but she would clutch at any straw.

"If I fail," said Lily matter-of-factly, "probably I shall; but I do not intend to fail. And what is that position in society worth when we are no longer able to feast and entertain? How many of those whom we feasted and entertained at our last ball will seek us out when we live in poverty and obscurity?"

Poor May could think of nothing to counter this.

"If you would only look at all the obstacles," she said feebly. This was all Lily needed to confirm her resolution. "No, I am looking above and beyond them, and I only see duty in their place."

May knew that there was no help for it now. Lily had heard her voices, and though they led her to the stake—which to May would have been infinitely preferable to a hall full of staring people—she would follow them to the end.

"Young as my sister was," Anna Cora recorded later, "she saw the force of my arguments, and sorrowed in silence."

Anna Cora was neither sorrowful nor silent. During the next two weeks, for hours of the bright October days, she paced up and down the brick path under the arbor, exercising her voice on the numbers she had chosen for her program. If the housemaids and gardeners of Melrose had been amazed by the rehearsals for *Gulzara*, what must they have thought now as hour after hour their chatelaine promenaded under the grapevines, proclaiming in loud clear tones,

The way was long, the wind was cold,
The Minstrel was infirm and old. . . .

What they or anyone else thought was just now of small importance to Anna Cora. She had committed herself to an unprecedented step, and if she failed it would not be for lack of effort. Meticulously she analyzed every line of every poem she would present, trying innumerable readings until she had the one she felt was right. At night in the library she would try out the results on James; and when in his judgment a stress had been misplaced, a tone was pitched too high or too low, she corrected the reading and next day under the arbor rehearsed the change.

Epes Sargent had been most helpful. He was enthusiastic about the plan. Although not present at the production of *Gulzara*, he had been a guest at Melrose many times since then and had witnessed often Anna Cora's talents. He had no doubt she would enchant a wide public quite as much as the more intimate gatherings at home. He highly approved the idea of presenting largely the works of American poets, and promptly offered to assist the project with an original work of his own.

At the outset Lily had opposed the thought of making her début in New York. As she had pointed out to May, she had no illusions about the reaction of their friends. Few would come to hear her with any real interest in what she was trying to do. Some would deride her for making a shameless exhibition of herself, which was bad enough; and others would pity her because she was reduced to such an exhibition, which was even worse. Besides, even the best New York society was rather deficient culturally and could hardly be expected to appreciate a genuinely artistic performance even when they saw it, unless it was supported by a famous name and an established reputation. The place to start, Lily felt, was Boston: the Athens of America. In Boston taste was still pure, and people could recognize true merit without having it labeled in advance.

Epes Sargent concurred in this plan. He was himself a native of Boston, and he agreed that Boston people were superior to New Yorkers in their capacity for appreciating intellectual and artistic worth. Furthermore, he had a wide circle of connections there whose influence, while it might not guarantee success, would at least insure a fair hearing. Sargent was as good as his word. He not only wrote his friends, and particularly his newspaper friends, but he provided letters of introduction to a number of persons whose attention would be valuable.

On the 24th of October, 1841, the Mowatts bade farewell to Melrose. May and Lily took one last stroll through the gardens where a few late blooms brightened the fading landscape. Near the door of the greenhouse a heliotrope was still covered with blossoms. Lily gathered a sprig of the heavy-scented flowers and added it to a little bouquet of asters and chrysanthemums she had collected. It had been planted and tended by James from a spray which Lily had worn in her hair at the first ball they had given in their new home.

From the garden the girls passed on to the stables where they gave final pats to the ponies and the dogs. Then they came back to the house and walked once more through the silent rooms. May was weeping quietly, but Lily could not shed a tear. She had a feeling that she might never enter the door of Melrose again, but she accepted the idea calmly. Once again, as when she left her father's house to run away with James, her life had taken a new turning.

There was a strange similarity in the pattern of events. As on that other October morning, her great concern was for her father's good will. She had not told him of her plan to go out into the world and make her own way; she feared he might disapprove. And while that would not have made her change her mind, it would have weakened her confidence—and she needed that most desperately now. So once more she left the news of her decision to be given him by someone else, after she and James were gone. May, still sorrowful but resigned, was left to deal with Papa. And so the three of them, James, Lily and May, early in the morning set out in the carriage for New York. At Samuel Ogden's house the horses paused an instant for May to step down. Then Lily and James drove quickly to the steamship landing where they took the boat for Boston.

CHAPTER SIX

"An Entertainment of a
Somewhat Novel Character"

The Boston *Atlas* for October 18, 1841, carried at the top of
its front page the following notice:

Mrs. Mowatt's Recitations.—The public are invited this evening
by the advertisement of Mrs. Mowatt's performance, to an entertainment of a somewhat novel character, and one which we have
no doubt will be interesting, not chiefly from its novelty, but
from its adaptations to gratify a refined taste. It consists of reading and recitations in poetry, with introductory remarks upon
the respective pieces, by a lady who is most respectably recommended, for her eminent literary acquirements, and for those
accomplishments which are most highly esteemed in fashionable
society. We learn that she resorts to this employment of her
talents and acquirements with a view to rendering them productive

of pecuniary emolument, in consequence of reverses to which her family has been subjected.—There is no more laudable object to which the talents of an accomplished woman can be devoted than this, and we trust that she will meet with sympathy and encouragement in it, from those who are best capable of appreciating both the motive, and the success of her courageous effort. This we understand is her first public effort, and although it is made among strangers, we hope it will not be the less kindly met and rewarded. The following is handed to us as a specimen of the lady's poetical talent:

TIME
by Anna Cora Mowatt

Nay rail not at Time, though a tyrant be he
And say not he cometh, colossal in might,
Our beauty to ravish, put pleasure to flight,
And pluck away friends, e'en as leaves from the tree;
And say not Love's torch, which like Vesta's should burn,
The cold breath of Time soon to ashes will turn.

(A second stanza informs us that Time is a robber of youth and beauty but also a bringer of wisdom.)

Though cares then should gather, as pleasures fleet by,
Though Time from thy features, the charms steal away,
He'll dim too mine eye lest it see them decay,
And sorrows we've shared, love, knit closer love's tie;
Then I'll laugh at old Time, and at all he can do,
For he'll rob me in vain, if he leave me but you.

This effort by the fair authoress of *Pelayo* was nicely calculated to engage the Transcendental spirit. Its merits as poetry need no comment (greater writers than Anna Cora had written worse), but the sentiment was clear. The young lady from New York knew where to lay the emphasis so far as Boston was concerned. Youth and beauty were all well enough, and rumor, which had preceded the lady, credited her with both; but it was manifestly Mind which summoned listeners to the Masonic Temple.

Thanks to Epes Sargent, not only the *Atlas* but the *Transcript*, the *Bee* and other Boston papers noted the coming attraction in a dignified and friendly way. Sargent's letters to his friends had also produced results. When James and Lily arrived at the hotel they found numerous letters, cards and even bouquets to welcome them. Judge Story wrote a very encouraging note and Mr. Longfellow, the poet, expressed regret that illness prevented him from calling personally.

The day before the début Lily went to the Masonic Temple to rehearse. There was a chill in the great empty hall, and as she mounted the rostrum the rows of vacant seats seemed to stare at her with disapproval. Her heart began to throb violently and when she advanced to the edge of the platform to try her voice, she could scarcely utter a sound. Only James and an old doorkeeper were present, which made the place seem even bigger and emptier. Lily began to speak, but she could hardly hear herself. The words came in gasps, with no semblance of proper intonation. She grew sick at heart, for she could do nothing to fight off the fear that threatened to paralyze her. Again and again she tried to recite, selecting first one poem and then another from the program in the hope of finding some passage which would lift her out of the depths of hopelessness into which she was slipping deeper every moment. But it was no use. Finally, when she could control her trembling legs no longer, she sat down on the steps of the rostrum, sunk in despair. She was too miserable to weep.

The old doorkeeper was the first to speak. "You're only a bit nervous," he said kindly, "you'll get over that. I've seen great speakers look just as pale and frightened as you do now when they got on this stand here—but they soon warmed up."

But Lily felt that nothing would ever warm her again. She had staked everything on this venture. In imagination she had pictured the whole situation over and over, with perfect confidence. Now that she was faced with the reality—the reality of doing what no lady in America had ever done before—she was consumed with self-mistrust. All she could think of, was what failure would mean. She could hear the whispered comments of her sometime friends, the "whatever-made-you-think-you-could-do-its," the "I-told-you-sos."

On the way back to the hotel, she was too unhappy even to

heed James's efforts to console her. How preposterous it all was! and to all their other misfortunes disgrace would now be added. When they were in their rooms again and she saw the calling-cards and the flowers, a fresh wave of horror swept over her. Nothing could be undone: she was irrevocably committed.

At this instant, when she might at last have given way to tears, a knock came at the door and an envelope was handed in. When she saw the inscription and recognized the handwriting, her fingers trembled so that she could hardly break the seal. It was the long-awaited answer to her letter to Samuel Ogden. For a few seconds she could not bear to read the words he had written. In the state of her feelings, she knew that if her father should reproach her all would indeed be lost. But the first sentence set her mind at rest, and as she hurriedly skimmed the beloved script her spirits began to rise. Papa not only did not disapprove, he congratulated his little girl with all his heart for her splendid courage. He had not the slightest doubt that she would have a great success; who better than he knew her exceptional talents? But more important than talent was the purpose behind the venture. To seek independently to overcome adverse fortune—to strive by one's own efforts to save hearth and home —was so noble a motive for action that no one knowing the circumstances could possibly reproach her or fail to rally to her support.

Almost at once Samuel Ogden's prediction was proved correct. The only person with whom Anna Cora was personally acquainted in Boston was Mrs. Joshua Bates, wife of the Boston financier and partner of the London banking firm of Baring Brothers. Anna Cora had met Mrs. Bates in Paris two years before. It had been a pleasant though purely social connection. They had frequented the same salons and had met from time to time at Ambassador Cass's. When she had decided to come to Boston, Anna Cora, in some hesitation, had written to Mrs. Bates. At most she had expected a mere courteous acknowledgment. It was more than a happy surprise when, shortly after she had read her father's letter, a hotel attendant announced that Mrs. Bates had come to call.

"I had known her merely as a woman of fashion, chasing the butterfly of pleasure, even as I was doing, in Parisian salons, but now that I had a more earnest, a higher pursuit . . . she came to me in her true guise."

In her true guise Mrs. Bates took Anna Cora—figuratively at least though probably literally, for it was a custom of the times —to her bosom. She was not only full of admiration for the undertaking, but she made it seem that Boston was indeed fortunate to have been chosen for the début. She was confident of its success, and promised that all her friends would come to the recital. This was reassuring, for it was obvious that Mrs. Bates, whether chasing the butterfly of pleasure or engaged in good works, could exert pressure where and when it was needed. In this case she went to work with a will. As a token of good faith Mrs. Bates herself took a hundred tickets for the first reading. Well might Anna Cora record, "I was strengthened and cheered by her untiring kindness; her hearty enthusiasm gave me new faith in my own success. Beyond price, at that moment was such a friend; and the impetus which she gave to my first efforts had their effect upon my entire career."

Papa's letter and Mrs. Bates's more tangible encouragement were all Anna Cora needed to bolster her waning resolution.

The day of days dawned bright and fair. Having regained her composure, Anna Cora was determined now to let nothing disturb it. She stayed secluded in her room throughout the day, while the flow of cards (doubtless stimulated by Mrs. Bates) was handled by James.

When evening came she was still calm. She dressed herself with great care and without haste. Knowing advisors had insisted she wear her most elaborate toilette and all her jewels; people would expect a certain effect. On the latter point Anna Cora was in agreement, but she had her own ideas about the kind of effect. If she appealed to the Boston audience it would be on their own terms. She had promised an evening of intellectual and esthetic pleasure, governed by refinement and taste. Also she was a lady in reduced circumstances, a fact which called for a certain sartorial decorum. Accordingly she wore a simple white muslin dress, with a white rose in her hair and another at her bosom. With her pale face and large dark blue eyes, she looked younger than her twenty-three years. The vestal muslin added still further to her youthful appearance. Nothing could have enhanced her air of innocence, which was genuine; but the white roses—in lieu of diamonds—gave her a look of other-worldliness which Bostonians must have approved.

In the retiring-room of the Temple the Mowatts found a number of well-wishers, principally gentlemen, who felt especially protective towards the lovely stranger. There was some anxiety on their faces. The Temple, they informed Anna Cora encouragingly, was thronged "with one of the most fashionable audiences ever assembled within its walls." They entreated her to retain her self-possession. They urged this in such earnest terms that she might well have been frightened out of her wits; only fortunately her mind was on the details of the program and she scarcely heard what was said.

At seven o'clock the gentlemen departed, with the injunction that she not keep the audience waiting. "Bostonians dislike nothing more!" On this helpful note Anna Cora, accompanied by James, made her way to the foot of the stairs leading up to the rostrum. There James left her and took his seat in the front row. She mounted the steps, turned to the sea of faces and curtsied. The audience burst into a storm of applause. Half-stunned, Anna Cora curtsied again. Another storm. When she lifted the book from which she was to read there was still more applause. Although, as she said later, she felt as if she could scarcely have been "more unconscious in a state of complete inanition," the audience was determinedly enthusiastic.

Then she began to read. In a thin, half-choked voice came the opening words of *The Lay of the Last Minstrel:*

> *The way was long, the wind was cold . . .*

Never had that line been delivered more feelingly! The audience listened with rapt attention, unaware that the opening effect was due less to art than to stage-fright. Glancing up from her page and seeing the look of unmistakable enthrallment on every face,

Anna Cora's self-possession suddenly returned. People were actually enjoying it! With each succeeding stanza her voice grew stronger; and when she reached the climactic

Breathes there the man with soul so dead . . .

she was no longer a touching young lady reduced by circumstance to display in public a talent hitherto exercised only in the home; she was an artist.

Indeed she was the creator of a new art, which soon was to sweep the country and for half a century would be the delight of American audiences, as well as the support of innumerable gentlewomen in reduced circumstances or otherwise. The first lady elocutionist had appeared in the United States, and not until the twentieth century had run for more than two decades, and Chautauqua had had its rise and decline, would her voice be silent in the land.

The second and third night audiences were as large and as delighted as that which had come to the début. After the first awful moments, Anna Cora was completely self-assured. It was as though she were reading to a very large group of pleasantly indulgent friends. Even though she knew that she read extremely well, she was also aware that the enthusiasm of Boston was less for her artistry than for herself. The spirit of chivalry, evinced by the group of gentlemen who had met her on the opening night, characterized the Boston public as a whole—at least the masculine part of it. E. P. Whipple, a young literary light of the city, summed it up when he told her, during the first intermission that evening, "There is not a man in the Temple that wouldn't fight for you!"

If she was elated by her success, Anna Cora could have wished that the Boston press, at least, had been a little more precise in its comments on her reading. The newspapers teemed with notices, "but they were eulogiums, not critiques." And though Anna Cora left the city with the satisfaction of having made an impression of a sort unparalleled there before by one of her sex, she was not really certain it was all due to her art.

Generous Boston would have paid gladly for another series of readings, but Anna Cora was determined now to push on to further fields. Until she had braved New York, she could not feel justified in the course she had taken. If she really had something on which to base a career, she would find out in New York—where people would not only be less likely to understand her motives, but where the appreciation of art was less keen than in Boston. If she really had power to move men—and, she hoped, women—New York was the place to prove it.

Meanwhile, in a one-night stand at Providence, she received most literal evidence of her abilities. One number on her program was the piece by Epes Sargent written especially for her, entitled *The Missing Ship*. This work had a topical interest; it was inspired by an event which had created great public excitement a short time before. The steamer *President*, largest and finest packet in the North Atlantic service, had sailed from New York early in March, 1841, was sighted by another ship on March 13th, and was never heard from again. Though shipwrecks were not uncommon still, it was unusual that a vessel should meet its doom in the most frequented ship lane, with no indication of what had happened. Surmises were rife. Although a violent storm was reported at the time of the *President's* disappearance, it was certain that she could have weathered this. The assumption was that the ship had either struck an iceberg or caught fire.

Sargent, who was after all a successful journalist, treated both conjectures with a free hand. And Anna Cora made the most of all the details. The poem (which the historian fain would leave to merciful oblivion) begins thus:

> *God speed the noble President!*
> *A gallant boat is she,*
> *As ever entered harbor*
> *Or crossed a stormy sea.*

Then follows a description of the splendid spectacle made by the ship as she sailed out of New York Harbor, her guns saluting, on the way back to England and a welcome by a proud citizenry (she was a British ship):

Alas ye watchers by the strand,
Weeks, months have rolled away,
But where, where is the President?
And why is this delay?

It is difficult in the perspective of more than a hundred years to reconstruct the art by which this specimen of inanity was made moving to an audience which after all possessed some literary tradition. Yet move it did, as the sequel shows, when Anna Cora read it.

Through three more stanzas the poet develops his picture as fancy dwells on the various possibilities of disaster. Was it an iceberg that loomed before the helmsman's eyes—too late to be avoided—or was it fire bursting without warning from within that soon engulfed the hapless vessel? Both alternatives are given in lurid detail; but of what use, asks the poet, are these conjectures?

No answer cometh from the deep
To tell the tale we dread;
No messenger of weal or woe
Returneth from the dead; . . .

Did the recitalist on the Providence platform detect some strange disturbance in the rear of the auditorium as she reached this point? If so, the impetus of emotion would not have permitted a halt until the last sad note was sounded.

But faith looks up through tears, and sees,
From earthly haven driven,
Those lost ones meet in fairer realms
Where storms reach not—in Heaven.

With upturned eyes and lifted hands Anna Cora finished the reading. There was a moment of deep silence while the audience recovered its stricken senses. And then, before the applause could burst forth, there was a wild high shriek from somewhere in the back of the house. This was followed by another and still another. The startled performer gazed anxiously in the direction of the sound, and noted a sudden rising of gentlemen in the back row. The next instant she saw a female figure, gesturing frantically, being conveyed from the hall, while the shrieks mounted higher and higher.

It was some time before Anna Cora learned exactly what had happened. When it became known that the cause of the disturbance was a female auditor, of such delicate sensibilities that she had been reduced to hysterics by the reading of the poem, Anna Cora was sympathetic but not dissatisfied. Here indeed was incontrovertible proof of her dramatic powers! As for Mr. Sargent's poem, "it proved one of the most valuable in my *repertoire* for it never failed to impress an audience."

The Mowatts went straight from Providence to New York, but they did not return to Melrose. Despite the fact that Anna Cora's "pecuniary emoluments" from the Boston and Providence readings had been eminently satisfactory—she had realized more than a thousand dollars from the four appearances—they were not enough to stave off foreclosure of the mortgage on Melrose. Perhaps it was just as well. Although she would always treasure the memory of the happy years in Flatbush, the house and all it represented marked a point in her life to which she could not return. In after years she always said she had decided to become a public reader because there was literally nothing else she could do. But having once tasted the freedom of the new life, never again would she have been satisfied with the normal confined existence of most women of her day, not even as mistress of Melrose.

The Mowatts took up residence at the new Astor House on Broadway at Park Place. Unrivalled in magnificence by any other hostelry in the world, it had been built by John Jacob Astor as a civic enterprise and a monument to himself. It was typical of the Astor genius that he should have realized both these aims and at the same time developed a highly lucrative investment. The hotel had been completed five years before James and Lily moved there, and was the last word in luxury. It had piped water, supplied from its own wells, in all the bedrooms, and there were baths on every floor. The building soared to a height of six stories and was a source of lyrical ecstasy to men like N. P. Willis, New York's fashionable newspaper columnist, who also lived in it. "To those who inhabit the upper stories of this great caravanserai," wrote Willis in *Godey's* for May, 1843, "the hotel must seem but the ground floor of the stars—the Astor a corruption of ad astra."

Of course the Astor was very expensive, but it was comfortable and highly respectable. Indeed it had a considerable clientèle of New York's best families, who when the hotel opened had simply sold their houses and moved in—unable to resist the temptation of baths, steam heat, and lavish gas illumination. For Lily and James, living at the Astor was undoubtedly a lift to morale. It provided them with an atmosphere of luxury and associations with their own kind, with at the same time a touch of Bohemianism. The Park Theatre was close at hand, as was Florence's Oyster House where the world of fashion mingled with the literati. Nearby was the bowling alley at the Masonic Hall: a favorite resort of the sporting element, and so luxurious in its appointments as to resemble "a chamber of Aladdin's build."

On November 18, 1841, Anna Cora gave the first of a series of readings at the Stuyvesant Institute. The house as might be expected was full, with a goodly representation from the Mowatts' extensive acquaintance. For indignation at Mrs. Mowatt's conduct had not stifled curiosity.

Anna Cora had been prepared for this attitude on the part of their friends; she had steeled herself to it even before the Boston venture. But it was worse than she had expected. In the eyes of her own circle she had suddenly become nothing less than a freak, and completely shameless. It was inconceivable that the wife of James Mowatt and the daughter of Samuel Ogden should be reduced to such an extremity that she must exhibit herself publicly for money. There was obviously something wrong with Anna Mowatt, and people, many of whom had been close friends, met her after the first reading with averted faces.

In such an atmosphere it was difficult for Anna Cora to do her best, no matter how she struggled. Nevertheless she went bravely through the engagements at the Stuyvesant Institute, which were well attended and attracted flattering attention from the press.

Philip Hone, a leading citizen and later mayor of New York, was present at the début. In his diary, which has something to say about nearly everything that happened in the city in the forties, there is this note:

> November 18, Having nothing better to do this evening I went over the way to the Stuyvesant Institute to hear Mrs. Anna Cora Mowatt recite poetry. This lady is the daughter of Samuel G. Ogden, young and genteel in appearance, and handsome for aught I know, for a black curtain of curls hanging down the side of her face, like an unsightly wig of an English judge or barrister, concealed her features from all except those who were immediately in front of her. A vile fashion.

Hone, a man of taste and humane sympathies, might have been expected to offer some comment on the reading itself. The slight air of disdain with which he records merely Anna Cora's appearance typifies the attitude of most of the Ogden-Mowatt circle at this time.

The strain of preparing the programs and of the actual readings, and the gulf which had now been created between the Mowatts and so many of their former friends had their effects on Anna Cora's health. She had not been able to shake off a cold which she had caught earlier in the winter, and this, added to her general state of exhaustion, completely drained her strength. Shortly before the last recital at the Stuyvesant Institute she collapsed, and the few friends who remained close to her despaired of her life. Yet sheer determination, as was so often to prove the case, pulled her through. In December she staggered to her feet and with a heavy shawl around her thin shoulders gave a reading, many times postponed, before the Rutgers Institute for Young Ladies. The atmosphere here was different from the patronizing air of the Stuyvesant Institute audiences. "The hall was filled with an assemblage of lovely-looking young girls, and their evident enjoyment inspired me to read with more energy and feeling than I had done since my nights in Boston. The effort caused me a relapse of some weeks."

BROADWAY IN 1845

from Meyer's Universum, c. 1850

It was just over a month later that Anna Cora resumed the career which seemed already nipped in the bud. *The Evening Post* for January 13 supplies the record:

Mrs. Mowatt's Readings.—This lady appeared on Wednesday evening after a month's indisposition, and she far surpassed all her previous performances. She was not the reciter, but the poet herself, conceiving anew all the Bard's conceptions, which gained additional force and brilliancy from her mind and feeling, and portraying his passions and emotions with an intensity and vividness which carried the coldest reader captive. Byron's dream was given in a manner perfectly new and original, and we may add in one at least equal to any we have ever heard. The Brothers was a masterpiece; the expression of intense agony and horror depicted on the face of Mrs. Mowatt, at the sight of the dead brother seemed reflected on that of a large part of the audience; and The Missing Ship, by one of our own poets, was electrifying; The Fall of Babylon, also by an American poet, evinced a power and volume of voice which we would have pronounced it impossible for so young and delicate a being to possess. . . . The very modesty of her appearance, and her abandonment to her subjects, are calculated to impress the audience with a fear of disturbing her with clamorous applause.

This notice reflects the general tone of the New York press when it now said anything about Mrs. Mowatt. The January readings were given at the Society Library. Every appearance found the hall crowded with eager and demonstrative spectators. No matter what her own acquaintances might think of her, New York as a whole had taken her to its heart. Regardless of the quality of many of her selections (of which the less said the better), there is no doubt that Anna Cora Mowatt was creating a public for poetry with her art as a reader. If this seems an insignificant art to us, that is because we really know nothing about it and judge it by the vapid elocution of a later tradition. Anna Cora's audiences may have been emotionally less complicated than people of the present day (which is debatable); but the fact that she could stir them to depths of feeling which they had seldom experienced is indicative of a great gift.

Since Anna Cora was completely self-taught there were naturally flaws in her performances. However, judging from the newspaper accounts there was steady improvement throughout the winter of 1841-42. This meant that despite the wretched state of her health she was constantly working to perfect her art.

But it was a bitter struggle. The wagging tongues would not leave her alone. Some of the newspapers refused to criticize her work at all, devoting themselves entirely to a condemnation of Anna Cora personally. They accused her of setting a precedent which if followed by other women would lead to the dissolution of the home and a general relaxation of moral standards. In an article in *The Ladies' Companion* she was denounced in scathing terms. It was bad enough that Mrs. Mowatt should read poetry in public, but that she should do so before mixed audiences seemed nothing less than depravity. If she must read let her do so before audiences of her own sex—leaving the gentlemen outside, presumably, with the canes and umbrellas; a notion which Anna Cora found rather amusing.

On the other hand there were many encouraging voices. J. W. S. Hows, a leading New York dramatic critic and authority on elocution, heard her and wrote a letter to her full of high praise. Perhaps the greatest tribute of all came from Mrs. Frances Sargent Osgood, a leader of the New York literati, friend of Poe, and a poetess highly esteemed by all readers of the ladies' magazines. In chaste lyrics Mrs. Osgood pronounced her judgment:

TO ANNA CORA MOWATT
(on hearing her read)
Ne'er heed them, Cora, dear,
The carping few, who say
Thou leavest woman's holier sphere
For light and vain display.

Mrs. Osgood, like others, had gone to Anna Cora's readings expecting to see "a being bold who braved the wide world's blame." Instead,

A being young and fair,
In purest white arrayed,
With timid grace tripped down the stair
Half eager, half afraid!

> *As on the misty height*
> *Soft blushes young Aurora,*
> *She dawned upon our dazzled sight,*
> *Our graceful, modest Cora!*

> *The loveliest hair of gold*
> *That ever woman braided,*
> *In glossy ringlets, richly rolled,*
> *Brow, neck and bosom shaded.*

She dwells on Anna Cora's modest attire, and the beauty of soul—"more than mortal"—which looked out of her pure blue eyes. She notes the profound hush that came over the audience when Anna Cora spoke and:

> *That voice of wondrous music gushed*
> *Now soft as murmuring dove—*

> *Now calm in proud disdain—*
> *Now wild with joyous power—*
> *Indignant now—as pleasure, pain*
> *Or anger ruled the hour.*

> *High in the listener's soul*
> *In tune each passion swells;*
> *We weep, we smile, 'neath her control,*
> *As 'neath a fairy's spells.*

If we make due allowance for Mrs. Osgood's uncontrollable tendency to gush, these verses give us an idea of Anna Cora's charm and physical appearance. It may appear in one instance that the demands of rhyme take precedence over cold fact. "The loveliest hair of gold" is not in accord with Philip Hone's "black curtain of curls," or with the dark hair shown in the various portraits. However, Mrs. Osgood first saw Anna Cora late in the winter of 1841-42; and her description may be accurate, since all references after this time specify that Anna Cora had light, or light auburn hair. From this one gathers that sometime during this first season a change in color took place—not wholly the work of nature. This in itself would have been no cause for alarm to Anna Cora's friends. Dyed hair was common enough in the 1840's. It was as usual for a lady to alter the shade of her tresses as the contours of her torso. Any good cook-book of the time told her just how to go about it. The fact that Anna Cora was abandoned by the world of fashion did not mean that she herself had ceased to be fashionable. Henceforth in this chronicle she will be blonde.

Despite Anna Cora's success on the platform, the winter of 1841-42 must have been wretched for the Mowatts. We do not know that Samuel Ogden contributed more to the support of his daughter and son-in-law than hearty words of encouragement. It seems unlikely that he did, for in after-references to this time, Anna Cora makes clear that their financial situation was most precarious. If she struggled through readings between bouts of illness, it was not wholly in the interest of art. The bills at the Astor House had to be paid, and Anna Cora was the one who paid them.

Although her work suffered from frequent interruptions, it attracted ever wider notice. By the end of the year half a dozen ladies were launched on careers as elocutionists throughout the Union. One of these advertised "Readings and Recitations in the Style of Mrs. Mowatt." Anna Cora was particularly interested in this unknown disciple, and had her health permitted she would have travelled some distance to hear the lady; for, as she tells us, "I was rather curious to get an idea of my own style."

One occurrence must be noted for its reference to the future. A reading at the Society Library was attended by a gentleman described as "one of the managers of the Park theatre." This gentleman, through an intermediary, made Anna Cora a highly lucrative offer to go on the stage. The offer was spurned with great indignation. The very fact that it should have been made must have added fuel to the fires of humiliation already consuming Anna Cora. To be thought even susceptible of becoming an actress! Necessity had driven her far—but not that far.

The unnamed representative of the Park theatre was not *one* of the managers, but the sole manager and lessee of the theatre —none other than Mr. Simpson, the "gentlemanly" neighbor of childhood days. Anna Cora may not have been aware of this fact, for her distress at the suggestion probably deafened her to all details. However, by 1841 Stephen Price, who had been co-manager of the Park with Simpson, was dead. Simpson was therefore in sole command; and that particular season he was having very rough sailing. As far as that goes, it was a bad season for everybody. The depression launched by Jackson's bank reforms in 1837 was still running its course. In New York there was real suffering, and this was reflected in the theatre. The season had begun well enough in September. At the Park, Charlotte Cushman had drawn good houses as Oberon in *A Midsummer Night's Dream*, and later in the fall had had another successful week as Lady Teazle to the Sir Peter of Henry Placide. "Jim Crow" Rice (the original black-face comedian) had returned from triumphs abroad, and had brought cash to Simpson's till with his plantation antics. Yankee Hill had also done well in his ever-popular impersonations of "native" American types, and there had been a truly dazzling success with Boucicault's *London Assurance*, in which Charlotte Cushman had again figured. But these were momentary flashes. The day of the long run was still far off, and an occasional good week was not enough to offset the bleak intervals when the house was almost empty. Furthermore one of Simpson's greatest successes of the season had almost ruined him, paradoxically. This was the engagement of the terpsichorean divinity Fanny Elssler, who could pack a house like nobody else and fill her own pocket-book proportionately. Simpson had had to guarantee her $5438 for her engagement, and because of a miscalculation on his part, had lost more than $2000 on the deal.

Faced by imminent bankruptcy, it is small wonder that Simpson by mid-winter was casting about desperately for an attraction that would fill the Park without too great an initial investment. Mrs. Mowatt's extraordinary success, not only as a charming personality but as a woman with undeniable dramatic gifts, must have suggested ideas. The stir caused by her daring venture had a distinct publicity value, and this added to her genuine attainments made her seem the answer to his prayers. But the prayers were vain; Simpson was left to struggle as best he could.

Meanwhile Anna Cora had new struggles of her own.

CHAPTER SEVEN

Men and Angels

The illness which finally brought Anna Cora's career as a
reader to a halt was no passing affair. Throughout the
winter and spring of 1842 her condition was so precarious
that recovery seemed unlikely. The trouble had started back in
November when she returned to New York from her Boston
début. She had scarcely begun her readings at the Stuyvesant
Institute when the old threat of consumption rose again. By
Christmas, in the midst of the desperate struggle to gain a footing
in her new profession, the threat had become a painful and
terrifying reality. Even so, she might have gone along by the
sheer exercise of will-power. But it was the mounting nervous
tension that finally broke down her resistance. She managed
to finish her series of readings at the Society Library in January
and then collapsed.

This is not surprising. The constant preoccupation with James,
who was still far from well though his malady was temporarily
arrested; the gruelling ordeals of the public appearances; the
sheer labor involved in preparing the programs; finally the

strained relations with many old friends who had never forgiven her boldness in seeking a career as an entertainer—any one of these would have been a heavy burden on a normal constitution. Altogether they quite overwhelmed little Lily.

Dr. Valentine Mott, who had known Anna Cora since girlhood and had helped James so much in Paris, was now in New York. But by this time Anna Cora's case was beyond the reach of any treatment that he as an orthodox practitioner might have been able to prescribe. He probably told Anna Cora as much. If he did not do so, she was well aware of the fact anyway; and that is why early in 1842 she turned to mesmerism.

Everyone was discussing the amazing phenomena produced by the mesmeric healers and animal-magnetizers who were holding forth in halls, in empty shops, on the very street corners—and in respectable consulting-rooms as well. It was part of the atmosphere of the time. Mesmerism was but one symptom of the vast psychological upheaval through which the country was passing. America had waked up to the need for something to offset the deadening effects of the crude materialism that had developed in the feverish rush of national expansion. Now, in the most varied ways—ranging from the Transcendental contemplation of the Over-Soul to the emotional orgies of camp-meetings—America was striving to express its inner life.

Mesmerism, in the belief of untold thousands, offered the very key to that life. In the state of hypnosis (which was the basis of the mesmeric experience) the everyday personality was laid aside and a new being emerged. This other self, a higher and rarer nature, had no preoccupations with material existence, but floated freely beyond time and space and could communicate with other spirits similarly liberated—even with those who had been supremely liberated by death.

But this was not the chief significance of mesmerism—at least not at first. In the state of trance, in which the higher nature dominated, it was believed that one could receive magnetic currents emanating from the mesmerizer, and that these, if properly directed, had a beneficial effect on the body. Thus mesmerism had a therapeutic value.

Neither James nor Lily knew anything about the "science,"

except what they had heard from Epes Sargent who had for some months been studying hypnotism. It was through Sargent that the Mowatts met young William Francis Channing, a mesmeric healer who was also a student at The New York College of Physicians and Surgeons. Channing had already been practicing medicine for some time (which was in no way discreditable to him since New York was full of respectable physicians without degrees or even formal medical training) and it was in anticipation of medical treatment that Lily followed Sargent's suggestion to consult him. Both Lily and James were impressed by the young man's intelligence and his professional manner; but they were taken aback when Channing, after carefully examining the patient and talking with her, turned to Mr. Mowatt and said: "If she is susceptible, I think she can be relieved by mesmerism more readily than by any medicine that I could administer."

Lily was frightened. She had heard enough about mesmerism to know that it reduced one to a state of helplessness through a complete abandonment of the will. She felt that without her will she would indeed be lost, for what else had kept her alive up to now? James too was uneasy. But as Dr. Channing explained the fundamentals of mesmerism and briefly described the hypnotic state, it appeared less alarming. Moreover, Lily's case was so serious that any straw must be grasped.

Young Channing was an accomplished hypnotist. Despite her skepticism and her nervousness at the first treatment, Lily was made unconscious in about twenty minutes. The experiment took place in the Mowatts' parlor in the Astor House. The blinds had been drawn so that the room was in darkness save for a tongue of flame from an astral lamp on the center table. James sat in a dim corner, while Channing placed himself directly in front of Lily with the lamplight full in his face. He talked to her for a few moments in a low reassuring voice. Then he made a series of motions with his hands before her eyes. Lily saw the room begin to grow hazy; the furniture seemed to lose its normal outlines, to sway and dance about her. She felt a little dizzy, but it was not unpleasant . . . and that was all she remembered.

When she awoke it was as though she had had a long, refreshing sleep. For the first time in weeks she felt actually rested. It was several minutes before she was aware of the pain in her chest and began to cough.

With each succeeding treatment Lily noted an improvement in her condition. She coughed less, and soon the tell-tale red flecks no longer were on her handkerchief when she took it away from her mouth. The temperature which she had been running for some time subsided.

But she was still uneasy. She could not rid herself of the fear that she was slipping into the grip of mysterious powers from which she might not be able to escape. However, both Channing and Epes Sargent, who was now assisting the healer at the treatments, assured her that nothing but good would result from the mesmeric experience. Gradually, Lily came to look forward to Channing's daily visits, for they meant a blessed break in the weary pain-wracked hours; and when by the middle of February her health had so far improved that she could give a poetry-reading in Brooklyn, she was convinced that a miracle was taking place.

As the results of Channing's ministrations became apparent, she found herself the center of much curious attention. Ill and weak as she was, she shrank from exposing herself to others. But she was so grateful to the young healer and so anxious that his powers should be recognized that she allowed witnesses to be present from time to time when she was under hypnosis.

Among those who followed the proceedings with keen interest were the Mowatts' neighbor Nathaniel Willis, the journalist, and the poet William Ellery Channing (nephew of the great preacher of the same name, and a relative of the healer). Still another observer was Dr. Valentine Mott, who examined Lily a few weeks after the treatments began and was so interested in the changes already wrought that he asked to be permitted to assist at the sessions. The great surgeon—for Mott had achieved international renown through his advanced operative techniques—was a man of imagination and open-mindedness. At this time he was experimenting with anesthetics, and he received valuable hints from what he saw in the Mowatts' parlor at the Astor House. Dr. Mott was impressed by the fact that when Lily was under hypnosis she often described her symptoms with medical accuracy, all the while giving evidence of keen suffering. Yet he noted that she was insensible to pain produced externally. Once he verified this by probing her arm deeply with a lancet. There was no reaction. When she came out of the trance Lily shuddered at the sight of the wound, but she had no recollection of any pain.

For the next three months Lily lived increasingly in a strange world of dreams and fantasies. Soon she developed a distinct trance personality which called itself "the gypsy." In her normal state she knew nothing of this other self, except what was reported to her by James or Epes Sargent. But "the gypsy" was fully aware of Anna Cora's waking personality, which she always referred to in the third person and in not very flattering terms. Almost as soon as "the gypsy" became articulate, she christened the conscious Anna Cora "the simpleton."

There was perhaps some ground for "the gypsy's" sense of superiority. She could perform feats which left "the simpleton," when told of them, completely baffled. "The gypsy" possessed a wealth of lore and special talent which the conscious Anna Cora knew nothing about. She was equally at home in medicine and metaphysics. She communicated with angels and wrote poetry of considerable merit. And this was not all. Soon "the gypsy" developed powers of a more spectacular kind. In a good deal of excitement Epes Sargent wrote to his friend E. P. Whipple of Boston on January 18, 1842:

> . . . The magnetic experiments are still continuing, and daily new phenomena are developed. It is rare that a subject reaches the high stage to which she has attained. In her case we see daily proved the most ultra and incredible facts reported of magnetism— facts which we dare not tell her in her waking state nor anyone else—so of this let nothing be intimated. This I will tell you, however, as one of the least remarkable. I have conversed mentally with her for several minutes—she replying vocally to my un- uttered questions, and sometimes even anticipating my thoughts by placing her hand on my head. . . .

Anna Cora may not have been informed of this particular development, but she knew enough to make up her mind. Perhaps "the gypsy" did possess remarkable powers, but "with womanly perverseness, I preferred my everyday imperfections to this mysterious and incomprehensibly brought-about superiority. For the former I was at least responsible—to the latter I could lay no conscious claim. I say conscious claim; though it must be admitted that there are *separate states of consciousness.* In the phenomena of this separation, the student of human nature may, I believe, find the clew to momentous truths." Little did Anna Cora know what "momentous truths" would emerge from the separate states of consciousness which she so clearly identified. Freud was still far in the future.

More than ten years later when she set down some of the events of this strange winter Anna Cora was still awed by what had happened to her. She was convinced that through mesmerism she had been brought in touch with mysterious forces which might one day be known and utilized for the benefit of mankind. But she had too much commonsense to go off the deep end as did so many of her contemporaries. She was revolted when Harriet Martineau, who was a militant atheist, proclaimed that mesmerism would eventually do away with the necessity for God. Miss Martineau held that clairvoyance, which was believed to accompany the mesmeric state, could be developed to the point where men might look freely into each other's most secret minds, thus making conscience superfluous. Anna Cora indignantly rejected this because she knew from her own experience that clairvoyance, if it existed, was "always involuntary—flashing and vanishing like lightning," and would be a poor substitute for the steady scrutiny of divine Omniscience.

One effect of Lily's mesmeric experience was to quicken her religious sense. She had inherited from both her father and mother a devout nature, and this had been fostered by childhood contacts with vigorous spirits like the Reverend Dr. Eastburn. In her struggle with disease and misfortune she had never lost her firm belief in a just and eventually merciful Providence. In this latest and severest illness she was more than ever conscious of the nearness of God.

There is poignant evidence of this in a manuscript poem dated February 1, 1842, and entitled "Impromptu, by Anna Cora

Mowatt, on hearing some lines read by Epes Sargent upon her recovery from a dangerous illness." The work is evidently a first draft; there are no corrections, and there is no punctuation except for a dash and two periods. The poem exhibits a technical freedom not to be found in Anna Cora's other verse. This, and the very nature of the subject, suggest that it was written under hypnosis. Be that as it may, the lines give us a clear insight into Lily's mind in the depths of her misery:

> O wonder not that soul inspired strain
> Should move me thus with mingled joy and pain
> Oft of that holy happy hour I think
> When standing on eternity's wide brink
> I saw—O heaven that one transporting glance
> The spirits of the cherished dead advance
> And spread the portals of that bright abode
> Where blissful souls may nearer view their God
> While firm within behold an angel band
> With radiant looks each waved a beck'ning hand
> Above me shone a heaven of peaceful joy
> Beneath a world whose very pleasures cloy
> But when my struggling soul would soar on high
> Earth bound anew her half dissevered tie
> And love's imploring look affections prayer
> And duty's pleading voice still chained me there
> While one lip murmured life hath woes to give
> Yet brave them for their sakes and dare to live.
> I heard and wept but yielded to that voice
> What pains hath earth for me while they rejoice
> I bowed my head the vision of delight
> Slow faded from my grieved but willing sight
> And I was yours again to cheer to bless
> To soothe you with unchanging tenderness
> Prepared content to bear life's store of ill
> My earthly mission nobly to fulfill.

One thing this poem makes clear. Whatever benefits may have come from mesmerism, one of which was release from the terrible tensions which afflicted her, the thing that determined Lily's final restoration to health was her love for James. In all the confusion, pain and despair which filled the winter of 1841-

42 she never lost sight of his need for her. He was only thirty-seven at this time, but the disease from which he was suffering, and of which his near-blindness was but one symptom, called forth all her pity and tenderness, and this strengthened her will to live. If she were to go there would be nobody to look after James.

Love of James and faith in a blessed hereafter were inextricably linked together in Lily's mind. While under hypnosis she frequently talked for hours at a time with James. Her conversation—it was of course "the gypsy" speaking—was chiefly of religious matters. Much that she had but dimly grasped before her illness was now clear. On the question of immortality all doubts were resolved, for Lily was in close communication with those "spirits of the cherished dead" mentioned in the "Impromptu." Through them she had been able to glimpse that luminous realm where there was no pain and no cruelty, and she was eager to share her visions of future bliss with her husband.

He listened with patience to "the gypsy's" revelations, though not with much interest—at first. Like most men of his generation and position he had received a classical education, one effect of which was to develop an attitude of rational skepticism toward religion. He had little sympathy with the mystical tendencies of the modern age. But in the last few months he had witnessed a good many things for which reason could find no explanation. As time went on he found himself listening more intently to what Lily had to say; and his views began to change. Exactly what happened Lily never knew, nor was he able to explain it himself. But before the winter was over James, through Lily, experienced a great spiritual awakening.

Shortly after one of these conversations James happened to meet an old friend, a clergyman, and related to him some of the ideas expressed by Lily in a state of trance. The friend listened very attentively, and when James had finished he said quietly: "Mrs. Mowatt must have read Swedenborg's works, for those are the doctrines Swedenborg promulgates."

James denied that Mrs. Mowatt had ever read Swedenborg. He could be quite positive about it since he had supervised her reading since she was fifteen years old. But his friend was insistent. He suggested that Mr. Mowatt put certain questions to his wife at the next opportunity.

James followed his friend's instructions and recorded Lily's replies. When he showed them to the clergyman, the latter was amazed. "Those are the very doctrines revealed through Swedenborg."

James's curiosity was thoroughly aroused. He knew nothing about Swedenborg, but he promptly purchased a copy of *Heaven and Hell* and began to read. At his friend's suggestion he attended a service of the New Church; and from that day until his death he was an ardent Swedenborgian.

Lily, at least in her conscious state, was less enthusiastic. Her faith was based on *The Book of Common Prayer,* and in her weakness and melancholy she could not struggle with the complexities of Swedenborg. She grew weary of the one subject which now absorbed her husband's thoughts, and which he insisted upon discussing with her on all occasions. Besides it worried her to see him strain his weak eyes poring day after day over the ponderous volumes of *The Arcana Coelestia* and *Divine Love and Wisdom.* When she grew stronger she resumed her practice of reading aloud to him in order to spare his eyes. Since he had no interest now outside his new religion, Lily— despite her own aversion—had perforce to read from Swedenborg's works.

But as she read she too came under the spell of the great mystic whose visions of other planes of existence and conversations with angels touched a responsive chord in her. She had the feeling that she was treading on long-familiar ground, and that the ideas she now encountered in Swedenborg had been at the basis of her thinking ever since she could remember. In a matter of weeks Lily also became a convert to The New Jerusalem Church and when she could get about became a regular attendant at the services conducted by Mr. Barrett, leader of New York's little Swedenborgian congregation.

Late in February, after having seemingly made progress for several weeks, Lily had a relapse. Her cough became so bad that each spasm threatened to carry her off. She could find relief only during the mesmeric treatments, but the effects of these no longer extended into the normal state as had been the case for some time past. One day, when Lily had been in a trance for about two hours and Sargent, who was now in complete charge of her case, was preparing to recall her to consciousness, Lily begged to be allowed to remain as she was. Although Sargent was not sure what risk might be involved, he decided to do as she asked. He reasoned that since the symptoms of her disease disappeared during the regular periods of treatment, permanent healing might take place if the trance were sufficiently prolonged.

The experiment was tried, and for more than two weeks Lily remained in the somnambulic state without once returning to her normal condition. At the end of two or three days she was so much better that she was able to get out of bed and walk about the room. When a week had passed James thought that an excursion in the fresh air might be good for her. It was early in March and the weather had suddenly turned very mild. So one Sunday afternoon he and Sargent took Lily in a carriage to the steamboat dock where they boarded a ferry for Hoboken. Lily was swathed in a heavy veil in order not to attract attention, for in her hypnotic state with her eyes rolled up and only the whites showing, she presented a very strange appearance. The trip was a great success. Lily seemed delighted to be out in the open and chatted merrily in a high other-worldly whisper as they walked up and down the graveled paths of the popular riverside resort.

But the experience of prolonged hypnosis almost ended in disaster for Lily's nervous system. When she had gone into the trance one of her last recollections was the view of Broadway through her hotel window. The street lay deep in snow which also banked the window ledge. Just in front of the window, inside the room, stood a little rosebush in a pot. There was one green bud on the plant and Lily had been waiting patiently for it to bloom.

When more than two weeks later Sargent decided it was time to bring her back to her normal state Lily happened to be standing in exactly the same spot by the window. The snow had completely disappeared and the green bud on the rosebush had become a bright crimson flower. As she returned to consciousness Lily saw first the rose, and then the street outside the window. Into her eyes came a look of bewilderment, quickly followed by one of terror. She had no sense of the interval that had passed since her last sight of the rosebush and the snow-covered street. The apparently sudden transformation so upset her that she became frantic. Sargent realized at once that she should have been prepared for what had taken place, and that the only thing to do was to mesmerize her again as quickly as possible. This he managed, but only with great difficulty for she was so agitated that he could scarcely control her. Then, as Sargent relates:

> After a somewhat prolonged state of profound coma, the well-known change in her countenance and the unconscious child-like smile, admonitory of the coming of her second and higher self . . . appeared, and after a breath of relief she took my hand and said, "You should have known better than to wake her so suddenly. You should have guessed that the changes to which you were to introduce her would bewilder and astound her. Now put your hands on her head and ordain that she shall be reconciled to the change and take it as a matter of course." I obeyed the direction, and "the simpleton" . . . returned and accepted the situation as if nothing remarkable had occurred.

By April Lily was able to leave her room and go about. But there was no question of making further public appearances —not, at any rate, for the present. She saw with despair that the career on which she had embarked with such success must be abandoned just when it was getting fairly under way. But although she did not know it, the apprenticeship as a reader had served its purpose. Above all it gave her confidence. It also taught her that she had something in herself which appealed to the public, and it enabled her to develop, in a professional atmosphere, some of the techniques of the actress, which would later be of great use. The platform exploits also brought her name before the public: a fact which stood her in good stead when finally she made her début on the stage.

When Lily had sufficiently recovered from her relapse the Mowatts made a trip to Flatbush to visit Melrose. It was a sad pilgrimage. Although Lily had earned enough from her read-ings to take care of current expenses during the winter, the dream of rescuing their beloved home was shattered. This would be a farewell look; Melrose would soon pass into other hands.

Spring was late that year. As they drove out along the rutted highway after leaving the ferry slip at Brooklyn, they noticed that the buds had scarcely begun to swell. When they passed up the avenue to the house they could not help contrasting the general dreariness with the gorgeous coloring when they had left for Boston in October. "The gardens which I had seen in all the richness of their autumn bloom, were bare of leaf and flower, excepting a few crocuses that had pierced through the slowly-melting snow. The favorite arbour appeared even more bleak and desolate than the gardens. Brown and withered vine stems alone covered the trellis, where huge clusters of grapes had hung in purple luxuriance. Even the greenhouses had a deserted air. Many of the flowers had been removed, many more had died, and those that remained were suffering from neglect. We looked around for the heliotrope of hair-decking memory—it was gone!"

They went into the house, and keeping close to one another moved forlornly from room to room. It was very cold, and dust lay thick everywhere. The ballroom, where *Gulzara* had been performed, which had so often echoed to music and happy laughter, was peopled with ghosts. They quickened their steps and were relieved when they stood outside again on the carriage-block.

When June came Lily and James were strong enough to want to get away from New York. They were weary of the Astor House which for all its satin-brocade and crystal-chandelier opulence was like a prison after the long winter of confinement.

As soon as the weather was really warm, they took the steam-boat up to Troy. From there they traveled overland by diligence to Lenox, Massachusetts. This picturesque village in the Berk-shires had been recommended for its pure air and peaceful social atmosphere. Some of the Mowatts' Boston friends had summer homes there, and the calm of rustic gentility was more appealing than the hubbub of a fashionable watering-place like Saratoga.

Besides it was cheaper; and nearly everything Lily and James now did had to be reckoned for the cost.

Epes Sargent joined them during the course of their stay. The summer was also "brightened," to use Anna Cora's own term, "by pleasant friendship with the gifted Miss Sedgwick and her genial relatives." Mrs. Charles Sedgwick, mother of the authoress, kept a seminary for young ladies. Lily soon made friends with a number of the girls, and they became devoted to her. She found it refreshing to have the companionship of young creatures still untouched by care. "They made me listen to their grievances, or join in their games, or read aloud for their amusement. Then came the usual schoolgirl interchange of locks of hair and pressed flowers. I still preserve a goodly pile of curls, ringlets, and braids of various hues that remind me of lovely Lenox schoolgirls, now wives and mothers."

There was—inevitably—some theatrical diversion. Miss Sedgwick had written a play for her mother's pupils, and Anna Cora was persuaded to direct it. The rehearsals proved very amusing since the play (as might be expected) involved a good deal of stabbing and dying in attitude, the techniques of which had to be perfected under Mrs. Mowatt's tutelage. But the piece came off in fine style. Anna Cora was touched by a simple but feeling address of thanks made to her by the leading lady, who also placed a wreath of flowers upon her head.

A guest at the performance was Dr. William Ellery Channing. The presence of this great divine, the most influential preacher of his day in America, caused a fine flutter among the young ladies and others who had been invited that evening. Lily recalled that some of the guests "in watching him . . . forgot to watch the play."

As the weeks passed the Mowatts and Dr. Channing became very friendly. The Channings were stopping at the same hotel with Lily and James, and many long summer afternoons were spent in conversation on the vine-covered piazza of the hotel. Channing was a fascinating man and even now in his old age very handsome. Lily never tired of watching his fine expressive face as he discoursed on Transcendentalism and other themes.

The interest was mutual. Channing had never met anyone

like Lily, ethereally beautiful and almost child-like in her expression, yet able to discuss knotty metaphysical problems with vigorous clarity. More than once the godfather of Transcendentalism was hard-pressed to defend his ideas of the higher realms of being. The theories which he had arrived at in the quiet of his study Mrs. Mowatt seemed to know about from actual experience, and her views carried a special conviction.

One day when Lily was reading aloud to James from Swedenborg's *Divine Providence*, a slight sound caused her to turn her head towards the doorway. There was Dr. Channing leaning thoughtfully against the wall with a look of intent interest on his face. Lily halted abruptly, but Channing begged her to continue reading. When she came to the end of the chapter he asked, "Do you understand what you are reading?"

Lily thought that she did.

"Do you believe it?"

"Yes."

"What makes you believe it?"

"Because I *can't help it*."

Dr. Channing laughed. "That's a woman's reason, but I believe it is the strongest you could give."

They talked for some time of Swedenborg, and then the subject led to mesmerism. Channing was deeply interested in Anna Cora's case, of which he had doubtless heard from his nephew namesake who had been present at some of the treatments at the Astor House. Twice he persuaded Anna Cora to allow Sargent to mesmerize her, so that he might see the effects for himself. One point on which he was very skeptical was the possibility of communication between minds without the aid of material signs. After several experiments in which Lily gave answers to Sargent's unspoken questions, he appeared convinced that this could be done.

Dr. Channing was fascinated by the effects of mesmerism on the personality, particularly when Sargent told him one evening at dinner of an episode that had occurred during the afternoon. Lily had been suffering from a severe pain in her chest and had asked Sargent to hypnotize her. As soon as she was in a trance there was relief. She then proposed to Sargent and James that they take a walk. The party started out along the highway to Stockbridge. It was the height of the season and there was considerable carriage traffic on the road. The walkers were just stepping out of the way to let a heavy diligence pass when Lily happened to notice a large snake sunning itself in the dust directly in the path of the oncoming vehicle. In her normal state she had an almost paralyzing fear of snakes. But to "the gypsy" fear was unknown. Without the slightest hesitation she grasped the squirming reptile and quickly carried it to the side of the road where she deposited it in safety behind a large stone.

Sometimes in the evening Anna Cora—who was by now rather celebrated herself—recited for Dr. Channing and the other hotel guests. Channing, unquestionably one of the finest speakers America has ever produced, made useful suggestions which Anna Cora was quick to follow. With great tact he pointed out one or two faults in her elocution, and a few errors in pronunciation. To the end of her life Anna Cora could never speak certain words without thinking of Dr. Channing. She profited by his corrections, as by all instruction, and listened with a sense of awe to his own reading of Bryant's "Future Life". In less than a month after leaving Lenox, Channing himself had entered

> ... *The sphere that keeps*
> *The disembodied spirits of the dead.*

But there was no premonition of this when the Mowatts parted from him.

The months at Lenox had brought Lily and James back to the world. Rest and sun and fresh air had halted the course of Lily's consumption and though there was no improvement in James's sight he was stronger than he had been in more than two years. But what had helped most was the companionship of people with normal backgrounds, and the stimulation of exciting personalities like Miss Sedgwick and Dr. Channing. When the Mowatts went back to New York in September they felt that they might really begin to live again.

CHAPTER EIGHT

The Unfettered Muse

L ily hoped to resume her readings in the fall. But she had scarcely begun to work on a new program when it became evident that she was not yet strong enough to stand for two hours on a rostrum and keep an audience entertained. The summer in the Berkshires had brought healing and strength, but she was still unable to use her voice for more than a few minutes at a time without beginning to cough.

It was a bitter disappointment to be forced to give up a career that had cost so much effort and heart-ache. Besides, the long months of enforced idleness had made her restless. There was also the question of money, more pressing than ever. By the end of the summer something had been salvaged from the wreckage of James's fortune; but it was very little, at most only enough to keep them going for a few months. James had almost lost the sight of one eye, and the other was so weak that he could use it to read only for brief intervals. There was little hope that he would be able to contribute to their support.

But Lily was not despondent. One effect of the crisis of the previous winter and the experiments with mesmerism had been to quicken her imagination and reveal new sources of power. At Lenox she had had long talks with William Ellery Channing whose sensitive mind had enabled her to see her experience in a new light. She could look back upon her fantasies not as the wanderings of a sick spirit, but as the extension of ordinary experience onto a higher plane. As a result the most common-place happenings now had a sharpened meaning, and life had acquired an overtone of excitement which she was anxious to share with others. It is therefore not difficult to understand why, in casting about for a means of livelihood, she determined to try her hand seriously at authorship. She had so much to say!

But Lily was practical with it all. Since she needed money, she made up her mind at once that she would be nothing if not a popular writer, and that she must appeal to the widest possible public. She thought first of the newspapers, but they were practically a closed domain, for men only. A more likely field was the magazines, which were multiplying daily. These catered largely to women; and their pages—which Lily studied with great care—were filled with the effusions of female authors. Some of these ladies were actually making a career of writing. Mrs. Lydia Sigourney had become, via the magazines, one of the most successful authors in the country. Lily's friend Miss Sedgwick was making a very good living with her sketches and tales infused (in the words of one critic) with "an amiable home sentiment". Lily decided she would take a leaf from Miss Sedgwick's book.

Among the papers in her desk she found some jottings from her Bremen winter and the letters she had written to James at that time. With this material for background as well as other letters which she recovered from her sisters, Lily set to work on a series of articles. The first of these, "Bridal Customs of the North Germans", was submitted to *The Ladies' Companion*. The article was at once accepted, and the editor wrote a very friendly letter saying that the pages of the magazine would welcome further contributions from Mrs. Mowatt.

Before the winter was over Lily had become a regular contributor to *Godey's*, *The Democratic Review*, *The Ladies' Companion*, *Graham's* and other periodicals. She wrote sketches of celebrities she had met—Mrs. Trollope, Lady Bulwer, Lafayette, Joseph Bonaparte (whose home she had visited at Bordentown, New Jersey)—and essays contrasting the manners of Europeans and Americans. Everything was based on her personal experiences which she related in a brisk, faintly sardonic style. Most of these contributions appeared under the name of "Helen Berkley". She also wrote poems which she signed "Isabel" or "Cora" or "A.C.M." and, sometimes "Anna Cora Mowatt". One of the Cora poems entitled *A Wish* expresses nostalgia for Melrose and the bucolic life of Flatbush:

> *Oh, I would have a cottage small,*
> *With creeping ivy twined:*
> *A crystal stream before it glide,—*
> *A shady brook behind.*

"Cottage small" hardly describes the mansion of Melrose, but "Cora" was expressing her "wish" in terms of the general experience of the readers of *Godey's*, who for the most part did not live in mansions. However the references to the Mowatts' country estate are unmistakable in other details such as "a sparkling fountain", "hinds and hares" (Melrose had a supply of both) and "a gentle steed to ride".

The poem ends on a note reflecting Lily's deepening sense of spiritual values, the result of her conversion to Swedenborgianism:

> *And had I then my wishes all,*
> *And happy might I die,*
> *No more I'd want except the heart*
> *To thank the ONE on high.*

Articles and poems were only a beginning. Epes Sargent told Lily about a contest which *The New World* was launching, for a novel to be entitled *The Fortune Hunter*. The prize offered was a hundred dollars, and the chief conditions were that the novel should be original (sometimes works submitted to American publishers were not original) and that it should not exceed one volume in length. This was *The New World's* way of striking a blow at the two- and three-volume novels which though still popular in England were beginning to strain the attention of American readers.

"Write a story in your Mrs. Berkley style," said Sargent; "you can easily make the title apply. Ten to one your novel will be the one accepted."

This might have seemed a somewhat optimistic prediction to make for a mere novice, but Sargent was an experienced journalist and he recognized the essential reader-appeal in Lily's work. Furthermore, he was on intimate terms with the editors of *The New World*, and he knew that a word on behalf of a friend would not go amiss. So Lily drew up a plot which she submitted to Sargent. He approved the general idea, with one or two changes, and Lily set to work. At the appointed time *The Fortune Hunter* was completed and in due course won the prize, which was the "most agreeable evidence of its acceptance."

Meanwhile she continued to turn out articles at a furious rate. In addition she composed—"compiled" is her own and perhaps a more accurate expression—several volumes for the publishing-house of Stringer and Burgess. This firm had on its list a very popular novelist and writer of household manuals, Mrs. Ellis. The lady's name had acquired such selling power that she found it impossible to meet the publishers' demands for her works. Stringer and Burgess, in order to resolve the difficulty, decided to engage a ghost-writer to supplement Mrs. Ellis's output. Lily was offered the assignment and under Mrs. Ellis' name wrote several works, including *Housekeeping Made Easy*; *Book of the Toilette*; *Book of Embroidery*; *Knitting, Netting and Crochet*; *Ball-Room Etiquette*. There were also other titles which she was unable to recall in after years, and which the modern researcher has sought in vain.

These works were all very profitable, most particularly the

volume called *Housekeeping Made Easy*. The book was nicely timed, for by 1842 the American woman had made a good start on the long road to emancipation from the shackles of housework. While her European sisters were still spending hours turning a spit in the fireplace, the American housewife was in possession of a self-basting roaster, in which she could place her ten- or twelve-pound Sunday roast, and a patented oven into which she could put the roaster, while she finished ironing her husband's frilled linen shirts—a wonderful saving of time. Lily's personal experiments with these new home-making techniques were probably limited, since at Melrose there had been a staff of well-trained servants, and at the Astor House she and James occupied a two-room suite. Nevertheless she presented the details in such a lively and intimate style that it seemed as though they were the fruits of her own trials and errors as a housekeeper, and this made the book attractive to readers.

When James saw what a good thing Lily's writing was turning out to be for Stringer and Burgess, he conceived the idea of publishing her works himself, thus keeping the whole profits of her pen in the family. Lily agreed heartily to the plan, because she would be able to write as she pleased—or so she thought. The firm of Mowatt and Company was therefore established, and the first work to appear under its imprint was a *Life of Goethe*. Since a lady could scarcely write the biography of a man with propriety, Lily used the pseudonym "Henry C. Browning" for this work. Her next effort, *The Memoirs of Madame D'Arblay*, appeared under the name of "Helen Berkley". Though these studies were doubtless more to Lily's taste than *Etiquette of the Toilette* and *Housekeeping Made Easy*, neither volume appealed to a very wide public. In order to keep Mowatt and Company solvent Lily had to return to compiling manuals of useful information. Two of these which proved quite popular were *Etiquette of Matrimony* (purporting to be extracted from the works of Lady Blessington) and *Management of the Sickroom* by "Charles A. Lee, M. D".

Mowatt and Company also drew heavily on the talents of Epes Sargent. The firm published the first two volumes of the

Modern Standard Drama, under the editorship of Sargent. This was later taken over by Samuel French and is the most important source of early nineteenth century plays popular on the British and American stage. Sargent also edited for James, *The Drawing Room Library* and *Sargent's Weekly*. The former was designed to present periodically works not easily available otherwise. The first (and only) issue was devoted entirely to Sargent's poems, including *A Life on the Ocean Wave* and the famous *Missing Ship*. *Sargent's Weekly* was a literary review aimed at the most elevated taste. It survived less than a year.

Mere compiling, even with subjects as attractive as Goethe and Fanny Burney, was largely drudgery, and for relief Lily turned to fiction. The result was a two-volume novel entitled *Evelyn, or a Heart Unmasked*. This was inspired by the works of Frederika Bremer, the Swedish novelist who was immensely popular both in England and America at the time. Lily borrowed something of Miss Bremer's method in telling her story through a series of letters, as well as a theme dear to that lady's heart. The emphasis in *Evelyn*, as in Miss Bremer's *Hertha*, is all on a more liberal attitude toward the frailties of women.

Evelyn is a story of the idle rich, or people aspiring to that status. It purports to show the corrupting effects of high society on the tender moral fibre of a young girl. Much of the story's action takes place in a fashionable boarding-house just off Broadway. This strikes the proper note of decadence, for as Lily makes clear, a fashionable boarding-house is no place in which to bring up a young girl of delicate principles. The setting is also a useful device for introducing a wide variety of characters and incidents into the story. *Evelyn* is a novel in which a great many things happen. There is a seduction, a duel, an attempted murder (with vitriol), a suicide, and experiments in welfare work.

Although Lily frankly admitted her debt to Frederika Bremer, *Evelyn* had a substantial basis in fact. It was the story, as Lily tells us, "of one whom I had dearly loved—over whose tomb there are few to weep, but whose sin we may dare to hope was forgiven, 'for she loved much'."

Evelyn occupied Lily's leisure time until late in 1844. It was accepted for publication by Carey and Hart of Philadelphia, but there were delays in getting it into print. This, as it turned out, was fortunate. By the time the novel did appear, Mrs. Mowatt had made her spectacular début as an actress. The widespread publicity given this event was useful in promoting the book, which had a large sale.

Before *Evelyn* appeared in America, an English publisher who had seen the manuscript wanted to bring it out in London. Lily would have liked this, but unfortunately she could not meet the British publisher's requirements. He insisted that there must be a third volume to the novel, and this Lily was unable to supply. Her heroine had already died at the end of volume two in the original, and her imagination, which could take care of most situations, was unequal to the task of resuscitation. One suspects also that no matter how much Lily may have loved *Evelyn*'s prototype, she was relieved to have the lady safely buried at last, in fiction as in reality.

Evelyn had a somewhat curious history, which is a commentary on the cavalier practices of book-publishers in mid-nineteenth century America. The novel was pirated, shortly after it appeared, by a publisher in Cincinnati. This gentleman brought out the story in a shortened version with a London imprint on the title page. It was issued as a gift book for young ladies and apparently had some sale in the West. In its mangled version it did not reflect great credit on the author and Lily would willingly have taken measures to suppress it. Unfortunately at that moment she was establishing her reputation on the stage and felt that she could not afford to become embroiled in a law-suit.

September 1842 to February 1845 was Lily's most active literary period. The statistical account of her writing during this time is staggering. In addition to articles, which taken together would have made more than a volume, she compiled eleven books (possibly more), wrote two original novels including the two-volume *Evelyn*, and composed an unknown number of poems. The period ended with the composition of *Fashion*, her

one remembered work and the most important play written by
an American up to that time.

Between the daily grind of hack-writing (and Anna Cora
Mowatt's work was mainly that) and illness, there was little
time for social activity. Until the appearance of *Fashion*, Lily
was not known as a literary figure except in her own circle and to
the editors of the magazines to which she contributed. Connections with the writing people of her time were very limited.
She was a close friend of Epes Sargent and his brother John,
editor of *The New York Courier and Enquirer*. Early in her
career as a reader she had met Mrs. Sarah Whitman, one of Edgar
Allen Poe's later loves, and for a short time carried on a correspondence with this lady on exalted literary and religious
subjects. She also knew Mrs. Osgood, another Poe amorata who,
as we have already seen, wrote a poem about her. But with both
these ladies the bonds were largely those of mutual professional
admiration.

There is no record that Lily had any close contacts with the
various literary cliques which flourished at the time in New
York. Although Poe later set her down as one of the "literati",
she did not frequent the milieu of ethereal ladies and melancholy
gentlemen who gathered on Saturday nights in the salon of
Mrs. Seba Smith. Nor did she participate in the "flow of soul"
which rarefied the atmosphere in the drawing-rooms of Miss
Lynch or Mrs. Ellet, two other literary ladies who with Mrs.
Osgood divided the sway in Upper Bohemia.

Nathaniel Willis she certainly knew, not only as the editor
of *The New York Mirror*, but as a fellow-guest at the Astor
House during the winter of 1841-42. She had dealings with
Park Benjamin and Parke Godwin, both prominent in the New
York newspaper world. She had little regard for Park Benjamin,
and with some reason. In the spring of 1842, while she was
slowly recovering from the illness which had stricken her that
winter, Benjamin, an inveterate gossip, spread a malicious story
about her. Sargent reported the matter in a letter to E. P.
Whipple in Boston. After commenting on the state of their
friend's health which was "very delicate, and her tenure of life
seems extremely frail", Sargent went on to say:

To show you how the spirit of detraction can pervert a very blameless act, I will mention a little incident. When in Boston she [Lily] wrote an impromptu consisting of some four lines in a lady's album. Subsequently in New York, she gave a copy of it to a lady at the Astor House, simply inscribing the lines in her album without calling it an impromptu—and at the same time giving the lady to understand that it was a copy of lines written for a Boston friend. It seems that an individual of her own sex, who chanced to see the lines inscribed both in New York and the Boston album, thought fit to put a malicious construction upon the simple fact— and has got up against Mrs. M. a charge of duplicity in passing off as an impromptu what was an elaborate composition. Park Benjamin has got hold of the story and is singing it in every- body's ears to Mrs. M.'s disadvantage. The mischief done by the *individual*, who chose to put this false, malicious and absurd con- struction upon a perfectly blameless act may not easily be repaired. Fields can tell you the name of the Boston lady, for whom the lines were written. Mrs. M. assured me in her somnambulic state that that lady (Miss P.) did not believe anything to her discredit in connection with the matter—and repudiated the idea that she was guilty of deception. Mrs. M. (somnambulic) is fully aware of the source where the story originated, and has disclosed to me the name of the inventor of the charge. For the *lady's* sake I will keep silent. . . .

This incident curiously parallels another involving Benjamin, who imputed to Edward J. English, a New York merchant, a slanderous remark about Poe. According to Benjamin's story, English was supposed to have accused Poe of forgery. The story was proved false and Benjamin, only the middle man as in the present instance, did not get into difficulties. But his reputation as a dangerous tongue was well established. As for Lily, the most malicious rumor he could spread about her was that she was guilty of self-plagiarism. Fortunately she had Epes Sargent on her side. Though Sargent discreetly kept silence about Lily's clair- voyance in discovering her detractor (for this was a subject on which she was extremely sensitive) he managed to set things to rights. The true version of the "impromptu" was given wide circulation and her good name was not damaged. Yet in the still provincial atmosphere of New York in the eighteen-forties, it paid to watch one's step.

Fortunately Lily had too many things on her mind to be concerned with the gossip of the literati. In the fall of 1842 the Mowatts left the Astor, which was a somewhat conspicuous residence for people of their quiet tastes, and rented a small house on Fourth Avenue. Here Lily submerged herself in writing and in the study of Swedenborg. The rigorous daily routine was broken only by an occasional visit with friends, a walk or a drive with James.

Late one afternoon in November the Mowatts returned from a drive and found a little girl sitting on their doorstep. The child was in rags, miserably thin and half-frozen. She was weeping bitterly. Lily was recovering from an attack of influenza and dared not stay outside to question the child, so she had her brought into the drawing-room. Here in the warmth of the open fire the waif was gradually able to tell her story. It was the familiar one of the hundreds of "cold victual" children who were roaming the streets of New York, begging food to eke out meagre family larders. She had rung the Mowatts' bell, but the cook had turned her away. Now she must return home empty-handed. She explained that her mother was very ill—dying, the neighbors said—and that her father was out of work. Something in the little ragamuffin's manner touched Lily deeply. As she had not removed her cloak and bonnet, she determined to accompany the child home to see what could be done.

In a wretched hovel only a short distance from her own house Lily found a young woman, pale and emaciated. Her cheeks were brightly flushed, and there was a glaze of doom in her eyes. In her arms she held a wizened baby, not more than two or three weeks old. The child was whimpering but seemed too feeble to cry. The mother could only speak in gasps, but she managed to say that they had had nothing to eat for days, except what little Esther had managed to beg. Lily stroked the woman's hand and tried to comfort her. She promised to help her and told her to send Esther back to the house in Fourth Avenue the next day.

Esther arrived early the next morning. Lily gave the child a warm meal and a basket with food and clothing to take home. As the child was leaving Lily suggested that she come every day for a visit and a hot meal. Esther was so tiny and forlorn, and there was something in the shy way in which she responded to a word of affection that went straight to Lily's heart. So Esther began to come every day to the house and stay until evening. She played by the fire and ran errands about the house to keep herself occupied. Lily did everything to make the child happy. She replaced the filthy rags with warm clothes and saw that Esther was properly fed. She visited Esther's mother and did what she could to brighten the sordid sick-room. When the unhappy creature died a few weeks later, Lily was at her bedside.

A few days after this event, Esther's father, an Irish immigrant, rough and ill-featured, came to see James. The purpose of his visit was soon made known. He demanded back wages for little Esther's "services" and threatened to keep her at home if he were not paid. He knew that Lily had become attached to the child and he assumed that she would yield to his demands rather than part with Esther. James was indignant. He saw that the man was capable of anything, and he refused to allow Lily to have any further dealings with him. So little Esther was sent back to her wretched home.

The episode haunted Lily. The thought of the miserable existence to which the child was doomed, doubly miserable after her brief taste of warmth and affection in Lily's comfortable house, would not leave her. And there was something else. The presence of the child, the sound of the small bright voice echoing in the rooms, the thin little arms clutching her in a burst of affection—these things had momentarily stilled a hunger in Lily. It was something of which she had scarcely been aware until Esther had come to them. Now that the child had gone and the house was silent again, she found it intolerable.

Lily was twenty-four years old, and she had been married for nearly ten years. She and James had had no children, and it seemed unlikely that they would ever have any now. Devoted as they were to each other, there had been an incompleteness in their life together. At the time of their marriage Lily, though in many ways mature beyond her years, had been still too much of a child to respond wholly to the passion of her husband. When she had grown, physically and emotionally, after the year in Europe, James had become a sick man. Sickness and trouble, as well as intellectual congeniality, had drawn them closer together during all this time; yet something was lacking. The energy and abandon with which Lily had thrown herself into her work as a reader was due in part to financial necessity, partly to the urge to express a genuine artistic impulse. But there was more to it than that. The intensity of passion which had electrified her listeners was not altogether histrionic. On the platform with an audience before her Lily had found means of emotional release which to some extent had been denied her in the course of everyday existence.

Lily was too circumspect, too full of inbred reticence, ever to be explicit on this subject, but it is easy enough to read between the lines of the *Autobiography*. It was not simply an instinct of charity that led her to welcome little Esther into her home. She had a great need to give herself unreservedly to something, to someone. Neither her work nor her devotion to James could quite satisfy this longing. But the child might have done so. When Esther had to be sent away the longing became an ache.

But she did not suffer for long. Through a seamstress who worked for a neighbor, Lily learned about another household, where poverty was acute and children were hungry. She could not resist seeking them out. Again she found squalor and wretchedness; but the people were of a different breed from the villainous father of Esther. The Greys were English with a modest but respectable background. The father had been a small tradesman in the old country, but falling on bad times he had decided to emigrate to America "to dig gold in the streets", as he put it. However, ill-luck had followed him across the Atlantic. Not long after he arrived in New York his sight had begun to fail. When Lily came upon him he was totally blind.

The family lived in a dilapidated shanty in Harlem, which Lily's coachman found with difficulty. It was a bitter January

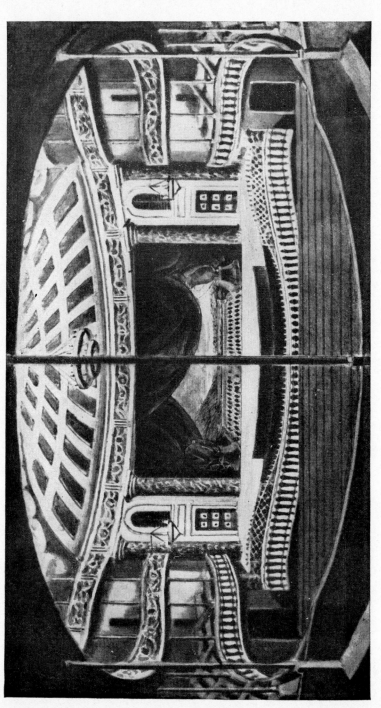

THE PARK THEATRE, NEW YORK, INTERIOR VIEW

This water-color by Alexander J. Davis was copied *circa* 1850 from a rare wood-engraving by Lansing.

Courtesy, The J. Clarence Davies Collection, Museum of the City of New York

day when Lily set out to visit the Greys, and though she was wrapped in furs and shawls with a hot stone at her feet, she had almost frozen on the long drive. Inside the Greys' shanty it was colder still. She found Mr. Grey sitting by an empty stove. At his feet lay a little boy, half-naked and shivering. On a small wooden box sat a baby strapped by its waist to the back of a chair.

When Lily spoke, the father rose with a kind of dignity she had not expected. From his first words it was obvious that he had known better days. In answer to her inquiry he explained that his wife and their nine-year-old daughter Margaret were out hunting something to burn in the stove. The winter weather was very hard on the little boys, he told her, and his own teeth were chattering as he spoke.

The combination of circumstances, the poverty, the cold, the blindness, the faint shred of human dignity which in some people survives with the last breath of life, caused her to make up her mind at once. She told Mr. Grey that she would like to have Mrs. Grey come to see her the next day. She was to bring little Margaret along, and if everything was satisfactory the child might come and live with her.

Next day Mrs. Grey and Margaret called. Lily was less favorably impressed with the mother than she had been with Mr. Grey. But she found little Margaret irresistible. Although badly under-nourished, the child was pretty, with great blue eyes and masses of golden hair down to her waist. There was no mistaking what lay behind her. Lily was stricken to find that suffering could leave its marks so early on the human face.

She told Mrs. Grey at once that Margaret might come to live with her. She also promised that she would enlist the aid of her friends in finding better quarters for the rest of the family and some steady employment for Mrs. Grey herself.

The woman was delighted at this miraculous change in their fortunes. But Margaret seemed heart-broken at being left behind. She made no sound, but Lily saw the terrified look in her eyes as her mother went out the door. Later Lily realized that ill-usage had broken her spirit. When she undressed Margaret for bed that night she saw that the thin little body was covered with ugly bruises, the result of continued beatings. In answer to Lily's questioning Margaret explained haltingly that she had not been mistreated by her parents, but by strangers with whom she was sometimes left when her mother went out to work. Lily understood then why Margaret was so frightened at being left again with people she did not know.

All that first day "busy fingers plied their needles", and if some of the fingers were more used to the pen than the needle, they worked no less eagerly for that reason. That night Margaret sat by the fire with James and Lily. She made no sound but shyly held out her hands to the blaze as though "she were making a new acquaintance. In her neat blue dress and white bib, with her fair hair smoothed and cut, it was only in the painful expression of her face that the little Margaret of the morning could be recognized."

It was months before Margaret smiled, and longer than that before she was heard to sing. When Lily came into the room, drawn by the unfamiliar sound, Margaret looked at her in terror as though she had been caught in some criminal act and burst into tears. The winning of Margaret was a slow process and was only accomplished by unceasing kindness and tact. But in the end the child accepted her new life and became a member of the family, "beloved and learning to love".

Lily made good her word to help the others. A house was found for the family in New York and Mrs. Grey was given work. But the struggle with poverty had gone on too long. Within a year both parents died, and the two little boys were left alone. There were two older sisters, but neither was in a position to help the little brothers. Lily was able to place Willie, the baby, with friendly neighbors of the Greys. John, the older boy who was about six, was brought to the house on Fourth Avenue. The child had just come down with pneumonia and for the next two months Lily and Margaret had their hands full taking care of him. Sometimes the pressure of work and her own ill-health obliged Lily to leave him to himself for long hours, but when she returned she would find him happily turning the pages of a picture book or feebly singing a little song. Unlike Margaret he responded at once to the new atmosphere, and as soon as he could wander about the house he tried to show his gratitude by inventing small tasks to make himself useful.

Margaret was sent every week to visit the baby. One day she returned in tears to announce that the friends with whom he had been left were moving away and Willie was to be placed that very day in an orphan asylum. Margaret begged that he might be allowed to stay with her and John for a few days before they were parted. The child's entreaties were so pitiable that Lily despite the struggle to make ends meet, agreed to let Willie come to them to stay. Within an hour Margaret staggered in the front door bearing the two-year-old Willie in her arms.

Lily had no fixed ideas about the children, and at this time she probably had no intention of assuming permanent responsibility for them. It was enough that she and the children needed each other so intensely. And after they had been under her roof for a few weeks, it was as though they had been there always. The latest arrival, little Willie, was a rosy-cheeked apple-dumpling of a fellow who prattled ceaselessly in a happy, unintelligible way and got into everything. But the children made few demands, and in that day before the advent of scientific child-care one could assume the responsibilities of parenthood without passing into a state of abject slavery. So the Mowatts willingly accepted the burden of three more mouths to feed and three rapidly-growing bodies to clothe.

From the first, James seems to have been as much attached to the children as Lily. When, two years later, events once more broke up the Mowatts' home, their first concern was for the children. Though James's and Lily's own future at this time seemed uncertain, there was no question about the welfare of the little Greys. The children were placed in safe and friendly hands, and James took precautions for their future by legally adopting all three.

Now Lily's pen had additional inspiration. With a family of five to think about, the words must be kept flowing in an unceasing stream. Lily ruthlessly omitted all superfluous activity, so that she might spend more hours at her desk or with the children, whose education she took over entirely. By adhering to the strictest schedule, she managed to increase her output of stories and articles. The checks from *Godey's* and *Graham's* and *The New World* came in regularly, but before they arrived Lily knew how the money would be spent down to the last penny. Household expenses were met principally by articles and sketches for the magazines, and these occupied most of the scheduled working hours. But often late at night, long after the children and James were in bed, Lily would sit by the dying fire in the little drawing-room, writing verses. Into these would go the ideas and feelings which had no place in her more prosaic day-time writing. Although she was very happy, she still was under the shadow of the disease which so many times had threatened to take her away. And so, inextricably, the theme of death was mingled with that of love, and the two would find expression in such lines as

> *Oh wear for me no sable hue*
> *No part of blazoned grief—when I*
> *Shall bid the gladsome earth adieu*
> *And fling my spirit's garment by!*
> *Nor mark the spot with grass or stone,*
> *Where worthless dust unconscious lies:*
> *Within your loving hearts alone,*
> *The monument I ask should rise!*

But whether her muse was bright or sad, the end was never lost from sight. Even death must be turned to account to fill the needs of the living. These trifles for the *Columbian Magazine* or *Graham's* would often be printed with elaborate ornamental borders or as accompaniments to etchings of maidens embracing tombstones. But each of them ultimately would be translated into a new dress for Margaret, a pair of shoes for little Willie, or the bill at the apothecary shop on the corner.

CHAPTER NINE

Fashion

When the Mowatts moved to Fourth Avenue in the fall of 1842 New York was in the midst of the greatest wave of expansion it had yet known. In the decade since their marriage, James and Lily had seen the population increased by more than a third (it now stood at around 300,000) and the physical appearance of the old town changed almost beyond recognition. In the early thirties most of the Mowatts' friends still lived around the southern end of Manhattan Island. Prince Street marked the northern boundary of civilization. But after the great fire of 1835—the most devastating in a long series of holocausts—the center of gravity shifted. The fire destroyed more than six hundred buildings and the loss was estimated at twenty million dollars. Yet the disaster merely acted as a spur to the city's development. The burnt-over section was rapidly rebuilt, mainly with business structures. By 1840, lower Manhattan had ceased to be a desirable residential section. A few diehards among the old Knickerbocker families still clung to houses in Bowling Green and Hudson Square, but the majority of residents who had lost their homes in the fire migrated northward into the tranquil reaches around Union Square.

The Fourth Avenue house to which James and Lily had moved from the Astor was located just north of Twentieth Street, around the corner from Gramercy Park. This section had been developed largely through the initiative of Samuel Ruggles, an old friend of Lily's father and one of New York's most far-seeing and influential citizens. Ruggles himself lived in Union Square, but it was he who had established Gramercy Park, deeding the land to the owners of surrounding lots in such a way as to insure its maintenance and make it the center of a highly restricted neighborhood. By the mid-forties this section, from Union Square on the south to Twenty-third Street on the north, was the most fashionable quarter of New York. Close neighbors to the Mowatts were Washington Irving, Peter Cooper, Cyrus W. Field, Horace Greeley, the Roosevelts and a dozen other families whose names were conspicuous in the city's history. The Mowatts' back garden joined that of Mayor James Harper, whose beautiful house with its delicate iron-work tracery still adorns Gramercy Park.

The houses in this district were all new and very different from the mansions in Warren Street, where Samuel Ogden had first settled on his return from France in 1825. The spreading dwellings of the earlier day, surrounded by gardens and trees, had given way to narrow row houses. These were mostly of brick with small porticoes. Occasionally one saw a front of brownstone which was now becoming fashionable. Except for the most pretentious mansions these houses were monotonously alike. Each had the same uniform series of rooms, which were ranged one above the other to a height of four stories—thus inaugurating the vertical existence which has been a distinctive feature of New York ever since.

But the change in the appearance of the city was as nothing compared to the change in the complexion of society. Many of the old pre-Revolutionary names were still prominent—people like the Schermerhorns, the Stuyvesants, the Ogdens and the Beekmans. But in the late thirties the solid phalanx of old patrician families had begun to give way under the pressure of a host of newcomers, vague as to antecedents but impressive in their display of wealth. This new group was composed mainly of people of simple origins having none of the traditions of the old Knickerbocker and sometimes very little education. What they did have unmistakably was a sharp eye to the main chance, developed in the rough-and-tumble ways of the frontier, or against the hard background of competitive European life. Whether they came from the hinterlands of America or from the Old World, they were keen enough to see the opportunities in the mushrooming city, and many had pulled rich plums from the golden pie of New York's booming economy.

The tastes of these new people reflected their wealth and their lack of cultivation. Their houses became repositories of all that was biggest and heaviest and shiniest and most patently expensive. Fringed damask curtains cascaded from ornate cornices at high drawing-room windows. Velvet ottomans, bulging and buttoned, cumbered the rooms, along with chairs and tables in rosewood and black walnut, tortured into fantastic shapes by the new wood-turning machinery. Intricately fretted screens and what-nots loaded with bric-a-brac lurked in dim corners, while sconces and chandeliers were festooned with crystal prisms, whose brilliant glitter and high bright tinkle more than anything else symbolized the wealth and aspirations of the owners.

But it was not only the furnishings of their houses, or the handsome carriages that jostled one another on Broadway, or the extravagant costumes of the women that advertised this new element in society. Manners also reflected the rapid climb to wealth and position. As they mingled with the older citizenry, these new people sensed their lack of background and sought to make up for it in various ways. Culture was not purchasable, but some of its by-products were. One might not have read books, but one could patronize poets and novelists. The blood in one's own veins might not run blue, but one could give balls and dinner-parties for visiting European aristocrats. Thus lion-hunting became an exciting, and sometimes deadly, pursuit.

The effects of foreign travel were prominently displayed. Not only did the drawing-rooms of Gramercy Park and Union Square bulge with European knick-knacks; they resounded to the echoes of exotic words and phrases, tossed off with the greatest aplomb, if not always with accuracy. Fashionable conversation was now charged with French words and expressions, some of which were to become fixed in the American idiom. The time-honored term "eating-house" which had been good enough for Hamilton and Jefferson, was now employed mainly by provincials and members of the lower orders. Even the conservative Philip Hone uses the new word "restaurant" with increasing frequency as his diary moves toward the mid-century. After Ole Bull's triumphant tour of the Union in 1843, Americans who were really *au fait* no longer spoke of "fiddlers". They showed their appreciation of the finer music (Bull's specialties were variations on "Yankee Doodle" and the "Carnival of Venice") by using the word "violinist".

Sometimes a new term was imported along with the practice it designated. *Déjeuner à la fourchette* was delightful to roll off the tongue, if one could manage it, while the institution itself was something very special indeed. The *déjeuner à la fourchette*, or luncheon party, was a French importation which had undergone considerable sea-change. This remarkable innovation, which gave a new tone to social life, began at two o'clock with a meal which consisted of oysters, pheasant under glass, game, pâté de foie gras, salads, ices and elaborate confectionery—with continuous interlacings of champagne. When the luncheon was over the party rose, if it was still capable of standing on its feet, and adjourned to the drawing-rooms for dancing until seven.

In the eyes of conservative old New Yorkers the *déjeuner* was a shocking practice—not because of the excessive consumption of food and drink, but because of the inroads it made on the working-day. However, by this time there was a whole generation of New Yorkers who lived in happy oblivion to the idea of remunerative employment. In society now, there were many young men of inherited wealth, or with good prospects thereof, who had less concern for the counting-house than for the race-track and the ballroom. They found a visit to the tailor more diverting than checking bales and barrels in a musty warehouse. With young ladies the situation was similar. Housewifery, once an important part of the education of all females of good family, had been largely supplanted by cultivation of the social graces. Hours once spent in fine sewing were now given over to French, or novel-reading, or the study of fashion-plates. The flamboyant forties, crude, extravagant, vulgar, with a thick coating of sentimentality, were under way.

Lily, always a sharp observer of people and manners, had watched the show from the beginning. She thought a good deal about what she saw. There may have been a trace of bitterness when she observed how many of her sometime friends welcomed these vulgarians without any show of distaste, while they continued to regard her with disapproval. But usually she was greatly amused by it all, for so much that met the eye was ridiculous.

Despite the coolness of some of their acquaintances, the Mowatts had managed to keep a toe-hold in society. Illness and hard work prevented much going about, but James and Lily saw enough of New York high life to appreciate fully the changes that had taken place. Often after some particularly extravagant affair which she had attended, Lily would regale the Sargents and other close friends with imitations of the people she had met and with sharp-edged descriptions of the costumes and interiors she had seen. Her sense of social values, whetted by her experience of society in America and in Europe as well, combined with her bubbling wit, gave a particular charm to these commentaries. After listening to one such account, Epes Sargent made a suggestion to Lily.

"Why don't you write a play?"

There was nothing remarkable in this idea, since Lily had already written several plays. She might now blush at a piece of juvenilia like *The Gypsy Wanderer* or her doctoring of *The Mourning Bride*. But *Gulzara* had proved thoroughly stageworthy, at least in an amateur production, and had met with approval on the printed page. What Sargent had in mind, however, was not a play in the pseudo-Shakespearian vein such as made up the chief fare on the stage at the time. For years critics and public had been asking for plays dealing with contemporary people and situations. Everybody was getting a little weary of noble savages like Augustus Stone's *Metamora* (of which Edwin Forrest had practically made a career) or exotic melodramas like Willis's *Tortesa, the Usurer*, which was set in Peru.

Sargent believed there might be a play in what was going on right in New York, particularly in the doings of that fantastic society Lily could talk about so amusingly. If the piece were well done and effectively staged it might take. It would at least have the virtue of novelty, and this was what the New York theatre-goer of 1845 was beginning to yearn for.

So Lily sharpened her pencils (she had given up writing with a pen) and set to work. We do not know how long it took to write *Fashion*. It was probably done in three or four weeks, for Lily wrote rapidly and this was material she had well in hand. We know that this task was no drudgery. In a letter to James Sargent, younger brother of Epes, written a year after the appearance of the play, Lily remembered what fun it had been:

> Every line [of your letter] and every word, ay, the very hand-writing itself conjured back to life those happy evenings when you, and Epes, and husband, used to sit in solemn judgment over such portions of "Fashion" as I had concocted in the morning. What delight I took in hearing you predict "Fashion's" success. Alas! the verifying of that prediction gave me more pain than pleasure. I have now seen Fashion so often murdered in all its minor and greater parts before a gaping throng, that the only pleasant thoughts connected with it are linked with its first perusal before my beloved fireside judges of the Fourth Avenue —which by the way is one of the largest avenues laid out by memory and affection in my heart. . . .

Epes Sargent's assistance was undoubtedly valuable in writing the play, though it is impossible to say just what his contribution was. Poe, in his celebrated review of *Fashion*, believed he detected touches by the hand of the author of *Velasco*, and Lily herself tells us that Sargent offered "suggestions". He probably helped her with such technical matters as entrances and exits and "covering scenes", or in pointing the dialogue so as to insure the proper emphases. It is quite certain that the best of the high-comedy scenes with their crisp and oftentimes epigrammatic dialogue are Lily's. The style in these closely resembles that of the articles on people and manners which had appeared in the magazines during the two years immediately preceding the writing of *Fashion*. Indeed the whole tone of the play, with its unsparing yet good-natured caricatures of the nouveau-riche, its keen perception of weaknesses behind a front of pretence, its passionate avowal of the principles of sturdy democracy, is a reflection of Lily's personality.

Fashion is set in New York in the opulent mansion of Mr. and Mrs. Tiffany, newly rich, and but recently established in the metropolis. Mrs. Tiffany has but one object in life—to be fashionable. This leads her to wild expenditures that result in the blackmailing and ultimately the bankruptcy of her husband.

Though she pursues her goal in majestic oblivion to all lesser matters, Mrs. Tiffany has harassments. There is the inadequacy of her colored flunkey Zeke, who, despite a dazzling new uniform, does not function in the polished manner Mrs. Tiffany desires. But as she says, "to obtain a white American for a domestic is almost impossible; and they call this a free country!" Zeke continually forgets that he has been re-christened Adolphe and that an arm-chair must be called a *fauteuil*. On one critical occasion he confuses a "fo-tool" with a table, to the peril of his mistress's dignity just as she is about to sit down. Mrs. Tiffany also bears the cross of a spinster sister Prudence, who is slow to lose her rustic ways and constantly brings up inopportune reminders of days when the Tiffanys occupied a less exalted position in society. But the great lady's real burden is her husband who talks eternally about money and the necessity for economy.

Despite all these trials Mrs. Tiffany is sustained by the conviction that she has surrounded herself with the atmosphere of the "ee-light". Her house contains the cushioned ottomans and crystal chandeliers, as well as the human appendages prescribed by fashion. The latter include a haughty young man-about-town by the name of Fogg who maintains his dignity by refusing to be interested in anything. "I consider operas a bore, madame," says he in response to Mrs. Tiffany's enthusiastic comment on the subject. And to Miss Seraphina, the daughter of the house who has just discovered the charms of poetry, he remarks: "I am indifferent to verses, Miss Seraphina." He is a creature of rare distinction.

Mrs. Tiffany also has a tame poet who frequents her drawing-room. "Poets are the aristocrats of literature," she reminds us, and "I dote on all aristocracy." The poet's name is Twinkle—T. Tennyson Twinkle—and he scarcely utters a word that does not reflect his lyrical genius. No moment is too insignificant to afford him inspiration. Thus he greets Miss Seraphina with

> Fair Seraphina! the sun itself grows dim,
> Unless you aid his light and shine on him.

But the crowning glory of Mrs. Tiffany's menagerie of lions is Count Jolimaître, a dashing Frenchman whose brilliance throws even haughty young men-about-town and poetic geniuses in the shade. Count Jolimaître's knowledge of the world is exquisite: "Why at the very last dinner given at Lord Knowswho, would you believe it, madame, there was an individual present who wore a *black* cravat and took *soup twice*!" In the presence of such unspeakable refinement Mrs. Tiffany is wax. Yet she never wholly loses her presence of mind and almost engineers a marriage between the lovely Seraphina and the handsome exotic. Her hopes of an alliance with the nobility are thwarted, however, when it turns out that Jolimaître is not a count but an ex-barber-cook-valet, who has already promised to marry Mrs. Tiffany's French maid Millinette.

Yet there are worse things in life than having one's daughter almost married to a count who turns out not to be a count. To meet the extravagant outlay of his wife in pursuit of fashion, Mr. Tiffany has been forging notes. He has been detected in this malfeasance by his clerk, Snobson, who has been systematically extracting handsome rewards for keeping silence. Poor Tiffany is at his rope's end, and is only rescued at the last moment by the intervention of his old friend, Adam Trueman, a rich farmer from Cattaraugus County, New York.

Trueman has turned up earlier in the play for no very clear reason unless it is to add to Mrs. Tiffany's trials. His brusque manners and strong republican principles, expressed in somewhat oratorical set-speeches, disturb the *recherché* tone of her drawing-room. But his uncouthness is overlooked when, rather in the role of *deus ex machina*, he digs into his capacious pockets to save his old friend. Being himself the soul of virtue, Trueman is quick to detect wrong-doing in others and he promptly points out (for some reason this has occurred to no one else) that Snobson by his blackmailing is an accessory to his employer's crime, and thus a candidate for the penitentiary. This is enough to send Snobson on his way to parts remote—California, to be exact, than which in 1845 nothing could have been remoter. In strict logic Trueman himself could probably be regarded as abetting his friend's crime by offering to cover it up. But in Lily's time, as now, the prime ingredient of the drama was illusion, not logic. Judging by the reactions of audiences and critics, Trueman was the most appealing character in the play. By the mid-nineteenth century the ideal of American manhood had become fixed; and Trueman personified that ideal, since in addition to being virtuous and shrewd he was also rich.

Added to the other elements of the play is a love affair between the poor but beautiful Gertrude, companion to Miss Seraphina, and an upstanding colonel in the American army. The fact that Gertrude turns out to be the long-lost granddaughter of old Trueman is an incidental but pretty detail.

No mere résumé of the plot of *Fashion* can convey the liveliness and bright humor that carry the whole thing along. Despite its sentimentality it has a vigor and freshness not to be found in any previous American play. In the very opening scene *Fashion* sets a mark for high-comedy that is still unsurpassed in our native drama. This scene centers about the attempt of Twinkle, the poet, to read a stanza of his latest masterpiece to Seraphina and her mother. This is an agonizing process, since the reading is constantly interrupted as one character after another enters the drawing-room and is greeted effusively by Mrs. Tiffany. With each interruption poor Twinkle must begin all over again, managing to get out one additional phrase before the next break. Finally in a desperate outburst he recites the whole stanza which consists of two lines:

> *Around my heart thou weavest a spell*
> *Whose magic I can never tell.*

This is certainly the first example in American comic writing of the tremendous build-up to absolute inanity, a device which has become the stand-by of much modern radio and motion picture humor. In *Fashion* the device is merely a means to an end, a satire on the vapidity and pretentiousness of the general literary taste in America at this period. Since Lily herself contributed a large number of effusions to meet the popular demand, one may conclude that she sometimes poetized herself with tongue in cheek.

When *Fashion* was completed, sometime in February, 1845, Epes Sargent took it to Simpson, the manager of the Park Theatre. Sargent's recommendation carried weight since he was not only a playwright whose works had been produced by Simpson, but also an important figure in the New York press, on whose good will the theatre greatly depended. But there were other reasons why Simpson at once gave serious attention to Lily's play. He was well aware that Mrs. Mowatt's name had a distinct publicity value since her daring appearances at the Stuyvesant Institute and the Society Library in 1841-42. She had also some literary reputation by now. Although most of her writing had been pseudonymous, she was generally known, at least in New York, to be the author of the sprightly "Helen Berkley" sketches in *Godey's* and *Sargent's Magazine*. Finally, she was a woman of social position whose comments on New York's upper stratum might be revealing.

But it was the play itself that won Simpson. When his stage manager, Barry, had also read it and was enthusiastic, Simpson felt he had a sure thing. He made up his mind to do it at once and to spare no effort to ensure its success. The play would have the finest cast available, and it would be mounted lavishly.

When *Fashion* was officially accepted, Lily was invited to call at the theatre and discuss the details of production with Mr. Barry. In those days the function of stage manager also included that of director, and Barry was responsible for getting the play on the stage. When the interview was over Lily was in "an agreeable state of bewilderment". She was so excited by the prospect of having a play produced in a real theatre that she scarcely took in all he had to tell her. The details he described, the professional jargon he used, were in large part meaningless; she could only beam and nod her head approvingly at everything he said.

Fashion was put into rehearsal at once and the opening set for March 26, a little over a week away. The day before the première Lily became so agitated at what might be happening to her brainchild that she determined to brave Mr. Barry and the actors and visit the theatre. "It is an author's privilege," she tells us firmly in the *Autobiography*, "to attend the rehearsals of his own production, his acknowledged seat being at the manager's table, upon the stage. He is also at liberty to make suggestions to the actors explanatory of his ideas."

Lily was not aware of her prerogatives as an author until after *Fashion* had opened. She was too shy and too overcome by the mysterious atmosphere of the darkened theatre to dare approach either Barry or the players. She watched the rehearsal from the dim recesses of a box, unseen by the people on the stage. This was her introduction to the working theatre in which before many months had passed she was to take her place as a regular member of the theatrical profession. But of this she had no inkling at the moment. She was aware simply that she had crossed the threshold of another world as remote from that of her everyday life as a dream.

The stage was lighted by a single branch of gas, shooting up to a height of several feet in the centre of the footlights. It sent forth a dim, blue, spectral light, that gave a phantom-like appearance to surrounding objects. On the right of the stage was the prompter's table—on the left, the manager's table. Beneath the

ghastly light sat a pale-faced prompter, with the manuscript of
Fashion in his hand. At his side stood the call-boy, a child of about
ten years of age. He held a long strip of paper, somewhat resem-
bling the tailor's bills of young spendthrifts, as they are represented on the stage. This was the "call" for the actors, and directed him which to summon from the greenroom.

How little the scene has changed in a hundred years. The
spectral gas-light has given way to a more prosaic, but equally
dismal electric work-light suspended from the flies. The arrangement of the tables is the same; only the titles and something of
the functions of the officiating personalities have changed. The
prompter as such has disappeared. The stage-manager holds the
"book" both at rehearsal and during performances, and he has
yielded his position as director to an individual who has no other
responsibility. It is the director now rather than the manager
who sits at the second table (when he does sit, which is rarely
and only from extreme exhaustion). As for the manager, he has
become the producer and he usually remains out of sight, sunk
in depression in a back-row seat. But these are details; essentially
the production of a play follows the same pattern today as it did
a hundred years ago.

The rehearsal of Fashion had begun. It was singular to see these
kings and queens of the stage, whom I had been accustomed to
behold decked in gold-embroidered robes and jewelled crowns,
glittering in the full blaze of the footlights—now moving about
in this "visible darkness," some of the men in "shocking bad
hats," and the ladies in modern bonnets in place of tiaras or
wreathes of flowers, and mantles and warm cloaks instead of
peasant petticoats or brocade trains. I found it difficult to recognize the romantic heroes and injured heroines in whose sufferings
I had so often sympathized.

Lily was seeing the other side of the dramatic illusion now,
and she was astonished to find it somewhat prosaic and not a
little tawdry. Had she not had a practical interest in these pre-
liminaries her fastidious nature might have been revolted, and
she would have slipped out of the dark musty atmosphere of the
old theatre never to return. Yet she was held by the fact that a

creation of her own was being brought to life in this strange world of half-light and hollow voices, and she watched with fascination as the miracle took place.

> . . . I soon discovered that a rehearsal is a very serious affair. There was no laughing, except now and then at the situations of the play—at which, by the by, I was particularly flattered—no talking, except in reference to the business of the scene, and now and then the remark from some critical malcontent, which was never intended for the author's ears . . . .

Although this was the day before the opening of the play, the actors were still reading their parts from rolled-up scripts which they carried in their hands. This gave Lily a slight feeling of panic. If they must read the parts now, how could they possibly have them memorized by tomorrow night! But the actors seemed quite unconcerned. They treated the matter with routine casualness, though they were very business-like in following Mr. Barry's directions. They executed each movement with the precision of long custom. Indeed all stage movements at the time were highly stylized. First entrances of characters were nearly always made on the diagonal, from upstage right or left to center (if one were a principal), or straight on from the wings, if one merely had a minor part, that of a messenger or domestic. An actor almost never let a "line carry him"—i.e. move while speaking. Long speeches were usually delivered from upstage center, if they involved matters which other characters on the stage were supposed to hear. If they contained information designed only for the ear of the audience, they were spoken directly down at the footlights.

While one actor spoke, particularly a leading character, all the others remained frozen in their positions, like automata waiting for a switch to be pulled. At the end of the speech, as the action of the play required, there would be a general shifting so as to bring the actors into new alignments. The whole effect was that of a formal dance in which each step is measured, with the figures forming and dissolving according to a set pattern. To one accustomed to the easy flow of movement in a

modern play this old technique seems stiff and crude. Yet in a
finished production (and there were occasionally such productions, though the theatre generally was a rather slap-dash
affair), this formalized movement had an abstract quality which
was very charming in itself, and largely offset the sometimes
ridiculous pomposity of the play's dialogue.

As she watched the rehearsal Lily was deeply troubled, for
she realized that *Fashion* did not lend itself to this traditional
style of acting. It was a modern play dealing with contemporary
society in present-day situations. In the dialogue she had tried
to capture the rhythm of everyday conversation; and this was
remote from the rhetorical prose or heavily accented metre of
blank verse to which the actors were accustomed. There were
plenty of "set speeches" it is true, especially in the part of Adam
Trueman. But the play was not studded with "points", those
moments in the action when an actor could draw the whole attention of the audience to himself and win a round of applause.
And so, she observed, there was a good deal of jockeying among
the principals for positions which would enable them to extract
the maximum effect from the few brief moments permitting
"solo" performances. This was a matter of deadly seriousness
and created so much tension that before the rehearsal was over,
Lily began to fancy she "had made a mistake and written a
tragedy."

When at last she stumbled over chairs and benches to the
door, she had the impression that it was indeed all a dream—
bordering on nightmare. Certainly it was a very "sober dream,
and while it lasted I received a lesson upon the vanity of human
wishes. Of the probable success of the play I could not form the
faintest idea."

CHAPTER TEN

"A Sensation Unexampled

in Theatricals"

Most of the New York papers noted the approaching premiere of *Fashion* with comments. Not all of these were calculated to raise the morale of the playwright. On March 15, *The Spirit of the Times* made the following observation under "Green Room Intelligence":

> A Native Comedy, by a Mrs. Mowatt is rumored to be in rehearsal at the Park. We have little confidence in female dramatic production of the present time, but we wish the lady a happy debut although it may be in five long acts.

The Albion, a week later, was more encouraging. The critic of that paper had read the play in manuscript and was of the opinion that *Fashion* would "satisfactorily solve the query, 'Are there materials in American society for constructing a successful comedy?—and is there a writer capable of adapting these materials?'"

The writer of the foregoing was a person of consequence in the New York literary and dramatic world. He was John William Stanhope Hows, an Englishman of background and attain-

133

ments who had emigrated to America some years before. He was passionately devoted to the theatre and was considered an authority on the art of acting. In addition to his position on *The Albion*, he held the post of professor of elocution at Columbia College. It may be recalled that he had written Lily a congratulatory note after her first reading in New York. This seems to have led to a personal acquaintanceship, which accounts for the fact that Lily had submitted the manuscript of *Fashion* for his opinion.

This was not an uncommon practice at the time. A dramatic critic was expected to do more than sit passively through the first performance of a play and pass judgment on the *fait accompli*. If he knew his business and was really dedicated to the theatre, he had a responsibility toward budding authors in helping them shape their work for production. Copies of *Fashion* were shown to at least three other critics, the most important being the editor of *The Broadway Journal*. He apparently was not solicited for his opinion but wrote Mrs. Mowatt for permission to see the manuscript. We do not have his letter, but Lily's reply is treasured in the archives of the Boston Public Library.

Thursday Evening

Edgar A. Poe, Esqr.

I regret that I have not a more legible manuscript of the Comedy to submit to your perusal—or even one containing all the corrections made at the suggestion of critical advisers. The only fair copy is in the hands of the managers, and that I could not procure.

Your criticisms will be prized—I am sorry that they could not have been made before preparations for the performance of the Comedy had progressed so far.

Will you have the goodness to return the manuscript at your earliest convenience, addressed James Mowatt, care Messrs. [?] Judd & Taylor, no. 2 Astor House?

Respectfully Yrs Ec

[Anna Cora Mowatt]

4th Avenue—5 doors above Twentieth street

Perhaps it was unfortunate that Poe's suggestions could not have been received in time to be incorporated in *Fashion* before the play opened. There is evidence that he did offer constructive comments and that these were utilized in preparing the printed edition of the play. But of this we have no precise knowledge. Neither the original manuscript nor any autograph copies of *Fashion* have come to light.

The day of the opening found Lily in a state of understandable agitation. This was shared by the actors. The presentation of a new play was a rare occurrence in New York; both the public and the theatre managers preferred to put their money on products of proven appeal. So for the players the hours before curtain time were filled with unusual tension. All would be playing new parts, and not a single "point" was certain.

Fortunately the cast selected by Simpson was highly experienced. The part of Mrs. Tiffany was played by Mrs. Barry, wife of the stage-manager. She was one of the most versatile "old women" (as this line of acting was technically designated) of the time. Her range was very wide. She could play Mrs. Malaprop or the Queen in Hamlet with equal facility—though not, we trust, with the same effect.

Another old favorite with New York audiences was Mrs. Knight, who was assigned the part of Prudence, Mrs. Tiffany's spinster sister. Her performance, according to Lily—and the critics—was "irresistibly comic". The part of Adam Trueman was performed by William Chippendale, who was certainly one of the finest "old men" on the stage. He was to become a fast friend of the Mowatts, and his path later crossed that of Lily many times.

Twinkle, the poet, was performed by T. De Walden. This gentleman later won some fame as a playwright. He was also an effective comedian, though he does not seem to have made the most of the role of soulful suitor for Seraphina's hand. Zeke, the colored flunkey, was done by George Skerrett, another comic actor with a devoted following in New York. The pampered Seraphina was played by Miss Kate Horn, a clever and graceful actress. Gertrude, the nominal heroine, was so conventional and uninspired a part that Lily herself always hated to play it. But

Miss Clara Ellis made a great deal of little and was so enchanting that, according to one wistful recollection of the opening, "everybody forgot she was nearly six feet tall."

Count Jolimaître was performed by Mr. W. H. Crisp, a light comedian and romantic leading man who had lately come from Ireland. He had a charming stage personality, but no two critics could agree on his real ability. He played not only the important part of the pretended Count in Lily's play, but an equally important rôle in her later career on the stage.

The other parts were taken by actors of established merit. It was indeed an admirable cast, perhaps the best that had been assembled for a single production on the New York stage in many years. Lily paid generous tribute to its contribution to *Fashion's* success. When the curtain fell on the opening night and "an unequivocally brilliant success had been achieved, I was forced to admit that my laurels were not of my own earning." Stage history does not record many comments like this from successful authors. But Lily was deeply sincere. She had no sense of the fundamental merits of *Fashion*, no inkling of its historic importance. She only knew that she had not been attempting to create a work of literature. In her own words, "Fashion is, strictly, an 'acting play', and placed in the hands of an accomplished company, the characters were re-created."

The première of *Fashion* was a significant occasion in more ways than one. The play itself was the first attempt to view American society critically and to picture American life with some degree of naturalism. Earlier attempts at social satire, such as Royall Tyler's *The Contrast* and William Dunlap's *The Father* fell short of the mark mainly because at the time they were written American society had few fixed characteristics. But they were also less skillful efforts than Anna Cora Mowatt's play.

There was still another reason why the opening of *Fashion* was a landmark in the history of the American theatre. The Park Theatre on the night of March 26, 1845, was filled for the first time with an audience composed almost exclusively of people of education and taste. Of course there had always been some ardent theatre-goers in New York and in other cities too who sought intellectual and esthetic satisfaction in the drama. But they were in a distinct minority. The pit of the theatre was patronized exclusively by men—clerks, apprentices, commercial travellers, and almost always a good many rowdies. The upper galleries were patronized by shop-girls and their swains, or families with children bent on a holiday. The third tier boxes by long tradition were given over to street-walkers for purposes of assignation. Only in the second tier and stage boxes might one find women of good repute and social position; generally speaking, the theatre was not regarded as a suitable resort for ladies.

All this was changed at the opening of *Fashion*. The theatre belonged to John Jacob Astor (Simpson was merely the lessee) and the stage boxes were occupied by the Astor family and their friends. The parterre circle was taken over exclusively by what Nathaniel P. Willis called the "crème de la crème de société". The roster included such names as Schermerhorn, Bleecker, Stuyvesant, Mott, Duyckinck, Westervelt, Rutgers, Dominick, Lorillard, Janeway, Van Zandt and a dozen others, names which in some cases now exist only on street markers and public buildings in New York. The political world was there too: Mayor Harper, the Mowatts' neighbor; Recorder Tallmadge; the distinguished judges Betts and Dent. And still another element had seized the occasion to turn out *en masse*. The *Tribune* in its report of the event noted the presence not only of the "élite" but of the "literati" also—thereby drawing a nice distinction which we of a later day cannot help pondering.

The pit, as one witness recalled, "unprecedentedly . . . had been surrendered to the fair sex." Here, seated with the ladies, were such notables as General James Watson Webb, James Gordon Bennett, Mordecai M. Noah, Parke Godwin, Edgar Allan Poe, Nathaniel Willis, Park Benjamin and William T. Porter. These were the mightiest of all, for they were the gentlemen of the press, and on their judgment would hang the fate of the play.

The second tier had been made fashionable also for this evening by the simple expedient of raising the prices, and the third tier had been barred to its regular patrons. In place of the be-feathered and be-rouged ladies of the street, the section was filled with stock-brokers and collegians, young men from Columbia and even as far away as the college at New Haven. The name of Mrs. Mowatt and her fame as a remarkable personality had already penetrated into curious corners.

Lily did not witness the performance from the front. She stood all evening in the wings. She wanted to be close to the center of operations in case anything went wrong, though how she expected to assist in such an event was not at all clear to her.

The performance began with a prologue in verse, a device archaic enough by now to be quaintly appealing. This was written especially for the play by Epes Sargent and was properly credited to him on the program.

When the house lights were lowered and the footlights turned on, Mr. Crisp was seen to walk out upon the apron of the stage, reading a newspaper. He was not for the moment Count Jolimaître, but a sophisticated New Yorker in search of an evening's entertainment. He was scanning the theatre announcements:

> "Fashion, a Comedy"—*I'll go: but stay—*
> *Now I read farther, 'tis a native play!*
> *Bah! Homemade calicoes are well enough,*
> *But homemade dramas* must *be stupid stuff.*

(This referred, of course, to the well-known prejudice against all forms of native art. It was a particularly strong prejudice with drama critics, and this remark was for their particular attention.)

> *Had it the* London *stamp, 'twould do—but then,*
> *"For plays we lack the manners and the men!"*
> *Thus speaks one critic. Hear another's creed:—*
> *"Fashion!" What's here?* (Reads closely) *"It never can succeed!*
> *What! From a woman's pen? It takes a man*
> *To write a comedy—no woman can."*
>
> *But, sir! but, gentlemen!—you, sir, who think*
> *No comedy can flow from native ink,—*
> *Are we such perfect monsters, or such dull,*
> *That Wit no traits for ridicule can cull?*

Have we no follies here to be redressed?
No vices gibbeted? No crimes confessed?
"But then a female hand can't lay the lash on!"
How know you that, sir, when the theme is FASHION?"

There was more in this vein as well as instructive remarks on the nature and function of the drama—"a daguerreotype of life and man". The prologue ended with these lines:

> *Grant that some wit may grow on native soil,*
> *And Art's fair fabric rise from woman's toil,*
> *While we exhibit but to reprehend*
> *The social vices, 'tis for you to mend!*

Mr. Crisp bowed gracefully and disappeared between the folds of the curtain. In the audience Parke Godwin was heard to remark to a neighbor: "Now let's see if society here tonight will be magnanimous enough to applaudingly see and hear itself satirized." By the end of the first act Godwin, as well as other friends who had been uneasy about the reception of Mrs. Mowatt's play, were set at rest. The applause was loud and long. It was perfectly clear that society was going to be magnanimous no matter how closely the shafts hit home. As a matter of fact people were so thoroughly entertained by the play that many only realized later that they had spent the evening laughing at themselves.

One observer noted that "different parts of the play evoked different reactions from the various sections of the audience. Mayor Harper, the Recorder [Tallmadge] and James W. Gerard [a witty lawyer and keen drama enthusiast] vigorously applauded the sarcastic repartee of the farmer, Adam Trueman, and the Yankee spinster, Prudence, when she attacked 'fashion,' while social leaders reacted rather coolly to the hits which so often struck home. Society belles were delighted at the depiction of the false count and intriguing maid, characters which they recognized as part of their world." There is no information on the reactions of the collegians and stock-brokers, but these must have derived satisfaction from the performance of the lissome Miss Ellis, who managed to give plausibility to the role of the virtuous Gertrude without wholly obscuring her own personal charms. Zeke, Millinette and Snobson supplied plenty of comedy broad enough for everyone's taste.

Only for one person was the evening something less than an unmixed delight. To Lily standing in the wings the noisy approval of the audience was scarcely perceptible. She was conscious only of what was happening on the stage. More than once her hand went to her throat in anguish as she heard the familiar lines of her own text giving way to improvisations or being mixed up in such a way that even she could not make head or tail of the meaning. Once Skerrett casually interpolated lines from *Grandfather Whitehead* (a familiar comedy of the period) into his part of Zeke; and once she thought she heard Snobson, the comic villain, embellishing his rôle with what sounded like echoes of *Richard III*—but of this she could not be certain.

What she did realize was that the actors, regardless of their somewhat spotty mastery of the text (which, after all, they had only rehearsed for a week) had thoroughly entered into the spirit of the play. They sailed blithely along, each one squeezing his part for all it was worth. If memory occasionally failed as to a line or phrase, or even a whole speech, they nimbly substituted others, of which their heads were full. To Lily this was little short of marvelous, and her anxiety at what might be happening to *Fashion* was largely offset by her admiration of the players' ability to keep the play going at a lively pace and to extract the full effect from every situation.

Most wonderful of all to her, as she listened, was the way in which the characters came to life. It was an extraordinary experience to see and hear living embodiments of what but a short time before had been merely faint stirrings of ideas in her head. For the audience, too, it was quite evident that Mrs. Tiffany, and Trueman, and Count Jolimaître were real people. Through a hole in the flat behind which she stood, Anna Cora could see the pale lines of faces in the darkened auditorium, bent forward in complete absorption with what was happening on the stage. She caught too the sound of laughter, increasing in volume as the play progressed, and the ripples of applause at the conclusion of some particularly amusing scene.

Yet she could scarcely grasp what it all meant. The whole experience had been like a dream of which she was only an observer. She did not even understand the full significance of the ovation at the final curtain. She heard the sound of shouting and clapping, as the actors took their calls, but she had no idea of the meaning of the final wave of applause. When Simpson, red and panting with delight, appeared and tried to lead her on to the stage she gave a cry of horror and ran for the door. It was impossible to explain that the audience was calling for the author. After the curtain had risen, she had felt that the play had passed completely out of her hands, and that she had no part in it after that.

Minutes later the stage was inundated with her friends, but she was still too dazed to do more than smile weakly and extend a somewhat limp hand to her host of well-wishers. She was immensely relieved when James arrived to take her home. It was not until they had jounced along the pavement for some minutes while James commented on various aspects of the evening, that she became fully aware of what had happened.

Lily did not exaggerate when she later set down that the play was "an unequivocally brilliant success." The press reports, both in terms of space allotted and liberality of encomiums, exceeded anything heretofore offered New Yorkers by way of dramatic criticism.

J. W. S. Hows was of course elated to have his prophecy, made earlier in *The Albion*, fulfilled. "It is with no ordinary feelings of satisfaction," he wrote, "that we record the triumphant verdict of the public in favor of Mrs. Mowatt's comedy. . . . It has created a sensation unexampled in theatricals and has decidedly established the fact that the time has arrived when a strictly American drama can be called into existence. . . . Upon the whole, Mrs. Mowatt may lay claim to having produced the best American comedy in existence, and one that sufficiently indicates her capabilities to write one that shall rank among the first of the age."

The Express, somewhat more pontifical but in the same spirit of jubilation, regarded the première as a milestone in the development of American culture. "The production of a new play, written in our own city, by one of our own citizens, with our own society, hotels, houses, customs, virtues, vices, foibles and follies as the subject matter, is an event looked forward to as a thing resting somewhere on the outer verge of possibility, but far beyond the known limits of the probable. The presentation last night at the Park Theatre, of *Fashion* by Mrs. Mowatt, was a realization of the practicality of this hoped-for undertaking. . . ."

The majority of the reviews were along these lines. Through nearly all there runs a note of gratified patriotism, as though the appearance of *Fashion* were a complete vindication of America's claims to cultural self-sufficiency. It is certain that one of the effects of the play, consistently overlooked by historians of American literature, was to give American writers new confidence in themselves and to salve the wounds made by British critics like Sydney Smith. Indeed one has the impression in reading the reviews of *Fashion* that everybody felt a personal share in this triumph of the national genius. The least that can be said of *Fashion*, viewed in its historical setting, is that it gave a boost to the morale of American writers eager to explore the native scene and character, such as had not been provided by any single work which had appeared in the country up to this time. It is probably quite safe to say that no play ever written by an American is comparable to *Fashion* in the immediate sensation which it created or its long-range effects on the course of American drama. It was followed naturally by a host of imitations, the majority of which were insignificant. What the play demonstrated was that audiences were ready to fill a theatre night after night to witness native drama which was something more than a vehicle for the display of athletic prowess and lung power. With *Fashion* the drama as an *art* had its birth in America.

There were two or three dissenting voices. The critic of *The Spirit of the Times* could not easily back down from the position he had already taken in expressing his "little confidence in female dramatic productions." In the March 29 issue of his paper he insisted that *Fashion* was not really a comedy because "the language of comedy is not the ordinary slipshod conversational stringing together of words employed in everyday life. . . . Comic writing should be terse, epigrammatic. . . . The plot should comprise a narrative of real events intermixed with those of a decidedly artificial nature. . . ." There is some uncertainty as to what school of esthetics was represented by this gentleman. It is only clear that he objected to realism, and that the mere attempt to catch the tone of every-day life in a play was an offense against the high proprieties. (The author of the review may have been George Wilkes who was the owner of the paper. He held fixed views on a variety of subjects ranging from poetry to prizefighting. The latter found expression in *The National Police Gazette* which he co-founded. But let us not confuse the issue.)

A far more important critic must be noted in the small group of those who had not been swept completely off their feet by Mrs. Mowatt's play. Edgar Allan Poe's review in *The Broadway Journal* pointed out the parallels between *Fashion* and *The School for Scandal.* The latter "was comparatively good in its day, but it would be positively bad at the present day, and imitations of it are inadmissible at any day." Unlike the reviewer in *The Spirit of the Times*, Poe thought Mrs. Mowatt's play too conventional, "a well-arranged selection from the usual *routine* of stage characters, and stage manoeuvres," without "one particle of nature beyond greenroom nature, about it." He pointed out the palpable weakness of the dénouement which depended on long-winded explanations rather than action. A good deal of what was supposed to be comic (at which the audience presumably had laughed uproariously) Poe found distinctly un-funny. Perhaps he had the Twinkle episode in mind, for Poe was touchy on the subject of the public attitude towards poets. Yet despite this and some other objections, Poe was forced to conclude that "there is much merit in *Fashion,* and in many respects (and those of a *telling* character) it is superior to any American play."

This report appeared on the day following the opening. In the next week's issue of *The Broadway Journal*, he published an article-length criticism entitled PROSPECTS OF THE DRAMA—MRS. MOWATT'S COMEDY. This began: "So deeply have we felt interested in the question of *Fashion's* success or failure that we have been to see it every night since its first production; making careful note of its merits and defects as they were more and more distinctly developed in the gradually perfected representation of the play." This sounds like the preliminary to a complete reversal of position. Yet Poe was not one to abandon easily his original views on any subject, particularly if he had stated them publicly. Despite his close study of the play in a more finished state of production (by the end of the week the actors had apparently learned their lines, and forty minutes had been lopped from the running time) his opinion was essentially unchanged. But—

> In one respect, perhaps, we have done Mrs. Mowatt unintentional injustice. We are not quite sure, upon reflection, that her entire thesis is not an original one. We can call to mind no drama, just now, in which the design can be properly stated as the satirizing of fashion *as* fashion.

Having made this remarkable recantation (which must surely be unique in the history of dramatic criticism) Poe promptly hedged by saying that in actual presentation the aim of the satire was lost. The characters were still conventional stage types. Had Mrs. Mowatt depended on her own understanding of human nature, he intimated, they would have been worthier instruments for the development of the theme.

The significant matter for Poe, quite apart from the merits or defects of the play, was the reception which it had received. This was indeed a subject for rejoicing, since it provided the "clearest indication of a revival of the American drama—that is to say, of an earnest disposition to see it revived." The review ended with a brief essay in Poe's usual clear sharp style, on what the drama could and should be. He challenged American playwrights to abandon their sickly imitations of the Elizabethans and let the spirit of the age speak out—the inference being that Mrs. Mowatt had shown the way.

Poe's two reviews of *Fashion* combined represent the most mature and genuinely perceptive dramatic criticism which had appeared in the United States up to this time. Despite the ambiguity of his views on *Fashion* in particular (which reveals rather an ambiguity in Poe's views of himself) his remarks are those of a man who had pondered the subject and was determined to treat it seriously. One or two of the ideas expressed in the second review belong among the great dicta of criticism: ". . . . A complex art can never be great in its primitive stages," and "only pedants admire simplicity for simplicity's sake" are as valid today as in Poe's time—and probably more applicable to art in general.

If Poe went to see *Fashion* for eight consecutive performances he must have found real significance in the play. Despite the simplicity of its plot Mrs. Mowatt's work was full of suggested complexities. There was more than just an evening's fun in the picture drawn by Mrs. Mowatt of the idle rich in a country where only a generation before no one had been idle and few had been very rich.

Poe did not elaborate these deeper meanings of the play. He did not wish to give Mrs. Mowatt more credit than was her due, or than was good for her. He did not know her personally, but he had observed her from afar. His intuition told him that she was of a different breed from the other "literary ladies" of New York, including those with whom he was emotionally involved. Given a chance she might accomplish something of real importance. He had observed that the flower of feminine genius was apt to fade under excessive praise. It is evident from the tone of deliberate restraint in his reviews of *Fashion* that he hoped Anna Cora Mowatt would keep her head.

Had he really known her, Poe would not have worried. No one had a better perspective on her accomplishment than Lily. She was flattered by Poe's attention, but she thought him unduly severe. She apparently did not perceive that he had paid her a great tribute by using *Fashion* as a springboard for a philosophical discussion of the drama. She was piqued that anyone might suppose she had intended *Fashion* to be a work of art; she had only wanted to write a play that could be acted. (She apparently did not realize that this was the first and final test of any play's merit—work of art or otherwise). She was a little annoyed about the comparison Poe had drawn between *Fashion* and *The School for Scandal*. Poe had said her play resembled Sheridan's in the same degree that the shell of a locust resembles the living locust. "If his severity were but *justice*, it must be that the spirits of the performers infused themselves into the empty shell, and produced a very effective counterfeit of *life*."

This was apparently the way the public thought about it. Within an hour after the box-office had opened on the next day, the Park was sold out for the evening. The same thing happened the next day, and the next. By the end of the week Simpson, who for years had not known whether he could pay the next month's rent, was planning a trip to Europe.

NIBLO'S THEATRE, NEW YORK, INTERIOR VIEW FROM BALLOU'S PICTORIAL
FEB. 24, 1855

Courtesy, The J. Clarence Davies Collection, Museum of the City of New York

CHAPTER ELEVEN

A New Star in Old Drury

Fashion ran for twenty nights, an unusually long engagement for the times—an unprecedented one for a new play. It would have lasted even longer had the Park not been contracted for a starring appearance of the young English tragedian James R. Anderson. He had done a turn in New York the previous fall and seemed likely to develop a following. But this was a mere hope. We can imagine poor Simpson's anguish at being forced to give up a sure thing like *Fashion* which was filling the theatre night after night with cash customers, for a tragedian of doubtful drawing power.

Meanwhile news of the hit had travelled. A few days after the New York opening an offer came from E. W. Marshall, manager of the Walnut Street Theatre in Philadelphia, for an immediate production of *Fashion* in the City of Brotherly Love. James drew up an agreement which was satisfactory to all parties and the play was put into rehearsal before the end of the New York run.

From now on, James's legal training was devoted almost ex-

clusively to his wife's affairs, and it speaks well for his astute-
ness that not one of his contracts was ever called into question.
We do not know the details of the agreements with either Simpson or Marshall, but they were probably similar to a proposal
made at this time by James to Smith and Ludlow, the impresarios
of the Southwest. In a letter of April 7, 1845 (while the play
was still running at the Park), James offered these gentlemen
the following terms: for the author, "15% of the gross receipts
of the house on each of the first 3 nights of performance and
10% on each night the play is performed afterwards, the theatre to have the privilege of announcing the third night as being
for the author's benefit. . . ."

The benefit, a charming institution which has now passed
from the theatrical picture, was often a source of great profit
to the individual actor or playwright. Like all customs in which
money is involved, it eventually was much abused. But in Anna
Cora's time it was still a device whereby audiences could show
their devotion to a popular player or writer. At the benefit performance all profits were turned over to the beneficiary. If the
latter's following was large the reward would be proportionate.
But if the house was poor the beneficiary might be out of pocket,
since on this occasion he was responsible for the running-expenses
of the theatre. In proposing to Smith and Ludlow an option of
announcing a benefit for Lily, James was guaranteeing the managers that should the play not draw, they would at least be sure
of no loss on the third night. If the play made money they
would have a healthy profit, since Lily still would take only the
stipulated 15%. James knew that the tastes of audiences in the
Southwest differed from those of Easterners, and that a play
based on New York life might not appeal in Louisiana. But he
was willing to take a chance.

He took no chance in Philadelphia. Philadelphia society was
as eager to see itself on the stage as New Yorkers had been.
Marshall gave the play an excellent production with new settings and a first-rate cast. Among the players was Miss Susan
Cushman, younger sister of the celebrated Charlotte. She performed the part of Seraphina.

The play was again a hit. Although Philadelphia papers at this period paid scant attention to the drama, which they regarded as a minor art, *Fashion* made them sit up and take notice. *The Inquirer* only got around to reporting the play on April 30 (it had opened on April 14), but it had this to say:

Mrs. Mowatt has achieved a triumph in its [*Fashion's*] production and has boldly ventured into an untrodden path of American literature. The success of a comedy purely local was problematical until Fashion was written. We now have evidence that in this department of literature, the talent of our country, if properly fostered, will take rank with that of Europe, as it has already competed successfully in every other walk. [Hail Columbia!] Mrs. Mowatt is still in our city and will be present at the Walnut St. Theatre this evening.

This item appeared the day after Lily's benefit which she and James had come to Philadelphia to attend. The note that she would visit the theatre for a second time, was to give those who had missed the ovation on the benefit night an opportunity still to see the famous lady.

The Mowatts spent three days in Philadelphia as guests of the theatre management, which lavished attention upon them. They were entertained as Lily fondly recalled "at one of the first hotels, in the most courteous manner. Our suite of apartments were the best that could be procured—our table was sumptuously provided, and a carriage stood always at the door at our disposal."

On the benefit night the Mowatts had found in their box special programs of white satin, printed in gold. They were accompanied to the play by Mr. and Mrs. George Mason, to whom they had been introduced by Marshall. This couple had a somewhat special history. Mason, scion of an old and wealthy New York family, had married an actress, the beautiful Emma Wheatley. As a result of this alliance young Mason had been cut off by his father, who had subsequently died. Mason was now in litigation with the heirs of his father's estate. Emma, who had energy and talent to match her good looks, had returned to the stage in order to keep the pot boiling and pay the lawyers' fees. She was well rewarded in the end when her husband came into a handsome slice of the family fortune. She spent her latter years looking comfortably down her lovely nose at most of the people who had tried to snub her earlier. At the moment she was still a glamorous stage figure. Her brother William Wheatley, also a fine actor, was performing the role of Count Jolimaître in the Philadelphia production of *Fashion*.

At the final curtain there were loud cries for the author. Anna Cora was greatly taken aback. She had no idea what she was supposed to do. When she saw all heads turned toward her box, which was in the center of the first tier, her impulse was to flee. James and Mr. Mason urged her to rise and curtsey, but Anna Cora could not move. The crowd grew noisier with the delay. Finally Anna Cora clutched Mrs. Mason by the arm and said that she would stand if the latter would accompany her. So the two ladies, amidst great acclaim, rose to their feet and curtsied deeply.

After the performance Anna Cora graciously thanked the cast for their contribution to the play's success. The following day she sent to each of the ladies in the company a little gold pencil in token of her gratitude. She had presented similar gifts to the ladies of the New York cast of *Fashion*. Doubtless in both cases this charming gesture was greatly appreciated, and if some wearable trinket might have seemed more appropriate, one must remember that Anna Cora had a practical turn of mind. After all, she had written *Fashion* with a pencil.

For a week after their return to New York the Mowatts moved in a state of high exhilaration. Anna Cora was a genuine celebrity now, and when her name was mentioned in the drawing-rooms of Upper Ten-dom, it was in a tone of healthy respect. Royalties were pouring in from the two productions of the play, and it seemed as if life were at last to hit an even keel. But Anna Cora had no intention of resting on her laurels. For some months past she had steadily gained strength, and the excitement of having a hit on her hands brought a surge of energy and a sense of well-being such as she had not experienced since girlhood. She immediately began to think about another play. Both she and James were sure that it would be nothing at all to turn out hits regularly. After all *Fashion* had come so easily!

Neither seemed aware that the play though written quickly had
been the result of long reflection, and represented the cream
skimmed from a lifetime experience of society.

James's optimism is reflected in the letter already mentioned
to Smith and Ludlow:

> . . . Of one thing you may be certain, that should Mrs. Mowatt
> or any other writer produce two such comedies a year it will ef-
> fectually put a stop to foreign stars taking all the profits which
> are made by our theatre, and leaving the theatres almost in a
> state of bankruptcy. . . .

One may not quite follow James's reasoning here, since he
merely proposes to re-channel the profits for plays from the
pockets of foreign stars (who frequently had monopolies on
the plays they produced) into those of native playwrights and
not necessarily into those of the theatre managers. But who
could be expected to reason in such a glow of confidence?

The glow had scarcely reached full brightness when catas-
trophe again descended upon the Mowatts. The publishing business which James had established failed. Neither of Lily's major
contributions (the biographies of Goethe and Madame D'Arblay)
had sold well, and in the general excitement over *Fashion* James
had been too distracted to give his full attention to the enterprise.
The subsidiary undertaking, *Sargent's Magazine*, had already
quietly ended its career—unable to stand the competition of the
better-established literary journals. For the second time in less
than five years James was bankrupt.

Overnight the royalties from *Fashion* disappeared to satisfy
the creditors of Mowatt and Company. Once more Lily had to
find some way to make money quickly, for she had not only
herself and James to think about. There were also the three little
Greys to be regularly fed.

Frantically she tried to get on with the new play, the hit
which would follow *Fashion* and which Simpson had already
agreed to take sight unseen. But for some unaccountable reason
the new play refused to be written. The more agitated Lily became with the increase of pressures, the more her imagination

balked. Hour after hour she sat with pencil in hand and a pile of paper before her. Try as she would, she could not get beyond a first sketchy scene.

Yet something must be done; and after all she was in a more favorable position to earn a livelihood than at the time of the first débâcle when they had had to leave Melrose. She had experience behind her, and something of a name both as a dramatic reader and as a writer. Briefly she contemplated a return to the platform, but the notion was soon discarded. Although her health was better now than it had been for years she shied at the strain and fatigue which reading involved. As for writing, she was at this moment in a vacuum so far as her imagination was concerned—and this might be prolonged indefinitely.

Inevitably the idea of the stage was suggested. Whether it developed spontaneously within Lily herself or came from the outside, we do not know. It is highly probable that ever since she had witnessed the rehearsal of *Fashion* at the Park, she had subconsciously pictured herself performing the parts which the actors were re-creating (not always according to the author's intention). In observing fine players like Chippendale and Mrs. Knight, she must have perceived that the basic equipment of a real stage artist consisted of imagination and the physical capacity to project conceptions across the footlights. She was confident of her own interpretive powers, even though the more purely creative faculty was proving balky at the moment. As for her physique, though slight, even fragile, it had already proved remarkably effective before large assemblages of people. There was the additional advantage of being beautiful. In the long run this was of secondary importance even for an actress, as Charlotte Cushman had demonstrated but it could assist one's progress at the outset.

The longer she reflected the more certain she became that she could make a career for herself as an actress. She may have expressed this conviction openly. She had certainly discussed the question, at least on a theoretical basis, many times with James and Epes Sargent. There is no doubt of Sargent's views. In a notice of one of her readings he had written in *The New World*, January 22, 1842:

We believe that she would be eminently successful on the stage. There never was a period when a lady of extraordinary talent, like herself, could so rapidly acquire fame and fortune in a profession distinguished by a Siddons, a Stephens, and an O'Neill.

This notice had appeared early in their acquaintanceship. Sargent was now a very close friend of the couple. His feeling for Anna Cora was deeper than admiration for her gifts. But of these he had the highest opinion, and as he was now consulted on all professional matters, he must have urged her on the course she was contemplating.

As for James, he seems from the beginning to have had none of the current prejudices against the stage. "Mr. Mowatt's appreciation of the drama was, I think, even greater than my own. His only fear was, that I had not physical strength to endure the excitement and fatigue of an arduous vocation." This was always, of course, the important consideration. But Lily had come to the conclusion already that acting would be less wearing than elocution. By arithmetical calculation (not without a touch of fantasy), she figured that it took twice as much strength and energy to give an evening of recitations as "to perform a light part in a five-act drama." By a "light part" she meant Beatrice or Rosalind as opposed to Lady Macbeth, her innocent assumption being that tragedy required more endurance than comedy. She was shortly to be disabused of this notion.

There remained the inevitable final point. What would Papa think of the idea? Anna Cora had now been supporting a family for several years by her own efforts, but she still made no decisive move without Samuel Ogden's consent. As usual she was afraid to approach him personally, and made James act as intermediary. She waited in the hallway while James interviewed Papa in his study. After what seemed an interminable time she could endure the suspense no longer and burst into the room. "My father spoke but two words as I silently put my arms about his neck. They were 'brave girl!'"

Whatever else life held for Samuel Ogden, there must have been satisfaction in being thus always deferred to by his favorite daughter, and in having her projects—which nearly always turned out successfully—hang upon his consent. He seems to have accepted it all pretty much as a matter of course.

Having made up her mind at last, Lily went ahead with the practical details of the venture. While she had been struggling with the idea of a new play, Mr. Crisp, leading man of the Park company, was a frequent caller in Fourth Avenue. Simpson, in agreeing to take the play before it was even written, had merely specified that the leading part be tailored to fit the talents of Mr. Crisp. Simpson had Crisp under a long-term contract and he was having trouble finding suitable roles for the romantic Irishman. So Crisp came frequently to discuss the part which Anna Cora hoped to write for him.

When Anna Cora in frustration had abandoned the play, Crisp was naturally disappointed. But when he learned of Mrs. Mowatt's desire to become an actress, he was prompt to seize on a new possibility. He expressed complete sympathy with her decision, and at once placed himself at her disposal for any points on which she might wish to be advised. In fact he had a practical suggestion to make at once. The question of a time and place for the début was all-important. June 6th would be the last night of the season at the Park. On this evening Crisp was scheduled to take his benefit. What more auspicious occasion could be found for Mrs. Mowatt's first appearance? Her first essay as an actress would be a fitting climax to a season which had witnessed her success as a playwright. And what could be more appropriate than that she should have her introduction to the public at the benefit of the actor who had played the role of Count Jolimaître in her own *Fashion*! (Indeed what more certain means could be found by Mr. Crisp, as yet without a real following in New York, to fill the house on the night of his profit-taking! But this happy thought was doubtless expressed by Mr. Crisp only to himself.)

At first Anna Cora recoiled at the suggestion. Her idea had been to seek an engagement in one of the distant towns—New Orleans or Saint Louis, perhaps—where she might gain experience with a stock company, and then come to New York. But Crisp, in a fine flow of Celtic reasoning, brushed this notion aside. Where but in New York before the discriminating and cultivated public of the metropolis, could she really gauge her powers? And what theatre but the venerable Park—"Old Drury" as it was fondly called—could give the seal of professionalism and distinction to her career at the very outset? Mr. Crisp's ways were winning, and in the end he prevailed.

Simpson, when informed of the plan, was delighted. He stood to lose nothing in any event, since Crisp was responsible for the expenses of the theatre on the night of his benefit. But Simpson might be the gainer in other ways. After the success of *Fashion,* Mrs. Mowatt now had a distinct publicity value. Her name on the bills would turn the public's attention once more to the Park, from which of late it had been wandering.

The question of training now arose. Despite her conviction that she could become an actress, Lily had no precise notion as to how to go about it. But here again Mr. Crisp was prompt with a suggestion. *He* would teach Mrs. Mowatt the routine of the theatre and coach her in the part in which she would make her début. There could be no doubt of Mr. Crisp's qualifications for the task. Though relatively young, he had played the whole range of romantic leads in the standard drama (so he informed the Mowatts). He had acted with such distinguished English stars as Miss Faucit and Miss Glyn. He had also had considerable experience as a stage-manager and director in the best provincial theatres of England and Scotland.

Crisp had no difficulty in bringing James and Lily to eager agreement in this proposal also. But he did not stop there. Before the début had even come off, he had signed a contract with Lily whereby he was to be her leading man for a year, sharing equally with her in the profits of all engagements.

For one thing we must give Mr. Crisp complete and unequivocal credit. He knew how to pick a winner.

Now came the delicate matter of selecting a play for the benefit. If she had been the usual novice, Anna Cora would have been content to start with a small part containing one or two effective scenes in which to display her ability. But Anna Cora was in a different situation. In deciding to go on the stage she had put all her eggs in one basket. Her own fate, and that of four other people, depended on the income she could produce.

As a bit player this would be negligible. Besides she was twenty-six years old. There was not time enough to start at the bottom. She had to take a short-cut. She must not only demonstrate at once that she could act; she must do so in the most decisive way. It was imperative that she make her first appearance in a part demanding both power and range—one associated in the public mind with an actress who had *already* arrived—in short, a stellar role.

Again Crisp was sympathetic—and useful. In the standard repertory no part was so ideally suited to Anna Cora's physique, personality, and the distinctive style she had developed in her readings as that of Pauline, the heroine of Bulwer's *Lady of Lyons*. The play itself was one of the most popular on the boards. It had been written in 1838 for Macready and Ellen Tree, and had since been acted by nearly every star in the English-speaking theatre. Like most plays of the period it was a jerry-built conglomeration of borrowings from Shakespeare and the other Elizabethans, with a dash of Byron to give it a modern flavor. It was mainly written in lumpy prose, interspersed with patches of sticky blank verse like the filling of a cake already made indigestible by everything in the pantry. But our great-grandfathers loved it.

The Lady of Lyons is set in France at the beginning of the Napoleonic era. It involves the love of a poor but upright peasant lad, Claude Melnotte, for the haughty daughter of a rich merchant. Pauline, the lady, is tricked into marrying Claude whose true identity she does not suspect. When she learns that he is not a prince, as she had been led to suppose, but only a gardener's son, there is indignation, humiliation—heartbreak. Claude, remorseful at having lent himself to the trick which enabled him to marry the lady of his heart (the trick had been thought up by a rejected suitor for the hand of Pauline), sends her back to her father with permission to get a divorce. Claude renounces everything and goes off to the wars. At home Pauline finds that her father is almost bankrupt, and that to save him she must marry a rich roué, one Damas. And so more heartbreak, but also opportunity for heroic self-sacrifice. The situation is saved by the arrival of Claude in the nick of time. After two years in the army he is now a colonel, and rich to boot. He bursts into the room just as the marriage contract between Pauline and Damas is about to be signed, and flinging a bag of gold louis down on the table before the ruined merchant cries: "I outbid yon sordid huckster for your priceless jewel!" Whereupon Pauline, who until this moment has been ignorant of the handsome officer's identity (so effective a disguise is a colonel's uniform), rushes into his arms. She has learned to love him *in absentia*. Damas, duped in the hour of his victory, stalks from the stage with "Curses on ye both!"

This was the fine flower of early nineteenth-century British drama. When we compare its dingy heroics with the fresh honesty and spontaneous realism of *Fashion* we are inclined to echo the patriotic sentiments of *The Philadelphia Inquirer* in proclaiming that the native drama was now able "to take rank with that of Europe"—at least!

It would never have occurred to Lily to compare her casual little effort with the masterpiece of the mighty Bulwer, though she certainly had no illusions about the intrinsic merits of *The Lady of Lyons*, as we shall see later. For the moment, all that mattered was that the play never failed to draw, and that the part of Pauline had become the show-piece of every leading young actress. As for Claude Melnotte, this was precisely the sort of romantic hero part in which Crisp fancied himself at his best. Given the time and the circumstances, *The Lady of Lyons* was on the whole a good choice.

The night of the début was less than three weeks away. Happily, Anna Cora had a phenomenal memory and in a matter of hours was letter-perfect in the part. Every afternoon Crisp came to the house and worked with her, going over every detail of every scene in which Pauline appeared. There was nothing he could teach her about reading. Since childhood she had shown an acute sense for word values, and her speech was full of variety and color. But Crisp drilled her in all the traditional stage devices for handling her voice in speaking dialogue, teaching her how to keep it level or raise it at the end of a line, and how to adjust the rhythm of a sentence so as to realize the full effect of the "points." These were the spots in the dialogue which long experience had shown would produce a definite effect on the audience: a sigh, a groan, a laugh. The "points" were as familiar to actors as the story itself—and for the actors sometimes even more important, as she had observed during the rehearsal of *Fashion*. Crisp also taught her all the movements required of Pauline. He showed her the time-honored ways of making entrances and exits, how to cross the stage, and the mechanics of handling properties.

Anna Cora listened to Mr. Crisp with great respect. These were the tricks of the trade, and her commonsense told her that craftsmanship was as important to acting as to any other art. She may have had her opinion of the play's tawdry emotionalism, but she kept this to herself. However, as she studied the part she realized that there were moments when the actress might, with intelligence and genuine feeling, rise above the strained artificiality of the language and characterization. She determined to make the most of these.

She threw herself into the work with an intensity and concentration that even those who knew her habits could only marvel at. In addition to learning the part she drilled herself in other ways. For four hours a day she exercised her voice in order to increase its volume, taking care not to roughen the timbre. For this her early singing instruction proved valuable. She also took fencing lessons to improve the co-ordination and flexibility of her body. She exercised vigorously with dumbbells to strengthen her delicate chest. Throughout the day, she trailed around the house in a voluminous train to acquire ease and grace in handling stage costumes. All this she did with that meticulous attention to detail and stern self-discipline which marked all her efforts.

It was not until the day before the performance that she went to the theatre to rehearse with the full company. This was through no choice of her own, but was simply a matter of circumstance. The company at the Park was thoroughly familiar with the play, having acted it many times either together or separately with other companies. They needed only a couple of rehearsals to refresh their memories for the lines and stage business. It would have been unprecedented to call extra rehearsals for the benefit of one person, even though she might be the leading lady. It would probably have been impossible to find time for such rehearsals, since the Park was a stock theatre, changing its bills nightly or at least two or three times a week. This meant that almost every day must be spent in rehearsing a different play, which would have to be ready for the next day or the day following.

When Anna Cora stood at last on the gloomy stage and saw peering from the shadows the faces of the other actors, touched by the pale glow of the gas-light, she felt the beginnings of the same paralyzing fear that had struck her years before in the empty Masonic Temple in Boston. Only this time it was worse. There had been two friendly faces to encourage her then. On the stage of the Park she was surrounded by expressions of antagonism or amused contempt, which even the shadows could not conceal. She knew what the actors must think of her. She was a newcomer presuming on sacred territory which they had won by long endurance and hard work. She could understand and sympathize with them. She was attempting to reach in one step the place which for most of them was as far away now as when they had first entered the theatre, the coveted position of star. They could not know how humble she felt and how frightened at her own hardihood. Even if they had known, she doubted that they would have taken more kindly to her—for she was still an intruder.

After a few brief words with Mr. Barry, she sat down quietly on a wooden stool in a corner by the wings. She saw the stage manager in whispered conversation with one of the actors. The latter presently retreated into the shadows. For a moment Barry riffled the pages of an open script that lay on the table before him. Anna Cora could feel the momentum of her heart increasing. Then Barry raised his head and cleared his throat. He gave a little nod and the prompter called: "Act one, scene one!"

Anna Cora saw a slight, middle-aged figure detach itself from the shadows and move toward the center of the stage. When she stepped into the circle of the work-light, Anna Cora saw that it was Mrs. Vernon, the veteran actress who had been assigned the role of Madame Deschapelles, Pauline's mother. She appeared in the very first scene and Pauline appeared with her.

Mrs. Vernon sat down at a bare deal table, then glanced at an empty chair on the other side of the stage. This was supposed to represent the sofa in the Deschapelles drawing-room on which Pauline must be languorously reclining when the curtain rose. Anna Cora wondered if her trembling legs would take her to it.

As she moved across the stage she could feel the white, shadow-bound faces in the wings following her. Yet somehow she managed to reach the chair.

Mr. Barry looked up from his table near the proscenium. "Madame Deschapelles and Pauline," he read from the script. Then in a tone of great dignity he said, "Commence, ladies, if you please."

Mrs. Vernon opened the scene. The dumpy middle-aged figure suddenly straightened. With an imperious gesture Mrs. Vernon became the haughty Madame Deschapelles giving an order to a servant: "Marion, put that rose a little more to the left."

Another actress stepped from the background and began making gestures as if arranging something in Anna Cora's hair. Mrs. Vernon continued her speech, tripping along with the ease of complete familiarity; she had played Madame Deschapelles a dozen times. In a moment Pauline's cue would come, but Anna Cora did not know whether she would be able to speak. Her eyes were fixed on Mrs. Vernon's face. As the veteran actress came to the end of her speech, to Pauline's cue, she gave Anna Cora a broad wink with her upstage eye, while the rest of her face remained fixed in the expression of the haughty *grande dame*. This was all Anna Cora needed. Suddenly her blood thawed, and she was amazed to hear her own voice speak up promptly when the cue came. With each succeeding moment after that she gained confidence. As the act progressed, with other actors making their entrances and exits, she felt herself moving more and more easily into the rhythm of the play. To her dying day she would never forget her gratitude to Mrs. Vernon for that encouraging wink.

Anna Cora played her second act scenes completely at ease, oblivious to everything except her part and the action taking place on the stage. Once or twice she caught murmurs from the wings, but these no longer disturbed her. Presently there were no sounds at all, except the voices on the stage.

In the third act, in the climactic scene where Pauline discovers that her prince is only a peasant and her future home a rude hovel, Anna Cora let herself go. When the scene was over she was startled by a burst of applause from the wings. She turned and saw that the actors were all huddled together clapping vigorously. Their eyes were all on her and they were smiling. Anna Cora felt a great wave of relief and gratitude pass through her. No applause of later triumph was ever to mean so much as the noisy approval of that handful of actors on the dark stage of the Park. It was her accolade.

There was another brief rehearsal on the morning of the début. The rest of the day Anna Cora passed quietly at home with her sisters who had come to be with her in the last hours before the great ordeal. There had been mixed feelings when the other girls heard of their beloved Lily's decision to go on the stage. They wanted to be loyal, and they understood Lily's motive in becoming an actress. But they had also heard the remarks that people were making; and they felt, if Lily did not, that she was making a dreadful sacrifice. People had finally forgiven her earlier exploit as an elocutionist. But the theatre was different. The girls feared that even Lily's oldest friends would not swallow that, and she would be an outcast forever.

Only Julia of the whole family accompanied her to the theatre. Samuel Ogden had said he would not go, since he felt that his presence might disturb her. (Only afterward did Lily discover that he had witnessed the performance from the dark corner of a side-box.) As Lily and James with Julia in the carriage drove to the Park, they made a detour so as to pass the Ogden house. In an upper-story window they saw the patriarch, surrounded by his remaining daughters. There was a great deal of solemn waving of handkerchiefs until the carriage was out of sight.

At the theatre Lily was ushered into the star's dressing-room. If she had had any previous notions of possible refinements in this apartment, she was promptly disillusioned. The room into which she was shown was scarcely more than a closet, dark and none too clean. There was a strip of faded threadbare carpet on the floor, and a rough wooden shelf ran along one wall to serve as a dressing-table. Propped up on this, beside a feeble gas jet, was a peeling mirror. A broken-down washstand and a couple of rickety chairs completed the appointments. In view of her health, Lily had to have a sofa on which to rest between acts. James sent a request to the management, but all that could be provided was a truncated article used as a stage property—thinly upholstered and without springs. Thus the star's dressing-room in America's most famous theatre in 1845.

James and Julia did not linger in the dressing-room with Lily. Julia's offer to help her sister dress had been gently declined, and Julia did not insist. It was understood that Lily wanted to be alone. So after tender embraces all around, with many repeated assurances that all would be well, James and Julia departed for the front of the house.

When the door closed behind them Lily took a deep breath and looked about her. There was little to indicate that this dingy little room was the ante-chamber to that "ideal" world which she was about to enter. Yet as she sniffed the musty air she felt a deep thrill of excitement. How many great ladies of the stage had hung their clothes upon those pegs above her head, had studied their faces in this same dim glass! Why, in this self-same room Fanny Kemble must have dressed for that never-to-be-forgotten performance of *The Hunchback* which Lily had braved the devil himself to see, on that far-off evening of her childhood!

But these awesome and romantic reflections did not hold Lily for long. She saw that the hands of her little travelling clock, which she had set up on the dressing-table, were moving towards seven. Frantically she snatched at the hooks of her street dress, and as she did so her lips began to move in Pauline's opening speech.

CHAPTER TWELVE

" . . . The Stuff of Which Great Actresses Are Made"

There had been too little time for Lily to master the details of such matters as make-up and costume. Customarily players supplied their own wardrobes, except for very special period productions. For these they might rely to some extent (in the matter of armor, or special headgear, or shoes, for instance) upon the costumer of the theatre. Women nearly always dressed themselves entirely—and pretty much as they pleased. Mrs. Vernon, the first of the Park company to make overtures of real friendliness to Lily, had been consulted as to suitable costumes for the part of Pauline. But Lily had relied mainly on her own good taste. She had spared neither effort nor money on the gowns for her début, and it gave her no small satisfaction to know that, whatever else happened, she would at least look her best.

Make-up presented a rather different problem. Crisp had given her a few pointers, and Mrs. Vernon had probably made suggestions as to procuring necessary supplies. But as she surveyed the strange array spread out on the rude dressing-table, she felt a little bewildered. There were so many refinements used by professionals, for which her amateur experiences had not prepared her.

Lily carefully checked each item to see that nothing was missing. There was a small pat of fresh butter, a box of fine rice powder, an envelope containing powdered Chinese vermilion, a steel knitting-needle, a candle, a packet of wax matches, half a dozen corks, and a rabbit's foot. No young surgeon with his first set of instruments could have felt greater pride than did Lily as she began to handle the equipment of her new profession.

She had removed her street gown and was swathed in a loose wrapper. She sat down at the dressing-table and turned up the gas flame to its full height. Then with a somewhat tentative finger she took a dab of butter and began to rub it over her face. Most actors were content with lard for a make-up base, because it was cheap. But ladies, anxious to run no risks with delicate skins, generally preferred butter.

When her face was well covered, she removed the excess butter with a towel which she had brought for the purpose. Then, proceeding very gingerly—for it was such poisonous-looking stuff—she took a little of the powdered vermilion (it had been boiled in milk the night before so as to make it more workable) and blended it into her cheeks, spreading it with great care upward and outward from the cheek-bone, as she had been instructed. When this was done she was amazed to note how her face, which had been so blank and spectre-like in the harsh flame of the gas, began to acquire a tone of warm naturalness. When she was satisfied that her color was right—after all Pauline was no ruddy-faced country girl—she took the candle and lighted it.

Now came the really delicate part of the operation. Over the candle flame Lily held the steel knitting-needle until it was covered with soot. With this she carefully lined her eyes just back of the lashes. It was almost like magic to see how they came to life, and how brilliantly they shone. The next step was to burn one of the corks until it was a rich dull black. With this she darkened her eyebrows. Then she took the rabbit's foot and dusted her face with a light layer of powder. When this was done the gleam of the butter had disappeared and the bright vermilion had softened to a rosy pink. As a last touch Lily mixed a little of the vermilion with another dab of butter. This she worked into a paste and applied to her lips.

The process had taken longer than she thought. The hands of the clock were almost at seven now. Hurriedly she slipped off the wrapper and began to put on the gown which she would wear in the first act. As she fastened the last hook a tap came at the door and a shrill voice piped: "Pauline, you are called."

Lily opened the door and saw the call-boy standing with his long strip of paper. She could not help feeling a little irritated at the interruption. She asked what he wanted.

"You, ma'am; you are called."

Lily stiffened slightly. The boy had addressed her as "Pauline," which she considered a singular piece of familiarity. She might have read the lad a short lesson in good manners (she had not yet learned that the theatre has its own manners), but time was pressing.

"Called for what?" she asked impatiently. It was unnerving to have these last-minute distractions.

"Why, for the stage, to be sure! That's *what*!"

"Oh!" she gasped. And that was all.

At this moment James appeared, and taking her by the hand led her toward the stage. As she walked into the set, she saw that Mrs. Vernon was already in her place at the table—not the plain deal table of the rehearsal but an elegant piece of real drawing-room furniture. And the sofa on which Lily took her place was also real. As she sat down, she was handed a large bouquet of magnificent paper roses—an important property for her opening scene.

James pressed her hand and murmured words of encouragement in her ear. Someone spread her scarf on the back of the sofa. Somebody else arranged the train at her feet. An unknown hand gathered a few stray curls into place.

Then came the order: "Clear the stage, ladies and gentlemen!"

Anna Cora felt her heart stop beating—or so she thought.

She began to choke, yet she managed to raise her hand and gasp, "Not yet—I cannot!"

Instantly the stage was thrown into pandemonium. Manager, actors, prompter, came rushing toward her. Some offered water; some, more invigorating stimulants. Ladies produced smelling-salts and scent bottles. Someone fanned her violently. There was fevered discussion as to whether she was swooning or hysterical.

In a moment her mind cleared. She was aware that she was making a ridiculous and humiliating exhibition of herself. She had earlier told Skerrett, the comedian of the company, that she was certain she would not have stage fright. Now when she saw the monkey-like face of the little actor peering down at her and heard him say, "Didn't I tell you so? Where's all the courage now?"—she burst out laughing.

"Are you getting better?" asked Barry anxiously. He was not certain but that the laughter was a symptom of some grave disorder.

Anna Cora straightened up on the sofa, then leaned back assuming the pose of careless ease called for in the script. She smiled at Barry. "Let the curtain rise!" The moment of panic had passed. As she saw the bright strip of light under the curtain slowly widen until the whole stage was thrown into dazzling radiance a feeling of complete security came over her. From the vast dim cavern on the other side of the footlights, she knew that hundreds of eyes were staring fixedly at her. But between her and them was a barrier of fierce bright flame. The footlights were a friendly protecting wall behind which the denizens of Lily's "ideal" world moved in their appointed ways without let or hindrance. To Lily it was as if she had come home at last.

Excitement in the auditorium had run as high as it had backstage during the last moments before the curtain went up. At the première of *Fashion* the audience had been unusual because of the number of people from literary and artistic circles as well as from the genteel world. Tonight the house was almost monopolized by the wealth and fashion of New York. Not a person in the audience failed to realize that he was about to witness an event unique in the annals of the city. Although opinion may have been divided as to why this was so, the sense of thrilled anticipation was no less keen for that reason.

There were few among the Dyotts and Astors, Ruggleses and Bleeckers and Livingstons, who did not view Anna Cora's decision to go on the stage as the abandonment of everything they held dear for their own womanhood. Position, security, protection from the rough contacts of the lower elements, the refined pursuits of a gentlewoman—all these were being left behind by Samuel Ogden's extraordinary daughter.

More than that, she was exposing herself to an atmosphere in which virtue could not last long unscathed. Of course ideas on this subject were changing somewhat. The ideals of conduct which had been general in the early days of the Republic were being weakened by the influx of wealth at the mid-century. Behavior was a good deal looser than it had been a generation before. Such things as drunkenness, gambling—an occasional murder, if suitably motivated—were more apt to be accepted in the natural way of things by this newer society. From time to time a discreet adultery, properly hedged by an atmosphere of romantic passion, offered a diversion from the routine of narrow domesticity. But persistent irregularities of conduct between the sexes were still frowned upon. The life of the theatre, to the minds of most of these people, was inseparable from such irregularities.

This notion had been fostered since Puritan days; and, though the theatre had always found some defenders among the highest of the land (Washington had been an ardent play-goer, and Franklin had believed the drama capable of a refining influence), the general attitude was one of deep mistrust. At the time of Anna Cora's début, there was a good deal of powerful opposition from press and pulpit. Horace Greeley regarded the theatre as a sink of the worst iniquities; and the voice of Henry Ward Beecher had been raised loud and long against its godlessness, though he was charmed to have one of his novels made into a play.

The view of the average middle-class citizen is summed up by a doctor from the western part of the state who visited the metropolis in the fifties and set down his impressions in a volume entitled *What I Saw in New York*. He apparently saw a good deal. The book is richly detailed with descriptions of the back alleys around the notorious Five Points, where grog-shops alternated with brothels. But at the theatre he stopped short:

> Of these places of amusement we have several in the city, but as to what has been seen *there*, the reader is probably as wise already as the writer, inasmuch as *he has never seen the inside of ONE*. He has, however, seen enough outside to satisfy him that he had better go down to his grave in his present ignorance, than to be enlightened by the performance within.

The author has his own ideas as to "what *might* go on within," but at this he draws the curtain.

The patrons of the Park on the night of June 6, 1845, can scarcely have felt so strongly, for society was increasingly finding the drama a welcome relief from the eternal round of whist and polka parties, heavy dinners and soporific lectures. But seeing a play from the front was a very different thing from taking part in a performance. The people of the theatre were beyond the pale socially; no one knew where actors came from or where they went. Their views of marriage and the more intimate relationships between men and women were understood to be casual in the extreme. Though Mrs. Mowatt's public conduct had offended the delicate sensibilities of a good many people, her private life was known to be irreproachable. In allying herself with the theatre she was running a risk which no lady—particularly one so delicate and so gently bred—could possibly hope to survive.

So it was in something of the spirit of a Roman holiday that the fashionable world, which was still the respectable world, foregathered this evening at the Park. They were about to witness the spectacle of one of their own kind throwing herself to the lions. Yet they could not forget that she was, after all, one of their own, and they were determined to give Anna Cora a rousing send-off to her martyrdom. In this spirit they had donned their diamonds and laces, their satin-faced frock-coats and white kid gloves, and packed the house.

There were a few at least of those present who had come out of curiosity to see whether Mrs. Mowatt could really act. There was no doubt that she had displayed great cleverness in everything else she had undertaken. She was certainly a remarkably fine-looking woman. . . . The motive behind this newest enterprise had to be considered, as well. It was known all over town that her husband for the second time had lost everything, and that his health was hopelessly impaired. There were also rumors that old Ogden was in trouble with William Astor over some real estate titles and that a big lawsuit was pending. If Mrs. Mowatt was hazarding everything in her decision to become an actress, it was not because of a mere whim. All in all, one had to admire her pluck.

Over everything hung the leaden pall of the heat. It was bad enough backstage, where the actors were gingerly removing the perspiration before the curtain went up, and praying that their make-up would not run before the first act was finished. In the auditorium the temperature suggested the proximity of a blast-furnace. Had the Reverend Dr. Beecher been present he would have pronounced it the radiation of infernal flames. But tonight that divine was cooling himself on a veranda in the Catskills, forgotten by those members of his flock who were beginning to fidget on the hard benches of Old Drury.

At seven-thirty, only half an hour behind schedule, the jets in the great chandelier were dimmed and the overture struck up. The chattering ceased. Presently one heard only the music and the swish of fans and the sound of squirming for more comfortable positions. Then in a high crashing fanfare the music ended and the curtain rose.

There was a moment's pause before the audience recognized the heroine of the evening. She was reclining gracefully on a sofa, contemplating a bouquet of roses. Slowly she raised her eyes and looked straight out at the house. There was a burst of applause. After a quick glance at Mrs. Vernon, who answered with a barely perceptible nod, Anna Cora rose to her feet, and gathering the skirts of her rose-colored velvet gown, curtsied deeply. There was another and louder round of applause. This, too, was gracefully acknowledged. Then the play began. Mrs. Vernon sailed into the opening speech in which Madame Deschapelles compliments Pauline on her appearance. Pauline's first line (she is still intent on the bouquet which has arrived from an unknown admirer) is:

You spoil your daughter, mother.

With these words, uttered in a low clear voice, with exquisite languor, yet with warmth, was launched the most remarkable career the American stage has ever known. Before the first scene was ended, New York had given its heart completely to Anna Cora Mowatt. Forgotten were all the fears for the débutante, the idea of social suicide—even the noble motive. After the first five minutes it was obvious to everybody that Mrs. Mowatt existed in a sphere far removed from all these considerations. She had about her that indefinable quality which sets one individual apart from the crowd, yet which gives everyone a sense of personal, unshared intimacy with her. To this rare essence were added intelligence and imagination, as well as beauty of face and form and voice. With all these elements concentrated in the delineation of an appealing character, and Bulwer's Pauline was enormously appealing to the audiences of 1845—the result was magic. From the moment she appeared upon the stage, it was perfectly clear to everybody that Anna Cora Mowatt was a great artist.

The press accounts of the evening form a unique chapter in the history of the American theatre. Never—not even on the first appearance of Fanny Kemble—had there been such excitement over a stage personality; never was language so tortured to express the sense of rapture evoked by Mrs. Mowatt's Pauline; never such manifest interest in the art of acting itself.

Summarizing the reports, and drawing on his own sharp memory of the evening, Oakey Hall (on whose account of the première of *Fashion* we have already drawn) gives us an idea of the general impression which Anna Cora made:

The signal feature of her Pauline was naturalness. . . . Both Pauline and Claude spoke their lines without caesural pauses, an unheard-of practice. Mrs. Mowatt, as the audience freshly perceived, was even mistress of the truest expression of dramatic art, pantomime. In the closing action Mrs. Mowatt rose to great dramatic powers and obscured the improbabilities of the plot, and made the stilted language forgotten, and then . . . the silence . . . of the audience was succeeded by a torrent of applause such as the traditionally stolid New York audience had never previously known. Usually impassive matrons sacrificed their gloves, maidens educated to believe enthusiasm was "bad form," sacrificed fans in beating applause upon the backs of seats; and the gentlemen in the pit realized what Edmund Kean remarked to his wife on his return from his greatest triumph—"the pit rose at me." . . . The occasion was the first and last really wonderful theatrical début in New York.

This account was written with the perspective of nearly fifty years. For the fresh savor of the triumph we must turn to the contemporary record.

Naturalness was the impressive feature of Anna Cora's acting. People had the sense that they were seeing Bulwer's shopworn play for the first time. There was a freshness and ease in Anna Cora's performance that set it completely apart "from the hackneyed Paulines of the stage," according to the critic of *The Sunday Mercury* who was impelled to add: "Pauline has not been played till now." *The Courier and Journal* attributed the extraordinary effect of reality to the fact that she played the part "throughout from her own feeling of what it should be and not in simple obedience to the rules. . . ." This was particularly notable in the quiet scenes which would have been "remarkable in any actress."

It was almost impossible to believe, as *The Post* put it, "that one with so little experience could acquire the ease and self-abandonment which is supposed to be the result only of long training. There was a great deal of soul in Mrs. Mowatt's acting, which proved to us, that with a little experience, she may make one of the best actresses now on the stage. Her conception of the character was perfectly true and sustained throughout, and in the more impassioned passages she exhibited very rare dramatic abilities."

There was no doubt that her personal charms contributed

much to Mrs. Mowatt's success. "Mrs. Mowatt has the body of a girl" (this, again from *The Sunday Mercury*), "with the air and expression of a self-willed woman. Her first glance gives you the idea of fragility, but watch the expression of that meaning [sic] face, and you see that it is of the body, not of the mind." The same theme was further developed by *The Evening Express*. "We do not know that we ever saw features better adapted than the débutante's to that by-play which is the charm of acting; to that silent, yet speaking illustration of the passing scene to which the quick eye, the flexible lip, the graceful form of the listener and observer, often contribute more effect than the most eloquent language could do."

Almost without exception, the critics spoke of Anna Cora's voice. N. P. Willis, writing in the *Mirror,* considered that the greatest of the natural qualities "which she brought to the aid of her intellectual conceptions, was her rich ringing voice, which gave precision and distinctness to every word."

One or two of the reviews tried to strike a tone of moderation, but without much success. *The Sunday Atlas* noted some excesses along with "much that was right excellent in her presentation." But it could find no fault that experience would not wear away, and concluded that "we are much mistaken if the débutante has not in her the stuff of which great actresses are made." *The Express* said that she "was somewhat stilted in parts of the dialogue and a little declamatory in colloquial passages, but these were lost in the general excellence of the performance."

A good deal of attention was bestowed upon the audience. *The Herald* called it "an array of beauty and elegance such as we have seldom seen at any place of amusement in this city." "An array of taste, beauty and intelligence" was *The Express's* variant.

The ovation at the end received a paragraph by itself in most of the reviews. It was "thunderous," "torrential," "stormy," and everything else that could be borrowed from the vocabulary of meteorology. This was doubtless a subconscious reflection of the heat which was also mentioned by everybody.

The high note of ecstasy was sounded by *The Evening Gazette*: "We wish we were a morning paper published tonight—that we might be the first to offer to Mrs. Mowatt, Mr. Crisp, and the public our congratulations on the triumph achieved at the Park last night. But we are not and therefore do the best we can, in writing our tribute immediately while the enthusiasm is yet unabated by sleep."

The notice in *The New York Republican* is a museum piece of dramatic reporting, and deserves to be quoted in entirety:

> Mrs. Mowatt's debut as Pauline last night, was one of the most triumphant we ever witnessed. Long before the commencement of the performance the house was filled in every part—lobbies and all were one dense mass of human beings. Hundreds went away without being able to gain admission. The heat was overpowering.
>
> We caught but one or two glimpses of the débutante; but ever and anon we heard the thrilling intonations of her melodious and powerful voice. It was asserted in the theatre that Mrs. Mowatt gave promise of becoming at no distant day, the greatest living actress. We could not remain in our uncomfortable position and therefore left the house at the end of the fourth act. Hence we give no critique.

The scene at the final curtain was as dramatic as anything else that had occurred during the evening. After a moment of profound silence, there was a blast of applause, increasing in violence as Anna Cora came forward for her first bow. It continued as the curtain came down again. Then a gentleman in one of the boxes called for three cheers. These were given with resounding force, the gentleman in the box taking the lead, mopping his face with a large white handkerchief between cheers. As though this were an agreed signal, the whole house suddenly became a sea of waving handkerchiefs. Then the audience rose to its feet. Someone called for another cheer. Again a mighty roar went up, continuing in prolonged shouts while the curtain rose and fell—no one counted how many times. Anna Cora had taken the first call by herself, the next with Mr. Crisp, the third with the entire company. But the rest of the evening was hers alone.

With each rise of the curtain the stage was showered with bouquets. Some of these had been prepared in advance, but the majority were nosegays snatched from lapels, from coiffures, from wrists, spontaneous tributes of delight and admiration.

Only one incident, not in Bulwer's text, marked the performance itself. Seated in the pit, fairly well forward, was an elderly gentleman of generous proportions. On one side of him sat a dowager in diamonds and brocade; on the other a sea-captain resplendent in gold braid and shining buttons. Throughout the play the old gentleman was observed to have in his hands two large white handkerchiefs with which he alternately mopped the sides of his face. As the play progressed the mopping became more frantic. In the third act, after Melnotte has taken Pauline to the humble cottage which is to be her future home (although she does not know it) she begins to shiver with premonition. To Claude's query whether anything is wrong Pauline replies: "The night breeze chills me."

At these words the portly gentleman suddenly ceased swabbing his face and shouted: "Chilled! By the lord Harry! I'd give a thousand dollars to be with you!"

In the *Autobiography*, written nearly ten years later, Anna Cora devotes two brief paragraphs to this momentous evening. She mentions the "call" at the end of the play and the fact that the audience complimented her by rising to its feet. She speaks of the rain of flowers on the stage, but she does not mention one detail noted by the newspapers; that she picked up the handsomest wreath thrown at her feet, and with a charming curtsey presented it to Mr. Crisp.

Her recollection was chiefly of the immense relief she felt when it was over. Now she had the proof she needed to go ahead. She had won the first round in the game on which she had staked everything. "The débutante had stood the test; she had not mistaken the career which had been clearly pointed out as the one for which she was destined."

CHAPTER THIRTEEN

Lily and the Raven

So far as the public was concerned, Anna Cora had proved that she could act. But this was only the beginning. The critics may have praised her mastery of technique, the finish of her performance, her veteran-like demeanor on the stage; but she still had a great deal to learn, and no one knew this better than she did. In one bold leap she had reached a great height. The question was, could she stay there? There was no doubt in Lily's mind that she could—if she worked. She began to plan her life so that all her energies might be devoted to this end.

If she had followed the advice of friends, and perhaps her own inclination at the moment, she would have retreated with James to some cool isolated spot to spend the summer studying and building up her health. But the one thing which her all-too-brief experience on the professional stage had taught her was that one learned to act by acting. A few days after her début, an offer of an engagement came from the management of the Walnut Street Theatre in Philadelphia; and though everyone foretold that she would collapse with the strain of continued activity in the summer heat, she promptly accepted the offer.

There were a number of reasons why the Philadelphia proposal was attractive. The most urgent, of course, was the need for money. The Mowatt fortunes had never been at a lower ebb; the expenses of the début in New York, particularly the cost of Lily's wardrobe and Crisp's fees for coaching her, had brought James and Lily to the end of their cash reserves. The Philadelphia offer would also give her a chance to play new parts: there would be four changes of bill during the engagement. She would be able to try out rôles which she meant to use on the tour James was arranging for the fall. There was a further advantage in continuing her novitiate in Philadelphia. She was personally acquainted with the company of the Walnut Street Theatre, all of whom had been very cordial to her at the time of the production of *Fashion*. A friendly back-stage atmosphere would help develop confidence. Most important of all, she felt the need of keeping contact with an audience. For Lily had also discovered in her few short hours before the footlights of the Park that the actor plays upon a double instrument: one part himself, the other part the audience. The fundamental interpretation of a dramatic role was of course the player's own—but the key and the tempo of a performance were set by the responses of the audience. Lily knew that every chance to study these responses was precious.

There was a matter of some delicacy involved in the Philadelphia engagement. Crisp would of course play the male leads opposite her, in accordance with their agreement. This meant that Crisp would displace, for the term of the engagement, the regular leading man of the Walnut Street Theatre—William Wheatley, an excellent actor and a great favorite with the Philadelphia public. Marshall, the manager, was greatly concerned about this. In those days the spirit of partisanship between an actor and his following ran high. Marshall feared that there might be resentment if Wheatley were dethroned from his established place in the company. But a contract was a contract. There was no alternative but for Wheatley to yield his position, at least for the moment. This Wheatley did with good grace. But his public, as events proved, accepted the change less willingly.

The house was packed on the opening night, and Anna Cora was greeted with an ovation similar to that of the début in New York. This augured well; and indeed the first two acts of *The Lady of Lyons* went off in fine style. But during the third act Anna Cora became aware that something was wrong. In this act Claude and Pauline are constantly together, and she had occasion to observe that something in Crisp's speech was not quite right. She noted also that when he took her hand his own trembled violently.

Her immediate conclusion was that Crisp must be suffering from stage-fright. She had heard that even veteran actors, under special conditions, were subject to this disorder. Crisp, she knew, was under considerable nervous strain, since he was well aware that he was replacing a favorite with the audience. Lily thought that he was beginning to be affected by the undertone of disapproval which she herself sensed in the reactions out front.

Lily's heart went out to her leading man in sympathy, and she did everything possible—by encouraging glances and surreptitious pressures of the hand—to bolster his courage. But somehow he failed to respond. Presently he began to miss cues and fluff his lines. This brought Lily to the verge of panic, for she was not experienced enough to improvise speeches to cover another actor's defections. By a supreme effort she managed to keep her own lines in order, but in so doing she ceased to act. She merely recited.

In the early part of the fourth act she did recover herself to some extent, since in this part of the play her scenes were with the Widow Melnotte and Beauseant, both of whom were performing with verve and assurance. Then came the moment for Crisp to appear again. The heroine, struggling in the arms of her rejected suitor Beauseant, called loudly: "Help! Claude! Have I no protector?"

This was Crisp's cue to enter, and enter he did—but in some uncertainty as to his objective. Instead of making a straight dash across the stage to the side of his beloved, he described a zig-zag course which sent him first almost into the perilous flames of the footlights, then recoiling to the back-drop. At last he located the struggling pair and came to a wavering halt. He managed to place an arm about Pauline and cry thickly: "Pauline —look up! Pauline! Thou art safe!"

At the word "safe" there came from the audience a sound more fearful than any Anna Cora had ever heard—a faint, low, but unmistakable hiss. Her blood froze. Yet her horror at the sound gave way at once to indignation. It was apparent now that Crisp was beside himself, utterly unnerved, and she felt a deep anguish at the audience's lack of humaneness toward his suffering. Once more she recited lines mechanically till the act was over.

By the fifth act the life had gone completely out of her own performance. She hardly knew what she was doing. Yet she continued to struggle through her scenes with the other actors until Crisp came on for his final lines. This time he barely opened his mouth when the house was filled with a deafening hiss. Anna Cora wrote afterwards, "The theatre seemed suddenly filled with snakes."

When the sound came, she had been facing upstage. With an instinct of defense she turned to the audience. At that moment she saw the pit rise in a body, presumably with every intention of doing violence to Crisp.

Anna Cora did not think twice. She did not know what Crisp had done to incur the audience's displeasure. Possibly people resented the fact that an Irishman should have displaced a native favorite? But that patriotic fervor should carry an audience to such lengths was shameful. Anna Cora had never encountered an exhibition of such provincialism, such pettiness and cruelty, especially toward one struggling so heroically to please!

As the hissing reached its height, Anna Cora walked quickly to the footlights and began to speak. Instantly the sound ceased. In a very few words, she entreated the audience's forbearance

LOUISVILLE, KENTUCKY

from Meyer's Universum, c. 1850

and appealed to its chivalry. She said that Mr. Crisp was simply fulfilling an obligation which circumstances had suddenly rendered very painful. She reminded the audience that her fellow-player was a stranger within their gates. She hoped she need not be more explicit on that subject to Philadelphians!

In a silence broken only by the sputtering of the gas-jets the audience resumed their seats. By ruthless cutting the actors brought the play to a quick end. Anna Cora rushed from the stage and started for her dressing-room, with a heartbroken sense of her own failure. She knew that only for a few brief moments had she risen to anything like a competent performance. She felt that the disaster was irretrievable. At the door of the dressing-room Marshall, the manager, caught up with her. He begged her to return to the stage. The audience was calling for her, he said. Anna Cora listened and could scarcely believe her ears when she heard the sound of applause.

Reluctantly she made her way back to the wings. There she met Crisp who offered to lead her out. She would have declined his company; but she did not want to wound him afresh after what he had gone through. The curtain was up when they reached the stage. Anna Cora curtsied and Crisp gave a slight bow. A number of bouquets were thrown, and these added to Anna Cora's sense of humiliation since they had obviously been prepared in advance to honor greater merit than she felt she had displayed that evening. One of the bouquets fell near Crisp's feet. Instinctively he reached down to pick it up and present it to Anna Cora. Then it was that she remarked for the first time the truly peculiar nature of his affliction. In straightening up, Crisp almost pitched into the footlights; only with Anna Cora's assistance was he able to resume an upright position. She was amazed—not only that his stage-fright should persist now that the performance was ended, but that it should affect his sense of balance.

The curtain was brought down with a crash and Crisp, sobbing loudly, rushed for the wings. Anna Cora followed close behind. As she left the stage she passed Mrs. Jones (who had played Madame Deschapelles) talking with another lady of the company. She heard Mrs. Jones remark: "He got no more than he deserved. I wish they had *brickbatted* him—the man was as drunk as could be."

Anna Cora stared at the two women and then rushed to James, who had just appeared. "Did you hear what that woman said!"

James smiled wryly at her. "Yes. And it is too true. I saw that you did not suspect his situation and I thought it better to leave you in ignorance."

Lily stared at her husband in horror. Was it possible! The idea had never entered her head that Crisp might be intoxicated. There was no reason why it should have. Although she was twenty-six years old and had grown up in a society of gentlemen who partook regularly of strong liquors, Lily had never been within close range of one in his cups.

The next night Mr. Crisp, hoping to save some shreds of a situation already completely lost, made a speech of apology to the audience. He explained that he had been led into unwonted indiscretion while dining out, and entreated the indulgence of the good citizens of Philadelphia. The apology was accepted; but it was noted that for the remainder of the engagement the audience displayed little warmth for Mr. Crisp.

As for Anna Cora, the rest of her stay in Philadelphia was depressing beyond words. Something had happened to her spirit, and though she struggled valiantly, she could not do her best. The fact that the houses were scanty was also cause for discouragement. She was haunted by the notion that she had made herself ridiculous by failing to diagnose Crisp's trouble correctly. But what weighed heaviest on her was the fact that she had been betrayed by the one person who was legally and morally bound to support her—at the most critical point of her career.

Crisp promptly returned to New York at the end of the engagement, only too happy to escape from the scene of the disaster. Anna Cora would gladly have followed, but Blake, the stage-manager, entreated her to remain for one more performance—his own benefit. Since he had been unfailingly kind, Anna Cora yielded to his request. The play selected for the benefit was *Fashion,* in which for the first time she played a part; that of Gertrude, the sweetly misunderstood companion of the elegant Seraphina. It was a typical "walking lady" part (what we would now term an ingenue rôle), more decorative than spirited. Anna Cora frankly detested it; yet she must have given it some special life and warmth on this occasion. Both public and critics were charmed with her acting in the part, and she was able to leave Philadelphia with a final impression which largely offset the earlier fiasco. The two other parts (besides Bulwer's Pauline which she had worked up for the engagement), were Juliana in *The Honeymoon*, a romantic farce, and Lucy Ashton, in a dramatization of Scott's *The Bride of Lammermoor*—of which we shall hear more later.

After the Philadelphia episode Crisp was a chastened spirit. But so far as Anna Cora was concerned he ceased to exist outside his professional capacity. Behind the footlights the two were often locked in passionate embrace; but once the green baize curtain had fallen, that was the end of it. For the rest of their contract, which ran for more than nine months—during which time they traveled thousands of miles together—Anna Cora never spoke to Crisp off-stage.

This may have been harsh treatment for one misstep. But in Anna Cora's code a breach of loyalty was the unforgivable sin. She had a wide tolerance for human weakness in general. In her life she received many injuries: she was defrauded, slandered, humiliated by those she had helped. Yet her treatment of Crisp is the only instance of any capacity to harbor resentment over a long period. When we realize how much depended on the Philadelphia engagement, coming as it did so early in the career on which she had staked not only her own fate but that of four other people, her attitude toward Crisp is perhaps not too difficult to understand.

The Mowatts returned to New York the day after Blake's benefit. There were innumerable details to be settled. Since the New York début, James had been busy arranging for a tour which would begin in October. He had secured an engagement for Lily at the Howard Athenaeum in Boston and another at the Charleston theatre. He was negotiating with the western impresarios Smith and Ludlow for turns in their Mobile and New Orleans theatres, and was exploring the possibility of brief engagements in Baltimore and Buffalo.

It was evident that the couple would be away from New York for most of the winter, and this immediately brought up a serious problem. In all the excitement over Lily's new career, the three little Greys had not been neglected. They had stayed with Lily's sister May during the two weeks the Mowatts had been in Philadelphia. But May and her husband Cephas Giovanni Thompson, a young portrait-painter who was beginning to achieve distinction, were making plans to go abroad in the fall. Proper care of the children during their own absence from New York now became James's and Lily's major concern: all the more since the children were not robust and required constant attention. Margaret and Willie had begun to show signs of their tubercular heritage and young John had never fully recovered from the pneumonia which had stricken him when he had come to live with Lily and James.

After long and careful search in which all friends and relatives were pressed into service, Dr. William Turner, the husband of Lily's sister Louisa, found a solution to the problem. The children were sent to Greenfield Hill, Connecticut, where they were placed in the hands of kindly and responsible farm people. The boys lived with one family and Margaret with another, but they were close enough together so that they saw each other constantly. Here the little Greys remained happily for the next several years. They were always in close touch with their foster-parents, who wrote to them regularly and sent exciting presents from remote places like Charleston and Cincinnati. Whenever they were in New York, James and Lily went to see the children or had them in town for visits.

The strain of the Philadelphia experience had made Anna Cora really long for a good rest. But the very fact that things had gone so badly during the second engagement of her career made her anxious to keep working, to repair as quickly as possible the damage she felt her beginning reputation had suffered. That she herself exaggerated this is quite evident from the fact that, three days after the catastrophic performance at the Walnut Street, the manager of Niblo's theatre in New York made her a very advantageous offer for a midsummer starring engagement at his establishment. Despite her fatigue, Lily accepted it thankfully.

To some of her well-wishers it seemed a mistake to undertake this off-season engagement. After the grand success in June many people felt that Anna Cora should not return to New York until the regular season had begun, and that she should appear only at the Park. Niblo's was really a summer theatre and did not cater to the sort of audience that frequented Old Drury. The building was a ramshackle affair, quite unlike the splendid edifice of a later day, with a beer-garden and ice cream pavilion attached. By long-established custom the second intermission lasted forty minutes to allow patrons a chance for convivial cooling-off. It was a popular family resort where dramatic entertainment with refreshments could be had for a nominal outlay. If its clientele was less select than that of the Park it was no less appreciative, and the greatest stars of the age were pleased to display their art at Niblo's Gardens.

Lily accepted the offer as a real challenge. She would have to learn more parts (there would be five changes of bill during the engagement) and she would have a chance to try her powers on a mixed public. Of course there was the question of money; and the hundred dollars an evening which she would be paid (in addition to what she might realize from her benefit) would help defray the expenses of getting the children settled in the country and purchasing the extensive wardrobe which she would need on tour.

Her judgment proved sound. The opening night the house was jammed. Those who had been unable to see her in June made the most of this new opportunity. Although the theatre was only a shed with sides open to the elements, on this evening it was like an oven. But—as earlier in the summer—the weather failed to dampen the excitement of the audience, and Anna Cora was greeted by a second ovation in New York almost as boisterous as the first. The opening bill, inevitably, was *The Lady of Lyons*.

The second and third offerings were *The Honeymoon* and *The Bride of Lammermoor*. During the second week a new play, Sheridan Knowles's *Faint Heart*, was added to her repertory.

The Honeymoon, second only to *The Lady of Lyons* in popularity at the time, was another hodge-podge of borrowings from the Elizabethans. The main plot was lifted bodily from Shakespeare's *Taming of the Shrew*, with touches of *As You Like It* and *Twelfth Night* thrown in for atmosphere. The part of Juliana, the heroine, must have presented some hazards for Anna Cora, since the tenderest moment of the play hangs upon the singing of the following ditty:

> *At the front of the cottage*
> *With woodbine grown o'er*
> *Fair Lucy sat turning her wheel,*
> *Unconscious that William was*
> *Just at the door,*
> *And heard her her passions reveal.*

However, any faults in her singing were ignored by both public and critics.

Despite the fears of her friends, this midsummer stint at Niblo's added greatly to her reputation. Practically the only discordant note amid the general acclaim was sounded by *The Albion*. This is somewhat surprising since the critic of that journal, J.W.S. Hows, had been such a staunch supporter of the new star from the beginning. However, it is evident that if Hows did not lavish the fulsome praise accorded by the other critics, it was because he had the newcomer's best interests at heart. He saw that she had great potentialities, but that these could be realized only if certain faults were corrected at the outset; and he took it upon himself to indicate at least the directions in which improvement was desirable.

There was a certain artificiality in her manner, Hows noted, which seemed to derive from instruction she had received; she would have done better to trust her own judgment in some of her interpretations. She tended sometimes to be declamatory where a casual delivery would have been more effective. Above all, he warned that she must be careful to select parts suited to her powers.

But with all this, Hows made it clear that there was no mistaking Mrs. Mowatt's extraordinary talent. Writing of the opening night of the Niblo engagement he said: "It must have proved a high gratification to Mrs. Mowatt to see that she could collect such an audience in her present novitiate stage, with the thermometer varying at blood heat." In the same review he pointed out that the audience had come "prepared to judge of her *real* merits calmly and critically" and that the first two acts of the play (*The Lady of Lyons*) had been coolly received. But from the third act on the applause was "loud and continuous". "She absolutely extracted the critical approbation of the audience, not inclined to be over-lenient." For her second performance Hows had nothing but praise. Her Juliana in *The Honeymoon* "was a bold dashing picture. . . . Her last act was exquisite".

Despite Hows's note on her artificiality, it is evident that Anna Cora was continuing to develop her own techniques in defiance of accepted stage tradition. *The Post* for July 25 (reviewing *The Honeymoon*) reported the disturbing fact that she moved about a great deal,—and that some of her movements were directly from upstage to downstage, instead of on the more graceful diagonal.

At Niblo's, Anna Cora repeated *The Bride of Lammermoor* which she had first tried in Philadelphia. In the intervening time she had worked hard over the part (entirely on her own, without benefit of Crisp's tutelage), and her interpretation of Lucy Ashton was sensational. Even Hows, though deploring the play itself, had to admit that—in the third act at least—it gave Mrs. Mowatt a chance to display "tragic powers, superior to any she has previously exhibited". But again Hows was nervous about the unrealized potentialities. He was unhappy that Mrs. Mowatt had returned to New York so soon, even though she had proved her "great powers of attraction" (she was playing to packed houses every night); and he warned again that she must study incessantly to master the details of her profession. If she did this, he prophesied, "we shall yet see her all her most ardent admirers desire." He concluded with a note to the effect that Mrs. Mowatt was leaving immediately for Buffalo.

Despite the slight pomposity and faint air of patronage in Hows's criticisms, he was a deeply interested and, as it turned out, useful admirer of Anna Cora. Eventually he became her instructor, in which capacity he exerted a great influence on her later career.

In another way which Anna Cora herself little suspected, this midsummer engagement at Niblo's Gardens was to have important consequences, extending beyond her own lifetime. Among the critics who recorded their impressions of Mrs. Mowatt's acting in the July heat of 1845 was the editor of *The Broadway Journal*, Edgar Allan Poe. What he saw and heard was set forth in the columns of his paper to form an important part of his critical writing and to insure for Anna Cora Mowatt a permanent record in the annals of the American stage.

We know already, from the two reviews of *Fashion*, that Poe had a more than casual interest in Mrs. Mowatt as an artist. This fact, added to a natural curiosity to see in the flesh a lady whose personal charms were being so widely discussed throughout the town, would have been motive enough to send him to Prince Street on that torrid evening of July 14. But Poe was doubtless impelled also by a desire to witness the new display of Mrs. Mowatt's talents which had created such a furore among his fellow-critics. In a matter of such high artistic interest it was certainly to be expected that Poe would have his word to say; that in his own mind, perhaps, it would be the final word. Or it may have been simply his instinct as a journalist that drew him to Niblo's to cover an event which would be of interest to his readers. Whatever his motive, Poe was in the audience when the curtain rose on the opening night of Anna Cora's turn at Niblo's and for all succeeding nights of the engagement as well.

The first of Poe's reviews appeared in *The Broadway Journal* for July 19. It began in the vein of Hows's criticism. Poe considered that Mrs. Mowatt had shown poor judgment in making her second New York appearance in a "summer theatre" and also "in appearing again after so brief an interval". It was important that Mrs. Mowatt maintain a certain dignity in the public eye. Of course, no one could dispute her *real* dignity, which resided in her position and in her character; but she would certainly be more appreciated if she made herself scarcer to the public view (a singular piece of advice to an actor whose living depended on such exposure). Poe felt that Mrs. Mowatt should have made her début in London for reasons of prestige, although he was glad, personally, that she had not. But he was deeply concerned lest any false step jeopardize a career which promised so much. He felt it unwise for her to continue acting with Mr. Crisp (an opinion in which Anna Cora herself doubtless concurred, though she could do nothing about it). She should appear with Mr. Forrest.

Poe took to task those who criticized Mrs. Mowatt for electing to follow a career unsuited to her background. "We have no sympathy with the prejudices which would have entirely dissuaded Mrs. Mowatt from the stage." And, as if to settle the matter, "The writer of this article is himself the son of an actress."

That she was justified in following this course was shown by her immediate success. Poe then devoted himself to more personal considerations:

Of Mrs. Mowatt and her acting we have to speak only in terms of enthusiastic admiration. We have never had the pleasure of seeing her before. Her figure is slight—even fragile—but eminently graceful. Her face is a remarkably fine one, and of that precise character best adapted to the stage. The forehead is the least prepossessing feature, although by no means an unintellectual one. The eyes are grey, brilliant and expressive, without being full. The nose is well-formed, with the Roman curve, and strongly indicative of energy; this quality is shown also in the prominence of the chin. The mouth is somewhat large with brilliant and even teeth and flexible lips capable of the most effective variations of expression. A more radiantly beautiful smile we never remember having seen. Mrs. Mowatt has also the personal advantage of a profusion of rich auburn hair.

There is no doubt that Anna Cora was very close to Poe's ideal of womanhood. She had that combination of beauty and good breeding, the appearance of delicacy with an underlying suggestion of strength, that he sought always but never quite found in the women to whom he became attached. He had found it perhaps least of all in the one he loved most, the little Virginia who at this moment was lying ill in the cottage at Fordham.

Yet despite the appeal of her personal attractions, it was Anna Cora's acting which made the profoundest impression:

> Her manner on the stage is distinguished by an ease and self-possession which do credit to a veteran. Her step is very graceful and assured—indeed all her movements evince the practiced elocutionist. We watched her with the closest scrutiny throughout the whole play and not for one instant did we observe her in an attitude of the least awkwardness, or even constraint, while many of her seemingly impulsive gestures spoke in loud terms of the woman of genius—of the poet deeply imbued with the truest sentiment of the beauty of motion.
>
> Her voice is rich and voluminous, and though by no means powerful, so well managed as to seem so. Her utterance is singularly distinct—its sole blemish being an occasional Anglicism of accent, adopted probably from her instructor. Her reading could scarcely be improved. In this respect no actress in America is her equal, for she reads not theatrically but with the emphasis of nature. Indeed the great charm of the whole acting of Mrs. Mowatt is its *naturalness*. She moves, looks, and speaks with a well-controlled impulsiveness as different as can be conceived from the customary rant and cant—the hack conventionality of the stage. If she does not suffer herself to be badgered out of this good path it will lead her inevitably to the highest distinction. . . .

The second week of the engagement also found Poe in regular attendance at Niblo's. On Saturday, July 26, another review appeared in *The Broadway Journal*. This was devoted to Anna Cora's performances in *The Honeymoon* (which as a dramatic specimen Poe considered "grossly absurd"), and *The Bride of Lammermoor*. Not throughout all the pages of Poe's critical works do we find such excited admiration for a subject as in his description of Anna Cora's performance of Scott's feckless heroine:

If in all the literature of fiction, there is a character for which Mrs. Mowatt is peculiarly adapted, it is Lucy Ashton. If the authoress of *Fashion* knew her own strength, she would confine herself, nearly altogether, to the depicting in letters as well as on the stage, the more gentle sentiments and the most profound passions. Her sympathy with the latter is evidently intense. In the utterance of the truly generous—of the really noble—of the unaffectedly passionate—we see her bosom heave—her cheek grow pale—her limbs tremble—her chiselled lip quiver—and nature's own tear rush impetuously to the eye. Nor is it this freshness of the heart which will provide for her the greenest laurels. It is this enthusiasm—this well of deep feeling—which should be made to prove to her an exhaustless source of fame! As actress it is to her a mine of wealth—worth all the dawdling instructions in the world. Mrs. Mowatt *as she now stands*, is quite as able to give lessons in stage *routine* to any actor or actress in America as is any actor or actress to give lessons to *her*. . . .

Like Hows, Poe was disappointed in the play-version of Scott's novel. The Lucy Ashton of the original had been changed to an operatic heroine. As a matter of fact the plot of this particular dramatization was closer to Donizetti's opera than to the novel. Yet the very crudity of the material was a challenge to Mrs. Mowatt's creative gifts.

With a bosom full of emotion she seemed to suffer from the total insufficiency of the words of the dramatist to give utterance to her thought. But what was done was done to admiration. The actress lost no opportunity. The appeal to the mother was very noble acting. The signing of the contract and the wild shriek at the entrance of Edgar, would have done honor to anyone. The apathetic and mute despair at the end of the play, and during the interview with Ravenswood in the mother's presence—the dumb incomprehending wretchedness—the half-conscious rendering up of the broken gold—the laboring anxiety for the relief of words—the final maddening confession, heartbreaking, and death in the lover's arms—were the teachings not of Mr. Crisp, but of Nature herself—speaking in tones that could not be misunderstood. The audience grew pale, and were betrayed into silence and tears—and if anyone went away sneering that night, it is at least quite certain that he felt ashamed of the sneer.

There is certainly no record of sneers at this performance. Everybody agreed that Anna Cora's Lucy Ashton was a deeply moving portrayal. The part was one in which she made a lasting impression wherever she did it. It may well have been at this performance witnessed by Poe that an incident occurred which is related by Mary Howitt in her memoir of Anna Cora.

The play had progressed through three acts with manifestations of steadily mounting tension in the audience. By the middle of the fourth act the excitement had become so great that the whole house had risen to its feet—pit, boxes and galleries. When Ravenswood, Lucy's true love, arrived on the scene and was shown by Lady Ashton the contract with Lammermoor which Lucy had been forced to sign, a man in the audience cried out in a voice shattered with emotion:

"Tear it up, Ravenswood! Oh! tear it up!"

Poe's third and final account of Anna Cora's acting appeared in *The Broadway Journal* for August 2. At the last moment the engagement had been extended to include a production of Colley Cibber's version of *The Taming of the Shrew*, under the title of *Katherine and Petruchio*. Of this production Poe had little to say since the play, as butchered by Cibber, was "beneath contempt." However *Faint Heart* by Sheridan Knowles, which he had not covered in the previous review, he found neatly epigrammatic and ingenious. But again the chief attraction was the star. "Nothing, we think, could be better than Mrs. Mowatt's personation of the Duchess." And he added a special note: "The beautiful lips of Mrs. Mowatt have, we fear, a singular facility in the expression of contempt." Mr. Crisp was intolerable as Ruy Gomez. "He entirely misconceives the part." (Perhaps in this instance it was Nature and not Art that made Mrs. Mowatt's portrayal of the scornful Duchess so very effective.)

Poe's concluding remarks are like a benediction—such a benediction indeed as few actresses have ever received:

> In taking leave of Mrs. Mowatt for the present, we have only to record our opinion that, if she be true to herself, she is destined to attain a very high theatrical rank. With the one exception of

mere physical force, she has all the elements of a great actress. Her conceptions of character are good, her elocution is excellent, though still susceptible of improvement. Her beauty is of the richest and most impressive character. Her countenance is wonderfully expressive. Her self-possession is marvelous. Her step is queenly. Her general grace of manner has never, in our opinion, been equalled on the stage—most decidedly it has never been surpassed. These qualities alone would suffice to assure her a proud triumph—but she possesses a quality beyond all these— enthusiasm—unaffected freshness of the heart, the capacity not only to think but to *feel*!

Poe's predilection for attractive women being well-known, it might be assumed that the fascination which Anna Cora exercised for him was not wholly artistic. Yet he never knew her personally, and, so far as can be determined, never saw her except across the footlights. That she appealed to him physically is evident from the nature of his remarks about her. But it is equally evident that he was very objective in his judgment of her art. His reviews are only more voluminous and articulate versions of the majority of opinions of her work even at this early stage. Besides, in his view of her achievements, Poe was able to make clear distinctions. His opinion of Anna Cora as a playwright we have already seen. In an article which appeared in *Godey's Lady's Book* for June, 1846 (a year after Anna Cora's début on the stage), he commented on her poetry. Although he felt that Mrs. Mowatt had latent poetical power, he was unable to find one of her poems "entitled to commendation as a whole". He was struck by a stanza from the lyric *To Isabel M. . .*:

> *Thine orbs are lustrous with a light*
> *Which ne'er illumes the eye*
> *Till heaven is bursting on the sight*
> *And earth is fleeting by.*

But in general her versification was "rough".

He could concede no particular merit to her novels, although they offered "glimpses . . . of a genius as yet unrevealed, except in her capacity as an actress".

The paths of Lily and the Raven did not cross again after 1846.

Poe died in 1849 while Lily was gathering laurels in London. Five years later, her career as an actress was ended. Had Poe survived to see her as a mature artist on her return from England in 1851, it is probable that Lily's name would be a by-word in the American theatre today, instead of a hazy reference in the minds of a handful of antiquarians. An actor's main hope for immortality rests on one of two chances. Either he must survive long enough before the public to create a body of legend, to be handed down from one generation to the next; or, during his life on the stage, he must have attracted the attention of a writer with the genius to give his memory enduring form. In this connection we have but to remember how much the reputation of Edmund Kean owes to Coleridge's unforgettable: "To see him act was like reading Shakespeare by flashes of lightning."

Despite the fact that Poe only saw Lily at the very outset of her career, his descriptions of her art—supported by the prodigal outpourings of lesser critics—are enough to dispel all doubts as to her intrinsic gifts. But the significance of the reviews which Poe devoted to Anna Cora Mowatt goes beyond any service he may have done the subject herself. Taken together, the notices in *The Broadway Journal* and the article which later appeared in Godey's in the "Literati" series form a landmark in the history of the American theatre and of American criticism. In these articles, for the first time, a great American writer looks upon the drama as a serious art. In them, also for the first time, the art of acting is made the subject of serious criticism.

Poe may have been generalizing from his own opinion when he said (in the *Godey's* article of 1846) that Mrs. Mowatt had "undoubtedly wrought a deeper impression upon the public than any of her sex in America". But as we examine the printed record, from which the details of her career now come thick and fast, we must agree that he cannot have been far wrong. During the next years Lily moved like a new planet across the American firmament, shedding a brilliance in which other native lights paled.

CHAPTER FOURTEEN

" . . . *The Minerva of the Modern Stage*"

Anna Cora had looked upon the mid-July engagement at Niblo's as a chance to try out new parts and, in general, as a sort of warming-up period before beginning the tour which had been planned for the autumn. She had expected at the end of the fortnight to go off quietly somewhere with James for August and September, to rest and digest the fruits of her further experience. All this would be merely preliminary to the serious professional life which, so Anna Cora thought, would not really start until November when she opened her engagement at the Howard Athenaeum in Boston.

But these plans were pointless. Anna Cora's professional career had already begun. There was to be no apprentice period. She had only played a week at Niblo's (with what success has already been indicated) when offers began to come in from all sides. The manager of the Eagle Theatre in far-off Buffalo had seen her at Niblo's, and noting the well-filled houses had conceived the notion of opening his own establishment for a late summer season—to be inaugurated by Mrs. Mowatt. His proposal was financially too tempting to decline. Besides, as Anna Cora reasoned, Buffalo was so far from the beaten track that she might experiment with additional new parts and not risk permanent damage to her reputation in case they did not come off. So with less than a week's breathing-time after the close of the engagement at Niblo's, Lily and James took the steamer again up the Hudson. If they gazed with wistful recollections as they puffed by Nyack, these must have been mingled with a certain sense of satisfaction. The ten years of their married life had brought vicissitudes which, had they been foreseeable at the time of the elopement, might have given greater cause for uneasiness than the wrath of Samuel Ogden. Yet they had survived them all— ill-health, poverty, and the disappointment of having no children of their own. In fact they had done better than survive. To the passengers aboard the steamer, many of whom doubtless recognized the beautiful Mrs. Mowatt, the couple must have presented a picture of success: Lily in her elegant bottle-green traveling dress and handsome pelisse, with the violet ribbons of her bonnet fluttering in the breeze; and James, thin and graying but so distinguished in his black frock-coat and tall beaver hat.

The Buffalo interlude was pleasant, mainly because the week spent in the cool wind from Lake Erie provided such a welcome relief from the heat of New York. There was also great professional success. Buffalo was already assuming importance as a theatre town; but her citizens had seen no one as yet comparable to Mrs. Mowatt, who not only charmed so completely on the stage but moved in an aura of romantic legend that thrilled the citizens of the drab raw town on the lake.

But the summer's activities did not end at Buffalo. On August 2 the New York papers announced that Mr. Simpson, the esteemed manager of the Park, had returned on the *Cambria* from Europe. It was conjectured that he had engaged distinguished artists there for the coming season—notably Charles Kean and Ellen Tree, who were scheduled to arrive in New York on August 4. This was true; but renowned foreign stars were not all Simpson had up his sleeve. On August 16, *The Albion* announced that the Park would begin its season on Monday the 18th, and that despite Mr. Simpson's "numerous and efficient engagements with distinguished *artistes* from abroad, he gives the precedent to Mrs. Mowatt who opens the season. This is a delicate compliment to the talents of this accomplished native artist. . . ."

Simpson's decision was more than a compliment to Lily. It was money in his pocket and he knew it. By what master stroke of greenroom diplomacy he managed to persuade the Keans to yield the honors of the first engagement to Mrs. Mowatt, we can scarcely surmise. But Simpson saw that the home-grown product had assumed a market value which even the British artists could not match, and he was determined to take advantage of the new star's availability, no matter what the cost.

So before she knew it, Anna Cora was back at the Park, facing the audiences of that famous institution for all the world like a distinguished alumna returning to a doting alma mater. Her reappearance was New York's event of the month: a month, one might add, not absolutely charged with excitement. On August 20, for instance, Lily's only serious competitor for the attention of the town was a cow which (if *The Herald* is to be trusted in the matter) "had been enraged in some way and stuck her horns into an old gentleman, Dr. Chapman, at the corner of Varick and Canal Streets. . . ." The location of this mishap was, one notes, perilously close to the Park; but even this event was forgotten when the carriages began to roll up before the gaslighted marquee of the theatre.

Lily's engagement marked the beginning of the forty-seventh season of Old Drury, and of the reign of Simpson the thirtieth. Of the two facts, the latter is on the whole the more notable. Witnesses are unanimously of the opinion that Simpson was the most ineffectual manager any theatre ever had, and a perfect babe among tigers in the New York business world. Yet strangely enough under Simpson's aegis the Park achieved its great reputation as a purveyor of the finest dramatic entertainment in the New World; and though Simpson's correspondence clearly indi-

cates that at any moment of his career nothing but a loan of
fifty dollars could hold him back from the brink of disaster—he
too had wonderful powers of survival. Perhaps, as in Lily's case,
the secret of his endurance lay not in any crude physical tough-
ness, but in the sheer love of what he had to do.

In one sense Lily's precipitate return to New York had its
disadvantages. So little time had elapsed since the triumphs at
Niblo's (and these following so closely on the brilliant début)
that the critics had had no opportunity to replenish their stock
of phrases. The reviews seem strangely repetitious of those called
forth by the earlier appearances. Hows, in *The Albion*, tried as
usual to be other than merely flattering. Although Mrs. Mowatt
had made extraordinary progress and there was no doubt that
she was "destined to be one of the brightest living ornaments of
the stage," at the same time, so Hows took pains to point out, the
true artist can never rest on his laurels, but must toil unceasingly
to develop the gifts provided by a generous Providence. In such
labor, it was delicately hinted, the artist might profit by the
guidance and criticism of a qualified mentor. (Crisp had long
since been dismissed by all the critics as having any real
prerequisites for this rôle.)

On the same page with this review, separated by the width of
two columns, appeared the following notice:

John W. S. Hows

Professor of Elocution at Columbia College will resume his classes
for private pupils on the first of Sept. next at his residence 476
Broome St.

The notice undoubtedly caught Anna Cora's eye. It may have
caused a slight lifting of the expressive eyebrows, but it did not
fail to make an impression. Eventually she did become a private
pupil of Professor Hows. And there is no question but that the
association was a valuable one. Hows was a broadly cultivated
spirit, a classical scholar and deeply versed in the literature of
the drama. He was also a competent voice teacher; and though
Anna Cora had done much independently to exploit her beautiful but not powerful voice, it was Hows who taught her how to

use it with maximum effect. It was also Hows who revealed to
Lily subtleties in Shakespeare which even her acute perceptions
had not brought to light. Her later renown as an interpreter of
Shakespeare's romantic and comic heroines—in which she was
unrivalled not only in her own time but for generations to come
—probably owed much to Hows's coaching.

On August 22, *Fashion* was presented with the author in the
rôle of Gertrude: the first time Lily had performed the part in
New York. As on the evening of her début in June the heat was
indescribable (at sundown the thermometer was hovering still
in the mid-nineties) and the theatre was pictured by *The Gazette* as "a well-heated retort . . . in which a thousand human
beings suffered distillation for the benefit of Mrs. Mowatt". But
the enthusiasm "though smothered in steam" was tremendous. It
was noted that there were changes and additions to the text of
the play and that "some of the actors made changes which were
not improvements . . ." but New Yorkers extravagantly showed
their satisfaction with this double display of the artistic gifts of
their native daughter.

At the end of August Lily was back in Philadelphia, again inaugurating a new season and a newly-renovated theatre. This
time it was the Chesnut (to use the then current spelling) Street
house which she graced. The management, apparently not sharing Lily's own view of the damage her reputation had suffered
in Philadelphia, hastened to secure her services to celebrate the
elaborate refurbishing which this theatre had undergone. The
interior presented an appearance of which a manager might
well be proud:

> Burnished Gold Ornaments, of chaste and appropriate designs,
> have been placed around the three tiers of boxes. The Proscenium
> is of gorgeous pattern, profusely decorated with Arabesque devices
> in green and gold. Stage doors have been added. . . . A New Drop
> Scene depicting the City and Bay of Naples, with a view of
> Vesuvius, has been painted by Mr. Hielge. . . .

The engagement was brief but highly successful. No one
seemed to recall the unfortunate circumstances of Lily's earlier
appearances, and Crisp himself—one cannot but admire his

courage in appearing in Philadelphia—was well received in *Romeo and Juliet*.

Meanwhile Anna Cora's literary career was catching up with her. In July, *The Fortune Hunter* was brought out by William Taylor. It met with a very favorable reception. Poe reprinted a whole chapter in *The Broadway Journal* and promised to publish a critique, but he never got around to this. In August, *Evelyn* at last saw the light of day and promptly became a best-seller. The publishers of both books utilized to the fullest the publicity attending Anna Cora's emergence as a theatrical star, and the rewards were gratifying. *Evelyn* was taken with great seriousness as a work of the new realistic school. "The whole novel [wrote the reviewer in *Graham's Magazine*] evinces more mental resources than usually characterize works of the kind. . . . The passions are represented with much power."

Lily was still fully confident that she would have some kind of rest before the autumn; but she had not reckoned with the pressure of success. Before she left for Philadelphia she received another offer from Niblo for a two-weeks' run in late September, and although she was nearly exhausted, she was afraid to refuse it. For the first time in years she and James were without financial worries; yet she did not dare cut off the golden stream even temporarily. So for three weeks she exerted herself in the friendly atmosphere of Prince Street. Where a month before an occasional vagrant breeze from the Hudson had not sufficed to prevent perspiration pouring from her face, now she shivered in low-necked evening gowns as the chill early-autumn winds swept through the open sides of the theatre. Yet the stimulus of working, the thrill of watching the effects of new parts on the responsive Niblo audiences, and—always—the handsome cash returns at the end of each week, gave her fresh strength and vitality. She had not felt so well in a long time. And the experience was invaluable. She had now more than fifteen parts in her repertory. At Niblo's she added the rôle of Lady Gay Spanker in Boucicault's *London Assurance*. She also appeared in a new play of Epes Sargent, *Change Makes Change*, which one of the papers described as "an interesting failure—written expressly to display her histrionic powers". The run ended September 17. A few hours after Lily left the theatre it burned to the ground.

Finally in October there was a break of three weeks. Most of this time Lily and James spent at Samuel Ogden's. Here they were joined by the little Greys, who stayed until the time came to leave for Boston.

Lily had looked forward to the engagement at the Howard with mixed feelings. She felt a sentimental pleasure in appearing as a full-fledged professional actress in the city where she had first stood, a trembling débutante, in the Masonic Temple. But she wondered if the critically-minded New Englanders would show as much indulgence for her now as when she was the courageous child-wife, displaying her talents to save hearth and home. She was still supporting a family (now increased by three adopted children) and her motives in embracing the stage, as her friends always hastened to explain, were those of duty: but in the dazzle of all the public acclaim and the prominence accorded her success by the newspapers, it was easy to lose sight of this fact.

Anna Cora may have expressed her apprehension to Boston acquaintances. Her mainstay of the earlier time, the energetic and generous Mrs. Bates, was no longer at hand, having departed for Europe. But there were others—and always, of course, those particularly susceptible to the promptings of Epes Sargent—to prepare the way. This was made evident by a poem which appeared in *The Transcript* on November 3rd:

TO ANNA CORA MOWATT

I ask for thee a welcome,
A welcome to our hearts
That bears in its intensity
That which our love imparts.

This vein was continued for several stanzas, ending with:

Let shouts of joy sing on the breeze
A welcome loud and free
And let it be Bostonia's boast
She welcomes worth with thee. . . .

Bostonia was certainly not disinclined to "welcome worth", but she would accept no ready-made judgments as to what constituted that commodity. The city was traditionally suspicious of New York opinions, particularly in cultural and intellectual matters, and the very lack of restraint shown by the New York press in dealing with Mrs. Mowatt put the conservative New Englanders on their guard. If the new star was as good as she was reported, she would have to prove herself according to Boston standards—which, as one or two of the papers chillingly reminded their readers, were perhaps somewhat different from those prevailing in the metropolis to the south.

Actually the tastes of Boston in matters theatrical were not perhaps all that her fondest admirers imagined. An examination of the dramatic bills-of-fare of the period reveal the city's penchant for circuses, and spectacles with liberal displays of fireworks rather than poetry on the stage. George Vandenhoff, the English actor, remarks on this state of affairs in Boston in his *Leaves from an Actor's Notebook*:

> It is, however, an unfortunate fact, that, in spite of the proverbial literary taste . . . the Drama, properly so-called—I mean the Drama of Shakespeare, Sheridan Knowles, Bulwer, etc.—does not generally attract the Bostonians. Show and spectacle, glitter, blue flame and pantomimic extravagance, have infinitely greater charm for them . . . and, I have no doubt that Mr. Barry cleared more money for the stockholders last season (1845-46), by the revival of the carcase of the old (one)-horse-piece of "The Cataract of the Ganges" without a line of poetry and scarcely of common sense in it, than he ever made in Boston by the most careful production of the highest Shakespearean Drama, or the most elegant Comedy.

If we may judge Boston life of this time from the picture presented by the daily press, it would seem that the city, like the rest of America, was more under the sway of Mammon than of the Muses. Advertisements, crowding each other for space on the front pages of the papers, proclaim the virtues of Bryant and Hemans' Hot Air Furnace (extraordinarily modern in design) and Lyndley's triumphant contribution to the eternal war

against bedbugs. Of the Lyndley Patent Bedstead it was proclaimed (by the makers) the "joints are so tight they afford no
resting place for the nocturnal family." In the most bewildering
variety the appeals of creature comfort are set forth: in nostrums
for every conceivable disease, in offerings of exotic foods, luxur-
iously upholstered carriages, self-adjusting nightcaps. If the publishers advertise their wares at all, it is with a discretion amount-
ing to timidity. The taste for lectures has in no way abated, but
the subjects are no longer Transcendental. Audiences crowd the
Masonic Temple, not to hear lectures on The Soul, but on "The
Stomach and Other Internal Organs" (with illustrations).

Yet it would be unfair to say that Boston's finer sense of
values was wholly smothered in the flood of mid-nineteenth
century materialism. There was still room, and apparently reason,
for a small advertisement in the papers announcing an exhibition at number 9 Milk Street of "Titian's Venus", a work praised
loudly by critics and connoisseurs and said to be "unsurpassed in
color and resemblance of a perfectly formed woman." Admission
for this display of a great European art treasure was 25c. A season
ticket could be had for 50c. Where but in Boston, one asks,
might a public be expected to purchase tickets not only for one,
but for repeated viewings throughout the "season" of a single
picture, even one "unsurpassed in . . . resemblance of a perfectly
formed woman"?

Inevitably, Anna Cora's opening bill was *The Lady of Lyons*.
Although the play had already been seen in Boston once during
this season and at least twice the previous year, the Howard
Athenaeum was packed; and this notwithstanding a torrential
rain. The inclemency of the weather restricted the feminine contingent at the opening, but the more hardy masculine element
turned out en masse. The audience, reported *The Atlas*, was
"particularly good-humored". Yet this show of friendliness was
not to be taken for an expression of unqualified approval. *The
Atlas* granted Mrs. Mowatt "much histrionic ability", but was
not able to accord to her "the rank assigned to her on the southern
boards. . . ." In fact, so this report implies, the critics to the
south had not been wholly discerning. There were serious flaws

in Mrs. Mowatt's acting. "Her by-play was not good. After she had spoken her lengths, she waited in apparent unconcern until the turn came again." This was indeed a serious matter—and so at variance with the oft-repeated comments on Anna Cora's complete identification of herself with the part, that we can only suppose she had begun to weary of the haughty Pauline! If this was the case, she showed very poor judgment in selecting the rôle for her Boston début.

But it may be that *The Atlas* had a particularly jaundiced eye on the evening of November 4. *The Courier* was unabashedly ecstatic. "We never saw the part so grandly performed, so felicitously embodied, or its pathos and passion so finely developed. Never was an actress so successful in completely winning the house."

Lily astonished the critics by her versatility when she did Lady Teazle in *The School for Scandal* on the next evening. In the audience at this performance was John Quincy Adams with a party of friends. Reports reaching the ears of the play-loving elder statesman had determined him to see for himself what was going on at the Howard. It was observed that he beamed with delight throughout the performance and that he applauded long and heartily.

With each succeeding night Anna Cora rose a notch higher in Boston's critical esteem. Her Juliet on November 11 placed her, in the sober judgment of *The Transcript* "in the very first rank of her profession". But nothing was comparable to the rendering of Lucy Ashton in *The Bride of Lammermoor* which "alternately stilled the theatre into the most eager attention and shook it with applause".

Boston was likewise greatly impressed with *Fashion* which it saw for the first time, even though the actors, as usual, were vague about their lines. Much of the epigrammatic quality of the play was lost due to the bungling interpolations; but nothing, *The Transcript* hastened to point out, "could be more unjust than to hold Mrs. Mowatt in the least responsible for these." *The Courier* was perfectly content with things as they were. The play was "exceedingly brilliant" and, as an afterthought, "interesting" (!). "Mrs. Mowatt was charming as Gertrude though the part does not show her powers". The audience was "the largest and [needless to say] most brilliant ever seen in Boston."

By the time she took the train for New York, Anna Cora was in no uncertainty as to the nature of her triumph. She not only had a reticule stuffed with gratifying press clippings. She also had a handsome draft on a New York bank. Furthermore, she had captured Boston so completely that the cool aloofness with which she had been greeted on her arrival had warmed to a passionate attitude of proprietorship. It was clear that, though a native New Yorker, Mrs. Mowatt the artist really belonged to Boston, not only by the historical fact of having made her first public appearance in the New England Athens, but by reason of her refinement, her taste, her intellectual endowments and her artistic gifts—all of which, Bostonians discovered, bore a remarkable affinity to the tone of Beacon Street and Louisburg Square.

As a matter of fact, Anna Cora herself felt this congeniality of spirit with the audiences that had filled the Howard during the ten nights of her engagement; and to the end of her career, though other cities lavished affection upon her and won their respective places in her heart, she felt always that she belonged artistically to Boston. That Boston felt the same way about her was amply demonstrated in the last chapter of her life, when long after she had been forgotten by the rest of the world, she received the most spectacular offer of her entire career from Boston.

In this pleasant atmosphere Anna Cora might have lingered; but the schedule of engagements worked out by James now drew her southwards. In New York she rested briefly at her father's house, and then early in December took ship for Charleston. Here, from December 4 to December 30, she played the most arduous engagement of her stage life. Opening in *The Lady of Lyons* (the part had now become so completely associated with her that managers automatically expected her to open in it) she went through a repertory of sixteen plays with constant changes of bill. Despite the rigors of nightly performances, with

breaks only on Sundays, she learned six new parts including Jane
Shore (in Rowe's tragedy of that name) and Belvidera in *Venice
Preserved*. With only twenty-four hours' notice and one rehearsal she gave an unforgettable performance of Otway's
poignant heroine. How profound an impression she created may
be judged from a communication to *The Charleston Courier*
signed "Old Drury", and probably from the pen of Charleston's
most notable literary figure, William Gilmore Simms.

After commenting in general on the success of Mrs. Mowatt's
season in the South Carolina metropolis, the writer describes the
thrill which swept over the audience at the final curtain of
Venice Preserved. "Delicate in physical organization, she has yet
by the force and versatility of genius made our theatre echo
with applause and admiration." In her rendering of Belvidera "all
was finished, mature". The writer was frankly awed by Mrs.
Mowatt's gifts. "Dramatic annals present no career more rapid-
bold and original. Her success is not the *result of elaborate
thought* but *creative genius*. The Minerva of the modern stage,
she sprang before its votaries . . . armed for conflict and for
triumph." Nothing, this author felt, so aptly described Mrs.
Mowatt's genius as the tribute paid to Mrs. Siddons by a great
English writer half a century before:

> Where there was little or no poetry, she made it for herself, and
> might be said to have become at once both the dramatist and the
> actress. Where but a hint of a fine situation was given, she caught
> up the vague conception, and produced it in a shape that was at
> once both ample and defined; and with the sorriest text to justify
> the outpouring of her own radiant and fervid spirit she turned
> into a glowing picture what she found but a comparative blank.

It is quite certain that Anna Cora's poetical talents, however
modestly displayed in her formal verse, enhanced her other gifts
for the stage. Critics speak again and again of her powers of
imagination in transforming a dull and threadbare character into
the living embodiment of poetic inspiration. That she actually
rewrote many of the impossible parts in which the tastes of the
time forced her to perform, there is ample evidence. On one

occasion, as we shall see later, she got herself into some difficulties through this practice; but there is no doubt that she had the capacity for seizing upon the merest wind-blown hint and transforming it into something real and exciting.

The experience in Charleston was Anna Cora's true introduction to the provincial American theatre; and though it taught her more than all her previous efforts put together, the sheer pace at which such a small stock company had to work would have crushed a weaker spirit. The labor of preparing the nightly changes of bill was prodigious. Most of the plays were rehearsed only once. But since the bills nearly always involved two plays—sometimes the main drama plus a short farce as after-piece, but frequently two full-length plays—the rehearsals were endless. They usually started at eight in the morning and continued until one or two o'clock; but sometimes they went right through till curtain time at night. The modern actor who finds a summer stock engagement wearing because he must rehearse for three or four hours during the day and then give a two-hour performance at night, might marvel at the vitality of our theatrical ancestors who sometimes plied their craft for sixteen or eighteen hours a day.

But this was not all. For Anna Cora, there were new parts to learn; and this meant further toil into the early hours of the morning. How she managed all this is best told by herself:

Often . . . I returned home from the theatre wearied out in mind and body; yet I dared not rest. The Character to be presented on the succeeding night still required several hours of reflection and application. Sometimes I kept myself awake by bathing my heavy eyes and throbbing temples with iced water as I committed the words to memory. Sometimes I could only battle with the angel who
> *"Knits up the ravelled sleeve of care"*
by rapidly pacing the room while I studied. Now and then I was fairly conquered, and fell asleep over my books.

Under this pressure the delicate Lily might have been expected to succumb; but the spirit of perverseness which had defied mere physical limitations before, was at work again.

Strange to say, my health, instead of failing entirely, as was predicted, visibly improved. The deleterious effects of late hours were counteracted by constant exercise, an animating, exhilarating pursuit, and the all-important *nepenthe* of inner peace. I gained new vigor and elasticity. With the additional burden came the added strength whereby it could be borne.

The "inner peace" of which Lily speaks came in part from the satisfaction she was finding in her new career, in part (and this the greater part) from her continued study of Swedenborg. Wherever the Mowatts went, on the table of Lily's hotel room were always half a dozen of the Swedish mystic's works. No matter how exhausted she might be, Lily could always turn to them for refreshment. In moments snatched from the exacting routine of the theatre, James and Lily read and prayed together. They encountered few congregations of the New Jerusalem Church in the south and west, but wherever the denomination was represented the Mowatts were faithful attendants at services. In a profession where piety was not common, this drew attention, and added to Mrs. Mowatt's reputation an ingredient, which appealed mightily to the respectable, church-going section of the American population. It was generally acknowledged later that Mrs. Mowatt had done more than any other figure on the American stage to open the doors of the theatre to people who previously had looked upon the institution as inimical to religion.

But this was an incidental detail in the real significance of Lily's religious life. In the isolated community of worship which they formed together, Lily and James were drawn even closer to one another. In Swedenborgianism the shadow of death which had so long hung over both lost its fearsomeness. Though Lily's own health, as she says, had greatly improved and though James, by taking every precaution, was holding his own against the disease which had undermined his constitution, neither believed that the tenure of life was for very long. They had faced this fact earlier with a stoicism which seems to have been a part of both their natures. But Swedenborgianism gave them something more. To the poetic imagination, which James as well as

Lily possessed in some measure, Swedenborg's vision of the after-life became so intensely real that the notion of earthly existence as a mere threshold to man's greater destiny was easily, even eagerly accepted. And this view—which by now had worked its way to the very core of their thinking and feeling—enabled them to live equably with the probability that death lay just around the next corner.

The effects of this immersion in the deep quiet stream of faith were manifest in Lily's personality. From the mid-winter of 1845 on, it was remarked that the characteristic sparkle of her nature was greatly heightened. At the same time—in her gestures, her glance, the very tone of her voice—there was also a new serenity. She had something of the air of an *exaltée* moving in an atmosphere of spiritual excitement. Yet she had also achieved greater control of herself. Her acting was more assured, her interpretations deeper and more mature. And over everything was thrown a luminosity which made her unique. Critics tried in vain to describe it. Poe had already seen it in the flash of her smile—"A more radiantly beautiful smile we never remember having seen. . . ." But nobody ever quite defined it wholly. The general effect when she walked upon the stage was as though the gas had been turned higher.

Lily not only learned a great deal about acting during her first season in Charleston. She became familiar also with the purely mechanical side of the theatre and with the ways of its people. Like all theatres of its day the Charleston establishment was completely self-contained. Every detail of a production was carried out in the theatre itself. Scenery was painted in a gallery, high up over the stage in the flies. This was a source of perpetual annoyance for actors who had to rehearse down below and who complained bitterly when their clothing and faces were spattered with paint.

Costumes likewise were made on the premises by the wardrobe-mistress or the property-man, who not infrequently was an ex-tailor. As a rule the theatre supplied only special items for period productions. The actors were supposed to dress themselves for all stock pieces. There was a standard wardrobe for men which was considered satisfactory for all parts in the normal range from Shakespeare to Boucicault. A handbook of the times designed for the beginner in the theatre describes the minimum sartorial equipment for men. Costumes (exclusive of modern clothing) were all vaguely Elizabethan or Italian Renaissance in feeling. The first requirement was "Three pairs of tights (red, white, and fleshings)." Then—indispensable because they seemed to enhance the virility of the masculine leg—"stage boots (russet or yellow buckskin)." "For old men" the regulation footgear was pumps with large buckles. Another important item was gloves: "silk, cotton, kid and buff-colored gauntlets." *De rigueur* for "shape dresses" (i.e. period costumes, particularly Elizabethan) was a stage collar of lace; and in the same connection "wrist ruffs, frills, and lace for boot tops." Also on the list were caps and feathers; of the former "one black, one plaid" represented the decent minimum. There must also be black and white plumes ("about three good ones will serve to set off a cap")—and "a jewelled ornament for the front of the cap." The list continues with "a dress coat faced with white satin (for gentlemen of the old English comedies)" and passes quickly to the all-important question of swords. Here the requirements, if we consider the novice's purse, are quite alarming. The actor should not only have a standard straight two-edged crosshilted dress sword, but a Roman sword, a Scottish claymore, a Turkish scimitar, etc. The author of the book, who describes himself as an ex-actor, is dogmatic on this point:

> Few characters can be considered completely dressed without them [swords]: perhaps more than one half the small parts in which novices are *cast*, are military officers, and how wretched and ineffective it is to see one of these personages, however subordinate, executing his orders, or *business* of the scene, or merely walking on and off the stage, without his characteristic weapon.

Precise instructions are given for suitable sword-belts and chains. For the latter, one "with links of good polished brass about two inches square is particularly recommended." Such an accoutrement the author points out "will always look showy and outwear half a dozen actors."

Since the most popular plays were "costume" pieces, demanding a frequent display of the masculine limb, the question of false
calves is treated exhaustively and with scientific detachment. The
most practical (in the opinion of this author, though the experts
seem not to have been in complete agreement) was the "built-up"
type. This was achieved by taking old stockings and cutting them
off in various lengths at about the region of the calf. The actor
then proceeded to draw on the longest section over his own calf;
over this came a slightly shorter length, then the next shorter—
and so on until a nicely graduated and distinctly athletic development was attained. The practice—deplorably careless—of merely
stuffing rags into one's stocking to fill out the calf was to be
avoided by any sincere artist. The rags tended always to fall
down about the ankles, particularly in a lively scene, and this
could—the records show that on numerous occasions it *did*—
excite the risibilities of the audience.

Even the professionally-constructed pad was not without its
hazards. One of the oldest bits of theatre folklore celebrates the
fact. The story concerns an actor husband and wife in their
dressing-room just as a performance was about to begin. The
husband was dressed and was running over his lines while the
wife busily stitched away at the costume in which she would
make her appearance later on. Habitually under such circumstances, the wife availed herself of her husband's leg for a pin-
cushion; at close range the false calf was unmistakable. Suddenly
came the husband's call. He dashed to the stage, while the wife
went on placidly with her needlework. Only in the midst of a
tender love-scene did the actor, upon some intimation from the
audience, realize that anything was wrong. Glancing down he
noticed that one stalwart calf was bristling with large, shiny pins.

A certain casualness, the result of the constant necessity for
improvisation, characterized stage dress of the day. Few managers
followed Kean's innovation in costuming a whole production
with uniformity and attention to historical detail. The women of
the theatre, as has already been noted, were given practically free
range in the matter and garbed themselves in what they considered suitable for the play or, more usually, for their own
personalities.

Anna Cora has left a vignette (in *Mimic Life*, one of her later works) of the provincial actress in her homemade costume, which suggests the informality of dramatic productions of the time:

> Mrs. Pottle next strutted on the stage. Her stunted, shriveled up figure was almost concealed in the folds of her far-spreading train, fashioned of flame-colored cotton velvet. She had prodigally adorned her diminutive head with a huge crown cut out of gilded foil. It was of her own tasteful manufacture and being somewhat limp in its construction shook and rattled at every movement. . . . Mrs. Pottle had been occupied in her leisure moments in the green room in the laudable pursuit of plain sewing. She chanced at the moment when Fish (the call-boy) made his call, to be more deeply engrossed by her housewifely avocation than her professional triumphs. The queen had pompously stalked upon the stage without removing the spectacles which glittered just beneath her gilt-paper crown. The hand which she lifted to give point to her declamation showed one finger crowned with a shining brass thimble.

James's negotiations with Smith and Ludlow had resulted in a contract for Lily to appear in New Orleans in February. Since the Charleston engagement closed on December 30, there might have been a month in which Lily could relax in the mild Carolina climate before continuing her tour. But before the Charleston engagement was half over, Lily had signed a contract to return for another ten days late in January. The interval between the two Charleston engagements would be filled by a run in Savannah.

Despite her assertions to the contrary, she must more than once have been close to collapse on this strenuous tour. During her second round at Niblo's in September, in the middle of a performance of *The School for Scandal*, she actually fell asleep on the stage. She was playing Lady Teazle to the Sir Peter of Henry Placide, whom she was to rejoin later in Charleston. She had had little sleep for several nights and in the famous scene where Lady Teazle hides behind a screen to prevent discovery by her husband, she simply lay down on the floor and gave way to an irresistible temptation to close her eyes. She was brought back to consciousness by the loud excited whisper of the prompter in the wings:

E. L. DAVENPORT AS "ADAM TRUEMAN" IN *Fashion*

Courtesy, Museum of the City of New York

"Wake up! Wake up! Mrs. Mowatt, wake up! Charles Surface is just going to pull the screen down!"

Through heavy eyelids she saw Jones, the prompter, dancing about in the wings in an hysterical manner, his whispers mounting almost to a shout:

"You'll be caught by the audience asleep! Wake up! Wake up!"

Looking up she could see the hand of the actor playing Surface already on the screen. More by reflex than conscious intention she sprang to her feet, kicked her train in place and pulled herself erect just as the screen came down to reveal a demurely contrite Lady Teazle all prepared to explain to her husband the imprudence which had led her alone to the lodgings of an unmarried gentleman. A split second later and she would have had to make explanations of a different sort.

After the Savannah interval, Lily returned to Charleston as an established favorite. A few nights before leaving for New Orleans she was asked to deliver a special address for the Palmetto Guard, the band of Charleston volunteers about to depart for the Mexican War. Lily gracefully accepted the invitation and a special tableau was arranged for the occasion. At the conclusion of the regular bill the curtain again rose, to display a tableau of Trumbull's *Signing of the Declaration of Independence*. After the singing of *The Star-Spangled Banner*, which had become very popular although it had not yet achieved the status of the national anthem, Lily moved from the back of the stage through the motionless figures of the tableau to the footlights. As she did so she could not but feel proud to note the character of her great-grandfather, Francis Lewis, prominently seated near the table bearing the replica of the immortal document!

New Orleans was the high spot of the southern tour. If the old Park in New York gave the hall-mark of professional merit to the actor, the St. Charles Theatre in New Orleans provided the most glamorous setting for his art. The building was the handsomest edifice west of the Alleghenies. No other theatre in the whole country could touch it for sheer magnificence. It had been built nearly a decade before by the first impresario of the Mississippi

Valley, James Caldwell—a sometime actor turned manager, and now one of the most successful businessmen in the west. Caldwell had built the theatre at an original cost of $325,000, largely as a promotion scheme to popularize gas-lighting which he was planning to introduce into New Orleans. He had ransacked France and Italy for ideas, materials and craftsmen. The theatre seated 4100 people; its stage was 53 feet wide and 44 feet high. There were four tiers of boxes with sumptuous drawing-rooms at the back of each tier. The boxes, hung with blue, red, and gold satin draperies, had handsomely-furnished boudoirs attached to each one, and were rented to fashionable families for the season at $1000 apiece. But the wonder of all was the chandelier. It alone had cost $10,750. It was 12 feet high, 36 feet in circumference, had 250 gas jets and 23,300 cut-glass lustres—a truly noble monument to this prism-hung era.

Sheer weight of grandeur and the vastness of stage and auditorium might well have swallowed up Anna Cora's slight physique and the subtle realistic style which she was developing: but the newspaper notices give no intimation of this. With its usual *esprit de corps* where Anna Cora was concerned, the world of fashion filled the house night after night. For Sol Smith, one of the managers of the theatre, the engagement was impressed on his memory by the fact that Mrs. Mowatt played to "good business."

In the regular company at the St. Charles during this season were two old-timers of the western circuit, Mr. and Mrs. Joseph Jefferson and their son Joseph Jr. In the latter's autobiography there is a note on Anna Cora's acting which was to have unfortunate effects on her posthumous reputation. According to Jefferson, Anna Cora had a mannerism of glancing down at the stage after delivering a line, instead of fixing the audience with a stare to force the point home. This, in Jefferson's view, was the mark of an amateur; and "once an amateur, always an amateur". James H. Hackett had the same trick and Jefferson bracketed the two players together in his condemnation of their art.

Jefferson's judgment here may perhaps be taken with some reservations, at least in the case of Anna Cora. It is quite possible that she ignored a practice as artificial as the one to which

Jefferson refers. Among the many tricks for which Jefferson himself is remembered was that of holding his gaze straight out front, after delivering a line, until the audience, in sheer nervousness, gave some sign of reaction. Forrest used the same method to bludgeon his way to effectiveness. According to the criteria of the day, this was art . . . but we may judge it otherwise.

As to the quality of amateurishness—Jefferson only saw Anna Cora during this one engagement, when she had been less than a year on the stage. From the point of view of the experienced actor, she doubtless still had much to learn. What is remarkable is that, if critics and public can be trusted, there was nothing in the impression she made "from the front" to reveal a lack of professionalism. Without disparaging Jefferson's own accomplishments, it might be stated for the record that Anna Cora in her ten brief years on the stage played three times as many parts as did Jefferson in half a century—and to the highest acclaim before the most critical audiences on both sides of the Atlantic. His note, drawn from the dim memories of his youth, may possibly be less indicative of Anna Cora's own shortcomings as an actress than of resentment which the Jeffersons, like the other "regulars" of the St. Charles company, felt towards the successful newcomer whose appearance had suddenly filled the huge theatre with the most elegant and demonstrative audiences it had known in a long time.

Ludlow and Smith at this time operated also the theatre in Mobile; and stars engaged by them had to play both houses, shifting from one city to the other as the management saw fit. On March 2, Anna Cora was in Mobile. Here she encountered old acquaintances, the Chippendales who had performed in the original production of *Fashion*, and the comedian Skerrett, who had played with her on her début. Otherwise the Mobile engagement was not rewarding. The weather was abominable, audiences erratic, and Anna Cora caught a bad cold.

In Mobile and again in New Orleans, where she returned late in March, *Fashion* was produced with the authoress in the loathed rôle of Gertrude.

To be forced to enact the walking-lady part of Gertrude was a severe punishment. To escape its infliction, I always withheld the production of the comedy until the solicitations of the public and the managers left me no alternative. Could I have foreseen, at the time the play was written, that I should be induced to enter the profession, I would have been careful to create a character which I could imbody with pleasure.

But there was no resisting the popularity of the piece which could always be counted on to fill the house. Since Gertrude provided the "love interest" in the play, and consequently the leading feminine rôle—and since there was no denying the drawing-power of a live authoress in a part of her own creation— there was nothing to do but grin and bear it. Sometimes, however, the sentimental colorlessness of the part would prove so embarrassing that Anna Cora could scarcely go through with it. In New Orleans, before the huge cosmopolitan audiences of the St. Charles, this was particularly the case. It may well have been in this rôle that Jefferson watched Anna Cora refusing to look the audience in the face.

On April 2, Anna Cora was again in Mobile for an engagement of two weeks to complete her contract with Smith and Ludlow. After three performances, however, the engagement was suddenly broken off. It is not clear what happened, beyond the fact that James had to pay a sizable cash forfeit in order to get Lily released from the contract. It may have been simply that Lily had gone as long as she could without a rest. The weather was still wet, and she had not been able to shake off the effects of the cold caught on her previous visit to Mobile. But there may have been other reasons. Perhaps she was beginning to feel the concerted antagonism which her unprecedented success was naturally arousing among many members of the theatrical profession. On March 9, *The Mobile Register and Journal* had published the following tribute to her:

> By the mere force of genius alone she has placed herself in the first rank of her profession, and now occupies a position which others have attained only after years of painful study and laborious effort. . . . The purity of her taste compensates for that want of

stage education which is too often apparent in unnatural starts
and tricks of so many good actresses. . . . [She] feels correctly
and trusts to feeling rather than to hackneyed precedent. . . .

Such remarks, no matter how gratifying to Anna Cora herself,
can scarcely have gone down well with the less generous-minded
old-timers of the company.

Maybe the trouble was with Crisp—although there is no reason
to think so from the *Autobiography*, or from James' letters to
Smith and Ludlow dealing with the business side of the matter.
Nevertheless, the sudden termination of the Mobile contract not
only brought an end to the tour, but also to the contract with
her leading man.

Crisp now disappears from Anna Cora's story. That he had
been a handicap all along, there is no doubt. In New Orleans,
Smith and Ludlow had attempted to use James E. Murdock, a
fine actor attached to their permanent company, in supporting
rôles of equal importance to those played by Crisp. But this
had not worked out. There were too few plays offering such
rôles, and Crisp had been adamant on his rights. Yet Crisp cannot be made out a villain by the record. His experience with
Anna Cora seems not to have damned him for all time. In a few
years he abandoned acting for management, and at the time of
the Civil War he was, ironically, manager of the theatre in Mobile. He was popular in the city and attached himself with devotion to the cause of the South. He served with distinction as
an officer in the Confederate army and lived to see his son a member of Congress and eventually Speaker of the House of Rep-
resentatives.

For Lily the year was not quite over. Beginning May 4, she
played a fortnight at the Park with George W. Vandenhoff. Together they did a round of the usual things—*The Lady of Lyons,
The Honeymoon, The Hunchback* and *The Stranger*. How such
stale, flat, unprofitable stuff could have appealed to any audience
leaves us wondering. But it must have appealed, and it cannot
have been wholly unprofitable. The houses averaged well over
$300 a night and for Anna Cora's benefit, May 8, the box-office
take was $584.37 (of which her share was nearly $300).

It was now just less than twelve months since the new star had bowed to the assembled members of New York society at the Park Theatre. In that time she had mastered over twenty rôles. Since the evening of her début she had played two hundred nights before audiences across the country. She had faced serious competition in the Keans whose tour almost exactly duplicated hers. In many rôles she followed Ellen Tree (Mrs. Kean) by only a few days. Yet people flocked to see her, and in the eyes of the severest critics she suffered nothing in comparison with England's greatest star.

There was no doubt that Anna Cora had written a unique chapter in the history of the American theatre. This was summed up by Laurence Hutton, the one critic who was personally acquainted with her work and lived to judge it in the perspective of half a century of subsequent experience of American actors:

> In the annals of the stage of all countries there is no single instance of a mere novice playing so many times before so many different audiences and winning so much merited praise as did Mrs. Mowatt during the first twelve months of her career as an actress.

CHAPTER FIFTEEN

The Great Circuit

Long before the contract with Crisp expired, Anna Cora had begun to look for a new leading man. Ordinarily male and female stars did not tour in pairs, unless bound by marriage or a reasonable appearance thereof. Anna Cora's arrangement with Crisp had been largely for educational purposes. He was to coach her in the various parts she would play and in the ways of the theatre, in addition to playing the male leads opposite her. In theory this was an admirable idea, but in practice it had misfired. The repeated remarks of the critics as well as her own judgment would soon have led her to dispense with Crisp's tutorial services, had not the episode in Philadelphia precipitated the break between them. For most of the year Anna Cora was her own teacher, learning simply through acting and by observing the work of veteran players like Chippendale, Henry Placide, Skerrett and others.

Nevertheless there were a number of reasons why Anna Cora still wanted a partner. As a newcomer to the theatre, it was always an ordeal for her to face a strange company, most of whom knew each other's ways and were more familiar with the repertory than she was. With an actor playing regularly opposite her, she knew that her own performances would be smoother and that she would not be forced constantly to adapt herself to new leading men with different interpretations of the various rôles. She also wanted an ally backstage, someone who would lend her countenance professionally as her husband did socially.

A number of possibilities had been considered, but the choice finally landed on a young actor from Boston—Edward Loomis Davenport. Several friends had recommended Davenport as the ideal answer to Anna Cora's problem. He was well known both to Epes Sargent and William Ayling, one of the managers of the Howard in Boston, to whom James had turned for advice. They could vouch for Davenport's background: he was the son of a respectable and well-connected Boston tavernkeeper—and for his professional abilities. Though he had been seen little outside his native Boston, both men believed that he would go far in the profession. In addition to talent, Davenport had good looks, education, and the instincts and manners of a gentleman. As a matter of fact Anna Cora had already had an opportunity to judge him for herself. In the first engagement at Niblo's the previous summer, Davenport had played the part of Beauseant in *The Lady of Lyons*. She had been impressed both by his handling of a thankless part and his quiet, unassuming air backstage.

Davenport was now thirty-one years old. He had been ten years on the stage; yet he had never managed to get either parts or engagements which would carry him ahead. When James Mowatt approached him with the proposal of a contract to act as leading man for his wife, Davenport did not think twice. He too had formed his opinion of Mrs. Mowatt. Despite the defects which the practiced eye of the actor might detect, some of which escaped the critics, he had seen the extraordinary qualities in the new star and was confident of her success. This private prediction had been more than justified in the reports that had come back to New York of Mrs. Mowatt's triumphal progress through the South and West during her first year on tour. He knew that nothing in the ordinary course of things could now hold her back; and in the offer he saw possibilities for his own future. If nothing else, it would at least give him a chance to escape from the routine of secondary parts in inferior theatres to which up to now he had been doomed.

Furthermore, he had liked Mrs. Mowatt from the beginning. He had seen that her reserve, which irked many of her associates, was the result of shyness and not a snobbish desire to keep aloof from the common herd. He admired her pluck, for he knew something of the handicap of ill-health under which she worked. Undeniably he had felt the power of her charm; and he can hardly have been insensible to her beauty. Yet it must be set down at once that no breath of scandal ever developed around their association. They became, and they remained, loyal and devoted friends, sharing professional triumphs and personal tragedies alike.

Throughout the spring, as soon as the agreement with Davenport was signed, James busied himself with arranging a tour for the coming season. This time he was in a position to make the terms himself, for Lily's box-office value had soared in the year since her début. By late June, except for one or two weeks still open, the tour was completely laid out. Both James and Lily were at last able to take their long-awaited vacation.

Most of the summer was spent on Long Island at the seashore. Lily took long walks and swam every day. She also took fencing lessons. As James wrote to William A. Frederick, manager of the Pittsburgh Theatre, she was "fully determined to accomplish herself in every way possible."

There were temptations to interrupt their stay, but these James firmly resisted. An offer of $100 a night from Niblo's in July was flatly turned down. "If it was every night for a fortnight I would accept," James wrote Frederick. But the offer involved only two nights a week, which was poor compensation for abandoning the cool breezes of Rockaway for the sweltering city.

But by the end of August Lily was impatient to be at work again. The tour was to begin in Buffalo on August 28; but a sudden proposal from Simpson for a night at the Park just before she left was eagerly accepted. The play was *Romeo and Juliet*, and marked Davenport's first appearance as Anna Cora's leading man. Although Davenport was not ignored, the plaudits—from established habit both of public and critics—went largely to Anna Cora.

In Buffalo the season got under way with every augury of success. Then suddenly, at the very next stop, Baltimore, an accident occurred which seemed likely to put an end not only to Lily's present season but all her subsequent ones as well.

The opening bill was *The Honeymoon*, which up until the final scene had gone off with great éclat. Lily had just made an exit and was dashing to her dressing-room for a quick change. She had been somewhat near-sighted since early childhood, and in the dim light backstage she did not perceive a sofa carelessly left in the passageway by the stage-hands—nor, more precisely, a pair of heavy boots projecting over the arm of the sofa directly in her path. Before she was aware either of the sofa or of the sleeping stage-hand whose feet were obstructing the passage at a considerable elevation, Lily collided full force against the boots. No blow with a nail-studded bludgeon could have been more effective. Lily staggered back and fell to the floor. Yet she scarcely felt either the blow or the fall. Her mind was filled with one purpose—which was to change as fast as she could and get back to the stage for her cue. She reached her dressing-room, changed and returned to the stage. She made her entrance on time, but when she began to speak she choked and could hardly utter a sound. To Davenport with whom she was playing the scene she just gasped:

"Cut the scene—I can't speak!"

Davenport took Lily at her word and they "came to cues" at once. The curtain came down, but it was up again for the call before Lily could stagger off. By a superhuman effort of will she managed to stand for the call. Then she was assisted to her dressing-room.

It was not until she and James had reached their hotel that

the full effects of the accident were realized. A blood-vessel in her throat had been ruptured and Lily had been almost suffocated by the flow of blood rising in her mouth. Only an effort of will had prevented the hemorrhage from becoming visible to the audience.

The Baltimore engagement of course had to be cancelled. This had never happened to Lily before and she was desolate. Yet in ten days she was up and on her way to New York where she was to do another brief turn at the Park. No one outside the family knew of her precarious condition. She performed Juliet to great applause, and played *Much Ado About Nothing* for the first time with Davenport. It was in the latter play that Lily was eventually to achieve the height of her fame. But there must have been a notable letdown in this whole round of performances. Most of the critics were complimentary; but Hows, in *The Albion*, took her sternly to task for the sudden deterioration in her work. Certain of the heroines were

mere declamatory elocutionized stage heroines, not the poetical creations of the author. They are *efforts* not *realities*. We would earnestly direct Mrs. Mowatt's attention to this fact. The mere conventional declamation and stage whining common among actors, are insupportable barriers to histrionic excellence in these days.

Probably no one was in a better position than Lily to appreciate how much her portrayals were "efforts." Yet she somehow went through the engagement and wound it up with a flourish. On the final evening at the close of *Man and Wife* (a new item in her repertory) she read Epes Sargent's *The Missing Ship*. One asks vainly why she should have dragged this metrical monstrosity out of the dust-heap; unless it was that her old friend was in the audience on that night and she wished to do him honor.

At whatever cost to Lily's health, the engagement made money and enabled Simpson once more to start a season in the black. This was not the case with other managers who complained uniformly at the indifference of the public to the choicest lures that could be dangled before it. There was—as usual in the theatre—an explanation for this. The chief cause of the diversion of cash from the theatre box-offices was laid at the door of A.T. Stewart's new white-marble emporium, which had opened for business on September 10. This establishment had become the cynosure of all eyes. "Nothing in Paris or London," noted Philip Hone in his diary, "can compete with this dry-goods palace." Yet Hone's admiration for this monument to the enterprise of a fellow-citizen was tempered by a slight disdain for what he termed a "useless piece of extravagance. Several of the windows on the first floor, nearly level with the street, are formed of plate glass, six feet by eleven, which must have cost four or five hundred dollars each, and may be shivered by a boy's marble or a snowball as effectively as by a four pound shot."

In early October the Mowatts were in Boston to fill an engagement made some time before. The city greeted its adopted daughter with jubilation. Lily had no doubt now that Boston was her special province and she saw to it that no one should dispute her sway. She was beginning to learn the ways of the theatre in this respect, as a note from James to Chippendale reveals very clearly:

Tremont House
Saturday evening
[October 24, 1846]

My dear Chippendale:

Before returning home when I told Mrs. Mowatt that her name was after Augusta's [Mlle. Augusta, a dancer, also appearing at the Howard] in the Posters as well as in the newspapers, she flatly refused to play on Monday Night—now it is an undeniable fact that Mr. Hackett applied to me to let Augusta in on our engagement, as a favor to the theatre.

The engagement was ours and not Mdmll. Augusta's and Mrs. Mowatt will not yield her right of position.

The small handbills, if printed must be suppressed and the names of Mrs. Mowatt and Mr. Davenport, be the first ones in the list of names in new bills—this is the only way the matter can now be reconcilable to her. On Tuesday she will expect to play Much Ado, and not substitute any other—

Yours very truly
James Mowatt

The newspaper advertisements show that Chippendale at once complied with James's request, both as to billing and as to the performance of *Much Ado*, about which apparently there had been some disagreement.

From Boston, James and Lily and Davenport went to New York; and then they moved south to Richmond. Here Lily met her brother-in-law, Isadore Guillet, and his three boys—whom she had not seen since the death of her sister Charlotte a year before. Guillet, Charlotte's second husband, was a wild Frenchman whose life, in which Charlotte had shared for a few brief years, had been a series of regular movements from the crest to the trough of the wave. Just now he was in the latter situation, as is evident from details given by Marion Harland in her *Autobiography*.

Marion Harland, now scarcely remembered but one of the most prolific writers of the late nineteenth century and the mother of Albert Payson Terhune, lived in Richmond as a child. At Mrs. Nottingham's private school for young ladies she was taught French by Isadore Guillet. She knew little about him except that he was the brother-in-law of the celebrated Mrs. Mowatt, and that a series of misfortunes had brought him to Mrs. Nottingham's. "He had lost wife and fortune in the same year." He was an extraordinary figure, "six feet something, superbly proportioned and heavily moustachioed. . . ." The latter detail was particularly glamorous for the young ladies of the school; for the mustache was at that time an exoticism in America. "I have never known a man who could, at pleasure, be such a savage and such a gentleman. . . ." Poor Guillet! If anything were calculated to reduce a vigorous and romantic Frenchman to savagery, it would have been the necessity of teaching French to a group of near-illiterate little girls in ante-bellum Richmond.

Lily makes no mention of the encounter with her brother-in-law. Perhaps it was not wholly friendly, for Guillet had led poor Charlotte a hard life. But Lily must have been happy to see the boys. She was a second mother to all her numerous nieces and nephews, at least half of whom at various times lived under her roof. Guillet's oldest son, Stanislas, was especially close to her later on.

There was another interest attached to the Richmond engagement, though Anna Cora may not have been aware of it then. In the audience at the performance of *Ingomar* was a young journalist, William Foushee Ritchie, son of the editor and publisher of *The Richmond Enquirer*. The elder Ritchie was an old acquaintance of Samuel Ogden, and it is likely that there was a meeting between his son and the beautiful Mrs. Mowatt. Whether they met or not, from the moment Foushee Ritchie first saw Anna Cora in the classic robes of Parthenia he was a man obsessed; and though in his wildest fancies he can hardly have conceived that this exquisite creature might one day be his, the passion aroused by this first glimpse of her persisted. In the end, as it happened, fate was on his side.

From Richmond the party took the steamer for Charleston. Here, after a round of nearly the same pieces in which Lily had been seen the previous year, they moved on to Savannah, where Lily appeared in a memorable performance of Kotzebue's *The Stranger*. This play, the German epitome of the sentimental melodrama invented by the French in the eighteenth century, had first been presented in America by William Dunlap, who had also translated the work. It had held the stage as a prime favorite for two generations, and still had some years of lively existence before it.

Anna Cora could scarcely have maintained her position as a star without appearing at least two or three times a season in the rôle of Mrs. Haller. This lady, the stage ancestress of Ibsen's Nora, was said to have produced more tears than all the wars and natural catastrophes of the nineteenth century put together. How she did this is hardly comprehensible to us now— unless it was by a process of infection. Mrs. Haller through most of the play is dissolved in tears of regret at having in a moment of unthinking waywardness abandoned her home and family. At the conclusion, when she is forgiven by her husband (the Stranger) and is reunited with her children, there is a veritable concert of weeping in which not only her immediate family, but relatives and servants, join in. Anna Cora did the part in her own fashion. She greatly heightened its effectiveness by portraying Mrs. Haller as a woman who has made her bed and is determined to lie on it—until gradually the consciousness of the destructiveness of her action comes home to her. Then her repentance becomes more believable and gives added force to her reactions when she finds she has been forgiven by her husband. This is not at all what Kotzebue intended, but it was the only way Lily could make the part palatable. It was enormously successful, and the memory of Lily's Mrs. Haller remained with people long after the play had dropped into oblivion.

But in Savannah the performance of *The Stranger* was remembered less for Mrs. Mowatt's original interpretation than for an unexpected development in the last act which Anna Cora herself recorded with gusto.

In this act the play calls for the appearance of two children. In Savannah, for some reason, the infants who usually played these parts were not available and the manager had not been able to find substitutes. At the last moment Lily was approached by the young mulatto maid whom she had hired for the engagement. With some hesitation the girl spoke about the problem of the children and offered to supply the deficiency. Lily brightened at the suggestion and inquired to whom the little ones belonged.

"They are mine, ma'am," answered the maid.

"Yours!" Lily was aghast. "Why, Mrs. Haller's children are supposed to be white." She did not mean to be tactless; but she was so astonished that the remark escaped her inadvertently.

The young woman did not seem to mind. She hastened to reassure Mrs. Mowatt. "Oh, my children are not *very* black, ma'am, seeing as how their father is altogether white. The little girl has blue eyes, and they have both got hair almost as light as yours; then you might powder them up a bit, if you thought best."

Since curtain time was near and the manager had failed to turn up any children for the parts, Lily told the maid to send her own offspring to the theatre. When they arrived, Lily saw that they were really lovely little creatures, with light cream-

colored complexions and long curly hair. Since the children had
no lines to speak, their accent would not reveal their origin, while
a judicious application of rice powder would render their complexions quite satisfactory.

Until their appearance in the last act, Lily had them bedded
down on a bundle of shawls in a corner of the dressing-room,
where they might take a nap until called for their scene. The
pair, plied with candy, went promptly to sleep. When the call
boy came for them he had great difficulty waking them and
setting them on their feet. However he finally succeeded in
getting them to the stage, where they were turned over to the
actor who would lead them on for the reunion with their
mother—in the grand scene in which Mrs. Haller makes her
climactic bid for her husband's (and the audience's) sympathy.
Still half-dazed with sleep, the children were led before the footlights. Suddenly confronted with the brilliant ramp of gas-
flames and the black maw of the auditorium, they became not
only wide awake: they began to scream with terror. They broke
from their guide and started to run wildly about the stage. They
were cornered at last by the stage servant who dragged them to
the door of the cottage where they were to be hidden until their
mother approached. But something in the shape of the painted
canvas hut, and the door swinging open, called up to both children fearful visions of the Savannah guard-house where captured runaway slaves were held pending return to their owners
and whatever punishment might be expected. They began to
struggle more frantically than ever, and to shriek in unmistakable accent:

"Oh, don't ee put me in ee guard-house! Don't ee put me
in ee guard-house!"

With these words the audience realized at once what the children were, and the house broke into uproarious laughter. Anna
Cora quickly made her entrance in the hope of somehow steer-
ing the performance back onto a normal course. But before she
had time to reflect, she had given the line that usually reduced
the house to a final flood of tears: Mrs. Haller's plea that she
might be allowed just once—before disappearing into oblivion

—"to kiss the features of the father in his babes." At this, the rafters fairly rang with laughter. The performance was beyond salvaging; and so, as Anna Cora relates, "We hurried the play to a close"—although by what means, short of a fast curtain, she does not specify.

There is a sequel to this episode which Anna Cora herself probably never knew. Ten years after her appearance in Savannah as Mrs. Haller, another popular actress, Eliza Logan, turned up to play the same part. At the rehearsal Miss Logan observed that the child engaged for the rôle of the little boy had a somewhat dark complexion. She questioned him and learned that his mother was colored.

"That's singular," remarked Miss Logan; "I seem to remember having heard that Mrs. Mowatt, when she played that part here, had a colored child for the part of William."

"Dat's so, missis; I is de bery chile."

"You? Why, it's ten years ago."

"Yes, missis, but I is a Quadroon Dwarf, an' I been playin' de Stronjer's chile for all de Stronjers wot been comin' to Savannah for de las' *twelve years*."

Despite the slight contretemps in *The Stranger*, the Savannah season was one of the happiest of the whole tour. The warmhearted town, in which Lily had many personal acquaintances, took her to its bosom. When the time came to leave, a group of leading citizens gave her a testimonial banquet. "We take this method of at once expressing our thanks for the exquisite enjoyment you have afforded us in your various personations, and our high respect for you personally." Thus read the invitation. "A lady of your character and attainments elevates and adorns the stage; and we have no doubt that your influence will be widely felt in purifying it from the abuses which sometimes mar its beauties, and that you will cause it to perform its proper task—'To raise the genius and to mend the heart.' "

This was not the first intimation that Lily had had of the rôle in which popular opinion had cast her. Being who she was and what she was, it was inevitable that she should be assigned the mission of making the theatre respectable. If the mission had involved any overt action on her part she undoubtedly would have shied away from it, for she had none of the impulses of the reformer. But since nothing more was involved than that she be herself, she was willing to let it go at that. She knew that, with a public eager for enjoyment but shackled by a middle-class ideal of respectability, the combination of an impeccable character, recognized social position, and the glamor of the theatre was irresistible.

Within the theatre there was less enthusiasm for the newcomer. Her extraordinary success at the very start had naturally excited jealousy among the meaner spirits in the profession. When to this was added the ingredient of an imputed motive "to reform the stage," there developed inevitably among many of her new associates an attitude of antagonism toward her. As time went on, this clouded Anna Cora's happiness in her work. Although she acquired countless staunch and devoted friends in the theatre, particularly among its more humble members who had reason to remember her kindness and generosity, she was never able wholly to overcome the sense that she was an outsider. For the next months, however, she was too deeply plunged in work, too filled with the satisfaction of living creatively and of making her own way, to feel the growing frictions.

Once again the chief objective of the southern tour was an engagement with Smith and Ludlow in their New Orleans and Mobile theatres. There was now an unfilled interval of ten days between the stop in Savannah and the date of the opening in Mobile. Anna Cora and Davenport decided to fill the time and break the journey west with one-night stands. From Savannah they traveled overland by stage to Macon, thence to Columbus, and on to Montgomery, where they took a steamboat down the Alabama River to Mobile.

In none of these towns were there regular theatres with organized acting companies. So Lily and Davenport appeared together in small halls where Lily recited and Davenport supplied interludes of ballad-singing, an art for which he had considerable talent. Lily found reciting a distinct bore, and somewhat uncomfortable. She missed the footlights, the atmosphere of the stage—above all, the excitement of a play. "I longed for the illusion," she writes, "the self-forgetfulness. On the stage I was *somebody else*—in the lecture room I could not rise out of myself."

Up until now the weather had been beautiful, clear and balmy. However, no sooner had the party arrived at Mobile than it began to pour—a repetition of their previous year's experience. James, writing to an unidentified correspondent, said that the "fog and rain melted away our audience." He spoke of Mrs. Mowatt's reluctance to play in Mobile, though he gave no reason for this. We can only deduce the weather, and the audiences that refused to come out in it.

Yet in New Orleans, where Lily opened early in February, everything was fine. Regardless of the weather (in New Orleans too it rained steadily), the St. Charles was well patronized. Ludlow writing of this engagement in his memoirs repeats what his partner Smith had said of the previous season in *his* memoirs: namely, that Anna Cora "played to good business."

For public and critics alike, the climax of the engagement was *The Stranger*. Lily's rendering of Mrs. Haller caused the New Orleans papers to overcome their usual taciturnity toward the drama and break into expansive tributes. James, who from the start had showed himself an adept in handling the business side of his wife's career, promptly forwarded a copy of *The New Orleans Commercial Bulletin*, containing a particularly excited notice, to his father-in-law, with instructions that he try to get the notice published by *The Courier and Enquirer* in New York. It was important now to keep Lily's name before the public during her long absences on tour. Ogden wrote to Samuel Ruggles, with whom Lily had long been a special favorite, to use his influence in getting the New Orleans notice reprinted. This, Ruggles was delighted to do.

The New Orleans engagement lasted nearly a month, one of the longest of any star in the history of the St. Charles Theatre up to that time. But at the end of February poor Lily was back in Mobile, the helpless victim of the Smith-Ludlow policy of keeping their stars shuttling from one town to the other. In the

Mobile company this time, were a family destined to occupy a very conspicuous place in American theatre history: Mr. and Mrs. James W. Wallack and their son, Lester. Lily played Portia to Wallack senior's Shylock, while Ludlow himself did Gratiano. Portia must have been a part ideally suited to Anna Cora's style and personality, but she never had more than one or two opportunities to play it. She rarely found herself in a company with an "old man" of sufficient stature to do Shylock. The same thing was true of her Desdemona—by all accounts one of her most moving performances—which she also did with Wallack senior in Mobile. Only once afterwards did she have a chance to play it with a first-rate Othello.

It had been planned originally that the tour would end, as in the previous year, at New Orleans. But in January James began negotiations to play the Mississippi valley to St. Louis and then on to Louisville and Cincinnati. Lily had never been in better form, and she was eager to enlarge her public to include the western cities. There was no difficulty in arranging with the St. Louis theatre, since this, too, was now part of the Smith-Ludlow chain, and Sol Smith was in active charge. But the only dates open were in the middle of June. James tried to secure contracts in Louisville and Cincinnati to fill the gap, but was unable to get satisfactory terms from J. C. Bates who operated the houses in both cities.

Bates was very canny in the matter. He knew about the St. Louis engagement and he knew that Mowatt would be willing to bargain in order to keep his wife busy in what would other- wise have been a long idle stretch of several weeks. But James had become a master strategist in these things himself. First of all, the gap was shortened by a re-engagement in New Orleans which would run until early April. Then James let it be known that his wife intended to come to Cincinnati in any case, to pay a long visit to her sister, Mrs. Wellman. This news, circulated perhaps by the Wellmans, immediately put Bates in an embar- rassing situation. He saw that, should it become known that the celebrated Mrs. Mowatt was in the city but that the public would have no opportunity to see her, his own position would be untenable. So he yielded at last, and met James's terms. Lily was engaged to open the new Athenaeum in Cincinnati. But he would do nothing about an engagement at Louisville. Bates had lost money steadily in that city all winter and he was unwilling to invest in such an expensive attraction as Mrs. Mowatt for a public which had shown itself so ungrateful for all his earlier efforts. This was not a very wise decision for Bates, as we shall see presently.

Meanwhile Lily and Davenport were reaping fat profits in New Orleans. *Fashion* had been produced again with great success and several new items had been added to Lily's repertory—including Milman's *Fazio*, another simulated pearl in the tinsel crown of nineteenth-century drama.

Shortly before she left New Orleans, Lily received a distinguished caller—Henry Clay. The meeting was probably prompted by Sargent, who not long since had written Clay's biography. Clay could hardly have required much urging, for he had more than a casual eye for a pretty woman. At any rate the visit gave much pleasure on both sides; and since Clay was preparing to go north to Kentucky at about this time, it was arranged that he would join the Mowatts and Davenport at Natchez, where Lily was to play for a couple of nights after leaving New Orleans, and they would travel up-river together. The Natchez rendezvous came off as planned. Mrs. Mowatt and her party were at the landing when the *Alexander Scott* hove in. A large delegation of citizens had turned out to greet the hero of the West (no defeated presidential candidate ever enjoyed greater popularity than Clay), and Lily boarded the steamboat under a shower of roses and cape jessamine.

The five-day trip to Louisville remained always with Lily as one of the happiest experiences of her life. The presence of two such celebrities, neither of whom encroached on the other's territory, kept the whole boat in a state of pleasant excitement. The *Alexander Scott*, named for one of the most notable early Mississippi River pilots, was among the finest and most luxurious of the many "floating palaces" plying between New Orleans and the Ohio. To honor its two famous guests the boat outdid itself in the matter of food, drink and entertainment. There was dancing every night, and concerts in the afternoon, and the warm spring air cast over everything a delicate balm, relieved by the plunk of the banjo and the popping of champagne corks.

Davenport shared honors almost equally with Lily and Clay. He was one of those rare actors with liberal social endowments. He could not only sing and dance a hornpipe; he was also a delightful conversationalist, and constantly bubbling over with good humor. He loved practical jokes and did not hesitate to play one on Clay himself. At a small landing below Memphis, a Yankee trader boarded the boat. He epitomized the type, complete with fringe beard, striped pantaloons, flame-colored cravat and clam-chowder accent. He at once signified his desire to be presented to the great statesman, and approached James:

"Stranger, I hear that's Harry Clay; I guess I'll scrape acquaintance with him, if you'll do the polite thing."

James, managing to keep a straight face, introduced the colorful stranger to the great man. The Yankee immediately launched an uninterrupted flood of questions so that the conversation was completely one-sided, with Clay doing the listening—probably for the first time in his life. The other passengers were thrown into convulsions, and Clay himself smiled at the demonstration. It was Lily who finally decided that the matter had gone far enough and whispered the Yankee's identity to Clay. With that the haystack wig and false whiskers came off and the saloon resounded with laughter, in which Clay heartily took part.

In such innocent pleasures the days sped swiftly. Clay was particularly attentive to point out all matters of interest along the way. When they paused to take on passengers at Memphis, he waxed lyrical over the booming river port:

"This western Memphis makes more gigantic progress than any town I know. She will be the queen city of the west by and by." Rather sternly he issued the injunction: "Never pass here again without appearing!" This Anna Cora dutifully promised, and she kept her word—though it took six years to do so and it would have been better, on the whole, had she not.

On the last evening before the arrival at Louisville, a gala entertainment was held aboard the *Alexander Scott*. Lily wrote a song which Davenport set to music and sang before the assembled passengers. Clay thanked Davenport in a gracious period for his contribution to the pleasures of the trip, not omitting mention of his illustrious companion whose charming presence was alone such an asset.

At Louisville, Lily and her new admirer parted company. Twice, during the day Lily stayed in Louisville, Clay came to call; and though they never met again, Clay's interest, manifested by "many evidences," remained unabated so long as he lived.

Lily and James spent the night in Louisville, a fact which was impressed on the mind of the populace, and then took boat again for Cincinnati. This was on March 28. The following day *The Louisville Morning Courier* noted the departure in a tone of high indignation. It was monstrous that the people of the city would allow such a "distinguished actress and authoress to pass through without performing." But *The Courier* knew where the blame lay. "We regret that in consequence of the parsimony of a selfish, obstinate, and illiberal manager, the citizens of Louisville will not have an opportunity of seeing this lady on the stage. Mr. Bates, according to his uniform custom, dictated terms which no person with proper respect could assent to, and hence Mrs. M. leaves the city this morning for Pittsburgh. . . ."

It would have been beyond the endurance of civic pride to add that on the way to Pittsburgh Mrs. Mowatt would play at Mr. Bates's Cincinnati theatre. How *The Courier* could know that Mr. Bates had "dictated terms which no person with proper self-respect could assent to" is a mystery. Could it have been the active pen of James that had conveyed this piece of information to someone close to the editorial chair? It is only a likely supposition; for in any case *The Courier* had a fixed attitude towards Bates and had been sniping at him for some time. Earlier in March for instance it had editorialized thus:

> During his three seasons here, he [Bates] has introduced no novelties, played no new pieces, but has been butchering up all the old tragedies, farces and comedies, which have been extant none less than twenty years.

If Bates had had qualms about introducing Mrs. Mowatt to Cincinnatians, they were dissipated on the opening night. The town flocked to witness (of course) *The Lady of Lyons*; and the subsequent nights were equally prosperous. In deference to the highly publicized cultural level of Cincinnati the engagement was well ballasted with Shakespeare. In *Romeo and Juliet*, Lily and Davenport swept the city off its feet. This seems to have been one of the few renderings of the play not accompanied by minor catastrophes. Though Juliet was one of Lily's favorite parts she never appeared for her first scene on the balcony without trepidation. She could not seem to do the scene without leaning on the balcony rail, and most of the balcony rails constructed by stage carpenters did not lend themselves to this practical purpose.

The play also required properties: ladders, and daggers, and vials of sleeping-potion or poison. These too presented complications. Lily developed a distinct complex about the dagger with which Juliet kills herself in the last act. She invariably forgot it. Usually she could extract Romeo's furtively from his belt and make use of that, but this was hazardous. Her stabbing was always carried out with a certain realistic emphasis. Once, having forgotten her own weapon, she reached down for Romeo's and holding it high above her head was about to plunge it against her bosom when the voice of the dead scion of the Montagues suddenly shattered the silence:

"Look out—it's very sharp!"

On another occasion Anna Cora almost came to grief with the sleeping-potion. At the last moment it was discovered by the property-man that he had forgotten the right kind of vial. Friar Laurence was just about to make his entrance to give Juliet the vial, and the distraught property-man seized the nearest small bottle he could find and gave it to the actor playing the Friar. The bottle was duly turned over to Juliet on the stage, with some whispered injunction of which Anna Cora caught only the words ". . . so take care." She thought no more about the matter until she had swallowed the potion. Then she noted a brilliant red stain on her fingers when they came away from her mouth. Viewed from the audience it must have been very picturesque. Lily's own reactions were less pleasant, when at the close of the scene the prompter rushed on, crying:

"Good gracious, you have been drinking from my bottle of ink!" She smiled bravely and uttered the words of the dying wit under similar circumstances:

"Let me swallow a sheet of blotting paper. . . ."

Both Lily and Davenport became great favorites in Cincinnati. At the end of the engagement, the young men of the town made up a subscription and presented Davenport with a handsome gold watch and chain. Anna Cora records this with tender recollections of her old friend and associate. With characteristic modesty she makes no mention of the token of esteem which she herself received from the Cincinnatians: a brooch in the form of a spray of enamelled forget-me-nots with diamonds at their centers.

In Cincinnati, Lily found a pleasant innovation in the new theatre. Bates—either by his own initiative or at the insistence of the citizenry—had abolished the notorious "third tier" which everywhere, for as far back as anyone could remember, had been the exclusive domain of the prostitutes. At whatever prompting, it must have required courage of Bates to eliminate the time-honored institution; and Anna Cora gave him full credit for his action. This somewhat offset her irritation with him when she learned, upon arriving, that she was not only expected to give the customary opening address at the new theatre—but that she must write it as well. In the midst of everything else, which included work on several new parts, she had to sit down and dash off an ode celebrating Cincinnati, the drama, the muses and everything else appropriate to the occasion. On top of that she had to memorize it. The work, as she pointedly explains, was not a masterpiece and only an "emphatic delivery" concealed its weaknesses.

The original engagement had been for two weeks. So successful was it that another contract was offered and accepted, and yet a third, before the team could proceed on its way to St. Louis. Here, in what was really the West, Lily experienced a new kind of audience—unbelievably crude, noisy, and unexpected in their reactions. But their enthusiasm was unmatched by anything she had ever known.

Finally, in July, they were back in New York. A plan which had been under discussion for some months now crystallized. Except for Charlotte Cushman, no native actress had received the recognition which had come to Anna Cora in her two years in the American theatre. But the ultimate mark of success on the English-speaking stage must still come from London, and to London Anna Cora determined to go. She had no illusions about the ordeal which an attempt to win acceptance in England would involve. Other American actors had tried it and nearly all had failed. Even Charlotte Cushman, who at the moment was still in England, had won her way only after the bitterest struggle, and despite the reports published by the American papers, was enjoying just then but equivocal success.

Yet knowing the hazards—above all, the long-established prejudice against American importations in anything relating to the arts (Mr. Irving's *Sketch Book* was the only specimen of American literary genius that had yet won unreserved acclaim) —Anna Cora was resolved to do or die. In the two years of trouping in America under James's careful management, she had amassed a tidy sum; perhaps twenty-five or thirty thousand dollars. The London venture would be costly! But .Lily and James and Davenport, who of course would come along, were confident that it would succeed.

Lily's closest advisers, among them Chippendale and other English actors, assured her that her style and personality, so different from those of the American emissaries who had previously landed on Albion's shores, would offset the disadvantages of inexperience—a matter which the British would, of course, consider very seriously.

In order to make all arrangements beforehand on the spot, James decided to leave at once for England. After preparing the way he would return in the early autumn for Lily and accompany her and Davenport back in October. So, armed with a variety of letters to all sorts of people and Lily's book of press-clippings, James sailed for Liverpool in early August. Before his departure he and Lily went to see the little Greys. It was at this time that James legally adopted the three children.

Lily retired at once to her father's house where, surrounded by her adoring family, she went immediately to work. The object of her labors was not a series of new parts, but a new play. She had had an idea in the back of her mind for some time; and since everyone had assured her that her reputation as an authoress would enormously enhance her prestige in the eyes of the British, she thought it would be useful to have another play in her trunk. She had no sooner let it be known that she was again in the throes of authorship than Simpson instantly offered her a contract to produce the new work before her departure for England. Since Mrs. Mowatt's name had become for Simpson personally a touchstone of prosperity, he did not even bother to inquire what the play would be about, and the contract was signed before a word had been written.

So all summer long in her high-ceilinged bedroom Lily wrote feverishly. Composition took place in the morning, revision in the afternoon, and trial readings before the assembled family, sisters and patriarch, in the evening. The general tone of the auditory was one of loving admiration, but this did not prevent a good deal of tart criticism from time to time. Some of the suggestions were good, and many scenes were rearranged and passages rewritten on the advice of the sisters. Lily never lost her ability to make the most of constructive criticism.

Armand, the work of this summer, was a strictly tailor-made affair. It was aimed specifically at the British public and incorporated all of the standard effects of Knowles, Tobin and Talfourd which were considered so artistic. It also contained parts especially designed for Davenport and herself (she would never make the mistake of writing another Gertrude!).

In *Armand* Lily turned her back on the contemporary scene. She had gotten away with it once, but she would not risk it twice. The new play was set in eighteenth-century France, at the court of Louis XV. It had a wonderfully serpentine plot centering about the beautiful Blanche, daughter of the Duc de

Richelieu by a clandestine marriage, who grows up in the care of an old peasant woman—in ignorance of her noble parentage. In the course of time Blanche, the village belle, attracts the roving eye of the king, whose pleasance is near the rude hut in which she lives. Conflict develops between the king and Blanche's peasant sweetheart, Armand (the Child of the People, as the play's subtitle had it). Armand is Adam Trueman in more youthful and romantic guise. He has republican ideas which he expresses in the presence of the king. For his subversiveness he is shipped off to the wars where he quickly achieves wealth, fame and high rank; and manages, in due course, to save the king's life. Before this, however, the king has tried to force Blanche into a marriage with a reprobate nobleman. Blanche's father, the Duc de Richelieu, who has watched over his daughter at a distance, in order to save her from this fate gives her a sleeping-potion which will create the semblance of death. Blanche takes the potion, is properly wept over by all not in the secret, and is then hurried off to the safety of a nunnery. In the end, happily, she is joined to Armand by the king, who is remorseful at his own vile intentions and grateful to his subject for saving his life.

"The plot," Anna Cora warns us, "is not strictly historical, but it has some slight historical foundation." At least the names of the noble personages were accurate, although some critics seemed to think that the piece followed Bulwer's *Richelieu* because a character of that time figured in it. Lily got rather weary of telling people that there were several Richelieus in French history, and that she was writing about the time of Louis XV, not XIII. There might have been a touch of Bulwer in the idea of sending Armand off to the army—but then this was a classic device for maneuvering a low-born hero quickly into a position of eminence. Of course there was a generous helping of Shakespeare—notably the affair of the potion, and the refuge in the nunnery (a neat telescoping of *Romeo and Juliet* into *A Winter's Tale*). But here too the play was adhering strictly to the requirements of the age, as in the matter of the dialogue which is mainly in blank verse. On this count the play must be ranked with the best which the times produced (a doubtful honor!). Anna Cora's verse is not only "correct" and "chaste," thus meeting the chief criteria of critical judgment of that day —it is also pleasing, and occasionally witty.

On September 1, 1847, *Armand* was put into rehearsal at the Park with Anna Cora in full command. The play was to open on the 7th. This meant an entire week of rehearsal, which the author had insisted upon. The cast in all likelihood did not take to the idea, since it meant double rehearsal time for those who were already playing an engagement with nightly changes of bill. On one point there was particular objection. Anna Cora insisted upon reading the play to the cast before rehearsals began. The attitude of the actors toward this practice (which a hardy playwright sometimes resorted to in order to save later arguments about points of interpretation) is set forth in *Mimic Life*:

> When rehearsal was over [i.e. rehearsal of the regular stock piece] the company reluctantly collected in the green room. Stella was surprised at the discontented tone of their remarks. What was the use, they asked, of Mr. Belton's insistence on the old-fashioned idea of a green-room reading? Hundreds of theatres got up new plays without the actors being bothered with anything but their own parts; scarcely any of them had the remotest idea of the plot. "What's the play about?" was a common question after it had been enacted for a week, and didn't everything go just as well? Leave the plot to the audience; the actors had enough to do attending to their own characters.

The cast assembled by Simpson was not up to that of *Fashion,* but there were good people in the parts that counted most. Davenport played Armand; the role "suited his vigorous and impulsive style of acting." Mr. Barry did the Duc de Richelieu; Mrs. Vernon was old Babette (Blanche's foster-mother), and lovely Kate Horn, who later achieved a fine name for herself, performed Babette's daughter. The house was sold out in advance for the première and for several subsequent nights.

The opening of *Armand* was an ordeal different from any that Anna Cora had yet passed through. As both star and author she had a double weight of responsibility. She was harassed with fears that the other actors might muddle their lines; that the sets would not be right; that properties would be missing; that the audience might not like the play. Consequently she had little awareness of the part she was performing. Nevertheless the consensus was that her Blanche was utterly delightful. Davenport as Armand drew the best notices of his career up to this point. The play itself was greeted as a work of genius.

At the close of the run, Lily and Davenport went immediately to Boston for their farewell engagement before sailing for England. They played a round of the usual things, including *Much Ado About Nothing*. Beatrice was now Anna Cora's favorite role, and she brought to the part—aided by Davenport's bright and vigorous Benedick—a sharp freshness, a kind of dancing gaiety, yet with an undertone of warm tenderness, that Bostonians never forgot.

Armand was also produced in Boston and was very much to the city's taste. *The Courier* said that it was "full of beautiful poetry" and "though romantic, its romance has the true energy of elevated feeling, not the sickly feebleness of sentimentality."

On October 27 *The Transcript* reported that Mrs. Mowatt was to sail shortly on the *Cambria* for England. *The Courier* took the occasion to pay special tribute:

> We are aware of no living actress who competes with her in the intense imagination of her embodiments of character, of the affections, of the brilliant grace and archness of her comic representations. She possesses qualities of mind and person that fit her beyond all her contemporaries in the representation of the highest *ideal* emotions of the drama. Her fame will eventually rest on her personation of such characters as Juliet, Ophelia, Desdemona, Cordelia, Viola, Beatrice and Rosalind.

In Boston, Lily had been rejoined by James on his return from England. He had secured a contract with the Theatre Royal in Manchester for two weeks at the end of November. He had done this at the advice of Macready, to whom he had presented letters of introduction. Macready, now the leading figure on the English stage, had not been encouraging about a London engagement, but he had heard much of Mrs. Mowatt and generously offered to do everything he could. It was Macready who pointed out that for a stranger without a London name, the only hope of obtaining an engagement in the capitol was to appear first in the provinces. This would give London managers an opportunity to see the newcomer before risking a commitment.

It was not altogether a heartening prospect, but the great success of the final American engagements, particularly the two weeks in Boston, cast a rosy glow over everything. Despite the outlook of an uncertain future in England, and the prospect of a rough November crossing of the Atlantic, the Mowatts and Davenport embarked on the *Cambria* with confidence. This was partly inspired by the ship, the fastest and most luxurious vessel in the North-Atlantic service. Her schedule from Boston to Liverpool was fourteen days, to which she adhered with amazing fidelity. She was an expensive ship to travel on; first-class passage cost $120. But no one begrudged the price, least of all Lily when she compared the *Cambria*'s size and speed with those of the little *Queen Mab* on which she had made her first crossing of the ocean.

Epes Sargent had come up to Boston to see them off. He was still Anna Cora's close advisor, and the indispensable guide in maintaining her health. Her chief medical resource continued to be mesmerism, and Sargent was the only practitioner to whom she now entrusted herself. There had been several times during the past two years when mesmerism had been needed to keep her going, and it was a matter of concern to both James and Lily that Sargent would now be separated from them by the breadth of the Atlantic. It was Lily who found the solution for the problem, and the last note in the record before the actual sailing tells us how. Sargent himself reported the story:

> Before their departure I imparted to . . . Davenport, by the direction of Mrs. Mowatt in her somnambulic state, all the information that would enable him to induce somnambulism in her case should she fall ill.

More versatile than his fondest admirers dreamed, Davenport henceforth would serve not only as leading man to Lily, but also as attending hypnotist.

CHAPTER SIXTEEN

The Siege of London

The *Cambria* arrived in Liverpool on November 15—a day late. The whole voyage across, she had battled violent gales and mountainous waves. In mid-ocean one of her engines had broken down; but it had been repaired. When she at last eased into Liverpool harbor, the passengers could scarcely believe they had reached safety. The same feeling was evident in the wondering looks of the throng that lined the dock to welcome her, for the *Cambria* had been reported lost. Indeed, another ship on the same run, the *Stephen Philip,* had gone down with ninety-one passengers.

Lily had been wretchedly sick throughout the crossing, and not until she had rested a week in a Liverpool hotel was she able to stagger to her feet. Fortunately the Manchester opening was not until December 6. But seasickness had not been the greatest of Lily's miseries. In the middle of the grey, storm-whipped

ANNA CORA MOWATT AS *Beatrice*
Collection of the Author

Atlantic, between the pangs of nausea—aggravated by the dreadful vibration of the ship's single functioning paddle wheel —the high courage with which she had embarked on this English venture began to wane. Away from the atmosphere of warm adulation with which she had been surrounded in America, she now saw the whole prospect in the cold light of reality.

· Many American actors had tried to storm the smooth hard rock of English opinion, and nearly all had been thrust back in ignominy. The classic instance was Edwin Forrest. The most popular star in America had twice made a bid for the favor of London and failed miserably. Only Charlotte Cushman, by a combination of daring and obtuseness—qualities which the British could appreciate—had made a place for herself. Even that place was none too secure. Few of the critics denied Miss Cushman's great gifts, but they generally found her heavy going. Their attitude toward her was often one of respectful irritation, such as was reflected in the critic-playwright Weston Marsland's later comment: "Her unrelieved, level earnestness of manner gave her Lady Macbeth a sameness of gloom which fatigued admiration." But there *was* admiration.

Anna Cora knew all this. When she thought of Edwin Forrest, she shuddered. Nor was she greatly encouraged by the example of Miss Cushman. She did not presume for a moment to think that, because Miss Cushman had won the reluctant approval of British playgoers, she could do the same. She had none of Miss Cushman's powerful physical equipment, and certainly none of "Captain Charlotte's" blunt manner and awe-inspiring determination which enabled her to roll over obstacles as though they did not exist. If Lily were to make any impression on the British it would be for different reasons. She could never (*would* never) play "breeches" parts. Miss Cushman had acted Romeo with a virility which charmed by its novelty: the critics had proclaimed her performance more convincing than Charles Kean's. But Lily was all woman. Whatever gifts she had were emphasized by her essential femininity. She hoped this would be recognized. But she had no way of knowing.

Meanwhile the date of the début was inexorably approaching.

Anna Cora felt the need of comfort and moral support to bolster her flagging spirits. In all difficult situations now, her first recourse was to her religion. As soon as the party arrived in Manchester she and James called at once on the leader of the Swedenborgian congregation and his wife. They were received warmly. The Reverend Mr. Smithson offered spiritual cheer, while Mrs. Smithson undertook to smooth the strangers' way in a purely practical manner. She assured Lily that the Manchester critics were ruthless, and that the most fearsome of all was the critic of *The Examiner*. However, she had some slight acquaintance with this gentleman, and promptly went to call on him. She had the notion that she might soften him towards the fair newcomer (he was notoriously anti-American) by giving him some details of Mrs. Mowatt's history. This was a tactical error. The critic was not touched by Mrs. Smithson's information. When she left his presence, she had the feeling that he might be very severe indeed.

In the same way, another anxious friend approached the critic of *The Manchester Guardian* with the suggestion that he might like to meet Mrs. Mowatt personally. This pleasure the critic declined on the ground that a personal acquaintance before the début might cloud his judgment. All of which indicated to Lily that she could expect anything from the Manchester press but sympathy.

Nevertheless the Smithsons did everything within their power to assure some sort of welcome for the Americans. They rallied the New Jerusalem Church to the cause, and the congregation pledged their support of Mrs. Mowatt if she "betrayed the slightest glimmering of genius."

If the advance notices in the papers were not frankly hostile, they were at least skeptical. The *Guardian* on December 4 published the following comment:

> The lady about whom high expectations have been raised by the encomiums of the American critics, makes her début in England at our own Theatre Royal on Monday next, and she is to appear in a round of well-known characters during her engagement here. The variety of Mrs. Mowatt's literary productions prove her to be

a lady of highly cultivated mind, and as she is understood never to have seen any of the parts in which she is to appear, performed by any other actress, we shall at least have the charm of originality in what she does: Monday night will prove whether she combines therewith the high histrionic powers for which American critics have given her credit. . . . [Here followed a passage from the introduction to *The Modern Standard Drama*—edited by Epes Sargent—giving the facts of Mrs. Mowatt's career. This had probably been handed the *Guardian* by the anxious Mrs. Smithson. The article ended on a note of suspicion.] Either Mrs. Mowatt's dramatic talents are of a high order or American criticism is deeply tainted with exaggeration.

Both Lily and Davenport had expected to be received coolly by the company at the Theatre Royal; but nothing had prepared them for the atmosphere of "impenetrable frigidity" when they walked on the stage for their first rehearsal. No hands of welcome were extended the newcomers. Instead there were tight-lipped smiles of contempt, and a few remarks of commiseration with the foreigners over their impending slaughter. Mostly, the company treated Lily and Davenport as though they did not exist.

The attitude of the audience on the first night was hardly more cordial. It said merely "let us see what you can do"—and no more. Yet it did promise the stars a fair hearing (Lily recalled this gratefully afterwards), and that was what they mainly asked. Still, for the first three acts of *The Lady of Lyons*, they might have been playing to empty seats, so icy was the silence. Manchester folk, including the small nucleus of Mr. Smithson's faithful, were apparently not going to make up their minds in a hurry. Neither Lily nor Davenport had ever experienced anything quite like this total lack of response. They went into the fourth act with the feeling that they were simply playing for each other.

Then with no warning, as the curtain fell on the act, there was a burst of applause, as complete and determined as the silence which had accompanied the preceding acts. At the curtain of the fifth act the applause was long and noisy and, as Lily put it, fully "atoned for the shyness of our reception." So cordial were the feelings now demonstrated that the visitors thought some sign of recognition on their part was in order. Accordingly Davenport, after he and Lily had taken their bows, advanced to the footlights and made an eloquent little speech, very gentlemanly and dignified. This display of good manners further heightened the audience's approval, and the evening closed with indisputable evidence that the stars "were in."

When the two left the stage they noted at once a change on the part of their fellow-players. There was a very respectful "making way" and "sneers and innuendoes were magically converted into smiles and congratulations."

The papers next morning confirmed the impression of the evening. Although the critic of *The Examiner* was as severe as he had warned Mrs. Smithson he would be, he was forced to admit that the Americans had made a hit with the British audience. The critic of the *Guardian* (whose conscience was so completely pure) devoted a long column to the newcomers' art, beginning:

> Exaggeration of a peculiar kind, if not rant, has been so uniformly a characteristic of all the American actors whom we have seen, that we have been induced to view it as an attribute of the American stage. That it is not an inseparable attribute, the chastened style of the artists . . . who made their English *début* at our Theatre Royal on Monday evening, in the Lady of Lyons, satisfactorily demonstrates. . . .

The critic then proceeded to comment on Anna Cora personally, going so far as to state: ". . . we know of none of our English actresses who stand a comparison with her except Mrs. Butler."

To anyone familiar with Mrs. Butler's (Fanny Kemble's) most recent experiences in Manchester, this might have seemed somewhat equivocal praise. This lady had preceded Lily and Davenport to England by some weeks and had opened the season in Manchester. There she had astonished (and in some quarters outraged) the audience by interpolating a southern plantation song and dance in the middle of *The School for Scandal*. Probably she had done this to jolt the audience out of its impassivity, which had gotten on her nerves. The effect had certainly been startling, but not as intended. A good many people had walked out of the theatre, and the succeeding nights of her engagement were played to almost empty houses. Nevertheless her general reputation in England was still high, and the critic of the *Guardian* had this in mind in comparing Mrs. Mowatt to her.

By the end of their fortnight there, the critic of *The Manchester Guardian* had assumed an almost paternal air toward the newcomers. For Lily his admiration was deep and sincere. In his final review he stated that she had "an ensemble of personal requisites not excelled by anyone on the stage." "She is the most refined American actor whom we have yet seen." Of Davenport, the *Guardian* critic was prepared to say that "with the exception of Mr. Macready there is no actor on the stage who *interests* us more powerfully than he does." He predicted that the visitors would make an early sojourn in London—which was of course precisely what Lily and Davenport fervently hoped.

James had been unable to arrange an engagement in the metropolis during the summer; but he had obtained a promise from J. M. Maddox, manager of the Princess's Theatre, that he would come to Manchester to see Lily, and that if he was satisfied with what he saw, the question of an engagement would be discussed. Maddox kept his word. He came to Manchester and was sufficiently impressed to offer Lily and Davenport a contract to open almost immediately in London.

It might seem strange that Maddox should have hesitated in the first place, since he took little if any financial risk in hiring the transatlantic stars. Though no details of the contract are known, James wrote later to Chippendale that he had spent eight hundred pounds before Lily and Davenport had attracted enough attention "to make it worth the while of the managers to remunerate us." It must therefore be assumed that both the Manchester and the first London engagements were financed by Lily herself. This was, of course, a perfectly normal procedure. It was the only way that a manager could be induced to risk his own reputation in presenting a newcomer of unproven merit.

Maddox, on the whole, had made rather a good thing of this method. He had brought out a number of foreign stars in London, all with fine reputations in their native lands but unknown to London audiences. But he had had the bad luck to present Forrest in his second visit to England, and the memory of that experience probably tempered his confidence in Mrs. Mowatt. Macready had put in a good word for her however, and when Maddox had seen her act in Manchester he decided at once to take a chance. It was arranged that Lily and Davenport would do a six-weeks' stand at the Princess's, playing alternate nights. The other evenings would be given to Madame Thillon, a French light opera star who was also trying to establish herself in London.

The Americans had hoped to open in *The Lady of Lyons*. No matter what she thought of the play, Lily knew that it was a test piece and the surest means of winning recognition among the English. However, the royalty for the play was twenty pounds, and this Maddox at the last moment refused to pay. Doubtless if Lily had chosen, James would have paid the royalty himself; but they both possibly felt that they were already in so deep that they must watch every penny from now on. So, as a compromise, Sheridan Knowles's *The Hunchback* was the first offering.

If Lily and Davenport had been taken aback by their reception at the first rehearsal in Manchester, the Princess's was an ordeal requiring all their courage. Here, no effort was made to conceal the contempt felt for the Americans; and it was evident at the outset that the company were tolerating them only because they were under contract themselves to Maddox. If it was known that Mrs. Mowatt was actually paying their salaries (supposing that the contract with Maddox was based on Lily's meeting the running expenses of the theatre on the nights she and Davenport appeared), this only heightened their antagonism towards the presumptuous foreigners.

The first rehearsal was like

... a lane of nettles, so narrow that we could not avoid getting scratched. The more gently they were touched the more deeply they stung. At the request, politely urged, of "Be so good as to cross to the right—I occupy the left"—the answer dryly returned was, "Excuse me; I played this part originally with Mrs. Butler at Drury Lane—I always kept this position—it is *the proper* situation." Then there was a significant look at the prompter which said, "This republican dust offends us! We must get rid of it!"

Finally, Lily could endure it no longer. She became so irritated at being told by one member of the company that Mrs. Butler sat this way, or Miss Faucit fainted another way, or Mrs. Kean did thus and such, that she turned on him and said firmly:

"Sir, when I have made up my mind to become the mere imitator of Mrs. Butler, or of Miss Faucit, or of Mrs. Kean, I shall come to *you* for instruction. At present it is for the public to decide upon the faultiness of my conception. I shall not alter it, in spite of the very excellent authority you have cited."

This declaration of independence was effective in silencing the spoken criticism of the company. What they thought was still obvious from their looks, but fortunately Lily was somewhat nearsighted.

The first rehearsal was made doubly agonizing by an incident involving a fellow-American. Susan Cushman, who had come to London to join her sister Charlotte, had for some months been a regular member of the Princess's company. Susan had little talent for the stage but she had good looks and a figure "to please the fellows," in the words of George Vandenhoff. Her particular line was that of "walking lady." She and Lily were not strangers to each other; Susan had played Gertrude in the Philadelphia production of *Fashion*. At this first rehearsal with Lily and Davenport, Susan refused to come, sending an excuse that she was ill. Maddox seemed to doubt this, and immediately decided to substitute Miss Emmaline Montague in the rôle which Miss Cushman was to have played. Wind of the substitution reached Susan and she came instantly to the theatre in a fury. There was a nasty scene between her and Maddox, who was notably blunt and short-tempered. Words flew fast and the quarrel became increasingly violent. Susan claimed her right to play the part whether she rehearsed or not, since she was under contract to play the "walking ladies." Maddox insisted that she would *not* play the part, suggesting that her absence had not been due to illness but to jealousy of Mrs. Mowatt and a wish to wreck the performance. He gave the order to clear the stage and Miss Cushman was literally forced off it.

All this time Lily had been seated at the side waiting for her first cue. She was horribly embarrassed and upset; not only for Miss Cushman, but because of the obvious enjoyment of the company. Suddenly, in the wings, Susan turned abruptly, stalked back to Lily and without saying a word grasped her hand and pressed it tightly. She then marched out of the theatre. Had Susan really been jealous of her? Was the silent handclasp one of remorse? Lily could not know. But the whole episode unnerved her; the atmosphere of hostility clung to her, and she could not shake it off either during the rehearsal or even after she had left the theatre.

When she came back that night, the bare, unheated dressing-room added to her depression. She complained of the cold to her newly-engaged maid. The woman replied that the stove smoked so much that it disturbed the other ladies and she had been afraid to light it. Just then the wardrobe-mistress entered and solved the problem by lighting all the gas jets—which did warm the closet-like room but consumed all the oxygen, so that Lily was soon gasping for breath.

The wardrobe-mistress was inclined to be loquacious and also critical. She disapproved of Mrs. Mowatt's style of wearing her hair in long ringlets down to her waist and assured Lily the audience would "guy" her. Then she glanced at the star's slender figure with the wrapper drawn closely around it, and disappeared suddenly through the door. In a moment she was back with an article which puzzled Lily.

"I made this for you to wear," said she, "for I noticed you hadn't much more figure than a beanstalk. You look as though a breath of air would blow you away."

She then proceeded to initiate Lily into the mysteries of the apparatus she had prepared. It was a wadded *jupon* designed to amplify and round out her contours.

Lily was of course very slight. At the time she weighed less than ninety pounds. But it had never occurred to her that her figure was inadequate. She tried to protest; but the wardrobe-mistress was already strapping her firmly into the *jupon*. When a dress went on over it, the woman proclaimed to Lily that it made a *great* improvement! In Lily's own eyes, as she studied the effect in the mirror, it made her look disproportioned. Her waist became waspish, her shoulders too narrow. But there was no time to do anything about it now. There was a knock on the door and she heard the cockney voice of the call-boy imperiously crying, "Julia, you are called!"

Lily's first entrance was with Miss Montague. When the two appeared on the stage, there was a warm round of applause. For an instant Lily's spirits rose. Then she realized that the applause was for Miss Montague, who was a popular figure in the London theatre. There was really nothing to show that the audience had taken notice of the newcomer. Suddenly she felt utterly alone—alone with a thousand eyes staring at her, through her. She tried to smile, but her features remained fixed as in a wooden mask. She opened her mouth to speak, but she could not hear her own voice. Black mists began to float in front of her eyes. She tried to focus them on her fellow-player, but instead of one Miss Montague there were three. She made an effort to move, but invisible chains seemed to hold her feet to the floor. For the first time in her life she had been seized with stage-fright in its worst form.

Long familiarity with the part of Julia enabled her to recite the lines and so get through the first act. When the curtain descended there was silence; and as she met James in the wings she caught ominous whispers from other actors. But there were no glances of sympathy or encouragement.

In a daze Lily changed for the next act. She heard James's voice, consoling and cheerful, but it seemed a long way off. When the call came for Act II she was waiting in the wings. Again she made her entrance to deadly stillness. She could now hear herself speak, but the lines were meaningless. And so it went throughout the act. She was like an automaton whose mechanism provided motion but no more.

The third act went no better. If she played with complete control, it was the control of habit, not of the imagination. In the back of her mind Lily ticked off the celebrated "points" of the play, those moments of high dramatic intensity to which the audiences of Boston and Charleston and New Orleans had responded so enthusiastically. All had been passed over in silence. By the end of the act Lily had lost all sense of the play, of the theatre, of everything—except the cold stillness of the massed figures on the other side of the footlights. "I seemed to myself to be gradually sinking on a shoreless sea, in a dead calm—the sea of public condemnation—without the power to grasp even a straw."

But the worst was yet to come. In Act III, Master Walter, the Hunchback, bids Julia look at herself in a mirror—a purely imaginary mirror out of sight of the audience. During rehearsal it had been agreed that the direction of the mirror would be the left side of the stage. When told to gaze at her reflection Julia would automatically turn to the left. Now the actor playing Master Walter pointed to the *right*—while Lily, who had been looking forward and therefore could not see his hand, turned her head to the *left*. It was a cruel trick, and the titter from the audience emphasized its meanness. But Master Walter had not finished. The next moment, according to the demands of the scene, he handed Julia a chair, telling her to be seated, and drew up another for himself beside her—placing a leg carefully on the train of Julia's gown. Lily continued with the dialogue, trying vainly to attract the actor's attention to her unfortunate predicament. But Master Walter was playing his part with such deep concentration that he could not be diverted. Now Lily was supposed to spring up from her seat in a burst of joy. But since she could not do so without the risk of losing her train—perhaps her skirt—she was forced to hear the happy revelation made by Master Walter in motionless ecstasy.

The crisis had to be brought to an end when the action of the play called for Master Walter to leave the stage. An instant later Davenport, playing Julia's lover, Clifford, appeared for his first scene alone with Lily. The feeling of release, plus Davenport's friendly face, suddenly restored Lily to herself. The paralyzing fears melted away. She went into the famous love-scene of the play with an intensity and an abandon that literally pulled the audience out of its seats. At the end of the scene there was a great gust of applause, and when the curtain came down on the act there were loud calls for the star. But Lily refused to take the call. She went quickly to her dressing-room, conscious only that she had recovered her freedom from the steel bands of stage-fright, from the hostility of her fellow-actors—above all from the legs of Master Walter's chair.

When she reappeared in the fifth act, the audience might have noticed that she had grown suddenly much slimmer. In her dressing-room Lily had also freed herself from the straitjacket-like *jupon*. Now completely at ease, mistress of every gesture and movement and intonation, she gave to the part everything that had made it so successful before. The applause at the final curtain indicated clearly that the bad impression of the first three acts had been thoroughly wiped out. But when Lily finally got to her dressing-room she was near collapse. The whole evening had been a nightmare, and the effects on her nervous system were so profound that it was six months before she fully recovered.

In view of all that had happened, she could scarcely believe her eyes when she saw the papers next morning. Although the approval of the audience was still sounding in her ears, it did not seem logical that a detached judgment could be anything but unfavorable. A few reviews were indeed distinctly reserved, like *The Literary Gazette*'s, which could have wished "for a softer and more subdued style of stage presentation." But most of the papers took the opposite line, commenting on Anna Cora's refinement, her personal charms and the intelligence of her conception of the part of Julia. The general view was summed up by *The Theatrical Times* when it said that Mrs. Mowatt was "a decided acquisition to the theatre, being free from coarseness and Americanisms."

This idea was important. No matter what other handicaps she may have started with, Anna Cora had none of the crudeness most American actors exhibited (at least in the eyes of the British). When she recalled the remarks about Forrest ("inflated ranter, . . . turgid tragedian, only suited to the precincts of Lambeth") she could breathe a sigh of relief. But refinement and restraint such as she had displayed in her performance of Julia were not enough to carry her to the heights of popular favor in London. She must also find out as quickly as possible whether her style would pass muster in the supreme test of Shakespearian interpretation.

The Hunchback was repeated on the second night of the Americans' engagement. Their third performance was *Much Ado About Nothing*. It was a daring venture, for the London stage had seen more than one actress with a greater reputation than Lily's go down to disaster in the rôle of Beatrice. But Lily had no misgivings. She loved the play, and of all Shakespeare's characters she felt the closest affinity with the lady at whose birth "a star danced." And she had worked hard on the part—which showed her special gifts better than any other in her repertory. She knew how completely unorthodox was her interpretation. Her Beatrice was no hoyden but a high-spirited lady whose wit flowed from an intelligence nourished by the joy of living. When she railed at Benedick it was in the sheer delight which a fine mind feels in the presence of its equal. Her best effects came from under-playing (a technique which Lily developed fifty years before it became the standard method for high comedy), and from concentration on the subtleties of the poetry.

Whether all this would go down with a London audience, she had no way of knowing. But on the whole she was optimistic. She and Davenport had played *Much Ado* in Manchester with gratifying success. There seemed to be every advantage in repeating the play now, while the memory of their first British audience's reaction was fresh in their minds.

Despite the fact that few of the Princess's players were familiar with the play and some of the parts were badly miscast, the performance went smoothly. But both public and press were sharply divided on the interpretation. At one extreme were people like the critic of *The Era,* who, wedded to the orotund manner of

Mrs. Nesbitt and Fanny Kemble, was nonplussed by the quietness of certain scenes and decided that Beatrice and Benedick were parts "beyond the reach of the parties venturing on the undertaking." The subdued manner of Mrs. Mowatt in the great scene in the church—in which the actress playing Beatrice usually filled the theatre with sounds of condolence for the betrayed Hero—led the same critic to decide that Mrs. Mowatt was "greatly wanting in sustaining powers" and that she relied "too much on her personal advantages."

In the opposite camp was Bayle Bernard, whose reviews in *The Weekly Dispatch* were widely read. He was enchanted by the whole conception of the rôle—by the spontaneity, the gaiety, the warmth of Lily's performance. He instructed his readers in oracular fashion that "Mrs. Mowatt is an artiste—there is no mistake about it. She has the ring of the genuine metal—she can act Shakespeare!"

With one exception, the London papers reported faithfully the progress of the newcomers during the six weeks' engagement at the Princess's. Opinions were mixed but spirited. There were those critics like Bernard, and Shirley Brooks of *The Chronicle*, who were ready to assign Mrs. Mowatt at once the highest rank in the profession. And there were also those like Heraud of *The Athenaeum* who felt that the lovely American's "style was more suited to the drawing-room than to the theatre, and that she would do well to confine her talents to the former." Of the leading papers, only *The Times* seemed completely oblivious of the presence of Anna Cora and Davenport. Not until the last day of their turn at the Princess's was this ominous silence broken. On February 10 a column appeared in *The Times* which began as follows:

> Mrs. Mowatt is a lady of great personal attractions, and all that she does evinces care and cultivation. Her voice is extremely pleasing, but the defect she should remedy is a tendency to lengthen syllables for purposes of accentuation. . . .

There was a good deal more about Mrs. Mowatt's depiction of Mrs. Haller (even London still went to see *The Stranger*) which was "nicely rendered"—but it was obvious that nothing could weigh the balance against a lengthened syllable.

Some weeks later Lily learned why *The Times,* after so long ignoring her, suddenly became aware of her presence. John Oxenford, the *Times* dramatic critic, had more than the current British distaste for American actors. When he learned of the visitors at the Princess's he thought it "too great a bore" to even bother to see them. This he told Lily herself, when he met her at a dinner-party at Macready's in the spring of 1848. He confessed that his interest was finally aroused by the intermediation of a friend of Mrs. Mowatt's. Lily was puzzled. Her circle of acquaintance in London at the time of her début was so limited that she could think of no one who might have approached the critic of London's most important paper.

"To what friend?" she asked.

"To the Earl of Carlisle," replied Oxenford.

The matter then became clear. Lily was not personally acquainted with the nobleman in question. But she had had an introduction to him from Henry Clay, who had met the Earl in America. She had forwarded the letter, enclosed in a brief note from herself, but had received no reply. Amid the general excitement of the first weeks she had given the matter no further thought, assuming the Earl's casualness to be due to the traditional bad manners of the English aristocracy. But Carlisle had after all acknowledged the letter in his own way. He had followed the Americans' career in the London press, and noting the continued silence of *The Times* had personally written to Oxenford suggesting that the omission be corrected. Oxenford had promptly followed his advice. Thereafter this critic became one of Lily's staunchest supporters, particularly after he noted that her peculiar intonation of vowels had been entirely rectified. Their acquaintanceship, begun at Macready's, became a pleasant friendship, which Oxenford crowned by writing a play especially for Lily.

But all this was some time later. Even with the eventual inclusion of *The Times* among the ranks of the friendly, the course to success was a long uphill drag. But at least by the end of the engagement at the Princess's, Lily and Davenport were beginning to pay their own way. From the time of *Much Ado* on, there was steady improvement in the houses. On February 5, *The London Illustrated News* noted:

> The engagement of Mrs. Mowatt and Mr. Davenport appears to have been a judicious one, as regards the interests of this establishment. On each night of their performance, the theatre has been well attended.

The fact that they were drawing paying audiences speaks more highly than any amount of press encomiums. For the season generally had been poor. The Keans were having a struggle to keep going; while at the Olympic the young tragedian Gustavus Brooke, who had cut a great swathe on his first arrival in London, was obliged to bolster *The Lady of Lyons* with interludes from *Venice Preserv'd* performed by a pair of infant wonders—"The Parisian Prodigies, J. and E. Duprez." The only place of entertainment which had done good business steadily that season was Madame Warton's *Walhalla* in Leicester Square. Madame Warton's specialty was living statuary and tableaux. She and her troupe were turning people from the door with such presentations as "Lady Godiva, from Edwin Landseer's, R.A., forthcoming picture." There were other personations—Venus, Sappho, Diana—to strike the high esthetic note. At the end of the season, but surely not as a mere afterthought, there was added an extra number called "Innocence."

The depressed condition of the theatre reflected the widespread misery in the city. The rich were still very rich, and their brilliant carriages made a fine show in Hyde Park. But in the back streets the pinch of hunger was everywhere. On the morning of January 17, *The Post* carried a story which could not but have caught Lily's eye, since it ran alongside the note on her own forthcoming appearance in *Much Ado About Nothing*. The item told of a starving seventeen-year-old boy who broke a window in order to be sent to prison. He had been duly arrested, condemned to hard labor and had immediately died. The prison chaplain had entered a protest to the authorities.

He felt strongly about the routine procedure of "committing prisoners, who were in a starving state, to hard labor." He thought a hospital or workhouse would be more suitable. The protest was properly recorded.

Lily usually looked feelingly upon the world around her; but these first months in London she scarcely ventured outside the rooms she and James had rented in Upper Baker Street, except to go to the theatre. There is no indication—either in the *Autobiography* or in her sparse letters of this time—that she was aware of anything beyond this closed existence.

Sometime in that spring of 1848, through Swedenborgian connections Lily came to know William and Mary Howitt, a remarkable pair of hack writers who by the sheer mass of their output had impressed themselves on the London literary world. Starting out as Quakers, they had run the gamut of religions and reform movements. They had been attracted to Swedenborgianism because half the radical political reformers of London belonged to the sect. At this time, the Howitts were running *The People's Journal,* a literary and political review, with a policy of reform to suit the most catholic tastes. They were opposed to "capital punishment, war, slavery and the slave trade, military floggings, hard labor conditions for children, cruelty to animals, the separation of children in workhouses and the mistreatment of chimney sweeps." Their social zeal was sincere and admirable, but weakened by their tendency to be carried away by more and ever more causes.

At the Howitts' house in St. John's Wood, Lily and James met a variety of London personalities. There were people of the stage (for the Howitts' liberalism knew no bounds), Members of Parliament, poets, writers, painters and a miscellany of crackpots. With some of these figures, Lily formed pleasant friendships. She was especially drawn to W. J. Fox, an ex-clergyman, now a Member of Parliament and (more important) the dramatic critic on *The Examiner.* Here also, Lily met Mrs. Gaskell and the poetess Camilla Toulmin. The following year, the poetess inscribed a lengthy ode to the actress. It was inspired by the rumor that Anna Cora might soon be returning to America:

Blow, western wind, athwart the wave,—
Blow, western breezes, still,—
And hold at bay the envious bark,
That seeks its sail to fill. . . .

Having pleaded with the elements, the poetess turned to her subject proper:

A bird,—a pearl—a "lily" flower!
We love to liken thee
To something fresh from nature's hand
In mystic purity,—
And Protean should be types, I ween,
Of thee, O richly gifted!
By triple rights and triple crowns
Above the herd uplifted.

And so on for eight stanzas. It was really quite a tribute and, for the biographer at least, a handy catalogue of Anna Cora's charms and accomplishments. The last stanza spoke of the "chains more strong than steel" binding the hearts of friends and the spell that "girds thee round with British love." Miss Toulmin was impressed by the latest addition to the Howitt circle. Lily was likewise taken with Miss Toulmin and for some years there was a continuous exchange of tokens of friendship between the two. But memory is short. When Miss Toulmin (then Mrs. Crosland) came to write her memoirs she, like the rest of the world, had forgotten all about Anna Cora.

Above everybody else, at first, Lily prized Mary Howitt. Such a generous nature! such vast capacities! What genius, to be able to plump all the problems of the world into one basket and solve them at once, through Chartism or Utilitarianism or whatever it was! Lily had never been able to manage this even with her own personal difficulties: each one had been a separate mountain to be shoveled away by grim, gruelling labor. There seemed only one direction in which the Howitts' genius was insufficient, and that was in the matter of finances. They were already having trouble with *The People's Journal,* founded a year before. In another year it was to perish—not, however, before it had dedicated long pages in two issues to a memoir of Anna Cora, written by none other than Mary Howitt herself. This memoir, based largely on material supplied by James, was useful in spreading Anna Cora's unusual history among the advanced British public which read *The People's Journal*. It was more useful in the long run to Anna Cora herself, since it gave her the idea later of writing her autobiography, and furnished her a framework of details which she might otherwise have forgotten.

It was not long, however, before a cooling-off took place between Lily and Mary Howitt. Though energetic, Mrs. Howitt tended to scatter her forces, particularly in the way of friendships. She was so passionately devoted to so many people! Like Camilla Toulmin, she too had a weak memory. Her autobiographical notes, later edited by her daughter, make no mention of Anna Cora whom she had once proclaimed an "undying inspiration."

Lily's and Davenport's engagement at the Princess's was to be followed by Macready in a round of his great tragic rôles. Macready had been very cordial and helpful to the Mowatts in getting established in London. By now he must also have seen Lily act and been strongly impressed. Shortly before the end of her original contract with Maddox, Macready, through Henry Wallack, the director of the Princess's company, proposed that Lily should join him as co-star for his engagement at the theatre. The offer was flattering and tempting. It would have afforded Lily "invaluable opportunities of improvement," as she put it. But she knew that she must tread cautiously. Her forte was high comedy and romance. This was the field she had come to conquer, and she did not mean to be diverted into bypaths. She knew that she lacked the force required by parts like Lady Macbeth and Queen Katherine; her qualities were those of Juliet, Beatrice, Desdemona. Furthermore, gratifying though Macready's offer might sound, it would probably be of little personal benefit to her in the end. For she knew enough of his style and methods of staging to realize that if she were given any chance to shine at all, it would simply be by reflected light. And this was not what she wanted.

Besides, an offer had now come from the Olympic Theatre for Lily and Davenport to join Gustavus Brooke, whose popularity was waxing. This would provide a far happier arrangement for her, since the two gentlemen could divide the honors in their own department, and she could shine alone in hers. There were further attractions. The Olympic had been made very popular by Madame Vestris and Charles Mathews, whose finished productions and excellent high comedy repertory had built up a clientele of discriminating West End playgoers. The theatre was under the nominal management of a man named Davidson, but the real lessee (who was careful to keep the affiliation secret) was Henry Spicer, a well-to-do man of letters. One suspects that Spicer's interest in the theatre was founded on the hope of having his own plays produced; this was about the only way that a new playwright could get his work before the London public.

At the Olympic Lily at last had a chance to show *The Lady of Lyons* to the London play-going jury. She assumed that after the notices of *Much Ado* nobody would question her right to present herself in the rôle of Pauline. But she had reckoned without the public's attitude towards Bulwer's masterpiece. It was one thing to pass muster with Shakespeare. He was after all a classic. But *The Lady of Lyons* was a sacred cow. Many were called but few indeed were chosen to preside at her shrine— and it was clear, when the notices came out, that Mrs. Mowatt had misinterpreted the call. ". . . her Pauline," said *The Era*, "is something more than a respectable performance and anything but a great one." *The Athenaeum* suggested that the applause at the final curtain was not for a theatrical demonstration but for a drawing-room entertainment. Both *The Post* and *The Examiner* questioned the taste of one presuming so far on such short acquaintance with the British public. Only Oxenford of *The Times*, who had the same disdain for his fellow-critics as for the majority of the stage productions he saw, showed any warmth. He found Anna Cora's Pauline "more charming than more elaborate performances."

The season ended with a production of Henry Spicer's *The Lords of Ellingham*. This was condemned all round—except by the public, which filled the house night after night. *The Era* called it a "poor play" and said that "Mrs. Mowatt, as the heroine, was evidently much excited and much in Earnest." *The Times*, reviewing the opening, again noted pleasing details of her personality and physique—and also that for the latter part of the first evening she wore a bandage around her head.

Once more Lily had met with an accident in the middle of a performance. This time she had fallen outside her dressing-room door as she was entering preparatory to changing for the last act. She had struck her head on a sharp corner and been knocked unconscious, to be revived by the warm blood trickling down her face and the call-boy's voice. She had barely time to bandage the wound, which despite "the most ingenious arrangement of curls" she could not wholly conceal. She thought, however, it would pass unnoticed—since her final appearance was as a corpse borne in on a bier, her face covered by a veil. Unfortunately, the action demanded that her lover Dudley, played by Davenport, should raise the veil for a last look at the visage of his departed one. There had been no time to apprise Davenport of the mishap and when he lifted the swath of tulle from Lily's face and saw the blood oozing down, he burst forth with a cry of horror. Lily was able to murmur cheerfully, "It's nothing—I'm not much hurt," and Davenport managed to continue with his part. For Lily it was all in the day's work.

At the close of the season it was not certain what the next step would be. Several prospects were in the air; but it was not until the end of July that a proposal which seemed exactly right came along. During the Olympic run, Lily and James had been introduced to a young man by the name of Walter Watts. He was known to be "somebody in the City." Lily was immediately struck by his good manners and the casual elegance of his appearance. He had very light hair, a tiny blond mustache and flashing blue eyes. He was quite small, but one forgot this fact when he began to talk—especially about the theatre, for which he evidently had a deep passion. His interest was more than that of a dilettante. He had had a financial share in one or two theatrical ventures, and was now determined to go into management on his own. He had secured the lease of a theatre in the West End, the Marylebone, and he offered Lily and Davenport an engagement to open the season—with the proposal of a re-engagement if he could break even on the contract.

The plan appealed at once to Lily because the Marylebone, though a small theatre, had a very fine reputation and a perma-nent high-class clientele. For several seasons it had been success-fully operated by Mrs. Warner, a well-known actress who had inaugurated a policy of having the best stars and the most fin-ished productions. In addition to everything else, Watts offered handsome financial arrangements with Lily and Davenport. All these details were attractive, but the most attractive feature was Watts himself. In him both James and Lily felt at once a kindred spirit. He had the soul of an artist, but he was also a gentleman. He wanted to bring a new atmosphere to the thea-tre—to restore it to its classic rôle as the temple of high poetry, and to surround it with the breath of refinement. Yet he was no mere dreamer. James could judge best of this when Watts began to talk of technical and business particulars, of which he had an amazing mastery.

Also, Lily would not have been human had she not been pleased by Watts's great interest in her. He had followed her closely from her first appearance in London. He had seen from the beginning that she had brought something new to the Lon-don stage which, if properly exploited, would carry her to dazzling success. Her acting had a quality of intimacy which gave the public a heightened sense of participation in the play, more than was produced by the broad manner of people like Miss Glyn and Ellen Tree. Such a gift could best be developed in a small theatre where there was closer contact between audi-ence and actor. In fact, Watts had really had her in mind when he leased the Marylebone.

Lily and Davenport opened their season with Watts in *As You Like It*—the play which they had prepared for Lily's benefit in June, but which had been cancelled because of Princess Sophia's death. The play ran for twelve nights with business more than justifying Watts's expectations. Although *The Athenaeum* pronounced Lily's Rosalind "pleasant, but wrong," the other reviewers were unanimous in praising the performance, noting the revelations of poetic beauty in the lines, and the wistful charm of the new Rosalind.

In *The Bride of Lammermoor,* the second feature of the Marylebone season, Lily came fully into her own. The very staidness of Oxenford's review hints at the effect she made. Like everybody else, the *Times* critic condemned the poor construction of the play.

> However, the last scene is so powerful, that with Mrs. Mowatt's acting, it more than compensates for the weariness of the introduction. This lady has not been nearly appreciated enough in London, but her improvement has been sure and steady. . . .

The greatest of her earlier faults,

> . . . . a certain drawling manner of speaking,—she has so completely subdued, that scarcely a trace of it is left.

Thus had Lily finally met Oxenford's highest criterion of excellence!

The engagement was renewed before its termination, and with most unusual conditions. Lily and Davenport were offered a contract (which both promptly accepted) to become the stars of the theatre for the entire season of which five months remained. So for the next hundred and twenty nights the partners —now established favorites with the regular Marylebone audience and drawing increasing numbers from the other houses— poured out their energies in rôle after rôle, in plays good, bad and indifferent, but with unqualified personal success.

In all this Watts played his part, and a most important one. He was determined from the outset that the productions in his theatre should be as nearly perfect as art and money could make them. Every detail was executed with the utmost care. Nothing slipshod was allowed. He made heavy demands on the actors; but also he did not spare himself. Everybody marveled at his indefatigability, his taste, his seemingly heedless disregard for expense. He out-Keaned Kean in his insistence on historical ac-

curacy in costume pieces. He experimented endlessly with lighting, developing all sorts of ingenious reflectors to obtain the
maximum power and flexibility from the gas flames. The sets
were of the finest materials and the finest workmanship. Wherever possible, properties were not mere imitations but genuine
articles. If a script called for a heavy silver cup to be dashed
with a ringing sound to the floor, Watts procured a real silver cup.
His fellow-workers marveled at his prodigality; but even more
at the astute business sense which enabled him to mount such
lavish productions on the box-office returns of the theatre.
Though the company played regularly to full houses throughout the season, it seemed that only a financial genius could make
ends meet. But somehow Watts did so, winning the admiration
and affection of all in the process.

The grand event of the winter was the production of Lily's
Armand. The elegance of settings and costumes outdid everything that had gone before. Moreover, the play was given ample
and careful rehearsals. Watts could not have expended more
thought and love on *Armand* had it been his own work. Lily
was deeply touched.

Davenport was struck by the differences in English and Amer-
ican production methods, particularly by the whole tone of the
Marylebone. To his friend Tom Ford, one of the managers of
Boston's Howard Athenaeum, he wrote:

I still hold to my original opinion that we have more natural
talent in America but [not] so much application. We are too
careless. I mean *all* concerned from manager to super. Here rehearsals are made of import and when a piece is to be done, the
scene men, the property men, musicians and actors must each do
their share. It is a system here that I would gladly see introduced
into our theatres—And if ever I have power I will strive to bring
it around—we can play Shakespeare almost *without* a rehearsal—
not so here—the actors and all know and feel their responsibility.
I am speaking of the genteel theatres. . . . Stage appointments are
all here more attended to—effects of scenery more studied—the
artist being for a period the director for his own purposes—then
the machinist and then with good acting requested by a stage

manager who knows his business—you see things done well, but remove anyone of the screws—it will lame the machine.

Armand put on the stage here in the little theatre was better than anything of the kind in our *largest* house. . . .

There was only one hitch to getting *Armand* before the London public. The Royal Licenser refused permission to produce the play until the sub-title was changed and several lines expunged. The original title, *Armand, or the Child of the People*, was felt to have an anti-monarchical tinge; so Lily re-titled the play *Armand, or the Peer and the Peasant*. On the same grounds it was necessary to delete such speeches as

> *A monarch's state that sanctions what would shame*
> *A subject, doubly shames itself! When Wrong*
> *And Crime usurp the garments of the state*
> *They grow more hideous in those glittering robes*
> *Than when they wear the branded felon's garb . . .*

and the following (when Armand spurns the King's offer of rank and title):

> *And why the trappings and the adjuncts vain*
> *With which the great enshroud themselves, to awe*
> *The gaping multitude, should I not scorn?*
> *Free thought—free will—the birth right true of all*
> *Manhood, the universal heritage—*
> *For them, nor for a million times their worth,*
> *I would not barter.*

One might suppose that these deletions would have somewhat weakened the play, the main point of which is that a subject may be a better man than a monarch and that freedom of speech is more precious than rubies. But no one, not even Lily, seemed to be disturbed by the Licenser's requirements.

Of course Lily submitted the play in advance to several critics who graciously read the manuscript and suggested improvements. Lily conscientiously tried to carry these out but soon gave up, since the suggestions were mostly in conflict with each other. So the play was produced as originally written except for the deletions required by law.

The Marylebone was sold out long before the opening, and the audience comprised not only the fashionable and titled world but most of the literati of London as well. This intelligence, brought to Lily just as the curtain was about to rise, so unnerved her that she might have succumbed to another attack of stage-fright had she not just received a note from the most admired of all the literati—the Reverend Mr. W. J. Fox, M. P., critic of *The Examiner*. This said in part: " 'Tis not in mortals to command success, but you have deserved it." To be told from such a source that she "*deserved* success" revived her fainting spirits.

At the final curtain, Lily received her first great London ovation. There were resounding cheers and the stage was showered with flowers. Among the wreaths was a chaplet of ivy woven by the younger daughter of Mary Howitt. Lily identified it at once, because it was the favorite headdress of this young lady when she went out in society. She was deeply moved by this simple token from the daughter whom she had come to esteem even more highly than the mother (". . . her philanthropy was more discriminating").

Next morning the papers recorded the triumph in full detail. W. J. Fox's review was the longest. He had most certainly written it well in advance; but it was scarcely more exalted than some of the others. Mr. Fox could not say that the play contained "a profound philosophy of human nature, the terrific war of stormiest passion" or "magnificent bursts of poetry":

> . . . But we have, instead, living and suggestive outlines of character, scenes of pathos whose power is testified by the emotions of the audience, and a pervading simplicity, truth and loveliness, both of thought and language, which act as a charm and are full of fascination. . . . On the whole, though dangerous themes have sometimes to be dealt with, there is an air of purity, refinement, and tenderness. The most religious parent might take his child to such a play. . . .

(When a drama critic has one foot in the evangelical ministry and another in Parliament, the effects on his style are curious.) Oxenford of *The Times* gave a complete synopsis of the plot—

in itself no mean achievement for a critic—and stressed the sublimity of the moral.

> The one grand object of this piece is to set native worth in opposition to artificial rank. . . . In pursuing this object the authoress has treated the characters as ideal beings of her own invention, and has not paid particular regard to the period or circumstances of the action. . . .

But this, of course, was unimportant.

> The personages speak with a generous enthusiasm as the mouthpieces of her own sentiments, and it is not the French peasant but the American citizen who rates so soundly the vices of a depraved Court, and insists on the "rights of man." . . .

Armand ran for twenty-one very profitable nights. While the play was still going it was published, and copies sold at the door. Lily immediately regretted this, for the constant fluttering of pages by members of the audience following the printed text so distracted the actors that they continually blew up in their lines. But this was one of the trials of success. With the publication of the play Lily found herself receiving income from three sources simultaneously: royalties from the theatre, royalties from the publisher, and the star's share of the box-office take.

The winter of 1848-49 was the high tide of Lily's career. She was the talk of London. She was secure in popular favor. She was on the way to becoming wealthy. She was adored by her husband and an increasing circle of intimates. Her little drawing-room in Upper Baker Street became a sort of shrine where her devotees gathered occasionally for small supper-parties. There were Davenport and Miss Toulmin, W. J. Fox and the Howitts, and a charming member of the Marylebone company, Fanny Vining. And increasingly regular in his attendance was Mr. Walter Watts—who was voluble with plans for the future—all of them centering about Mrs. Mowatt.

CHAPTER SEVENTEEN

"Our Little Mowatt"

B y mid-February of 1849 the Marylebone had become the most popular theatre in London. Watts had made good his promise to provide Anna Cora with the finest possible setting for her art. He had shown this in the careful and handsome manner in which he had put on *Armand*. In his next production he outdid himself in the opulence and ingenuity of costumes and scenery.

The play was *Ariadne* by Thomas Corneille, the forgotten younger brother of the great Pierre. It had been revived in France by Rachel and had become her favorite vehicle. John Oxenford had translated it into English and adapted it for Anna Cora.

The rôle of Ariadne was the most exacting that she had yet undertaken, for the play was practically a monologue by the heroine. Its effectiveness depended in particular on the flexibility of the actress's voice and on her gift for interpreting the verse with depth and passion. It was a part in the declamatory manner of the great French tradition—a tradition which Lily had absorbed in childhood and which she had intensively studied during her months in Paris in 1839-40. Oxenford as well as other critics had been struck from the beginning by a distinct Gallic flavor in Lily's style, a clean precision in her gestures and a clarity in her enunciation (once he had accepted her American vowels). These gave her acting a highly individualized quality. Combined with her natural grace and dignity they made her an ideal choice for the rôle of the Cretan princess.

Oxenford had retained the neo-classic simplicity of Corneille's original in his treatment of the name part, but he could not resist carpentering the action of the rest of the play according to the tastes of the day. The scene of Ariadne's death had all the excitement of the finale of a three-ring circus. In Corneille's play the abandoned Ariadne dies true to the legend, by falling upon a sword. But so many swords had been fallen upon in the Victorian drama that this method of extinction was abandoned for one with greater novelty and eye-appeal. Oxenford's Ariadne must jump off a high cliff into the sea, in plain view of the audience. To carry this out, the inventive talents of Watts were brought into full play.

The last act setting depicted the wild coast of Naxos, rendered with meticulous realism. Towering above the stage was a rocky crag, its summit approached by a zig-zag path. In the background gleamed the blue sea. Ariadne was seen pacing the shore when she received the news that her sister Phaedra and her lover Theseus had sailed away together. Presently in the background appeared the ship (a model pulled on rollers behind a profile wave). This was Ariadne's cue for self-destruction. The audience, wildly excited by the imminent event, now saw Lily dash across the stage, start up the rocky path, vanish for a moment in the wings, reappear at a higher level, and pursue her course until again she vanished behind a projecting ledge. An instant later her form was seen to rise up on the dizzy summit. Here she poised with draperies fluttering—and then, just as the ship disappeared, with a wild cry she threw herself into the sea, to the accompaniment of hysterical shrieks and deep groans from out front. On the opening night there was one clearly audible cry: "Good God! she is killed!"

The effect was managed with great ingenuity. When Lily started up the path and vanished in the wings, her place was taken by an agile-footed ballet girl dressed in a costume identical to hers and bearing some resemblance to her. The girl nimbly scaled the perilous ledge (Lily's near-sightedness forbade her making the attempt herself) until she, too, was lost from sight behind a jutting rock. The figure that appeared a second later on top of the promontory was a dummy, whose leap into the sea was precipitated by a spring mechanism.

From the front the illusion was perfect—and horrifying. When Mrs. Mowatt emerged to take her bow at the final curtain there were mingled gasps of amazement and relief—followed, of course, by a wild ovation.

Ariadne was a great success; and the rôle revealed to London for the first time Anna Cora's capacities as a tragic actress. In reviewing the production Oxenford was obliged to use some restraint, since after all the play was his own work. Consequently his remarks that "the excellent acting of Mrs. Mowatt will advance her reputation considerably in the estimation of the public" was the mildest comment of the press. Like everyone else Oxenford lauded the scenic effects; though his note that "an antiquarian might object to the arches in the palace of King Genarus" probably caused Watts to recoil. But his final word surely brought solace to the diligent manager. "The last scene is one of the most elaborate ever constructed."

Ariadne was followed by Sheridan Knowles's *Love*, which likewise showed happy results at the box-office. Lily's acting in this piece originally written for Ellen Tree was described as "effective in the extreme."

In March, the grateful and devoted Watts paid her a public tribute which touched her all the more because of the circumstances surrounding the gesture. A special performance of *Armand* was announced "in honor of Mrs. Mowatt." *The Times* records the unusual interest of the occasion:

March 12, 1849

We hope the partisans of Mr. Forrest will hear of the very handsome manner in which Mrs. Mowatt, the American authoress and actress, has been received in this country. Mr. Watts, the lessee of the Marylebone Theatre, without any stipulation at all as to a benefit gave her the whole receipts of his house on Thursday, paying the expenses himself.

However, the object of Watts's munificence was not a cash donation to Lily but a splendid silver vase. The vase had been ordered in advance on the basis of the calculated receipts for the evening and was presented to her when she took her curtain call. It weighed more than 120 ounces and was lined with gold. Its cover was surmounted with a statuette of Shakespeare. The cost of the vase was estimated at £100. On one side was inscribed the dedication:

Presented to Anna Cora Mowatt of New York, United States, by Walter Watts, Esq., lessee and manager of the Theatre Royal, Marylebone, in respectful and grateful acknowledgment of her services to the drama as authoress and actress; and as a record that worth and genius from every land will ever be honored in England. London, 8th of March, 1849.

On the opposite side of the vase were engraved the following lines from *Measure for Measure*:

> *In her youth*
> *There is a prone and speechless dialect*
> *Such as moves men; besides she has prosperous art*
> *When she would play with reason and discourse;*
> *And well she can persuade.*

That the presentation was not simply a device for giving Anna Cora a handsome gift which circumstances would have prohibited Watts from doing privately, is made clear by a report from the London correspondent of *The Boston Transcript*:

The theatres have been doing poorly, with the exception of the Marylebone, which with the attraction of Mrs. Mowatt and Mr. Davenport has been remarkably prospering. Mrs. M's [sic] performance last night completed her fifty-first consecutive night at this theatre, and she is engaged to play up to April first, when all the theatres close. In consequence of the unexampled success of her original play "Armand," the manager Mr. Watts, appointed last night for her benefit, when he gave her the gross receipts of the house, without any deduction whatever, an act of liberality the more gratifying, from the fact that it was entirely voluntary on his part.

There is of course a slight error about the "receipts" which were not given Anna Cora outright but in the form of a vase. The report ends with a description of the evening:

The play was Armand. The house was filled to its utmost capacity. The front rows of the pit were partitioned off for the occasion as stalls, and filled with the beauty and fashion of London. The enthusiasm of the audience was beyond all bounds, and, at the conclusion of the play, wreaths and flowers were lavished in any quantity. Mrs. M. has received most advantageous offers to remain in London another season, but she is anxious to see home once more and intends leaving in July. We Americans here are, I assure you, quite proud of her success.

Watts's policy at the Marylebone was to offer not only productions of high quality, but new plays as well. One of the most remarkable of these was a work by himself with the imposing title *A Dream of Life*. This was a temperance drama. Its plot revolved about the reformation of a drunkard (forcefully played by Davenport) through a dream. In a series of Rake's Progress-like scenes, the drunkard beheld the awful future unroll before him, and as a result was cured of his weakness. He was assisted in the process by his lovely and long-suffering wife, played by the charming Fanny Vining. In the final scene the pair setled down to a life of unalloyed bliss, thus foreshadowing the later years of the two leading actors whose real marriage took place a few months afterwards.

The settings for this play, notably the dream sequence, brought Watts indeed to the fore as the wonder-man of the London stage. Using a technique supposed to have been developed only in comparatively recent times, he produced a composite setting of several scenes at different levels, in which the various phases of the drunkard's dream—if the visions of *delirium tremens* may

be so designated—were acted one after another. Only the section
of the stage in use at that moment was lighted, which implies a
greater versatility in gas illumination than we are wont to
imagine. The last scene in the sequence depicted the drunkard's
end on the gallows. This apparently carried realism too far even
for the sensation-loving Londoners. "In future representations,"
remarked *The Era*, "we would recommend an abstinence from
too close an imitation of the details of execution, seeing that such
exhibitions are repulsive as well as impressive." Had *The Era* but
known, had Watts but known how far the grim scene would
project itself into actuality, with what horror might both have
contemplated this master stroke of the theatre! But just then the
future was guarding its secrets.

The whole atmosphere of the Marylebone was one of happy
excitement. For the Americans, the knowledge of their accomplishment was like a heady drink. Their exuberance is shown in a
letter written by Davenport to his friend Ford, on April 4, 1849.
Davenport was spending the Easter weekend in Brighton.

Well we are still here in John Bull-dom and are all better Yankees
than ever. Our last success has raised us in our own estimation
several feet and per cent to match. We feel that Yankees are some
punkins and dear old America in the dim distance looms up like
a 74 gun ship of nations amidst a whole squadron of Baltimore
clippers. Ford, we are a great people—and bound to be greater.
To any folk who dare to squint at us we will prove we are nutmeg
graters of the greatest sort. One of our orators said some years
back, I think during the pause in the events of nature and nations
previous to the Declaration being signed "England may as well
dam up the waters of the Nile with bulrushes as fetter the step
of freedom. . . . Open your eyes, O ye 2 week stars in America and
see the names of Mowatt and Davenport 16 and 17 weeks succes-
sively and successfully before an admiring Public. Bull-headed and
porter-sucking, wine-drinking and horse-racing, dog-fighting,
half-and-half destroying though they be, there are some here who
(the best compliment I can pay them) ought to have been
Yankees. I've seen only one actress yet that I would engage as
leading woman—I mean after stars, and her name is Fanny Vining.
She is a fine-looking creature, very talented. She will be a jewel

NEW

ROYAL INDEXED

OLYMPIC ✪ THEATRE

SOLE LESSEE, Mr. W. WATTS, NEVILLE LODGE, St. JOHN'S WOOD.

It is respectfully intimated that no charge will be made at the Box-office for Booking Places, neither will any Fees or Gratuities whatever be allowed to be taken by the Box-keepers. And any inattention or attempt at exaction on the part of the Servants will be immediately noticed.
EACH PERSON ENTERING TO EITHER BOXES OR PIT AT FIRST PRICE, WILL BE PRESENTED WITH A BILL OF THE NIGHT's PERFORMANCE.

GLORIOUS TRIUMPH
OF THE
NEW COMEDY!

☞ NOTICE — Mrs MOWATT's New and Original Comedy of FASHION: or, LIFE IN NEW YORK, continuing to be received with the most enthusiastic applause by crowded audiences, will be repeated Every Evening.

Thursday, Jan. 24th, Friday, 25th, & Saturday, 26th,
Will be presented (14th, 15th and 16th times) an entirely New and Original Comedy, in Five Acts, written by **Mrs. MOWATT,** entitled

FASHION
OR,
LIFE IN NEW YORK.

WITH ENTIRELY NEW SCENERY, COSTUMES AND APPOINTMENTS

Adam Trueman, (a Farmer from Catteraugus) **Mr DAVENPORT**
Count Jolimaitre, (a Fashionable European Importation) - **Mr A. WIGAN**
Colonel Howard, (an Officer in the United States Army) **Mr BELTON**
Mr Tiffany, - (a New York Merchant) **Mr JAMES JOHNSTONE**
Mr T. Tennyson Twinkle, (a Modern Poet) **Mr KINLOCH**
Augustus Fogg, - (a Drawing-room Appendage) - **Mr J. HOWARD**
Snobson, (a rare species of "Confidential Clerk") **Mr H. SCHARF**
Zeke, (a Coloured Servant) **Mr J. HERBERT.**
Mrs Tiffany, (a Lady who imagines herself Fashionable) **Mrs H. MARSTON**
Prudence, (a Maiden Lady of a certain age) **Mrs PARKER**
Seraphina Tiffany, - (a Belle) - **Miss A. GOUGENHEIM**
Gertrude, (a Governess) **Miss FANNY VINING**
Millinette, - (a French Lady's Maid) - **Mrs A. WIGAN.**
Gentlemen, Messrs Maurice, R. Greene, Haines, Collis, Barnes, Regan, Beckett, &c.
Ladies, Misses Mears, Douglas, Mandlebert, Webber, Coleman, Paris, Barton, Feist, Lovel, &c.

PLAYBILL, NEW OLYMPIC THEATRE, LONDON

to any one that can get her as his leading gal—she will. Both Mrs.
Mowatt and myself have taken quite a fancy to her and I shouldn't
wonder if we enticed her over. As to young men, I am not vain
but I see no one here that I need fear. Cushman can lick all the
tragedy ones (heavy) and our little Mowatt all juvenile and
comedy ones. I have not seen Helen Faucit yet and of course except Mrs. Nisbitt. There is no old man can compare with Henry
Placide and young Wheatleigh, and J. Murdock can hang em all
in a light comedy. So you see we go, and yet they are loth to
allow that Yankees have talent.

Davenport's high-spirited self-satisfaction was not mere brag-
gadocio. His reputation with both press and public was rising
steadily. If he waved the Stars and Stripes over-vigorously, he
had been goaded to it by the English critics with their monotonous drone about the mediocrity of American actors—even while
heaping praises on the heads of Lily and Davenport.

The remark on "our little Mowatt" can still be verified by
a mountain of evidence. At the moment, she was playing the
field so far ahead of the other women on the London stage that
the critics had ceased drawing comparisons. Ellen Tree and
Fanny Kemble were her only possible rivals. The former was
nearly smothered under the monumental productions of the
Haymarket, and Fanny Kemble was now so involved in her
libel-suit against Pierce Butler (for charges advanced in his
divorce-suit against *her*) that she had little or no interest in her
career. In the course of legal proceedings, she had tactlessly
alienated the public by saying that she had been forced by
Butler to resume "the distasteful profession of my youth" in
order to make a living. While appearing the previous year with
Macready, having accepted the offer which Lily had declined,
she snubbed her audience on one occasion by leaving the theatre
before her call, presumably because Oxenford had said of her
acting, "She wants that art by which art is concealed."

Daveport's opinion that Fanny Vining "will be a jewel to any
one who can get her as his leading gal" is a rather *ex post facto*
touch. If he had not already married the lovely Fanny, it was
high time for him to do so. It was probably to celebrate the

engagement of the pair that Lily sent to Fanny Vining a little piece of jewelry along with the following note:

> 40 Upper Baker Street,
> March 29, 1849

Dearest Fanny:

Will you wear my little gift in remembrance of me—a token of my friendship and esteem—and of my appreciation of your heart and talents?

It is an emblem of *night and morning* that I lay upon your bosom—should your eyes turn to it sometimes when you are in sorrow (for "sorrow comes to all") let it remind you that the darkest hour is one upon which morning is ready to burst, and the heaviest grief has its morning hour of consolation ever near.

I fear that I am wrong to speak of sorrow when I wish you nothing but gladness, and would like to see you (perhaps *make* you) forget past trials and look brightly to the future.

If there were magic in good wishes, dear Fanny, a brilliant destiny would await you through those of your warm and sincere friend

> Anna Cora Mowatt

Fanny Vining was one of the most popular members of the Marylebone company. She came of a well-known theatrical family; and though she had been on the stage since she was a young girl, she had been carefully brought up. She was a handsome, vivacious brunette, full of fun and high spirits, but with that same innate delicacy that Lily admired in Davenport. Lily had become deeply attached to Fanny and the marriage must have given her pleasure. What may have been the "past trials" to which she refers, is not known. But Fanny's marriage to Davenport was a real love-match. For the next thirty years, their devotion to each other steadily gave the lie to the popular notion that the theatre does not make for domestic bliss.

In April, Watts produced *Romeo and Juliet* with Fanny Vining as Romeo. This was the great era of "breeches" parts, and nothing so titillated the audiences of the forties as to see a handsome woman in tights. Everybody was delighted with the production, in particular the actors. Lily said she had never had a Romeo she "liked so well". Fanny herself seemed less enthusiastic. She had only done the part to please Lily, and it was her last venture of this sort. "I think women deserve to have men for lovers," she candidly told a reporter—a remark which must have pleased Davenport when he read it.

The last play of the season was a new offering, *The Witch Wife*, by Henry Spicer. The playwright-lessee of the Olympic had been much taken with Lily's performance in *The Lords of Ellingham* the previous year; and had written this new pseudo-historical drama about a noble lady falsely accused of being a witch, to display Mrs. Mowatt's delicate grace under strenuous emotions. It was only mildly successful despite general praise for her performance. The work was printed later in the summer with this dedication:

To
Anna Cora Mowatt
a name familiar
To the English Public as that of an
Accomplished Authoress and Actress
But to which a more select Circle Annex
The Better title of
Dear and Honoured Friend
This Piece is Dedicated
With the kindest wishes of
The Writer

Lily's appearance in *The Witch Wife* had followed a week's illness, or, in *The Times* version, "a severe indisposition". Whatever else may have been the trouble, overwork was certainly a contributing factor. Since September she had been acting steadily without a break. In addition to at least five new parts, she had the nerve-wracking responsibility of presenting *Armand* to the London public. Finally, James had begun to show alarming symptoms of a recurrence of his old trouble. The sight of one eye had much deteriorated, and his general physical condition caused Lily great anxiety. Her one thought, as soon as she was back on her feet and the Marylebone season had come to a close, was to get him out of London, away from the tense atmosphere of the theatre and worries about contracts and box-office receipts.

In July, the Mowatts went to Stratford to fulfill a long yearning to see Shakespeare's birthplace. Their visit almost coincided with the rescue of the birth-house from destruction. Lily had followed with breathless interest the events between the announcement that the house would be sold at auction, and its purchase by the association which had been hastily formed to preserve it as a national monument. She had a deep-seated reverence for the material surroundings from which men had moved to immortality. She felt always that in the rooms which had echoed to their voices, there still lingered vibrations through which lesser men with spirits properly attuned could strike contact with the yet-living presences. It may have been a primitive notion but it was to have interesting consequences. For out of this deep conviction that the *manes* of the great hovered about their earthly habitats to inspire and help those left behind, Anna Cora was to render a significant service to her own country. Her decisive share in salvaging Mount Vernon belongs to a later chapter; but during this visit to Stratford she got many of the ideas for this future crusade.

After Stratford, the Mowatts spent a month on the Isle of Wight. It was a time of pure enchantment. James's condition began to show improvement, and Lily for the first time in her life knew the meaning of "perfect health". The couple passed every moment they could out-of-doors. Lily rode horseback in the mornings before breakfast, galloping hatless across the downs with her long hair streaming in the wind. Afternoons, when the spirit moved, they hired a carriage and went sightseeing; but they did nothing under pressure. In the balmy warmth of the soft sea air, strain and tension magically disappeared.

The rest of the summer was spent in a blossom-covered cottage in Richmond. Here Lily worked on her repertory, pacing up and down the graveled path of their little garden while James sat in a basket-chair and cued her. Sometimes late in the evening, when the moon was full, they took a punt and rowed on the river—past Pope's villa at Twickenham or up to Kew. They saw few people. To be well and to be together was enough. The passing weeks seemed to lift them ever higher on a great wave of happiness.

People scarcely recognized Anna Cora when she returned to the theatre the middle of September. The little lines of strain which had begun to show about her mouth and eyes in the spring had vanished. The creamy pallor of her face had taken on a delicate bloom. She had gained weight so that her childish figure had filled out in becoming curves. "I have never seen her look so hale and hearty," wrote Davenport to Ford. "A regular bouncing English lass."

Anna Cora had signed another contract with Watts for a full year, an unheard-of engagement at that time. Watts, too, seemed to have blossomed during the summer. In the fine glow of success he was making ambitious plans for the new season. Among other things he had decided to change his base of operations. In the late spring the Olympic Theatre had burned and was now rebuilding. Watts had taken a lease on this new house to which he planned to move his company in December, when construction would be completed.

His motive for abandoning the Marylebone was twofold. The new theatre—which was being built according to Watts's own design—would offer superior facilities for the sort of productions he meant to do. The Olympic also had an established clientele, and, although slightly smaller than the Marylebone, would be more profitable. The pit would be given over to stalls, following the new fashion, and the cheaper seats would be relegated to the gallery. There was another reason for the change, perhaps not openly expressed. In the Olympic, situated nearer the center of the regular theatre district, Mrs. Mowatt would take her rightful place among the galaxy of London stars, dimming their lustre with her own particular brightness. For in all these plans—inseparably bound up with his passion for the theatre—the figure of Anna Cora occupied the central place in Watts's mind. By now he was madly in love with her.

If Lily knew this (and it is idle to suppose that she did not), her attitude towards Watts remained unchanged. She continued to have him to the intimate little suppers in Baker Street. In her eyes, he was simply a rare friend and a paragon among managers; and if she caught the echoes of stage-door gossip, she was perfectly confident of having the situation well under control. She enjoyed adoration—but most of her heart belonged to James; what was left belonged to her art.

Watts's enthusiasm was contagious. As he outlined his scheme for the Olympic—not neglecting the prospects for profit—the Mowatts listened attentively; for they admired more and more the combination of Watts's extraordinary business acumen with his high artistic ideals. Whether finally the suggestion came from Watts himself, or from James, or merely developed spontaneously from their long talks together, James became a secret partner in the new enterprise. His faith in the little man was certainly justified by the showing at the Marylebone. James had seen the theatre crowded night after night. Furthermore, Watts was not seeking capital from the outside. He was putting his own money into his share of the new association: that fact alone would have encouraged James to invest. But what really made it seem right was that Watts was such a true friend. So James turned over Lily's accumulated savings, to the amount of several thousand pounds, to Watts.

The Olympic was scheduled to open at Christmas-time. Meanwhile the season would begin at the Marylebone. During one of Watts's visits to Richmond to discuss details of the new theatre, Lily had laughingly expressed the hope that the star's dressing-room would not be the usual black cell. Watts promised·to take care of the matter. This he did—and without waiting to move into the Olympic. When Lily arrived at the Marylebone she found that her quarters had undergone a transformation "worthy of Aladdin's lamp". The small chamber off the greenroom (which as a star she did not frequent), had been assigned to her. It was carpeted in deep moss-green velvet with a pattern of roses. The walls were papered in panels with bunches of roses, and a garland of roses decorated the ceiling. The shades of the gas-fixtures were of glass shaped like water-lilies, and on one wall was a magnificent painting of the same flowers from the hand of Valentine Bartholomew, who enjoyed the title of "Flower Painter to Her Majesty the Queen". Large mirrors on the walls reflected gold furniture upholstered in pale-blue satin.

Lily gasped when the happy Watts threw open the door to

reveal his handiwork to her. She was much affected at this mark of his thoughtfulness, for the whole room bore the unmistakable signs of his personal supervision. But such magnificence had its drawbacks. Lily had merely wanted reasonable comfort. The exquisite appointments of the new dressing-room were so delicate that both Anna Cora and her maid were constantly afraid of breaking something. The latter put it clearly: "I don't like fairyland when there's *real work* going on."

The Marylebone season opened with *Velasco*, a play by Epes Sargent which had been presented some years earlier in America with Ellen Tree in the leading feminine rôle. For some reason Anna Cora did not act in this production, though she appeared on the stage with other members of the company for the singing of the national anthem which inaugurated the new season. She notes that the play "found favor with the public", although it may be inferred from the press that this public was not very large. *The Era* said that the play "partakes greatly of the general style of American writing. It is crude, extravagant and ill-digested." The friendly Oxenford asserted that the work "seemed to be founded on *The Cid*" and that "the author had shown much ingenuity" in turning a plot of the rigidly classical school into a melodrama abounding with palpable situations." At least Lily had done what she could for her old friend—whose reputation in London, even if he had had one, would not have suffered much since none of the papers mentioned the author's name.

Watts's next offering was *Much Ado About Nothing*. The play was a favorite with the public—and the house for this, Anna Cora's first appearance of the season, was crammed to the ceiling. At the end of the performance, *The Times* reported: "Mrs. Mowatt was vociferously called for by the audience and was led on by Mr. Davenport, when she received such a shower of bouquets that she was embarrassed to reduce them to portable dimensions." The sweeping acclaim of the critics meant more than her establishment as a popular favorite. Its true import can best be seen in *The London Illustrated News* on September 29:

This lady's acting is not to be judged by the ordinary rules of art, or by comparison with other artists. We must take it as it proceeds from her own idiosyncrasy which is both peculiar and pleasing.

She had at last won the right to her complete freedom as an artist.

(In connection with this production of *Much Ado* there is an interesting note in *The Theatrical Journal* which gives us insight into London performances of this time. It praises Anna Cora and Davenport especially because

> . . . they are always perfect in the text, the result of painstaking study only. When we see so much carelessness at other establishments as to this important particularity it is a fact worth noting.

Despite Davenport's remarks on the generally higher quality of British dramatic productions, in London—as in America—the indispensable man of the theatre was usually the prompter).

Lily might have taken a very human satisfaction in having the critics eat their words. "We now know what Shakespeare meant Beatrice to be," said John Heraud who had earlier declared that the part of Beatrice was entirely out of Mrs. Mowatt's reach. But any such triumph was blighted by the reappearance of an old enemy. The very morning after the opening of *Much Ado*, James had complained of severe pain in his right eye. The specialist who was called in was very grave when he finished the examination. Within a week, though the pain was relieved, James had completely lost the sight of this eye.

This was not all. He started to lose weight, and he seemed to be overcome by a terrible lassitude. Lily grew frantic. She was rehearsing *Cymbeline* now, and the part of Imogen was new to her. Usually, work on a new rôle was a thrilling challenge; but she found herself unable to concentrate at rehearsals. The moment she could leave the theatre she flew back to the rooms in Baker Street.

One doctor after another was consulted. The diagnoses were varied—but eventually there was unanimity as to the treatment to be followed. James must leave London. He must go to a milder climate where his resistance would not be taxed. Perhaps a long sea voyage would be beneficial; and so it was decided that James would spend the winter in the West Indies.

Lily was now in agony. She was terrified to let James out of her sight; but the added expense of his illness made it imperative that she continue to work. Everybody tried to reassure her. Watts was wonderful in his kindness. In the end it was James's own insistence that prevailed upon her to stay behind.

A number of things had to be decided quickly. James was chiefly anxious that Lily should not be left alone. A very happy solution to this problem presented itself. Davenport and Fanny were expecting their first child and were looking for a suitable place to live. They had found a pleasant house in Green Street near Grosvenor Square. It was too large and expensive for them alone, but with Lily to share it, it might be just the thing. So the house was immediately rented; and before James left Lily was installed on the first floor with the Davenports overhead. It was an ideal arrangement. For the first time in her life Lily would live alone—but with such devoted friends as Edward and Fanny under the same roof she would at least not feel lost.

James's going left a blank in her life which she filled simply by working twice as hard as she had before. Her Imogen, of which she had been so fearful, had a pronounced success. In the next play—Sheridan Knowles's *The Love Chase*—she also came off well, though she had to stand comparison with the great Mrs. Nisbett whose memory still evoked the militant loyalty of the critics. *The Love Chase* was followed by *Twelfth Night*, in which she was once again undisputed mistress of the field. It was an almost unbearable descent to have to do next a blood-and-thunder melodrama by Searle called *The Shadow on the Wall*. After Viola's exquisite poetry, Anna Cora found it well-nigh impossible to mouth the ranting lines of Cicely, the heroine of Searle's play; so she proceeded to do a little re-writing on the part, and made it at least endurable. From the reactions of the audience, she flattered herself that she had done a very good job—as indeed she probably had. But when a knock came at her dressing-room door after the performance and a gentleman was announced as Mr. Searle, author of the play, the glow of self-satisfaction disappeared. What went on at this interview may only be guessed at; it was too painful for Lily to record.

The season at the Marylebone was climaxed by a grand fête given by Watts for the entire company including ballet girls, stagehands and even the call-boy. The latter might have "preferred the luxury of going home to bed", but Watts omitted to ask nobody regularly employed in the theatre. It was an unheard-of procedure in a world where caste-lines were so rigidly drawn, and the invitations had probably been issued at Anna Cora's request. If so, she had reason to be proud of this exhibition of practical democracy. "Although the position of the subordinates was a novel one . . . the most fastidious observer could not have picked a flaw in their conduct. Their decorum was unimpeachable." At both the tables of the principals and that of the artisans and *corps de ballet*, champagne (Watts's favorite refreshment) was bountifully dispensed; yet—at least among the lowly —"no loud mirth was heard throughout the evening. Subdued enjoyment reigned in its place, with as strict observance of nice proprieties as would have been deemed necessary in an aristocratic ball room." We must forgive Anna Cora if she tempered her description of what in reality was a very lively party. She was writing this for her autobiography—one purpose of which was to convince the lay world that theatre people were not inevitably wanton gypsies.

The evening's entertainment included speeches, singing and "a few quadrilles and waltzes . . . before supper." The party was to break up early, since most of the actors were exhausted after their four-hour stint. Consequently there was but "one cotillion and a country dance after the collation."

The ceremony of leave-taking had just begun when a loud cry came from a group near the footlights. Suddenly a blazing figure dashed up the stage, screaming wildly. Instantly the theatre was thrown into panic. Women fainted or tried to rush into the streets. Some of the men attempted to seize the girl whose garments were in flames but were thrust back by the creature's wild clawing. Only the presence of mind of Mrs. Renshaw, the wardrobe-mistress, saved the girl's life. With a sweep of her hand she snatched off the heavy cloth from the banqueting-table and with arms outspread caught the girl and threw her to the floor, enveloping her in the folds of the linen. Though she burnt herself badly she extinguished the flames. As for the girl, a member of the ballet whose gauze skirt had come too close to the gas footlights, her arms were burnt almost to the bone, though her face escaped harm. A doctor was summoned and he did the best he could for her; finally in great pain she was taken home in Lily's carriage.

For a long time the dancer's life was in the balance. Lily went to see her almost every day and enlisted help from other quarters. A fund was raised, subscribed to most generously by Watts and by Lily, and the best medical care was obtained for her.

Anna Cora's interest in the girl brought her into contact with an element in the theatre she had never really known before. The Marylebone, like every legitimate theatre, had its regular *corps de ballet*, since incidental dancing was a part of each production. The girls also acted as supernumeraries, court ladies or servants, and occasionally played bit parts. Traditionally they were so remote from the regular actors, both professionally and socially, that the latter were hardly aware of their existence. They were treated often with contempt, and some of them in order to eke out their wretchedly inadequate wages sold their charms to a steady clientele. But, as Lily soon discovered, there were many who were honest, hard-working girls, usually with a family to support in the background. Such was the case with the poor creature whom Lily had now taken under her wing. The girl lived in a miserable slum with a semi-invalid mother; but Lily was struck by the cleanliness of their one room and the pathetic little evidences of the girl's efforts to make it cheerful and comfortable. She was also impressed by the patience and courage the girl showed in the long ordeal of her recovery. From this moment on, Lily made it a point to be friendly with the other dancing-girls in the company—a gesture which some of her player associates frowned upon or regarded as a mark of Mrs. Mowatt's eccentricity.

Her democratic principles revealed themselves in another way which her fellow-players probably welcomed. Before the opening of the new Olympic, she requested Watts to give all the regular actors of the company equal billing, thus—so far as formal designation went—abolishing the "star system". She did this partly to create a stronger *esprit de corps*, which she knew would improve the ensemble acting. But she was also prompted by indignation at the way in which critics constantly by-passed some of the finest players in a company, merely because the star was traditionally the center of attention. It was a pioneer move for which Anna Cora Mowatt has never been given credit in the history of the theatre.

In announcing the transfer of the company from the Marylebone to the Olympic, *The Times* referred to Watts's extraordinary contribution in raising so high the standard of the drama in London. The paper noted that, on the last night at the Marylebone, the audience in an unheard-of gesture had called Watts before the curtain to show its appreciation of what he had done. The article went on to say that the presence of Anna Cora and Davenport had established the Marylebone as one of the leading theatres in the city.

The opening bill in the new theatre was *The Two Gentlemen of Verona*, in which Anna Cora had no part. Then on January 28 occurred the inevitable production of *Fashion*—inevitable simply because wherever Lily went it was sure to follow. On other grounds this was a thoroughly daring venture which only Watts's devotion to the author could have justified. Practically everything in the play, from its satire on New York high life—towards which London was completely apathetic—to its ridicule of European manners—which could only excite hostility—made it a debatable offering. But Watts was determined to display this further proof of the many-sided genius whose gifts, as he believed, were such a perfect counterpart to his own.

As in the case of *Armand*, the play was done with scrupulous care. Every effort was made to re-create the feeling and the tone of the original. The actors were coached in Americanisms like "O.K." (heard in *Fashion* for perhaps the first time on any stage) and "I reckon"; and some pains were even taken to suggest the American accent. Davenport of course played Adam Trueman—to which he imparted all the native flavor of which he was capable, and this was considerable. Fanny Vining played the innocuous Gertrude. Mrs. Marston, the efficient "old lady" of the company, acted Mrs. Tiffany; and the other rôles were distributed as the special talents of the troupe permitted. Lily was uncertain about the whole business, but Watts assured her that the play would go. A good play would always go in London, if it were properly done. *Fashion was* a good play; and Mrs. Mowatt could see for herself how it was being treated. "The mise en scène was truly magnificent."

Lily may have had her doubts about the warmth with which *Fashion* would be received; but she did not expect the critics to break into open warfare over it. Yet this is exactly what happened —though most of the firing was over Anna Cora's own head. In the divided opinions of the press some of the critics' pet grievances against each other were brought into the open, and the sniping became fast and furious. This was especially so in the case of *The Morning Post* versus *Punch*. *The Post* attacked the play savagely as a piece of childish nonsense, prefacing its criticism with the remark that the occasion was not one in which gallantry should yield to integrity. "Genius", said Mr. Jenkins, the oracle of *The Post*, "is of no sex"; and informed his readers that he would discuss Mrs. Mowatt's work on a strictly impersonal basis. But this was exactly what Jenkins did not do. His remarks reached a climax of indignation not at the quality of the play but at the fact that the authoress when acclaimed at the final curtain had appeared on the stage *"ready dressed for the occasion"*.

At this *Punch* rushed to Mrs. Mowatt's defense:

> Why could you not have moderated the rancor of your pen a little, Jenkins? Why attack the lady and stranger personally? Is it your individual self, or your order,—Jenkins or flunkeydom, —that Mrs. Mowatt has offended? Jenkins, you say that "genius is of no sex." Neither is criticism, as personified by you. At any rate it is not manly.

The Times gave the play a long and careful analysis, taking pains to point out that while the types represented by Mrs. Mowatt were not English, they ought not to be absolutely condemned for that reason. In fact "the American tone given to all the characters endows the work with a freshness that distinguishes it from the many comedies produced on our stage."

The Examiner took a distinctly different view of the play but generously prefaced its notice by quoting one of *The Times's* encomiums:

> We are happy to give the lady authoress all the advantage desirable from this good-natured criticism of a deservedly high authority, but we are bound to add we do not in the least agree with it. The piece seems to us to have no merit whatever, negative or positive. For the most part it was nonsense, nor was it nonsense void of offense. . . . For what has here drawn praise and glory to Mrs. Mowatt, Mrs. Trollope would have been denounced to the tar barrel. . . .

The Sun bestowed on *Fashion* the highest tribute in its power:

> America is worthily repaying the dramatic debt she owes us. The seeds of the dramatic art, which have been scattered by all our best dramatic artistes broadcast on the American soil, have fructified, and are now bearing fruit. . . . Rough and ranting melodramas have formed the staple of what America hitherto has sent us; but last night this reproach was wiped out, and there was represented at the Olympic Theatre with the most deserved success, an original five-act comedy, the scene of which is laid in New York, and which delineates American manners after the same fashion as our Garrick, Colman, and Sheridan were accustomed to delineate English manners, and which, as regards plot, construction, character, or dialogue, is worthy to take its place by the side of the best of English comedies.

The Literary Gazette also championed the play. The critic of this journal was G. H. Lewes, who in addition to being the husband of George Eliot, was a distinguished writer for the theatre. In his review of *Fashion* he brought home to the English a rather unpalatable but undeniable truth:

> In the barrenness of home authorship, in the spirit of humiliation which attaches to our dependence upon the French for a mongrel dramatic literature, the public will greet with satisfaction the quasi-English production of an American author; and to this author even a qualified approval, tendered in spite of English self-love, must be gratifying. . . .

The controversy was prolonged by the weeklies and was finally brought to an end by an anonymous reader of *The Theatrical*

Times. Someone had written a letter to *The Daily Times* denouncing *Fashion* as immoral because the forgery detected by Adam Trueman was covered up, and the forger was not turned over to the police. The correspondent of *The Theatrical Times* cautioned:

> Good Christian folks, this lesson heed in time,
> That Forgery's a very shocking crime,
> And governesses well this warning mark,—
> Don't go with foreign counts in the dark!

The last couplet refers to an episode in the play in which the blameless Gertrude is almost compromised by hiding in a closet with Count Jolimaître.

If *Fashion* made little money for Watts, it provided Anna Cora with good publicity. It had been a long time since London had seen a woman who combined such varied gifts, along with beauty and charm—not perhaps since the days of the matchless Dorinda —so that when she appeared in the Olympic's next production as Desdemona to the Othello of Gustavus Brooke the house was packed. Desdemona is not a great tragic rôle; but in this instance she was the cynosure of all eyes—although Brooke's Othello was a powerful performance and Davenport's Iago one of the most impressive anyone remembered.

But the laurels which now crowned all Lily's work had quite lost their meaning. The one voice whose approval had had positive value since her girlhood was not there. Without James she was without her other self. And every actor—as Lily well knew both from her own experience and from Diderot's celebrated *Paradoxe du Comédien*—must have a second self always at a little distance to observe and check the personality acting upon the stage. This mystical second self is usually developed only with long practice. In Lily's case, it had been there, ready-made, from the beginning—in the person of her astutely critical and deeply loving husband. Without James on the other side of the footlights Lily felt depressed and insecure.

There was apparently nothing to mark this in her acting. But those close to her were aware of the strain under which she was working. The person most concerned about her was Watts.

Since James's absence he had increased his attention to Anna
Cora, though only as a friend especially anxious for her happiness
and welfare. Her longing for her husband doubtless made him
feel for the first time the real hopelessness of his own passion;
but this did not alter his conduct toward her. Whatever he did
was with circumspection and according to the code of a gentleman, and Lily was profoundly grateful to him.

Near the close of February, Lily's spirits received a lift from
a spree of clothes-buying. This was no common shopping orgy
since it developed from a somewhat special circumstance. In
December, Queen Adelaide, the widow of William IV and aunt
of Queen Victoria, had died. Her death occurred just prior to the
opening of the new Olympic. The theatre had been draped in
black; and regulations had required that the company, when it
emerged on the stage for the singing of the national anthem,
should also wear mourning. Lily's Swedenborgian principles forbade a display of the inky weeds of woe. So she paid her respects
to the deceased lady by wearing pure white. This created a mild
sensation but no scandal.

Now Queen Adelaide was to figure sartorially a second time in
Anna Cora's life. On February 9 at Marlborough House, the
Queen's effects were put up for sale. It was of course a most select
and dignified proceeding. There was no question of admission to
the general public. Invitations were sent to a very choice list, in a
graduated scale of importance, for the three days of the sale. The
first day was set aside for members of the Royal Household, the
second for the highest peers of the realm, the third for lesser
nobility and other people of distinction. Lily obtained a ticket for
the third day, probably through Lord Craven, owner of the
Olympic. Her purchase consisted of several of the late Queen's
court and ball gowns. It was really a wonderful buy; for Lily had
developed a streak of thrift, and she perceived that in the second-
hand gowns of royalty she would have a supply of stage costumes to last her whole life. The fact that the ball-gowns of
Queen Adelaide had no bearing on most periods of her repertoire
made little difference. The materials were sumptuous, and the
gowns were beautifully made. They would show off handsomely
on the stage; and in the theatre of those days that was the essen-

tial. There were other interesting purchases during the sale, including a set of Dresden dessert plates acquired by Queen Victoria. She had been offered her late aunt's table silver but declined to buy it, stating that her household was sufficiently supplied.

On February 19 a new play, *The Noble Heart* by G. H. Lewes, was presented with great acclaim. It seems to have been written especially for Anna Cora. Largely made up of borrowings from Spanish drama with a touch of *Ernani*, it was a brilliant success both for Anna Cora and for Watts. "The dreamy sorrows of the lady were beautifully and poetically rendered by Mrs. Mowatt," recorded *The Era*. "The costumes and scenery were magnificent."

But Lily's appearance in the play had been at a price she could ill afford. By the end of January, after the excitement caused by *Fashion*, she had been already worn out. On top of this had come discouraging news from James. She had been expecting his momentary return; but his condition did not seem to be improving, and he wrote now that he would not arrive in England until spring. There was also bad news from America. Margaret Grey had been ill for several months, and it was feared she was hopelessly afflicted with consumption.

All during rehearsals of *The Noble Heart*, Lily had to put forth a great effort to keep her mind on her work. For the first time in her life her phenomenal memory began to forsake her. She found herself struggling desperately to retain her lines. Every moment she was not onstage, she sat with the "lengths" in her hand. But her eyes seemed to look through the words, not at them. When the play opened, between each exit and entrance she frantically continued to study.

The Noble Heart ran for three nights and then was suddenly withdrawn. Another play was substituted, without Mrs. Mowatt. She had had to go to bed and rest. On March 1 she appeared once more in Lewes's play. The next day, as she was trying to gather strength to go back to the theatre, word came that both the Marylebone—of which Watts was still lessee—and the Olympic were closed. There was no clear story, but from the garbled details it appeared that Watts was in jail.

That night Lily went to bed with a high temperature. For the next four months life was a complete blank.

CHAPTER EIGHTEEN

The Long Way Home

Lily's malady was diagnosed as brain fever, a term covering a wide range of disorders but usually pointing to nervous collapse. It is not surprising that Lily should finally have been overcome, for she had been on the brink of a breakdown for weeks. The increasing pressure of work, the worry over James, and perhaps the uneasy sense that Watts's feeling for her might soon become unmanageable, all contributed to a state of affairs so frightening that Lily began to feel a yearning to escape. Watts's débâcle and arrest were merely the last details in the nightmare which was closing in on her. When the news came that the theatre was shut, Lily's hold on reality gave way.

For the next four months the personality she had years ago named the "simpleton" was put aside, and the "gypsy" ruled supreme. A nurse was procured to take care of her, and she continued to live in her rooms in Green Street under the loyal and ever-watchful eyes of Edward and Fanny Davenport.

After the doctors had made their usual pronouncement to the effect that "only time would tell," Davenport took matters in his own hands. Lily's psychopathic condition seems to have caused no trouble. She was content to remain within four walls improvising nonsense verses or singing to herself in a high, bird-like tuneless voice. But her physical condition had also broken down under the general stress. The symptoms of consumption manifested themselves again, and the singing was often interrupted by long terrible fits of coughing. This was the point at which Davenport began to use the techniques in which Epes Sargent had so carefully drilled him before the departure from America. In order to relieve Lily's agony when the coughing racked her worn frame beyond endurance, he placed her under hypnosis. In this state Lily prescribed treatments for herself and made predictions about the course of her illness. Once she foretold with absolute accuracy a hemorrhage which occurred several months later.

One episode of this time is of interest as revealing her continued powers of clairvoyance. Fanny Davenport had recently given birth to a daughter—that second Fanny Davenport whose lustre brightened the American stage in the later years of the century. Dr. Westmacott, Fanny's physician, had also attended Mrs. Mowatt on occasion, but he had never seen the effects of Davenport's "treatments." One day while calling on Fanny he learned Lily was at that moment in a state of trance. He expressed a wish to see her, for he had brought a little present for her. He patted a flat parcel in the pocket of his coat but did not reveal to Fanny what it was. Fanny immediately suggested that they go downstairs to Mrs. Mowatt's sitting-room. As they moved along the hall they heard her high childish voice chanting a meaningless little song.

Dr. Westmacott knocked on the door. Immediately the singing stopped and Lily called, "Come in, Doctor."

This identification of her caller was amazing enough—for she had not been told of his presence in the house—but it was nothing to what followed. Westmacott and Fanny entered the room, and the physician chatted for a few moments with the patient who was stretched out on a sofa. As he rose to go Westmacott said, "I have brought a little present for you."

Lily clapped her hands in delight. "Oh, let me have it!"

Westmacott took the package from his pocket, but held it close to him. "You must tell me first what it is," he said.

"Then you must let me have it," said Lily again and she snatched the package from the physician. Then as though playing a game she pressed the package, still wrapped in heavy brown paper with a string about it and sealed, against her forehead. For a moment her eyes closed. When they opened she said, "You have brought me a Jew, a lovely Jew."

She then tore away the wrappings and smiled with pleasure at a beautiful little engraving of Rembrandt's painting called *The Jew*.

One day late in July Lily opened her eyes from sleep, as she thought. Dr. Westmacott was sitting by her bed gazing at her intently. A nurse whom she did not recognize stood at the foot of the bed, and on the other side was Fanny. She heard the physician whisper, "Hush! She is coming to herself." He then asked Lily if she recognized him. She thought this an odd question, for she had known Westmacott for many months and was fond of him. She had no sense of the long lapse of time, or what had happened in the interval.

She herself relates what then occurred.

Dr. Westmacott wisely determined not to deceive me in regard to my illness or any of the events which had taken place during my long unconsciousness. At my eager inquiries he took up the broken chain of memory and supplied the missing links. Mr. Mowatt had returned to England some months previous—he was better—I should soon be allowed to see him.

The theatre—it was still closed. It had been opened but one night, and that was on the occasion of a benefit given to Miss Vining. The company were heavy losers. The manager—very gently the kind doctor communicated the fearful intelligence that related to him.

How much of the story Westmacott actually revealed is not certain. Lily sums up the principal facts in two sentences, keeping the whole thing in a cool impersonal light which gives no idea either of what really had happened or of her own reactions to the terrible details.

On March 16 *The London Illustrated News* noted in its column of theatre gossip that the Olympic and Marylebone theatres were closed "in consequence of a mysterious charge made at the Mansion House on the part of the Globe Insurance Office against the lessee Mr. Walter Watts for the last twelve years an accounting clerk in the establishment."

The question which agitated the theatre world was: who, in reality, was Walter Watts? It was a question that might well have been asked before. But Watts's cheery, open-hearted nature, his urbanity, his apparently solid financial background—above all his tremendous success, precluded the asking of such questions. His extraordinary achievement in the theatre had focussed attention away from the man himself. When the facts of his story were known, the achievement, to a detached observer at least, was more astounding than ever.

The *Illustrated News* had reported the matter accurately, so far as it went. In the following days the rest of the London press supplied the missing details.

Watts had always been regarded as "somebody in the City." In the sense that he was not absolutely "nobody" this was true. He was a clerk in the accounting office of the Globe Insurance Company, of which his father was an official. Since his earliest days, Watts had been hopelessly, passionately stage-struck. He had haunted the theatres for years and had eventually become a small investor in one or two dramatic enterprises. This had led him behind the curtain, where he had studied the details of dramatic production with a fanatical intensity.

It was not until he saw Lily in the winter of 1848 that his great scheme took shape. Watts was spellbound by that "peculiar fascination" to which the critics constantly referred in trying to describe the beauty, grace, intelligence and art of Mrs. Mowatt. Before the spring was out Watts determined that his life henceforth would be in the theatre, and that at the center of that life Mrs. Mowatt must take her place. The qualities which set her apart from the other women on the London stage were qualities which he alone could appreciate at their true value. But in a proper setting the rest of the world would also see her greatness. Watts made it his mission to provide that setting.

He took the shortest way to achieve his end; but he planned every move carefully. Large sums of money passed daily through his hands. One of his functions was to check the receipts of the insurance company as they were turned over to the bank for deposit. It was a simple matter to help himself to checks and cash, and the shortage would pass unnoticed—at least temporarily—since Watts himself handled the accounts. The borrowing was of course only for a short term, for Watts was certain that he would make money in his venture. But he was fully aware of what he was doing, and he made preparations in case his plan misfired. A few days before appropriating the money for the lease of the Marylebone he took advantage of the chance to acquire two shares in the Globe Insurance Company. Because of the nature of the company's organization, this made him technically a partner in the business. As such he would not be liable to arrest for larceny, since under the law theft from a business by one of the partners was tantamount to theft from oneself, a matter over which the courts had no jurisdiction.

The theft was discovered in the usual way, by the auditing of the company's books. Watts was immediately arrested and taken off to jail. He accepted this without protest, serenely confident that all would be well.

His trial occurred on May 10 in the Central Criminal Court of London. *The Times* on the following day gave a full report of the proceedings, at least so far as Watts's personal activities were concerned. None of his theatrical associates was mentioned. There were a number of witnesses for his character. Watts's father protested his son's innocence. It developed that everybody at the Globe office was aware of Watts's theatre enterprise, as was inevitable in view of the position he had attained. But it had apparently occurred to no one to inquire into the source of his capital. Watts's superior did state that he had remonstrated with the young man on the impropriety of the theatrical venture. The total amount of the defalcation was not mentioned (although it was later reported to be about £40,000). One check for £1400 was introduced as sufficient evidence of theft.

Up to a point everything went as Watts expected. There was no conviction for stealing money, but by a technicality which he had overlooked, the court did find him guilty of stealing a piece of paper—the check itself, which was an instrument belonging to the payor and not the payee. Watts was remanded to Newgate Prison to await sentence.

Part of the ensuing period he spent in the prison infirmary with *delirium tremens*. He was returned to his cell on the day before his scheduled appearance in court, apparently in good health and spirits. He confided to his cell-mate that he would probably get off with a few months more or less.

On July 11 Watts was sentenced. He appeared in court elegantly groomed and easy in his manner. When summoned to rise he sprang jauntily to his feet. The judge then made a few remarks on Watts's perfidy in coldly arranging matters so that his major crime would lie outside the law. In view of this circumstance it behooved the court to impose the maximum sentence allowable for the subsidiary and punishable crime—the stealing of a piece of paper. Watts was condemned to transportation for ten years.

There was no indication of any reaction to the sentence. Back in his cell Watts seemed too dazed to answer his cell-mate's questions. He lay down on his bunk and apparently went to sleep. Early in the morning of July 12 he was found by the cell-mate hanging from an iron bar over the water-closet. A doctor was summoned and Watts was pronounced dead.

He was hanging quite perpendicularly with his back to the wall. He was in his shirt with a napkin across his chest. Under the napkin was a locket with the miniature of a woman, young and beautiful with long curls falling about her shoulders. He had hanged himself with a woman's silk scarf.

How many of these details Lily learned from Dr. Westmacott, or indeed ever learned, is not known. She could not have been ignorant of the miniature for everybody in London knew that Watts had died with a picture of Mrs. Mowatt next his heart. There was also no doubt that the scarf too was hers, probably a memento lightly given, or purloined by him from her dressing-room.

Only the knowledge of her own innocence in the whole ghastly affair saved her from a relapse—that, and the urgent necessity of looking after James. For though there was some improvement in his condition Lily was shocked when she first saw her husband. He had lost more weight, and his step was so feeble that he tottered as he walked.

James too had found his beloved greatly changed. He was deeply distressed to see that the heavy mass of hair which had formerly hung to her waist was gone. During her illness she had often complained of its weight and had begged her nurse and Fanny Davenport to cut it off. They had thought the request simply a vagary of her condition and had paid no attention to it. One day when Lily was left alone in her room she seized a pair of shears that had accidentally been left near her bed and cut the hair completely away. When James saw Lily it was still very short, but Fanny had arranged it in little curls all over her head, tied about with a bright ribbon.

James had spent two weeks after his return to England at Malvern taking a water-cure. This was the great day of hydropathy, and its popularity as a universal nostrum was only comparable to that of psychoanalysis in our own time. James was convinced that the treatments he had received under Sir W. E. Wilson had benefited him, and he wished to return to Malvern now with Lily.

So, late in July, Lily was lifted onto the train, where a bed had been installed for her between two seats, and they made the trip into the west country. At Malvern they rented a small cottage surrounded by a large luxuriant garden. Here they remained until late October. James faithfully and desperately took the treatments. Lily, always casual about medical matters, was less diligent in following her regimen. She seemed to benefit more by long rides on donkey-back across the Malvern hills. Once or twice James accompanied her in a dog-cart, but the exertion was too great for him and he soon gave up the attempt.

About the first of November the Mowatts returned to London. Toward the close of their stay at Malvern James had grown rapidly worse. He could scarcely walk at all now and had to be carried from his sofa to the carriage. In London Lily found a specialist who for a while infused new hope in both of them. He was able to give James some relief from the constant pain he was now suffering, but from this time on James was confined entirely to his bed. Despite the relief which he had been able to obtain, he knew clearly that he could not last much longer.

He faced the end without melancholy. In his deeply established conviction, death was the beginning of a greater and happier experience. He talked long hours with Lily on the prospect ahead, and his own serenity kept her spirits from sinking. "A never-wavering trust had cast out fear and given to the foot of the Summoner the sound of music."

It was at this point that Lily learned the full extent of the disaster at the Olympic. James told her about his investment in the venture—representing nearly the whole of her earnings both in America and in England. The money of course had been swept away in Watts's ruin. But there was no time to lament this loss, as there was no inclination to blame Watts for it. Both James and Lily felt that somewhere in the inscrutable machinery of life a vital part had come loose, and that the three of them, Lily, James and Walter Watts had been caught in the wreckage.

But tragedy in Lily's belief was only definitive on the stage. In life, new ways were constantly opening up to lead one back into the light, if one had faith and the will to work. These were the dominant traits of her character and they now asserted themselves with typical intensity.

The London season was already well under way when the Mowatts returned to town. It was impossible for Lily to secure a profitable engagement in the city, but she had several offers in the provinces. After a long talk with her husband's physician she decided to accept one of these.

It was agonizing to leave James. Lily had no illusions about his condition, and the doctor had made her no false promises. But their desperate financial straits demanded that she take some action. The doctor was sure that James was in no immediate danger, though he told Lily frankly that recovery was highly improbable, as of course James himself well knew. But he might linger on for months. What mattered to Lily was that he should continue to receive proper care and that he should be comfortable until the end.

She therefore decided to take up an offer in Dublin for three weeks in January, at the end of which time she would hurry back to London. Davenport could not accompany her now. After the closing of the Olympic he had joined Macready and was rapidly rising to eminence on the London stage. Macready had returned to London early in 1850 from a tour in America, a disastrous venture culminating in the bloody Astor Place riot of which Macready had been the innocent cause. But it was typical of his generous nature that he bore no malice to Americans in general for this lamentable event. He had shown this by inviting the popular Davenport to play with him when he came back to London.

Davenport had been given every opportunity to display his gifts at the Haymarket. During a run of *Othello* Davenport and Macready had alternated the rôles of Iago and Othello. In both parts, according to many of the critics, Davenport had outplayed the veteran. This is all the more significant since Macready was making his farewell while still admittedly in his prime, before a public whose devotion to him had in no way abated.

However, Lily did not go to Dublin alone. The maid who had been with her since she opened in London at the Princess's had become James's nurse and would remain behind to look after him. But her sister, Mrs. Renshaw, the former wardrobe-mistress of the Olympic, was looking for a place. When Lily offered to take her to Dublin as companion and maid, Mrs. Renshaw was glad to accept although she had never been in service before. But she and Mrs. Mowatt were old acquaintances. Ever since the horrible accident to the ballet girl at the farewell party in the Marylebone, Lily had admired this woman whose courage and self-sacrifice had saved the girl's life.

Mrs. Renshaw was in her early forties. She had been a widow for nearly twenty years, and most of this time she had been in the theatre. Her vast knowledge of backstage life as well as her experience as a costumer would be of great service to Anna Cora. Altogether it was a most fortunate association. Mrs. Renshaw's loyalty and devotion form a consistently bright element in the closing chapters of Anna Cora's life.

On the evening before the journey James and Lily had a long talk, which, as James said, might be their last. He seemed full of the past, particularly of the dim far-off days when he had walked with Lily to Mme. Chegaray's school, and of the first years of their life together at Melrose. How few of the rosy dreams of those times had come true! How few of the things that he had promised her had he been able to give. He had never meant for her to shoulder the burdens which had been thrust on her; but he was proud of her—and confident, too, that all would go well with her when he was gone. Lily said little, for she could not trust herself to speak, and she had promised the doctor that no excessive show of emotion on her part should disturb James. So she listened and smiled and stroked his hand. A little past midnight he sank into a deep quiet sleep, and Lily stole out of the room.

The train for Liverpool was to start soon after daylight. James had awakened long before and for some time was closeted with Mrs. Renshaw. When Lily went in to bid him a brief farewell she did not inquire as to the subject of their talk. James too regarded Mrs. Renshaw as an old friend and Lily knew that there was an understanding between them. The nature of this understanding she only came to realize with the passing years. In those few brief moments before they left the house in Green Street, James had resigned his trust to Mrs. Renshaw.

From Liverpool the voyagers sailed to Kingston in *The Iron Duke*. Lily recorded that she found comfort in the name. Whatever was of iron in her own nature would be used now to carry her along.

They reached Dublin at half-past eight in the morning. Calcraft, the manager of the Theatre Royal, was supposed to meet the two women traveling alone and to assist them with their mountain of baggage. But Calcraft failed to turn up. So Lily and Mrs. Renshaw were left to shift for themselves. When they and their belongings were at last loaded into a carriage, they drove to the theatre to try to learn the location of the lodgings Calcraft had promised to find for them.

The doorkeeper of the theatre informed them that Calcraft had engaged no rooms. He had searched everywhere, but had been unable to locate quarters such as they had specified: three rooms opening together. The doorkeeper explained that Mr. Calcraft had been afraid to engage anything else for fear it wouldn't suit.

Lily and Mrs. Renshaw were in a dilemma, but they refused to wait shivering in the cold theatre. They got back into the carriage and ordered the driver to take them to Merrion Square. This was the one location Lily had heard of in Dublin. The name was attractive, as was the square when at last they turned into it. At the first green-grocer's Mrs. Renshaw got out of the carriage and made inquiries. The proprietor immediately supplied them with three names where they might obtain rooms. At the first address a pleasant-faced woman showed them to an attractive apartment on the second floor which was exactly what they required—three large rooms adjoining each other. So much for Calcraft's efforts! Somewhere, Lily remarked once that the Irish were only indefatigable at being Irish. She may have had Calcraft in mind.

Anna Cora's leading man for the Dublin engagement was Gustavus Brooke, with whom she had played in London. His presence in the theatre made her feel less alone, and less shy in rehearsing with the new company. But she noted that the atmosphere here was different from that which she had encountered at Manchester and at her first rehearsal in London. Calcraft, despite his casualness, was a gentleman; and his influence was felt throughout the theatre. "The actors were courteous in the extreme, and vied with each other in readiness to conform to the wishes of the stranger." Anna Cora might have attributed this to the fact that the stranger was now a great star, but she preferred to take it as a mark of good manners.

The opening bill was *The Lady of Lyons*, which Lily herself had selected—for the simple reason that in the first two acts she had little or nothing to do, and this gave her time to grow used to the audience and get over any incipient stage-fright. In the long months of her absence from the theatre she had become nervous about facing the public again.

From beginning to end the engagement was a huge success. Lily could not but contrast the attitude of the Dublin press towards an American with that of the London papers. Not, of course, that the Irish were not conscious of their own exalted standards of taste. *The Freeman's Journal* pointed out what an ordeal it was for any actor from abroad to face a Dublin audience:

> It might seem needless to remind the readers of this journal of the fastidious character of that same audience, the most considerate, as it is the most just and generous, of any before which true genius had ever presented its claims. We would not do so were it not that we wish to enhance the magnitude of the delicacy of the compliment paid on last evening by that audience to the fair and gifted actress who came before them as a daughter of America.

Near the end of the engagement *Armand* was played to a house literally bursting at the seams. The Irish still followed the archaic custom of allowing chairs to be placed upon the stage; they were so numerous on this occasion that there was scarcely room for the actors to move about. In fact, one scene in which Armand and Blanche dance about the Maypole on the village green simply had to be abandoned, but the enthusiasm of the audience made up for any minor shortcomings. All the speeches which had been deleted by the English licenser were restored, and Armand's anti-monarchical utterances raised such excitement that it seemed as though the galleries would make a descent upon the stage and carry him off on their shoulders.

The quality of the Irish production could scarcely stand comparison with that of the Marylebone. In the matter of settings Calcraft, gentleman though he was, did not worry too much over niceties. For the last act of *Armand*, which is supposed to take place in a drawing-room of Louis XV, he simply utilized the Elf King's Palace, left over from the Christmas pantomime.

But Dublin was just what Lily needed to lift her out of the dark state of mind in which James's illness and all the events of these last months had left her. She enjoyed the uninhibited exuberance of the Irish audience, even its habit of addressing the actors on the stage with critical or complimentary remarks.

The Dublin visit was a triumph in the grand manner. When Anna Cora drove through the streets she was instantly recognized and greeted with cries of "Bless your swate face!" or "The Lord love ye!". On the last night of her engagement a large crowd was gathered at the stage-door. The press was so great that "the gentlemen" (apparently several) who were escorting Mrs. Mowatt had difficulty in forcing a way to the carriage. There were a number of women in the crowd, many with children in their arms. As Lily passed along they touched her skirt or tried to kiss her hand. One woman raised up her baby and cried: "Look at the baby, me lady! Take a look at me baby!" The throng was so dense that Lily was seated in the carriage before she realized that Mrs. Renshaw had been left behind. Lily sent one of the gentlemen back for her. He found her with some difficulty, nearly trampled underfoot. The gentleman had to repeat her identity over and over before she was allowed to pass to the carriage. When at last they drove away the street was filled with shouts of "God bless ye!"—"Long life to ye!" which echoed until the carriage had disappeared from sight.

Meanwhile good news had come from London. James was better. He wrote every day, sometimes twice. He was immensely pleased by Lily's reception in Dublin. Once, he wrote that after a refreshing night's sleep he had been able to sit up and read—for the first time in months. He spoke always lovingly of Lily and the comfort he derived from reminders of her presence, a portrait which hung at the foot of his bed, and Valentine Bartholomew's lilies (rescued somehow from the dressing-room at the Olympic, whither the painting had been moved from the Marylebone).

The reports were so cheery and so encouraging that Lily felt she might dare delay her return to London to act a fortnight in Newcastle and then play a brief engagement in Edinburgh.

The journey from Dublin to Newcastle, via Liverpool and Carlisle, took the better part of two days. It was late at night when Lily and Mrs. Renshaw arrived in Newcastle. They went straight to a hotel and to bed. In the morning Lily sent to the theatre for her mail. There was but one letter from James. It was in the same placid, cheerful strain as the last ones she had received, but the writing seemed strangely irregular. James usually wrote a beautiful copper-plate hand.

The next day there was no letter. The following day was Sunday, but early Monday morning Lily sent Mrs. Renshaw to the postoffice. She was informed that all mail had been delayed. None at all had come in on Sunday. Lily's hopes now rose: here was the explanation for James's silence.

She went on to the theatre to rehearse. As she passed the doorkeeper he touched his hat and asked respectfully if she were Mrs. Mowatt. In his hand was a large packet of letters, which he explained were delayed mail that had just come in. Lily snatched the packet and hurriedly thumbed through it. There was nothing in James's handwriting but she recognized a letter from Davenport. Hastily she tore it open. It informed her that Davenport was writing for James who was too weak to write himself.

Lily moved on toward the stage where, she realized vaguely, the actors were waiting for her. The packet of letters seemed to burn her hands, but she could not delay the rehearsal. She spoke to the stage-manager and started to take her place on the stage when her eye caught sight of another letter in Davenport's hand with the notation across the top: "URGENT." Lily tore open the letter, too alarmed to apologize for keeping the company waiting. It was dated Saturday (the first letter had been on Friday). Davenport's note stated that he feared James was worse; he did not appear to suffer, but was very feeble.

Lily tried to retain her composure while she opened a third letter from Davenport. It too bore the designation "URGENT." The first lines were all she read. . . .

As soon as she could gather strength she returned to the hotel. She prepared to return to London at once. Davis, manager of the Newcastle theatre, was kindness itself, not only releasing Mrs. Mowatt from her contract but making all necessary arrangements for the journey.

At Green Street, she looked once more upon James's face. She listened to the details from Mrs. Renshaw's sister. He had awakened on Saturday morning much weaker, but able to inquire anxiously whether the postman had yet made his rounds. At ten o'clock the awaited letter was placed in his hand. He opened it and held it before him for a long time as though unable to see the words. Finally he looked up at the nurse and in a faint voice said, "Read me Lily's letter!"

Those were his last words. The nurse read the letter, and noticing that James's face had taken on an unusual pallor and that his head had sunk back on the pillow, she hastily sent a messenger for Davenport and John Mitchell, another of James's close friends. Fanny Davenport had come down at once from upstairs. When Davenport arrived he had a doctor with him. The latter looked at James and announced that he was going fast. Just then James raised his head slightly, and Fanny who had knelt by the bed slipped her arm beneath it. In her free hand she took one of James's. James smiled and his head sank back on Fanny's arm.

He was buried in a tree-shaded corner of the cemetery at Kensal Green, which in those days still had an atmosphere of rural peace about it. From the slight rise at the entrance of the cemetery one could look out over London whose spires in the silver mist had a suggestion of that Holy City where James had now surely found safe abode. Above his grave was placed a simple stone slab, rounded at the top but without decoration. The inscription was equally simple:

> James Mowatt
> of New York America
> A Member of the New Church
> Who Departed This Life
> Feb. 15, 1851
> Beloved and respected by all
> Who truly knew him
>
> "Blessed is that servant whom his Lord,
> When he cometh, finds watching!"

Among the few possessions which James had left behind was a little trunk. In this Lily found three letters, one inside the other, addressed to her. The first of these gave a complete statement of

ANNA CORA MOWATT, A DAGUERREOTYPE, *circa* 1845
Courtesy, The Players Club, New York

their financial affairs. The second contained a few wishes which James hoped could be carried out. The most important of these was that Lily should continue with her profession, no matter what pressure might be put upon her by family and friends to leave the stage. The final letter was a message of love to Lily and a statement of his absolute faith in another life.

After resting a few weeks, Lily embarked once more on a tour of the provinces which would last until she returned to America in mid-summer. With the ever-watchful Mrs. Renshaw she visited Newcastle, Leeds, Hull, Sheffield, Manchester, and Liverpool. In Manchester, she had the joy of seeing her old acquaintances the Smithsons once more.

In Liverpool she played with Barry Sullivan, since Macready's retirement the greatest name on the English stage. She made no further attempts to present *Fashion*, but *Armand* was given everywhere with success. At Lily's benefit in Liverpool, Davenport was released from his contract at the Haymarket to come down and play Armand with her. It was the last time the two acted together, but the friendship continued always. Davenport's second daughter was named Lily.

Anna Cora was joined in Liverpool by her brother-in-law, C. Kennedy Smyth, the husband of Julia. Smyth was in England on business, and he had timed his trip so as to be able to accompany his sister-in-law home. When the Liverpool engagement was finished Anna Cora went back to London with Smyth to spend a few weeks before embarking for America.

In the early summer she received a farewell tribute from the English press, in the form of a lengthy critical memoir by Bayle Bernard. This appeared in *Tallis's Drawing Room Table Book*, an annual of theatrical portraits, memoirs and anecdotes. It was accompanied by an engraving from a photograph made in 1850 by Paine of Islington. Lily is unrecognizable in the portrait because of her plumpness and the expression of beaming satisfaction on her face—so different from the wistful, inward-looking smile of all her other pictures.

Bernard's article contains, in addition to valuable biographical details, a summary of the judgment of British critics on her art. While admitting that her delicate physique prevented her from achieving great success in the higher walks of tragedy, Bernard stated the general opinion that

> she has a tenderness and pathos that render her Imogen and Viola scarcely equalled in our memory.

At the same time there was a quality in her personality,

> such an entire adaption of her whole person, look, and spirit to the blander sphere of comedy, that we cannot but feel it is her true one. . . . But her comedy has its distinction—we think it peculiarly Shaksperian, owing to that thrill of poetic feeling which winds through all its passages. That mixed exposition of the ideal and the true, which stamps all Shakspere's writings as the profoundest insight into man, receives the happiest illustration in the genius of Mrs. Mowatt. . . . It is in Beatrice and Rosalind that she must be witnessed, to be estimated—equalled by some in part, and surpassed in force by many, she alone has that poetic fervour which imparts to them their truth, and makes our laughter ever-ready to tremble into tears.

Such things mattered less to Lily now; but she must have found satisfaction in knowing that she had won the recognition she came to London to seek. She had impressed the English as had no other American actor before her. Even Charlotte Cushman for all the power and grandeur of her art never pierced the protective shell of British sensibility as did Anna Cora Mowatt.

Joseph Ireland had followed her English career with a careful eye. This is how he summed up her achievement in his *History of the New York Stage* (1866):

> Delicacy was her most marked characteristic. A subdued earnestness of manner, a soft musical voice, a winning witchery of enunciation, and indeed an almost perfect combination of beauty, grace and refinement fitted her for the very class of characters in which Miss Cushman was incapable of excelling, and in which *she* commanded the approbation of the British public. . . .

On July 9, 1851, with Smyth and Mrs. Renshaw she sailed aboard the *Pacific* for New York. The first two thirds of the voyage were made without incident. Then, somewhere off the coast of Newfoundland at about two o'clock one morning, a sudden blast followed by a terrible crash brought the passengers wildly clambering from their berths. The sound was repeated three times and it seemed as though the ship were being rent asunder. The passengers rushed for the main saloon which soon was filled with bewildered, frightened men and women in, as Lily says, "a not-to-be-described mingling of night and day costumes." Despite the terror it was noted that the women remained calm, awaiting orders from the captain, while some of the braver sex plunged headlong onto the deck and endeavored to save themselves by cutting loose the lifeboats.

It was half an hour before the condition of the ship could be ascertained, and the passengers informed as to what had happened. In the dark, the lookout had suddenly reported that the ship was almost upon a reef. Orders were given to reverse the engines instantly, though the vessel was moving full speed ahead. In this abrupt manoeuvre, one of the engines had been shattered to pieces. This had accounted for the sounds and the convulsive shaking of the vessel. The danger was now past however, and the passengers were told they might return to their beds, which Lily was content to do. With her experience of the sea, in both sailing vessels and steamships, by this time nothing short of actual sinking could cause her any uneasiness. As in the case of the *Cambria* in 1847, the *Pacific* limped into harbor with one paddle wheel.

The ship landed after a thirteen-day passage, at eleven o'clock at night. Most of the passengers expected to remain on board. But Lily and her brother-in-law could not endure the torture of waiting. For Lily particularly after nearly three years the thought of being so near those she loved, yet not able to see them, made even a few hours' delay unbearable.

Smyth, after some search, succeeded in hiring a coach to take the party to Ravenswood, New York, where Lily's father now had a country place. The way was long—nearly six miles—over roads that were almost impassable. But Lily was undaunted. By a liberal distribution of tips they were able to get their baggage removed from the ship and stowed on the coach.

She describes the trip to Ravenswood:

> The roads were newly made; and every few moments the carriage sank down into a deep rut, or rose sidewise over a high mound of earth. After several narrow approaches to an upset, we alighted from the carriage and walked, ankle deep in mud, over the worst portions of the road. When Mrs. Renshaw and I resumed our seats, my brother-in-law mounted the box, and himself took the reins as the only means of guarding us from the perils of an overturn.

It was after one o'clock when Lily, who had decided that the trip would last all night, heard Smyth call from the top of the coach: "Look out, sister! I can just see your father's house behind those pine trees."

In a moment the heavy carriage was rumbling up to the door of the house, the noise of its wheels accentuated by the complete stillness of the mansion and the dark grounds.

Lily jumped from the coach and rushed to the door. While she pulled frantically at the bell-knob, Smyth shouted beneath the windows.

Suddenly through the open windows above came the sound of pattering bare feet and a voice, familiar, beloved—but unidentifiable—calling, "Wake up! Wake up! They have come!"

The key was hastily turned in the lock and the door flung open. Lily was instantly clasped in somebody's arms—whose she did not know, except that they belonged to a sister. These were pulled away and replaced by others, and still others, and then any number of arms together. In the blackness of the hall Lily could only make out the pale shapes of billowing nightgowns and shadowy braids of hair. She cried, "Who is it? Is it you, Emmie? Is it May? Is it you, Jule?"

Smyth tried to locate his wife but seized one of her sisters instead, and this sent everybody into wild high giggles. In all the excitement nobody had produced a light. There was a frantic scramble to locate matches, but in the confusion none could be found. Then Lily happened to remember a packet of wax vestas in her hand-bag. A flame was struck and a lamp lighted. When all the beloved faces could be seen and identified, there were more cries of joy and more embraces.

The girls—Lily was still not certain how many were there— now led the way to Samuel Ogden's room. Always a sound sleeper, he had just been aroused by the uproar in the lower hall and had begun to guess its meaning. His arms stretched wide to receive his beloved Anna Cora. "There was joy enough in that meeting to make amends for all past sorrows."

The patriarch was in excellent health and apparently undiminished vigor, as was evidenced by new additions to his family— two more daughters. These, along with their half-nieces and nephews (for the married sisters had also acquired numerous offspring during Lily's absence), were now roused from their slumbers to be kissed and kissed again by their sister and aunt.

Lily had never seen the house at Ravenswood. But the strangeness did not affect her. The beloved faces, the voices, the clinging arms were everything that meant most to her in the world. All the past with its uncertainties, its sorrows, its triumphs, its excitement, vanished in the thrill of joy which swept over her. She had come home.

CHAPTER NINETEEN

"... Still Let Me Dwell
in Your Remembrance"

Lily found New York greatly changed after her four years abroad. But nothing more deeply affected her than the disappearance of the old Park Theatre—which for the third and last time had gone up in flames—and of its presiding genius, the gentle and enduring Simpson. Had the Park still stood, Lily would undoubtedly have made her re-appearance there. But there was an appropriateness in her choice of Niblo's; for it was there that she had said good-bye when she left for England.

The ramshackle shed-like structure had been replaced by a theatre almost rivalling the St. Charles in New Orleans in the splendor of its appointments. Although the night of August 19 fell in the middle of a record-breaking heat wave, New Yorkers packed the house to welcome home their celebrated daughter. Many of the fashionable world forsook their summer retreats to be on hand for the occasion, and the greeting Lily received was almost riotous.

The opening bill was not *The Lady of Lyons* but Anna Cora's own *Armand*. This was followed by a round of old favorites; and on September 5 she took her benefit. The theatre was filled to overflowing. People stood tightly wedged together along the walls and back of the auditorium, and more than five hundred were turned from the door.

Everybody noticed the changes that had taken place since the star's sojourn abroad. Willis wrote in *The Home Journal* of "an impassioned, earnest grappling with characters altogether new and startling with her." The critic of *The Mirror* saw her now as an artist of "consummate ability," remarking that "it was frequently impossible to realize the fact that she was acting." There were also references to Mrs. Mowatt's altered appearance. Despite all she had gone through in the past year, Lily had retained her graceful curves and seemed radiantly alive. J. W. S. Hows later recalled his impression when he saw her after she returned from England. "I found her to my astonishment developed into a magnificently formed woman, vigorous and healthy and beaming with geniality and hopefulness."

Hows had good reason to remember her at this time. At long last, the suggestive advertisements in *The Albion* and the pointed criticisms were having their effect: Lily saw Hows shortly after she returned to New York and made arrangements to work with him. That she could seek him out now must have been particularly gratifying to the critic-professor for it might be assumed that an artist "of consummate ability" had little to learn. Lily of course knew better. One never stopped learning. But it was difficult to work without the stimulus of real criticism. While James was alive he had supplied this. Without it, she felt herself beginning to dry up.

Anna Cora seems to have gotten what she needed from Hows —at least for awhile. On every return to New York, she worked with him two or three times a week. Whenever she tackled a new part or wanted to experiment with new effects, she tried them first on Hows. His dispassionate appraisal of the results had a refreshing disciplinary value.

Anna Cora started from New York in early September on a tour which was like a royal progress. Wherever she went, committees waited upon her with official greetings, and her hotel rooms were always filled with flowers. In Boston, where the tour began, she was welcomed as a national heroine whose triumphs abroad had indisputably raised the prestige of American culture. But Lily as an actress had a further significance for Bostonians. It was noted, again and again, that when she appeared the whole complexion of the theatre audience was changed. As *The Transcript* said, the throngs which "crowded to utmost capacity the Howard Athenaeum night after night" were individuals of "the most select and discriminating character. From the class of people she attracts it is evident that her fame is not confined to habitual play-goers." The truth is, that with Mrs. Mowatt on the other side of the footlights a great many people felt really safe in the theatre for the first time. This was implied in an article in *Gleason's Pictorial* which attributed the fact to Mrs. Mowatt's "admirable fireside life."

Boston also had a great deal to say about the development of her art, indistinguishable though that may have been in some eyes from her morality. Her Pauline was proclaimed by *The Transcript* as "the most brilliant impersonation of that character we have yet seen," which probably meant more than the comment that her Rosalind was "poetry not only in words but embodiment." *The Lady of Lyons* was still the supreme test.

The night of Anna Cora's benefit, September 24, a violent storm raged. Yet the Howard was packed and—this is *The Transcript* still reporting—"as many persons were sent away as would have filled it again." The play was *Armand* and it had to be repeated the next night to take care of the disappointed multitude. There is no record of Anna Cora's profits from these performances but the ticket speculators reaped a harvest.

During her three weeks in Boston, Lily managed to enjoy a little social life. The Thompsons were living in Brookline, and it gave May great delight to show off her illustrious sister to her friends. Among the people Anna Cora met at May's house was a shy young Boston girl, Annie Frobisher, who had ambitions to write. She had long worshiped Mrs. Mowatt from afar, and it was a rare moment in her life when she actually met the famous lady. The girl instantly aroused Lily's sympathies and affection, and out of this meeting developed a lifetime friendship between the two.

At the Thompsons', Lily found herself enjoying almost for the first time since her early marriage an association with people from the world into which she had been born. Lily was no snob—in fact "society" in large doses had always bored her—but she felt easier with people whose manners were more like her own than those of most of her stage associates. Boston society she particularly liked, because its members were less pretentious and more certain of their values than New Yorkers. Even the very rich in Boston were often able conversationalists; and Lily found it refreshing to talk about things outside the theatre.

Her departure from the city was accompanied by a flurry of last-minute tributes from the press, as though the critics feared they might not soon have an opportunity to air the fine phrases they had not yet expressed. *The Bee* noted that Mrs. Mowatt's final appearance was before a crowded house "more than half of which were ladies."

The tour continued from Boston to Providence; then on to Philadelphia, Baltimore, Cincinnati—and in December there was a long engagement in St. Louis. This was Anna Cora's second visit to the metropolis of the West. It was to be memorable for a number of reasons.

The St. Louis theatre was operated by Bates, the much-maligned manager of the theatres in Louisville and Cincinnati when Anna Cora had played the latter city in 1847. Bates had suffered long from the recriminations of the Louisville press because of his "niggardliness" in refusing to bring worthy attractions to that city. Something of the same thing seems to have been going on also in St. Louis. But with the announcement of Mrs. Mowatt's appearance, the press did an about-face. On December 6 *The Missouri Republican* published an indignant letter to the editor on the subject of Miss Jean Davenport (no relation to Edward), a popular young actress who had refused to come to St. Louis because Bates would not meet her terms—although Bates had offered her the same terms he made to all stars *including Mrs. Mowatt*. Who, asked *The Republican*'s correspondent, did Miss Davenport think she was? "Mrs. Mowatt has a great London reputation. We have heard of no London reputation of Miss Davenport." The writer then proceeded to note the superior claims of Mrs. Mowatt on American sympathies because her great-grandfather was a signer of the Declaration of Independence (Miss Davenport was English). If Miss Davenport needed more money because she had lately lost her father, it could be advanced that Mrs. Mowatt was in the same position, "having lately lost her husband, whom she had long supported by her exertions," and that furthermore Mrs. Mowatt had the care of three orphan children. Pursuing his chain of logic to its inevitable conclusion the writer then said:

> In view of these facts is it not fair to ask a just and enlightened public to witness the performances of Mrs. Mowatt at the Bates Theatre, performances on which the first critics and the literary world have sealed the stamp of their approval—and then decide if Miss Davenport has any cause to complain of any illiberality on the part of Mr. Bates when he offers her Mrs. Mowatt's terms.

Jean Davenport plays a part in the final pages of Anna Cora's story, and therefore merits some comment beyond that of Mr. Bates's defender, who can scarcely have been other than Mr. Bates himself.

The young lady had had a very difficult past, for she was the original—despite a lifetime protest to the contrary—of Dickens' "Infant Phenomenon" in *Nicholas Nickleby*. Born of theatrical parents of modest talents but great ambitions, she had first appeared upon the stage when she was eight as Little Pickle in *The Spoil'd Child*, a favorite exhibition piece for theatrical prodigies. From this she had graduated to *Richard III* and thrilled audiences with her treble piping of "Now is the winter of our discontent," and "A horse! a horse! my kingdom for a horse!" Despite a figure which with time exceeded the reasonable outlines even of an Infant Phenomenon, she continued to be billed as such. The increasing reluctance of managers to give her engagements forced her retirement from the stage until she properly grew up. When she returned some years later it was, surprisingly, as a lovely and winning actress of considerable talent.

While Miss Davenport was debating terms with other managers, Lily was culling new laurels in St. Louis. She played a round of the usual parts—Juliet, Mrs. Haller, Lucy Ashton—to delighted and profitable audiences. The enthusiasm of the public for Mrs. Mowatt gave Bates an idea for increasing his own prestige in St. Louis. He wrote Anna Cora asking if she would be willing to devote one of her last week's performances to a benefit for the city poor fund, offering her a benefit for herself on Monday, December 15, if she would remain over for that date.

On December 10, *The Missouri Republican* published Lily's answer:

> Dear Sir—
> In reply to your note desiring me to extend my engagement for a night longer, that I may take a benefit on Monday next, and devote one night of this week's engagement to a Benefit for the Poor, I am forced to say that it will be impossible for me to remain until Monday, but I will gladly give up one night of this week and act gratuitously in any parts which you may select to Aid the Poor of this city.
> I am, dear Sir, yours
> most sincerely,
> Anna Cora Mowatt

This was not exactly what Bates had intended, since it was Anna Cora who would now make the generous gesture, but Bates managed nevertheless to squeeze into the picture by donating the expenses of the benefit evening. On December 13, *The Missouri Republican* stated that Bates had handed over to Mayor Kennett a check for $407.75, the proceeds of the benefit, and commended Bates's generosity in turning over *all* of the receipts: "This gentleman deserves the applause of the public"—which was precisely what he wanted. The paper then continued:

> Nor in this connection is the liberal conduct of Mrs. Mowatt to be overlooked. . . . The impulses of a woman, always alive to the sufferings of the poor in large cities, were no sooner appealed to than her determination was made. . . . Mrs. Mowatt feels the sincerest gratification . . . at having been able to assist . . . and seeks no other commendation. But the public can reward her tonight when she takes her [regular] benefit. . . . We might add that Mrs. Mowatt's engagements are such as to have compelled her to de-

cline a complimentary benefit, tendered to her by our most eminent citizens, and this is an additional reason why she should now receive such a benefit as will justify her in holding us in lasting remembrance.

So everybody was happy. Bates seemed firmly ensconced in the good graces of the press, Lily had won the devotion of the city fathers, and the Poor were $407.75 better off than they had been before. Anna Cora also received an embossed scroll containing a resolution of the General Committee for the Relief of the Poor thanking her for her generosity.

The urgent reason for Lily's departure from St. Louis was a rendezvous with her family for Christmas in Philadelphia. It had been agreed that this year should be marked by special festivities in honor of Lily's return to America, and that the celebration should be held at the home of the Henry Meckes, who had come over from Bremen some years before and were now settled in Germantown. The feature of the occasion would be a production of *Gulzara, or the Persian Slave*. Lily herself would not take part (she rather shuddered at the thought of having to act with amateurs) but she had promised to direct the play. In order to reach Philadelphia in time to carry out this plan, she had to leave St. Louis at the earliest possible moment.

Anna Cora's last performance was on the evening of December 13. On the afternoon of that day, the steamboat *Robert Rogers* was scheduled to sail from St. Louis to Pittsburgh. The captain, on receipt of a little note from Mrs. Mowatt, obligingly delayed departure until after the theatre. Without bothering to change, though certainly with the makeup removed from her face, Lily, accompanied by the faithful Renshaw, hurried down to the landing and boarded the steamer. It was bitterly cold, and she was happy after the long hard week to snuggle down in the warm blankets of her berth. The next day it was snowing and Lily luxuriated in pleasant idleness, not bothering to leave her stateroom. The third day she was roused by Mrs. Renshaw exclaiming, "Good gracious! The river is one sheet of ice!"

Lily sprang from bed and looked out. The river was like a flat mirror, and the banks on either side were piled high with snow. The sun was now shining and the whiteness of the snow was almost blinding. The boat was cutting easily through the ice, though her pace had been somewhat slowed. Lily spent the rest of the day in the pilot-house (that choice retreat of privileged river passengers), watching the ice grow more and more solid.

The next morning when she awoke, the boat was barely creeping along, pushing and jerking as though battling every inch of the way. Lily went again to the pilot-house. At her anxious question the veteran pilot shook his head noncommittally. The boat was scarcely moving at all now. At about noon it stopped altogether.

Lily, thinking of the family already gathering in Philadelphia, grew very anxious. "How long may we have to stay here?"

The pilot looked kindly at her. "I'm right sorry for you, I am; but I'm thinking the boat may just have to lie here perhaps three weeks, perhaps a month—"

"Won't it perhaps thaw soon?"

"Well, it don't look inclined."

Lily pointed to a tiny cluster of houses on the Indiana shore, and asked what the spot was called. The pilot told her that was West Franklin.

"Are there any stages that start from there?" Lily was beginning to want action.

"Stages! I don't believe they've got anything better than a cart in the whole place. This is Indiana State . . ." Anyway, the pilot went on, no one could travel over the roads now in a stage; he'd be sure of being spilled every few miles.

"But will nobody leave the boat for weeks to come?"

"Some of the men will, *in course*. If they have to walk for it, they'll *get on*."

Then, thought Lily, I'll *get on* too. The idea of *Gulzara* without a director, and of the ball which was to follow the play without the guest of honor, sent her speeding back to the state-room and Mrs. Renshaw. The poor woman was gazing from the window in bewilderment. She had never seen a frozen river before. As Lily closed the door of the cabin, loud, piercing screams came from down the gangway. She remembered that among the passengers were two lunatic sisters who were being taken by an attendant to an asylum. The thought of possibly passing some weeks in their society spurred Lily to desperate measures. She began to consult with Mrs. Renshaw as to what might be done.

The discussion was interrupted by a knock at the door. It was one of the negro waiters with two cards on a tray for Mrs. Mowatt. Lily expressed her amazement at receiving a call in the middle of the frozen Ohio; but the waiter pointed his finger out toward the river where, as Lily saw, another steamboat was also frozen in!

The owners of the cards were two gentlemen who were passengers on the second ice-bound vessel. They had heard of Mrs. Mowatt's presence on the *Robert Rogers* and had ventured to call. Lily, relating the episode in her autobiography, refers to these gentlemen only by their first initials, and their identity still remains a mystery. But one of the gentlemen, Major R., had been presented to Mrs. Mowatt some six years before. "He was," she tells us firmly, "the father of a large family." The younger gentleman, Mr. N., was acquainted with one of Lily's sisters in New York. However, Lily was not inclined to be fussy about credentials—particularly when the gentlemen asked if they might be of any assistance.

Lily informed them that she must be in Philadelphia by Christmas, or at least before New Year's; and that she meant to get there at whatever cost. From the tone of her voice the gentlemen thought it better not to attempt to dissuade her. Instead they gallantly offered to escort her and Mrs. Renshaw to their destination—about eight hundred miles away.

Plans were quickly made to walk to the shore, thence to a nearby farmhouse where it was hoped a cart might be procured. The baggage was gathered together and the party climbed down from the boat onto the ice. A number of other passengers, all of the male sex, were disembarking with a similar project in mind. As they neared the shore, all seemed to be taken with the same idea: to reach the house before any of the others, since the number of available vehicles was probably limited. It was soon evident that the race would go either to Mr. N. or another fleet-footed gentleman; but Mr. N. outwitted his rival by calling in a loud voice as they neared the house: "I engage whatever conveyance you have got!"

The conveyance turned out to be an ox-cart. The owner was not eager to travel in such weather, but after a little persuasion by Lily, finally hitched up a pair of strong horses to the vehicle and the party set out. After some miles, during which Mrs. Renshaw and Lily both began to be conscious of the cart's hard bottom, they came to a barn. Here the cart stopped while the men jumped out and got armloads of hay. With hay between them and the rough boards of the cart-bed, Lily and her companion were able to endure the twelve miles to Evansville.

At Evansville they found that stages would leave the next morning for Vincennes. Unfortunately all the places were taken. But Fate stepped in, in the form of a Mr. C. This gentleman, too, still hides behind his first initial. But he was a Baltimorean, which should be enough; for, as Lily says, "I never knew a Baltimorean yet who was not a pattern of courtesy." Mr. C. had three places which he promptly turned over to Mrs. Mowatt, Mrs. Renshaw and Mr. N., while he engaged a small wagon for the Major and himself. Why the Major instead of the younger Mr. N. should have ridden in the open wagon is not clear. Perhaps Mr. N. was suffering from the exertion of his heroic sprint across the ice. If so, Lily makes no mention of the fact.

There were more stages at Vincennes. Into one of these the whole party was packed, including both the Major and Mr. N. They then started out for Terre Haute. As they traveled, the roads became progressively worse, and there was no doubt that the stage would soon upset; the only question was where. The situation was aggravated by the driver who while watering his horses had been seized with a "sympathetic thirst." This he satisfactorily quenched, but as a result he could not be left alone in the driver's seat. About midnight the stage suddenly sank into a deep gully. By utilizing the rails from a convenient fence the gentlemen managed to hoist the vehicle once more onto the road.

Major R.—who was a wit and occasionally wrote articles about the theatre—said, "I have been trying for years to *elevate* the stage and I have just succeeded, *with you upon it!*" This caused much merriment, which lasted until the road got so bad that everybody had to get out. The remainder of the journey to Terre Haute was made on foot.

It was four o'clock in the morning when the party arrived in Terre Haute. Lily would have liked to go to bed. Instead, she and her fellow-travelers started for Indianapolis at six, where they arrived late in the afternoon without accident. In successive stages they pushed on to Dayton, to Xenia, to Cleveland. They left Cleveland by—O blessed relief!—the railway cars. These carried them all the way to Alliance, which they reached the afternoon of the same day. But at Salem they had to take the stage again. They came to Palestine late at night, and were sorely put to it to find rooms. For these they were indebted at last "to that prompt gallantry, characteristic of Americans, which induced gentlemen already provided with lodgings to surrender them for our accommodation."

From Palestine they traveled once more by railroad to Pittsburgh, which they reached that night—Christmas Eve. Christmas Day was spent in stagecoaches. Christmas dinner consisted of frozen cheese and biscuits. At Johnstown, the travelers took the Portage Railroad, which by a series of ten inclined planes (Lily lost count and thought there were only nine) lifted them over the Alleghenies and set them down at Hollidaysburg. They traveled all Christmas night, and all the following day. At about six in the evening, with soaring spirits, they recognized the suburbs of Philadelphia. Then the train ran into a snowbank and could go no further.

Lily looked out of the window and realized that they were only about a mile from the Meckes' house, so she proposed that they walk the rest of the way. Major R. had become indisposed, but Mr. N. accompanied the two women to their final destination, thus fulfilling the gallant offer made two weeks before in the middle of the frozen Ohio.

At her brother-in-law's house, Lily found all the sisters gathered together and waiting anxiously. Their welcome of the wanderer was almost as overwhelming as that she had received at Ravenswood on her return from England, and their relief certainly as great. For the hazards of overland travel in the early '50's were quite comparable to those of an Atlantic crossing.

There were only three days left before the ball and the performance of *Gulzara*. After her cross-country adventures life in the harem of Sultan Suliman must have seemed rather tame to Lily, but she plunged with gusto into the production of the play which was as great a hit with Philadelphia society as it had been with the Melrose audience twelve years before. Only two members of the original cast took part this time, May and Julia. The leading role was played by Julia to great applause; but the real star of the evening was the author and director. To her family, no less than to their Philadelphia friends, Lily moved in a dazzling aura of fame and romance like a creature out of a fairy tale. For two weeks she was the center of a whirl of festivities such as she had never know before. This Christmas season marked the culmination of the glorious family gatherings that meant so much in the lives of all the Ogdens. It was the last time that Samuel Ogden and all his living children were under the same roof together.

When Lily started out again after New Year's, she was conscious of a drag on her spirits. The trip from St. Louis, the preparations for the fête in Philadelphia, the emotional strain of being surrounded by such intense affection and then being suddenly without it—above all the absence of James—took away her buoyancy. She was really tired now, and she was lonely. When the family party in Philadelphia broke up and she saw them all going their separate ways, father and stepmother, sisters and brothers, back to their homes and their family preoccupations, she felt that her life no longer had a real center.

She tried to find one in her work, but this now seemed to fail her. What she lacked was something only James had been able to give her. Without him she had no vital incentive for her best efforts. Yet it was the thought of James that urged her on; for she had promised him that she would continue her career. By an intense concentration of memory and imagination she could still see his face—and so long as she had his image before her and the sound of his voice in her ears, she could still fancy that he was near her, sitting in the wings or in the dim shadows of a stage box: that other self which like the sounding-board of a musical instrument gave depth and clarity and resonance to her playing. But she missed the tangible physical presence. And she needed love.

The first engagement of the New Year was in Richmond. The city had no particular associations for her beyond the fact that her brother-in-law, Isadore Guillet, and his three boys were there.

Richmond was merely a week's stand where she had before found an appreciative audience and hoped to find one again. When she arrived she was still under the spell of melancholy engendered by the breaking up of the family after the Christmas festivities. In such a mood she must have been taken off her feet by the reception she received.

If she recalled the tall, red-haired editor of *The Richmond Enquirer* at all, it was only casually. But William Foushee Ritchie had never forgotten the spell cast over him by Mrs. Mowatt on her first appearance in Richmond nine years before. When he saw her now in the glow of mature beauty, trailing clouds of dazzling triumphs, the feelings which she had first aroused returned with added force. It was like a dream that she should be back in Richmond, like a miracle that she should be alone in the world. Whether dream or miracle the opportunity was not one for Ritchie to let slip past.

Throughout the ten-day engagement he scarcely let Anna Cora out of his sight. He haunted the theatre and her hotel, and when he was not present there was an unending stream of notes, flowers and gifts to remind her of his adoration.

There was certainly no reticence in Ritchie's approach. Never had Lily experienced such treatment as she received from *The Enquirer*, accustomed though she was to having extravagant things printed about her. On January 13 that newspaper, after a flattering note on her performance in *The Stranger*, quoted in its entirety Bayle Bernard's long memoir which had appeared in *Tallis's Drawing Room Table Book* the summer before. The next day there was a whole column beginning: "This lovely woman and beautiful and captivating actress, won a complete triumph on Monday night." The article continued in the same unrestrained terms, with almost embarrassing references to her personal qualities. "Her attitudes brought to mind the finest specimens of Greek sculpture." And there was a note of tender solicitude: "We regretted to find her suffering from a severe cold . . . but it only slightly impaired the effect of her fine acting—set off as it was by the handsomest woman we have seen on any stage, in this country or abroad."

If this was not a declaration of love on the part of Mr. William Foushee Ritchie, it was the nearest thing to it that might reasonably appear in a newspaper.

The reporting throughout the week kept on in the same key. In reviewing *Armand*, Ritchie seems to have felt some reserve was necessary:

> We shall not again trust ourselves to speak of her personal attractions farther than to say that, in her piquant peasant's costume, she combined delicacy and softness of American beauty, with the glowing bloom and rich developments of the English mould[!].

When Lily left Richmond, it was probably with something like relief. She had never before been so passionately pursued, either in or out of print, and she must have found it strenuous, even assuming that she felt inclined to return Mr. Ritchie's feeling. There was no evidence that this was so—as yet. There is rather the suggestion that some precautions were needful; for in leaving Richmond Lily took with her the seventeen-year-old Stanislas Guillet as *cavaliere servente*. "He had arrived at the age of transition between youth and manhood, when the spirit of chivalry is newly enkindled in the breast, [and] proved the most energetic and efficient of escorts."

After a week in Baltimore and another in Providence, Anna Cora played a month's engagement at the Howard Athenaeum in Boston. The cold which she had caught in Richmond had settled into bronchitis. Despite the orders of her doctor to take a complete rest, she planned to allow herself only two weeks' break before going on to New York in April.

In the middle of March, she decided one day it would be pleasant to hire a horse and ride to Brookline. May, who was still living in Boston, accompanied her. There was heavy snow on the streets; and in Tremont Road, just as they were turning into Boylston Street, Lily's horse slipped. As she tried to pull him up, he began to rear. In a moment he had lost his balance and fell backwards on top of her.

A huge crowd immediately gathered. Lily was removed from

under the horse, a sofa was procured from a neighboring house, and she was taken back to the Thompsons' under the supervision of two physicians who happened to appear on the scene.

Reports instantly circulated that Mrs. Mowatt had been killed, and the telegraph busily relayed the information about the country. Next day the story was corrected; but everybody was excited over the accident and so concerned for the health of Mrs. Mowatt that the Thompsons' modest domestic staff was sorely tried attempting to take care of inquiring visitors. To remedy this inconvenience, daily bulletins were posted outside the house. These served the purpose but in some quarters, at least, did not make altogether the right impression. *The Spirit of the Times* printed the following reaction:

> The notoriety given during Mrs. Mowatt's indisposition and confinement to her house by daily posting bulletins on the outside of the door of her dwelling in regard to the state of her health . . . was not only a capital advertisement, but as clever a bit of diplomacy as I have seen in a long time, while I must say it smacked somewhat of ostentation to have it continued after the lady was convalescent.

If Anna Cora was pioneering with a now classic publicity device, it was hardly necessary. Boston was not only aware of Mrs. Mowatt's presence, but was deeply conscious of its responsibilities. A committee headed by the mayor drew up a letter to her on May 13, 1852, as "a public expression of your services and your worth in the sphere of dramatic art. . . . When we have seen you imbodying your own conceptions of tenderness and truth, we have felt that the charm of your performance flowed from the fact that your words and your voice were but imperfect expressions of yourself. And now that you have lately stood on the edge of another life, we feel that we should welcome you back to ours with more cordial greetings and more earnest voices." The committee then expressed its desire to offer Mrs. Mowatt a complimentary benefit at the Howard Athenaeum. The letter was signed by a group of citizens including Longfellow, George S. Hilliard, E. P. Whipple, E. C. Bates, Epes Sargent and a dozen others.

The benefit took place on May 2 with Lily in the rôle of Parthenia in *Ingomar*. As almost always on the occasion of such demonstrations, she was so overcome with emotion that she could scarcely act.

Early June found Anna Cora in Cincinnati. Then followed a long engagement in Louisville—a visit which coincided with the death of her old admirer, Henry Clay. The city was plunged in deepest mourning, in which Lily, after her own fashion, participated. The façade of the hotel was draped in long streamers of black. But in front of Anna Cora's suite hung festoons of white bunting, intermingled with violet bouquets; a garland of white and purple violets with ribbons of black, violet and white was draped along the window-ledges. *The Courier* explained next day that as a Swedenborgian Mrs. Mowatt could not display the conventional symbols of death. Her white banners and violets were greetings to one who had passed to a fuller and brighter life.

Throughout the tour, William Foushee Ritchie had been ceaseless in his attentions. By telegraph, by letter, and in person—when Lily played in Baltimore and Washington—he had vigorously carried on the courtship. When she returned to New York in midsummer, Lily found him waiting for her.

Obviously this development in the private life of a public figure did not pass unnoticed. Anna Cora found New York bubbling with rumors that she was engaged. She did what she could to put a stop to them, for she was determined to end her career, as she had already planned even before Ritchie reappeared on the scene, without distractions. Furthermore, even though the idea of marriage had begun to appeal strongly to her, she wished to keep the way open for retreat in case things did not work out satisfactorily.

She had been attracted to Ritchie; there is no doubt of that even if his headlong tactics left her somewhat breathless. In his courtship the ardent Southerner displayed accomplishments which her romantic nature found hard to resist. She found his vigor and singleness of purpose both stimulating and infectious. All along the tour, after leaving Richmond, she was aware of a renewed zest for her work and a fresh excitement in life. She was inspired by the fact that once again she was the center of another person's life. In Ritchie's passion there was also an element of flattery. Though Anna Cora's attractions were celebrated, she was after all thirty-four years old, and it was gratifying to have aroused in this handsome, virile man the sort of ardor usually associated with the first flush of youth.

Yet she did not lose her head. Anna Cora fully realized what marriage now would mean. She had achieved an almost unheard-of independence and had lived a full life in her own right. If she married she would have to give this up; and while she knew well that she had not the strength to continue her career on the stage much longer, there were always other things that she could do. Fond as she had grown of Ritchie, she suspected him of having a very possessive nature; if she yielded to him she would have to do so wholly. It was a step she could not take without long reflection. Ritchie, having waited nine years, was willing to give her a few more months, and this was the understanding on which they parted in the summer of 1852.

In the fall Anna Cora was back on the road again. She opened the new Metropolitan Theatre in Buffalo, played a brief engagement in Syracuse, another in Cleveland, returned to Boston for a single night (to give her services at the benefit of an old acquaintance, Mrs. Warner), and then went on to Philadelphia. Here she came down with an attack of bronchitis so severe that the engagement had to be broken off after the second performance. In December, though still ailing, she opened at the Broadway Theatre in New York. It was touch-and-go whether she could get through this commitment. Only the constant exertions of her brother-in-law, Dr. William Turner, enabled her to keep on using her voice.

But she did not stop. Before Christmas she went to Baltimore, where she gave a benefit for the Fireman's Library Association. On this evening the members of the organization presented her with a somewhat unusual token of their devotion. In the second act of *The Honeymoon* while she was singing beside the cottage door, a character named Lopez appeared on the stage leading a fawn. Accustomed to any and all manifestations of public approval Anna Cora did not pause, but took the fawn's leash and went on with the part. During the act she fed the fawn crumbs from a table set up on the stage. Once during a scene in which she sat on a low footstool, the fawn began to nibble her curls. Everybody was enchanted, including Anna Cora.

After Christmas there was another visit to Boston, her fourth within the year; then Lily started off on the great circuit of the south and west: Charleston, Mobile, New Orleans. She was ill again with a severe cold in New Orleans, but she grimly went through her round of characters—including Gertrude in *Fashion*, which she seemed fated to have to play always in New Orleans. Her condition was so bad at this performance that *The Picayune* said, ". . . she ought not have allowed herself to play." Yet the next night, when she was much worse, she volunteered her services for the benefit of Mrs. Estelle Potter, who had played Mrs. Tiffany in *Fashion*.

On March 16, accompanied by Mrs. Renshaw and the assiduous Stanislas, she embarked on the steamer *Magnolia* for Memphis. She had never forgotten her promise to Clay to visit some day this city whose people were noted throughout the Mississippi valley for their friendliness and urbanity, and she looked forward eagerly to the week.

Her cold had not improved and she was thoroughly worn out, not only with acting but with all the business details which she was forced now to take care of herself. She had written Charles, the actor-manager of the Memphis theatre, earlier in the fall to try to arrange seasons at Chattanooga and Nashville, and she planned to go into the hinterlands after the Memphis engagement.

On March 21 *The Memphis Appeal* announced the "First Night of the Engagement of the highly distinguished Native Actress and Authoress, Mrs. Anna Cora Mowatt." The play was *Ingomar* and on the same bill was the "Infant Drummer" (who had followed Lily up from New Orleans and who was said to perform in "an eminently scientific manner").

As the curtain fell on each succeeding act of *Ingomar*, Lily felt her strength ebbing away. But she still believed that by concentration mere physical disability could be overcome or held in check until the play was over. She did manage to get through the performance and was even able to make a graceful acknowledgment of the vociferous applause at the final curtain. But her teeth were chattering when she got back to the hotel and crawled into bed.

Next morning she had to sit throughout the rehearsal of *The Stranger*. When it was finished she went back to bed, where she remained until the evening performance. That night, Mrs. Renshaw and Stanislas got her to the theatre with difficulty. Mrs. Renshaw dressed her and put on her make-up and supported her to the wings for her first entrance.

As Mrs. Haller, Lily had little to do in the first act of *The Stranger*; but the few words she uttered sent her into such a fit of coughing that she had to hold to the side of a wing to keep from falling. In the third act as soon as she started to speak, she knew that it was all over. Charles, who was playing with her at the moment, had kept his eyes on her throughout the scene. As he saw her knees buckle under her he gave a quick signal to bring down the curtain.

Lily was carried back to the hotel, where she stayed for nine days battling a high temperature and violent fits of coughing. Her condition was aggravated by malaria, which she had picked up in New Orleans. The physician who attended her said that her one hope was to get out of the pestilential air of the Mississippi delta.

Twelve days after her arrival in the city, Lily was carried aboard a steamboat at the Memphis landing. She traveled by boat to Pittsburgh, then by train overland (including the ten inclined planes at Johnstown) to her sister's house in Philadelphia. The whole time, she was flat on her back.

It seemed obvious to everybody that this was the end. When she had rested sufficiently to be moved, her father and Ritchie, who had come up to Philadelphia to meet her, took her to Astoria on Long Island, where Samuel Ogden was now living. For several weeks Lily lay in the shadowy world with which she had long ago become familiar, waiting for the summons which would now surely come at any time. Then, as the weather got warmer, she began to mend.

One of the things she had promised James was to set down

the story of her experiences on the stage. As soon as she could be propped up in bed she began to write her autobiography. She wrote in pencil with feverish activity, scattering the pages on all sides as they were written. They were read by Ritchie, who in turn passed them on to May. When May had neatly transcribed the work in ink it was given to Epes Sargent for editing; for Lily still committed nothing to print that did not come first under Sargent's eye. The book was finished in the fall of 1853. Early the following year it was brought out by Ticknor and Fields of Boston. It was an immediate best-seller, and by May, 1854, had passed the twenty-thousand mark.

The true merits of *The Autobiography of an Actress* were recognized by the critics almost without exception. The simplicity and candor, the unceasing flow of humor gave the book its unique tone. It was a success story, but not in the regular American tradition, beginning with a strong arm and unlimited opportunity. It was the story of one on whom failure acted as the surest stimulant to action and for whom, to quote the review in *Graham's Magazine*, "mortification was made the basis of new triumphs."

It is still a very remarkable book. It gives us the most important picture of the theatre of the forties and fifties which we possess. Unlike most theatrical autobiographies it spreads out over the general life of the times. The world of fact and the world of fancy are shown side by side, and the result is a better perspective on both than we could otherwise obtain. *The Autobiography of an Actress* is a very personal story in which, strangely enough, the heart is almost totally hidden. This was the way Anna Cora meant it to be. She was after all a lady, and though she had gone so far as to expose her outer self to the public gaze, the rest must be decently veiled. At the end of the book she apologized for having had to use the first person singular from time to time; in so doing she hoped "to be pardoned as for an unavoidable literary trespass."

Almost the only negative criticism of the *Autobiography* appeared in *The Evangelical Review*. This was written by Dr. Mary Walker, the well-remembered crusader for woman's right to wear trousers. Dr. Walker was the only critic really concerned with the book's announced thesis. Mrs. Mowatt had set out to show that there was nothing in the theatrical profession itself which was absolutely conducive to immorality. Dr. Walker demolished the thesis with one blow. How, she queried, could anyone pretend that the theatre might be wholesome since dramatic performances were always given at night when, as everyone knew, the passions were so susceptible to excitement! This was, of course, before the days of the matinée.

Nathaniel Hawthorne, then American Consul at Liverpool, read the book and was so impressed he recommended it as one of half a dozen American works he thought his brilliant friend, Richard Monckton Milnes, ought to read.

Writing the book was hard work, and once at least Anna Cora thought it would be an epitaph and not an autobiography. But as so often before strenuous effort produced beneficial results. By the end of November Lily was not only out of bed, she was busy directing Renshaw in the packing of her trunks. She had said in the *Autobiography* that she meant soon to bid farewell to the stage. She was about to do this now, in a thoroughly professional manner.

Charleston was the starting-point of her last tour. The city was honored to be thus singled out, though it mourned the occasion of its distinction. *The Courier* published a notice of Mrs. Mowatt's approaching engagement on the front page, with a long excerpt from Bayle Bernard's memoir (beside a report of the signing of the Gadsden Treaty).

While in Charleston Lily appeared in a new play by William Young, editor of *The Albion*. This was entitled *Corinna, or the Improvisatrice*. Lily was a great success in the part, which ran the gamut of all the delicate emotions. One would like to know just what it was Corinna improvised—a question presumably in the minds of the audience which witnessed its single performance. But, as *The Courier* stated: "The limited time of her [Mrs. Mowatt's] stay with us, . . . forbids the reproduction of Corinna, to the regret of the many who would enjoy it more fully after the exposition of its drift and plot now afforded."

On March 13, Anna Cora was in Philadelphia at the Chestnut Street Theatre. The critic of *The Daily Pennsylvanian* found her "a star of resplendent beauty ... worthy of imitation in every respect." But *The Sunday Mercury* was not kind. The writer for this journal was annoyed by her effort "to startle by striking attitudes, accompanied by an elevation of the voice in keeping with them," and was outraged by the fact that Juliet wore her dagger throughout the performance.

There was probably justice in *The Mercury's* report. On the way up from Charleston Lily had caught her inevitable late-winter cold. By the time she opened in Philadelphia she could hardly speak. Only by exerting herself to the utmost was she able to make herself audible; but in doing this she lost all control of her voice, which occasionally would come through her hoarseness with piercing volume. The reporter for *The Sunday Mercury* assumed that this was a conscious effect. As for the dagger, Anna Cora was always nervous about hand props. More than once she had come on the stage for the last scene in the Capulet tomb without her needed weapon and had been obliged to borrow that of the recumbent Romeo. She was determined not to let this happen for her last appearance as Juliet in Philadelphia. She simply stuck the dagger in her girdle at the beginning of the play and left it there.

The Autobiography of an Actress was out now and was advertised along with a new edition of *The Fortune Hunter*, conspicuously near the theatre notices. Acting and authorship worked upon each other profitably for Lily all during the tour.

By the middle of April, 1854, Mrs. Mowatt reached Cincinnati. Here, night after night, the theatre was thronged with the city's élite. She took her benefit on April 22. Of the occasion, one paper reported:

> Such a blaze of beauty and fashion that thronged the walls of the old National we have never before seen. The box sheet for the first tier was *full* yesterday morning, and hundreds of ladies were compelled to take seats in the second tier.

As always, Anna Cora's ability to attract members of her own sex to the theatre drew awed comment. In Cincinnati and elsewhere, ladies were discovering the pleasures of the drama through Mrs. Mowatt; for they knew that when she was on the stage there would be nothing to offend the most delicate sensibilities. This is all the more remarkable when we note that Lily's repertory included the same plays in which every other actress of the time appeared. It seemed to have been her peculiar gift to enact the most improper scenes and speak the bawdiest lines without losing anything of the effect, and yet at the same time without offending the most squeamish disposition. It was of course a mark of her genius as an actress; for she could carry her audiences so far into the world of illusion that they completely forgot their everyday lives and the arbitrary code of conduct by which they were normally governed.

Mrs. Mowatt's magnetic attraction for a special kind of audience continued to the end to excite the antagonism of many members of the profession. But not all. One of the humblest actors in the Cincinnati company, a quite insignificant young "walking gentleman" by the name of Watkins, recorded in his diary for April 17:

> Performed Ingomar at Mrs. Mowatt's benefit and got through with applause. It is a pleasure to play with her; a kinder, more agreeable lady I have never met with. House crowded throughout with Cincinnati's wealth and fashion. Rumor has it that she is to marry Mr. Ritchie, editor of the Richmond Enquirer, and leave the stage.

On June 2 Anna Cora made her last appearance in Boston. The crush in the theatre had never been equalled, and again the speculators had their day. This time seats were auctioned, and the bidding was wild. Box seats brought more than $20 apiece. At the close of the performance it seemed as though the applause would go on indefinitely. Finally, Lily raised her hand for silence, and in the hush that instantly followed she came down to the footlights and spoke to the audience:

Ladies and Gentlemen:

I appear before you for the last time and to utter a last farewell. . . .

It was a simple speech but full of dignity, and it came straight from Lily's heart. She recalled to the audience that it was in

Boston that she had made her first public appearance, and she expressed her gratitude for the impartial hearing she had been given, even though she was a woman:

> It is for this—for that first warm greeting that I have now most deeply to thank you; for the events of that night gave their coloring to my whole future career. And now that my long day of trial has drawn to a close, I come back to you, my first public friends, to make my last professional efforts before you, and to tell you that you will ever remain first, in my grateful memory. . . .

She spoke of her hopes for the future of the drama in America and expressed her firm belief that it would be freed of the abuses which had prevented so many people from enjoying it. She was gratified that in Boston a start had been made in this direction.

> And now for the last time, farewell! May you sustain and cheer many who will follow me, as you have cheered me, and though some may more worthily fill the place I cease to occupy, I pray you to still let me dwell in your remembrance.

At Niblo's in New York there was also a solemn leave-taking. Lily's final benefit had been arranged by a group of the city's most eminent citizens. The letter proposing the benefit, which would mark the end of a career distinguished by "brilliancy of talent" and "elevated by loftiness of character," was signed by William Cullen Bryant, George Bancroft, Samuel Ruggles, Benjamin Silliman, James W. Gerard and nearly a score of other notables. Under the careful supervision of Samuel Ruggles, the ticket speculators were eliminated from the picture. Anna Cora's profits for the evening were reported at $6,000.

On this occasion also, Lily made a speech which left few dry eyes in the crowd of some four thousand who managed to get into Niblo's. Among those present that evening was young Adam Badeau, the close friend of Edwin Booth whose star was now rising. Badeau had been unable to get a seat and had stood in the passageway behind the dress circle. During the intermission he fell into conversation with "a fine gray-headed old man." Their talk turned naturally to the star, and Badeau wondered if her graces were natural or acquired. The old gentleman assured him that they were natural. Badeau expressed doubts that this would be her last appearance, and the old gentleman said quite positively that it would be, for Mrs. Mowatt would be married in a month. Badeau knew that, and mentioned the date which he had noted in the papers. The old gentleman corrected him by giving another date. Badeau was prepared to dispute the point for he was becoming a trifle irritated with the old gentleman's authoritative manner, when the latter quietly informed him, "I ought to know. I am her father."

All over the country the press paid tribute to Anna Cora's unique achievement, not only as an artist but as a personality whose effects on the public had been unparalleled in the history of the American theatre. The general impression was accurately summed up by *Gleason's Pictorial*:

> . . . If a comparison be made with contemporary actresses, it will be found that she lacks the thrilling energy of Charlotte Cushman, the perfect self-possession of Miss Davenport, the graceful style of Julia Dean, and the fiery earnestness of Mrs. Farren, and the deep and touching pathos of Miss [Eliza] Logan, and yet so cunningly has nature mingled these elements together in Mrs. Mowatt, that the impression she leaves upon the audience is more lasting than of all the others.

Despite some isolated exceptions, the critics to the end were baffled in their attempts to define Anna Cora's genius. The clue to the difficulty lies in the oft-discussed "naturalness" of her approach. This was the day of the florid style, the sweeping gesture, and vocal pyrotechnics. Lily's art all came from within, from intense concentration on the vision which her imagination had conceived and which her personality projected in its own way. That was what the critics meant when they repeatedly spoke of her "poetic embodiments." She was of course limited. High tragedy she did not even essay, for she lacked the physical powers necessary to develop an overwhelming effect. But where the rôle called for delicacy, grace, subtle intelligence, spirit and humor—she gave something which the theatre of her time had never seen. As Bayle Bernard, perhaps the ablest of the London critics, had pointed out, it was as Rosalind, as Viola, as Beatrice that she was unrivalled. She could not lead audiences into the regions of pity or terror; the world which she created was one of warm delight where poetry was the natural medium of communication, as easily understood by the citizens of Savannah and St. Louis as by the denizens of the Forest of Arden.

Anna Cora's marriage to William Foushee Ritchie took place at her father's home in Ravenswood on June 6, 1854. The event was truly the high spot of the New York social season. It was reported that four thousand invitations had been issued for the wedding. But this was newspaper exaggeration. Adam Badeau was present and estimated the number of guests at about two thousand.

The presiding genius at the wedding entertainment was the celebrated Brown, sexton of Grace Church. No picture of New York's social life of this period is complete without Brown prominently in the foreground. He was a personality and a power. In addition to his ecclesiastical function, Brown operated a livery stable and a catering business; no wedding, ball or funeral in Upper-Tendom was considered safe without his ministrations. He not only took care of such details as food and drink and mourning gloves, as the case required, but he could also assist with guest lists. He knew everybody in town, and was the unofficial master of protocol. If there were last-minute defections at a cotillion or dinner-party, Brown could always help. He kept a list of young men with suitable manners and wardrobes and could even supply an authentic nobleman—for a special consideration.

So Lily's wedding was in the right hands. But she had undoubtedly planned it all herself. She probably financed it too, for Samuel Ogden's means were straitened just then. He was heavily involved in a lawsuit with William Astor which he stood a good chance to win, but which in the meanwhile was draining his cash resources. Fortunately Lily's own situation had been greatly improved by her last benefit.

The details of the wedding were scrupulously reported in the New York press. Among those attending were Senator Stephen A. Douglas and Robert Walker, ex-Secretary of the Treasury, as well as five members of Congress. The guests were met at the door by Brown who led them into the large drawing-room, where Mrs. Ogden and Emma, Mrs. Mecke, received them. They were then distributed throughout the adjoining rooms and onto the verandas. At three o'clock, the bridal party came down the broad staircase and entered the main drawing-room. There were six bridesmaids including two of Lily's nieces, her step-sister Grace Ogden, and the sister of Epes Sargent. Matilda, Mrs. Wellman, who had stood up once before with Lily, was matron of honor. The bride entered on the arm of her "venerable and noble-looking father," as *The Tribune* phrased it. Her costume was described minutely for the public. She wore a gown of white silk, heavily embroidered, "with lace appliqué let in." Her veil was of Honiton lace, fastened by a wreath of white rosebuds and myrtle leaves. Her only jewels were a necklace of pearls and a pearl brooch, gifts of the groom.

The service was that of the Swedenborgian Church and was given verbatim by *The New York Herald*, which also repro-duced the hymeneal prayer. Except for the groom no members of the Ritchie family were present. They were reported to be in mourning at the time.

After the ceremony Dodsworth's band, imported from New York, discoursed sweet music while the guests flowed into the gardens where a splendid collation was spread under a marquee. Champagne was dispensed throughout the afternoon and eve-ning, and dancing continued until a late hour.

Obviously this was the wedding that Lily in her secret dreams had always yearned for. She had never regretted that hurried ceremony in Saint-Esprit Church, but the memory of that morn-ing—the furtive snatching of the veil from her reticule, the pantalettes showing beneath her little-girl dress—must have made her feel that she had been cheated of one of woman's most cherished prerogatives. So she meant now to have it all her own way, no matter what it cost. This time everything would be absolutely right, from bridesmaids and lace to champagne for two thousand people. Everyone agreed that there had never been a wedding like it.

"GORGEOUS MRS. RITCHIE," *circa* 1860
Courtesy, The Mount Vernon Ladies Association of the Union

CHAPTER TWENTY

" . . . But Seldom Wildly Gay"

The Ritchie family were people of importance in Richmond, though they did not belong to the oldest Virginia aristocracy. Thomas Ritchie, the father of William Foushee, was a self-made man, the son of a Scottish immigrant. He had started out as a schoolteacher, then turned to journalism in which he had made a brilliant career. In his youth Ritchie was a staunch friend of Thomas Jefferson, and his paper, *The Richmond Enquirer*, had been the chief mouthpiece for Jefferson's policies. The paper was still influential throughout the South, though its active leadership had passed from Thomas Ritchie's hands to those of his son, William Foushee, and a group of associates. But Thomas Ritchie, "Father Ritchie" as he was affectionately known in the town, continued to make his presence felt not only in Richmond but also in Washington, where he spent several months of each year.

The elder Ritchie was comfortably off, but not wealthy. William Foushee had nothing beyond his salary as one of the editors of *The Enquirer*. When he brought his bride to Richmond they set up housekeeping in a modest two-story frame dwelling (which Anna Cora always referred to as "the cottage") on Ninth Street, in the outskirts of the city. But they had periodical tastes of greater luxury when they visited the beautiful James River plantation of Foushee's sister, Mrs. George Harrison, or when they spent a few winter weeks in Washington. Father Ritchie had a house on Lafayette Square next to the mansion of the banker, William Corcoran. The house was frequented by everyone of importance in the capital and Anna Cora at once became a center of attraction. Her charm, her beauty, her romantic background and her fame made her much sought-after, and the Ritchies were proud to show her off. She and Foushee were frequent guests at the White House, at Lord Napier's and at the home of General Cass. Lily was an especial favorite with the latter whom she had known in Paris in 1839-40.

In Richmond it was not quite the same—at least not at first. As the daughter-in-law of Thomas Ritchie she of course had a position, though it would have been a little difficult to say what that position was. No one in Richmond society had ever married an actress before, and it took people a while to decide what to do about it. Everybody knew Lily's background, her Revolutionary ancestry, her important connections in New York; but this did not wholly offset the deep suspicion surrounding her theatrical past. There were a good many people who were sure that behind the charming manner, the air of innocence, the unselfish devotion to good works, there must lurk a streak of wantonness which sooner or later would make itself known. With young people especially, it was feared that Mrs. Ritchie's influence might not be for the best. Mothers with young daughters were careful to chaperon all conversations between their offspring and Mrs. Ritchie.

One of the young people who had been warned about possible danger was Mary Virginia Hawes, who was later to achieve literary fame and popularity as Marion Harland. Although she knew the Ritchie family well, for more than a year after Foushee's marriage she avoided meeting his bride. Finally an occasion arose which made a meeting compulsory.

Mary Virginia had already begun her writing career. In fact

she had just published her second book. It seems rather wonderful that a woman, however young, with two novels to her credit should fear the contamination of talk. But contamination had to be risked at last, because Mrs. Ritchie had published a very kind review of Mary Virginia's new book in her husband's paper, and good manners demanded a personal acknowledgment. Mary Virginia courageously made her way to the cottage on Ninth Street, hoping that Mrs. Ritchie would not be at home and that she might simply leave a card with a word of thanks on it. But Mrs. Ritchie was in; and despite the young writer's determination to show no more warmth than the occasion required, she was so disarmed by her hostess's radiant kindness and complete simplicity that she soon found herself talking as though with an old friend. When she returned home she burned with shame at herself and at the town for the stupidly cruel things that had been said about Mrs. Ritchie. Thereafter she was a frequent visitor at "the cottage."

Ritchie was forty-one at the time of his marriage and everyone considered him a confirmed bachelor. He was a tall, rangy, red-headed man, with courtly manners and a rather special eye for pretty women. Although somewhat indolent in his movements he had an impulsive nature. This expressed itself by flare-ups in his editorials. It may also have expressed itself soon at home. But in the early years of their marriage this was no bar to their mutual love and happiness. The only effect, apparently, was to make Lily feel the need for a frequent change of scene. From the beginning she was much absent from Richmond.

Most of the first summer Cora, as she was now called, and Foushee were at Fauquier Springs, Virginia, a watering-place much frequented by ante-bellum Richmond society. The visit was, or should have been, a prolongation of the couple's honeymoon. But it was difficult for Lily to adjust to the idea of unlimited leisure and no responsibilities; so she had brought her work along. She wrote to George Ticknor on August 4, thanking him again for his wedding present: "The group from Spencer's [sic] Faerie Queen stands upon a marble table in a most conspicuous situation in our cottage drawing room. It is universally admired, and I never tire of gazing upon it." But her mind was already elsewhere—"When the weather grows cooler and I am quite settled in my new home I shall resume my habits of industry and send you the fruits."

She did not wait either for the cool weather or the new home, for within a week she was writing Ticknor again to say that she was sending the corrected proofs of *Armand* and *Fashion* (which Ticknor and Fields were bringing out in America). Yet she was very conscious of her bridal state: ". . . would it not be well to change the name on the title to Anna Cora *Ritchie*?" she inquired.

As soon as the cool weather did come, Lily was in Brookline visiting her sister May, who was soon to leave again for Italy with her husband, Cephas Giovanni Thompson. On the way back to Richmond she stopped at Greenfield Hill, Connecticut, to see Margaret Grey. The forlorn little girl whose affection Lily and James Mowatt had worked so hard to win had grown up to be a charming young lady. But she had been ill for a long time and Lily was deeply concerned about her. She decided now to take Margaret with her to Richmond, in the hope that the milder climate would stay the course of the disease that had already marked the girl for an early end. In November, she wrote to her young friend Annie Frobisher in Cambridge: "Margery is no better, but not worse . . ." and mentioned that "our cottage is looking very charming and we are very happy."

Sometime during this autumn, either in Philadelphia or in Richmond, Lily made the acquaintance of a remarkable woman, Ann Pamela Cunningham. This lady, who had been a semi-invalid for sixteen years, was afire with a great purpose. It had become her mission in life to rescue the home of Washington, Mount Vernon—now threatened with dilapidation—and make it a national shrine. Mr. John Augustine Washington II, the present owner, had offered the estate for the sum of $200,000 to both the Congress of the United States and to the Virginia Legislature. Neither had been interested. Miss Cunningham, an ardent patriot, had brooded over the matter and decided that what the fathers of the Nation lacked the spirit to do, the mothers would undertake. She had begun writing letters to the newspapers which she signed "A Southern Matron," and the response was instantaneous. Money was already beginning to come in, and a rudimentary organization called the Mount Vernon Association had been created. This was composed chiefly of Virginia ladies, with a Central Committee established in Richmond. Miss Cunningham knew all about Anna Cora—who in America did not?—and she felt that a woman of Mrs. Ritchie's celebrity and winning personality would be invaluable to the Cause. The upshot of their first conversation was that Anna Cora accepted the position of secretary of the Central Committee.

Her enthusiasm is not difficult to understand. She, too, was deeply patriotic and had always been a passionate admirer of Washington. She had lived long enough in Europe to know that Washington's name was inseparable from the prestige of her country. Everything connected with that name was sacred. The place where Washington had lived and died was hallowed ground. It must be reverently preserved not only as a visible reminder of Washington's earthly connection with the nation over whose founding he had presided, but because—as she firmly believed—his spirit still hovered closely about the fields, the gardens, the rooms he had loved.

A second motive for her zeal to advance the Cause was Miss Cunningham. Nothing so stirred Anna Cora as achievement by the handicapped. She had attained success herself despite ill-health and social opposition. When she saw Miss Cunningham with apparently so little strength, giving that little—even to the last minim—to this noble purpose, her heart swelled with a desire to help.

Meanwhile Lily had her hands full with other matters. She was spending every available moment on a new book which she had promised Ticknor and Fields, and which she hoped would sell. She needed money badly, and she foresaw that she would continue to need it.

This was not because her husband was unable to support her, albeit modestly. Financial independence had become a condition of her life which she could not easily give up. Furthermore she had expenses which she could not ask Foushee to undertake, or which, maybe, Foushee had subtly implied that he would not undertake. Chief among these was the care of the young Greys. William was still at school, but she hoped that both boys would soon be able to fend for themselves. She had written Ticknor the previous summer to ask if he could not give John Grey a job. But the boy was not well, and it might be some time before he could make his own way. Margaret required Lily's constant care now, for the girl's health had not improved with the journey South. But this burden Lily would soon relinquish in sorrow. Late in February, she wrote Miss Cunningham that Margaret seemed "to be hovering on the border of the grave"; and in a few weeks she was gone.

The winter took its toll of Lily too. In March she came down with pneumonia, and for six weeks it seemed likely that she would follow Margaret. But the golden portals which she so often saw in her dreams were only ajar. They were not yet ready to open; and by June, after a fortnight at her sister-in-law's plantation, she slowly began to gather strength. She had no sooner returned to Richmond than her house was full of guests. When these moved out, another group took their place. It was, she explained to Ticknor, "an old Virginia custom." By the end of June she was longing to escape to the North.

At her father's house Lily worked feverishly on the new book, which was to be entitled *Mimic Life*. This was a series of three stories dealing with the theatre, and, as she informed everybody, strictly autobiographical. She refused to heed Epes Sargent's suggestion to change the name of a character from Trueheart to something less allegorical, because the character had been named that in real life and nothing else fitted!

It was late November when Lily finally left Astoria. When she arrived in Richmond, after a sea-trip which tried even the steady constitution of Renshaw, she discovered that serious difficulties had arisen for the Mount Vernon Association. The ladies might not be able to buy Mount Vernon even if they raised the $200,000 which Mr. Washington was asking for it. As a body, the Mount Vernon Association had no legal status, and without that they could not acquire property. The only solution would be for the Virginia Legislature to grant them a charter of incorporation. The big question was, would the Legislature approve such a charter? The staunchest admirers of Miss Cunningham were skeptical, for never in the history of the United States had a group of women been incorporated under the law, and it seemed unlikely that the Virginia Legislature would shatter this precedent.

But people had not reckoned with Mrs. Ritchie. This was precisely the sort of situation she had dealt with all her life. Nothing so stimulated her as the challenge of the impossible, and she began at once to plan a strategy. Miss Cunningham, for her part, had not been idle. With the assistance of John McPherson Berrien, senator from Georgia and a celebrated constitutional lawyer, a charter was drawn up which, it was believed, might pass the Legislature. It seemed a very innocent document, free from any suggestion of radical feminism (indeed the framers had apparently no idea how radical it was), and merely emphasizing the patriotic purpose of the organization.

Lily made it her special responsibility to see that the bill to charter the Association should be introduced during the present session of the Legislature. Despite the continued standoffishness of a few people, she now had many friends in Richmond. Some of the most devoted were members of her own sex, among whom she had won staunch allies for the Cause. Three Richmond ladies, Mesdames Cabell, Pellett and Robinson, she took into her confidence and with them worked out a plan of action.

It was January and the Legislature was sitting. The four ladies carefully went over the list of members, and each selected the names of those whom she believed she could effectively approach. Then the campaign began.

On February 29 Lily wrote to Miss Cunningham:

Now I must give you some scraps of good news.—I have been electioneering and very successfully. Night before last I gave a musical soirée. I desired my husband to invite as many of the senators and members of the Legislature as the house would hold.

My small but expansive rooms were well crowded—Everyone declared he had a delightful evening.—The music was excellent and supper good. Then came the grand coup. As the ladies began to retire Mrs. Pellett commenced the subject with Governor Floyd, and I managed to make it *general*. Governor Floyd pledged himself to use his best endeavors to pass our bill *and at once*—so did all the other members and senators present. After all the ladies had left the gentlemen still remained and talked to me. . . .

The effect of Anna Cora's conversation with the gentlemen was an invitation to come to the capitol and tell the Legislature about the bill and to urge its passage. Lily was horrified at the thought of making such a public appearance before an entirely male audience, but as she wrote Miss Cunningham, "I will not have it on my conscience that I left *one* stone unturned." So she agreed to go to the capitol.

From now until the middle of March, lights frequently burned late in the Ritchie house, as the legislators, replete with port wine and turtle soup, listened to Lily talk—with music in between. Lily began to fairly tingle with excitement, for the feel of victory was in the air.

However, the time was growing short. The Legislature was moving to the close of its session and as yet no action had been taken, though Anna Cora and her friends had long since secured the signatures necessary to have the bill introduced. Governor Floyd and Mr. Langfitt, an influential member, had assured her that the bill would be passed; but every day seemed to be filled with other business and the Mount Vernon charter was continually by-passed. Lily began to get nervous. Finally, on March 17 she could endure the waiting no longer. This was a Saturday; the House was due to rise on Monday. She told Foushee that he must go to see Langfitt and try to get the bill passed immediately.

Foushee went to the capitol. When he returned and reported to Cora what had happened she could not believe her ears. According to Langfitt, he had tried to introduce the bill but he had been opposed by Mr. Stanard—one of the members of whose support Anna Cora had been certain. After the session Langfitt had gone to Stanard for an explanation, and Stanard revealed that he had blocked the bill because he had been requested by some of the ladies of the Association to oppose it! Langfitt was thunderstruck and asked the names of the ladies who had made the request. But Stanard had been sworn not to reveal their identity.

Langfitt was of course thoroughly irritated by the whole business and considered the matter at an end. Foushee advised Cora that the Cause was now lost, and that the best thing would be to forget about it as soon as possible. But this was the last thing she would do. There had been treason in the very citadel and she meant to get at the bottom of it. Furthermore she was determined that, treason or no, the bill would be passed.

She asked Foushee to take her at once to see Mrs. Cabell. She had complete trust in this lady's integrity and believed that she could learn from her who had sabotaged the bill. Mrs. Cabell, when she heard the story, was as astonished and indignant as Mrs. Ritchie. She proposed to go to Stanard, whom she knew well, and get the truth from him. But Ritchie said that the important thing now was to get the signatures of all the ladies in favor of the bill. He wisely reasoned that many who had secretly opposed it would be afraid to do so openly. Mrs. Cabell, an energetic person, immediately summoned her carriage and started off personally to round up all the ladies of the Central Committee for a meeting at her house after church the next day, Sunday.

The ladies, including Anna Cora, duly met at Mrs. Cabell's. The only one conspicuous by her absence was a Mrs. Gilmer who, it soon developed, had been the ring-leader of the opposition— presumably out of pique at Mrs. Ritchie's dominant role in the campaign. There was some discussion; but in the end all the ladies present, a large majority of the Central Committee, signed the bill.

The next step was to see Governor Floyd and Mr. Langfitt. Once more Mrs. Cabell ordered her carriage, and the four ladies, Mrs. Cabell, Mrs. Robinson, Mrs. Pellett and Anna Cora rattled off to the Exchange Hotel, where they met the Governor and Mr. Langfitt just rising from Sunday dinner. The gentlemen were in an expansive mood. They listened kindly to the ladies' frantic explanations, and agreed that there might yet be hope. Governor Floyd proposed that they see the Speaker of the House, Major Crutchfield, and ask him to give the floor on the next day to Mr. Langfitt for five minutes.

Fortunately Lily knew Crutchfield well. He had been a very frequent recipient of her hospitality. In a matter of minutes the Speaker was located and Lily introduced him to the other ladies. Lily then begged the Major to grant them a favor "blindfold." (She had long ago discovered this simple technique for getting quick action from people). The Major was delighted to grant anything the ladies might ask, and Lily at once explained the situation. Crutchfield readily agreed that Mr. Langfitt should have the floor on Monday at eleven o'clock. He also suggested that it might be advantageous to have as many ladies of the Association as possible present in the House at the time.

The ladies were only too happy to follow this suggestion. They went back to Mrs. Cabell's where each got into her own carriage. They then scattered in separate directions about the town, alerting the other members of the Association for the next day's assault on the capitol.

It was very late in the afternoon when Lily arrived at "the cottage." Foushee was in an unquiet mood. He had sent a servant all over town hunting his wife, and complained that the dinner was cold. But as Lily wrote Miss Cunningham, "He forgave me . . . when he heard all we had accomplished."

At ten o'clock on Monday morning the ladies assembled at Mrs. Pellett's. Then in a body, escorted by Foushee, they made their way to the capitol. As they filed into the House there was dead silence, and a concerted craning of legislative necks as they rustled into the gallery.

Major Crutchfield then addressed the House. Gracefully bowing to the gallery, he called attention to the fair visitants who had honored the assembly with their presence and asked if the gentlemen would not set aside other business until the Ladies' bill had been attended to. There was a loud chorus of "certainly's"; only one or two voices were heard to mutter indistinctly something about "outrageous . . . ladies taking up the time like this." The bill was then presented and put to the vote. The ladies smiled charmingly, and fixed the members with unwavering gaze while the Ayes and Noes were taken. The bill chartering the Mount Vernon Association was passed with only two dissenting votes.

The ladies were now to pass into the Senate. Several members of the House jumped up to escort them. In the Senate after a wait of about five minutes the bill was again presented. One gentleman made a short speech, apparently against the bill, which Anna Cora could not hear. But no one else seems to have heard it either—perhaps not even the gentleman himself—for when the vote was taken the bill was passed unanimously.

It was a great day for the Association. As a matter of fact it was a great day for women throughout the United States. With the chartering of the Mount Vernon Association, for the first time in American history it became lawful for women to band together for legal action—even though the action involved nothing more than the acquisition of a shabby mansion and a few hundred acres of exhausted Virginia soil.

That night, Monday, March 19, 1856, Lily wrote Miss Cunningham: "Victory! Victory! beloved friend and fellow worker! Heaven smiles upon our efforts!" She then reported to the absent commander all the details of the battle, ending with "I am very *very* weary—but so happy! Mount Vernon is secure—is ours! We may be sure of that. All praise and honor be to you!"

Perhaps some praise and honor was also due the faithful lieutenant ("our little Mowatt," as Davenport had called her), whose powers to charm had contributed so much to the victory.

Anna Cora was very tired indeed, and Foushee was worried about her. He wanted to get her out of Richmond at once; and she agreed to go away with him as soon as one or two matters had been taken care of. With all legal obstacles removed, the question now was to raise the $200,000 as quickly as possible. Lily wanted to see the fund-raising campaign off to a good start.

The day the bill chartering the Association was passed, the greatest orator of the country, Edward Everett, came to Richmond to deliver his celebrated address on George Washington.

Everett had already met Miss Cunningham and had agreed to appear in Richmond for the benefit of the Mount Vernon movement. Lily may also have met Everett before. At any rate she had a long talk with him in Richmond, and the result of the conversation was that Everett agreed to donate all future proceeds of the Washington oration to the Cause until the purchase money should be raised. For the next three years he traveled up and down the country delivering his great oration before untold thousands of Americans. The proceeds of these appearances totalled nearly $70,000—all of which was turned over to the Mount Vernon Association. This accomplishment astonishes us now, but in Lily's day oratory was a great art—and one of the most popular forms of public entertainment. People paid and paid willingly to hear a powerful speaker; and Edward Everett— scholar, diplomat, divine—was, after Daniel Webster, the greatest of them all.

There was more than Mr. Everett's visit to hold Anna Cora in Richmond. She was hard at work on a new book, another work with a theatre background to be called *Twin Roses*. Although the story dealt primarily with the English stage, Lily had manipulated the plot so as to get her hero and heroine to America, and eventually to Mount Vernon. She wanted to sketch in this part of the story while still under the spell of Everett's oration. Everything must now be turned to the advantage of Mount Vernon, and *Twin Roses* would do its part. So Anna Cora's fertile imagination was busy weaving propaganda for the Cause into her romance of young love behind the footlights. While her hero and heroine were seeking theatrical employment in the New World, Anna Cora had them take time out for a sight-seeing trip to Mount Vernon. Once on the spot they were led to make appropriate reflections:

Herman [the hero] could not help but wonder and not wholly without indignation, that while the earthly dwellings of so many men, rendered illustrious by their genius or great deeds, were held sacred in the old world, this home of America's peerless patriot, the most hallowed ground of the new land, had not been snatched from the chances of profanation and ruin, and set apart as a shrine to which young and old might make pilgrimages and be inspired with patriotic and holy emotions as they visited the scenes consecrated by the memory and the virtues of the departed hero.

Always eager to pay tribute where it was due, Lily also had a few words for her associates:

> If governments are forgetful [this is still Herman in a reflective mood] there are too many gratified hearts in the breasts of American *women* for Mount Vernon, the home of their father, to become a ruin. . . . Let but a master-spirit (Heaven-appointed) lead them and mark out the way—one noble, self-sacrificing and wholly unselfish, patriotic woman, and thousands of hands and hearts will labor with her. They will share her laurels, but the work will truly be hers, and it will surely be accomplished.

All through the last exciting months when the Cause was really attracting attention, Lily had been distressed that the one who had started the movement should be confined to her invalid's room in Philadelphia, unable to participate in the active struggle and to share personally in the joys of achievement. At least she lost no opportunity to remind Miss Cunningham that it was *she* to whom the credit was due, that it was *her* example that had inspired her lieutenants to carry on with their mission. Never, never must anyone forget that!

In May, Cora and Foushee did get away from Richmond for a brief holiday in the Blue Ridge. When they returned early in June, Anna Cora was again plunged in innumerable problems, mostly of other people. Annie Frobisher was in dire need of employment and Lily was writing in all directions to try to find her a governess's position. In addition to Annie there were a couple of refugee Hungarians whom she was helping to get established in their exile. Then there was a poor dressmaker who had worked for Lily, but was now ill and had to be taken care of. Eventually Lily sent her to the seashore to recover her strength. There was also a music teacher. . . . How many more, nobody knows. George Ticknor may have had some idea, for throughout the summer Lily was constantly writing him to ask that he honor drafts on royalties due. Fortunately *Mimic Life*, after a somewhat slow start, was selling well. But the demands were so great that the money seemed to go into a bottomless hole.

As usual, Lily went North for the summer. She spent July and August in New York looking after Julia who had just had a new baby. In addition to nursing the mother Lily took charge of the housekeeping and looked after the other Smyth children. Although the excursion into the Blue Ridge Mountains had been refreshing, the summer proved a severe tax on her health. But it never occurred to her to try to ease some of her responsibilities onto others. Instead she went to the source of all needed strength, her religion; and there she found support for her flagging energies.

Perhaps one reason why Lily always looked forward with such yearning to the visits North was the fact that in her father's house, or with her sisters, she could more freely live the faith which increasingly filled her life. Her Swedenborgianism had contributed to the suspicion with which many people in Richmond continued to regard her; at least it set her apart in a community where religious orthodoxy was a paramount consideration. Actually she seldom discussed religion in Richmond. Even Foushee, who at first had tolerated Cora's Swedenborgianism as a mark of her fascinating individuality, was becoming more and more impatient with a belief at variance with many of the established *mores* of his native city. As time went on Lily avoided discussing religion with him altogether. But the less she talked, the more she thought. Even with Annie Frobisher, with whom she was so closely bound in affection, she was reserved. This did not prevent Annie from turning to her for advice when she was troubled by religious problems. In reply to a straight question, Lily would express herself sometimes. Once Annie wrote her on the matter of the communion, and Lily gave this clear reply:

> You ask my advice about taking communion. I should not be happy—could not be—were I not a communicant and had I not a *settled* religious faith. It seems to me incumbent on everyone to remember that the Lord has charged us to celebrate the Holy

Supper *in remembrance* of Him. Who can read his words and not feel bound to prepare themselves to obey?

But she scrupulously refrained always from proselytizing for her own faith. When Annie asked about specific points of Swedenborgian doctrine, Lily told her to consult the Reverend Mr. Huntington, Epes Sargent's brother-in-law, who was a professor at Harvard. "He can advise you better than I can."

In September, Lily's older sister Emma, who had been a widow for some time and was now Mrs. Levi Burridge, came on to New York. Lily was then able to leave Julia and go out to Astoria to her father's. Shortly afterwards, Matilda—Mrs. Wellman—arrived from Cincinnati. Lily was then able to report to Annie that nine of the sisters were together, all but "the dear wanderer in Rome, May." She told Annie that she expected to be very little in Richmond during the coming winter. Samuel Ogden was now 77 and she wished to be with him as much as possible—if she could "obtain Mr. R.'s consent."

Foushee came north the first of October, and he and Lily accompanied by Samuel Ogden and his wife took a trip to Niagara Falls, which Lily described as "delightful in the extreme." The trip had been preceded by a grievous leave-taking, however, for two of the sisters, Julia and Emma, were departing for indefinite stays in Europe. Lily was so desolate at the separation, that Julia at the last moment decided to leave her little two-year-old daughter Eugenia behind to console her.

Anna Cora's hope of spending the winter or at least of staying on through Christmas in Astoria was frustrated. Foushee refused to give his permission. There was to be a big Ritchie gathering at Brandon, Mrs. Harrison's plantation home, and Cora must be on hand. So, early in December, Lily mournfully turned her back on Long Island and started South. With her went not only little Neenie but another niece, Margaretta Ogden, daughter of Lily's brother, Charles. Margaretta, a girl of fifteen, was in delicate health and Lily hoped the milder climate of Richmond would benefit her.

Just before leaving Astoria she sent Annie Frobisher some

practical advice. Annie was writing a book and Lily urged her to "be sure and copy it in a clear large hand so that the publishers can read it without difficulty. . . . Many a good book has never seen the light because the ms. was not legible."

The Christmas at Brandon that year cannot have been very happy, despite Foushee's expectations. Lily was confined to her room for most of the time with a bad cough, and Margaretta Ogden was seriously ill. As if this were not enough, when they returned to Richmond Foushee was thrown from a horse and had his foot wrenched completely out of the socket—or so the doctors thought. Thus Lily now had two invalids to look after, as well as little Neenie. Somehow she bore up under it all—with, of course, the indomitable Renshaw ever at her side.

Still later in the winter, Lily was saddened by the death of her sister Matilda's youngest child. Her stoicism was sorely tried by this event. She could never really face the death of children with the same equanimity she accepted death for older people. She knew that Heaven was the rightful place for the pure and innocent, but she felt the world had need of them too.

The fact that she had no children of her own often shadowed her thoughts, and made her cling more fiercely to those that had been lent her by fate or her brothers and sisters. Once, Annie Frobisher in a letter had expressed regret that Lily should be childless, and had immediately written again to apologize for venturing on so delicate a subject. But Lily at once replied:

> You did not touch on too sacred a matter when you wished in one of your letters that I too was a mother. Children are a great joy to me. I should have been almost too happy if God had sent me one of my own. But he did not think it well for me and I do not murmur against the will of one "who doeth all things well".

Even more poignantly did she reveal her sense of deprivation to Marion Harland:

> There is something to me so mysteriously beautiful in maternity that I am impressed with a sense of reverence for a young mother

who is thankful for her great gift. Although it has not been the will of our Gracious Lord that I should be thus blessed, I feel as though I comprehend the thrilling sensations of one who clasps an infant to her breast with the jubilant cry, *It is mine*."

Strong as was her maternal instinct it did not dominate her feeling for her husband. During the first weeks when he was confined to the house after his accident she wrote Annie that he was "helpless as a child but good and patient and easily amused." As time wore on, however, and the foot did not mend, Foushee was less easily amused. Then Lily referred to him as "a big baby," with not quite the same implication of tender pity. Yet she felt keenly for his suffering, and when by June there was still no sign of real improvement she made him come North with her and consult a specialist in New York.

Besides the care of her husband and Margaretta Ogden and the two-year-old Eugenia, Lily had shouldered another responsibility during the winter of 1857-58. She had taken under her wing a charming young girl, Avonia Jones, whose parents were old associates of Lily's theatre days. The girl's father, an actor with more brass than ability, masqueraded under the name of Count Johannes. The mother, Mrs. Melinda Jones, was a respectable leading lady. Lily had played with her in Charleston in 1854 (Juliet to Mrs. Jones's Romeo), and she may have met Avonia then. Shortly after Lily's marriage, the girl had come to Richmond to be with relatives, and Lily had immediately invited her to the "cottage." This created talk in Richmond for it proved undeniably, just as the gossips had anticipated, that Mrs. Ritchie had not entirely broken with her theatrical past. But no one was less concerned about such talk than Lily. She not only had Avonia frequently to her house, but as the girl showed a marked talent for the stage, she offered to teach her to act. Avonia joyfully accepted the proposal, and the two had worked happily together all winter. In December, Lily's *Armand* was produced at the Richmond theatre with Avonia in the role of Blanche. Avonia performed like a veteran and Lily almost wept for joy at her success. She was with Avonia in her dressing-room before curtain-time. What it must have meant for her to smell the musty back-stage air again, one can only guess. Neither on this or any other occasion did she express regret for this closed chapter of her life. But there were those who observed an unusual brightness in Mrs. Ritchie's eyes that night.

Writing continued to absorb much of Lily's time. *Twin Roses* was due to appear in the spring, and she was also engaged on a series of sketches which eventually appeared in *The New York Ledger*. Her literary activities were stimulated by a small group of choice souls who had gathered about her soon after she moved to Richmond. Among these were Marion Harland, ex-Governor John Wise, J. R. Thompson (editor of *The Southern Literary Messenger*), and a young Richmond sculptor, Edward Valentine. The group was also augmented during this winter by the prolific and popular English novelist, G. P. R. James, who had been British Consul at Norfolk. He had often visited in Richmond and had found the literary and artistic atmosphere of Lily's coterie so stimulating that he had requested his government to transfer his consulate to the capitol. This the Foreign Office had obligingly done, and G. P. R. James was now a regular habitué of the cottage on Ninth Street.

There was no evidence, so far as these intimates could see, that Cora and Foushee were not perfectly happy. Ritchie seemed to take delight in the informal gatherings over which his wife's beauty and wit cast such a bright glow. It gratified his pride that his home should be the center of Richmond's cultural life and he gladly assisted Anna Cora in entertaining the group. In the winter, the Ritchies' hospitality was somewhat restricted by the size of their house; but in the spring and summer the soirées could overflow into the garden. Here Lily set out little tables under the trees from whose boughs hung gaily-colored lanterns, and sounds of polite revelry would often echo late into the night.

In the spring of 1858 a second obstacle arose in the work of rescuing Mount Vernon. Mr. Washington had begun to hedge about selling. Although Miss Cunningham had extracted a promise—or at least thought she had extracted one—that he would sell, it was not at all certain that the deal would go through. Mr. Washington was in a difficult mood, and not without reason. There had been a good deal of unpleasant, and some downright nasty, comment in the newspapers about the price he was asking. As real estate Mount Vernon was not worth $200,000, perhaps not a quarter of that sum; and Mr. Washington had been accused of trading on the honor of his distinguished kinsman to enrich himself. This had made Mr. Washington very angry, for he had earlier refused an offer of $300,000 from a group of speculators simply because he did not want the place to be exploited commercially.

Anna Cora was the one to smooth over this situation, both with Mr. Washington and with the public. She wrote an appeal which was widely circulated in the press, pointing out that

> If the price is deemed too great for the actual value of the estate, let us remember that it is to be paid by the whole nation, and to the Nation Mount Vernon is priceless. . . . We can put no market value upon a nation's attestations of gratitude, no price upon hallowed memories and holy associations—no price upon the footprints of Washington—and these give to Mount Vernon its value!

Mr. Washington had also objected to certain clauses in the Mount Vernon Association Charter which would have made it possible for the estate eventually to fall into the hands of Virginia politicians. But this objection was soon removed by the granting of a new charter, which left no loopholes as to future ownership. The estate would be maintained as a philanthropic, educational and patriotic enterprise by the organization whose new title was *The Mount Vernon Ladies Association of the Union*. The Association itself had now been reorganized on a nation-wide basis. The supreme commander was the Regent, Miss Ann Pamela Cunningham; and for each state there would be a Vice-Regent. The first Vice-Regent to be appointed was Anna Cora Ritchie, for the State of Virginia.

It had been a busy winter for Anna Cora. To all the varied activities—nursing invalids, training Avonia, writing, entertain-

ing, and crusading for Mount Vernon, Lily had given herself
without stint. Through it all had run a growing tension between herself and Foushee. This was heightened not only by the
differences in temperament which were becoming increasingly
apparent, but also perhaps by the suspicion that Foushee's affections were no longer centered on her. What it all added up to for
Lily was a sense that life had begun to pass her by.

She wrote to Annie Frobisher in the late spring of this year,
à propos of a joyous tone which had suddenly appeared in
Annie's letters, saying that she was reminded of herself at Annie's
age:

> I was mirthful to a fault. . . . Even my reverses of fortune failed
> to sadden me for more than a brief season. Now I am cheerful—
> lively perhaps—but seldom wildly gay.

The summer was to bring Lily further grief. When she arrived in New York for her annual visit she found that John
Grey, who was still living in Connecticut, was ailing. By September it was clear that his life was hanging by a frayed thread.
"We fear that he is hopelessly consumptive," Lily wrote to
Annie,—indeed slowly dying as his sister did. He returns South
with us towards the close of October. He may linger a long time
yet, but all that can be done for him is to smooth his way to the
great gate and to prepare him for the future life. He is a
good boy. . . ."

October came but John did not go South. He was not strong
enough to move, and by the end of the month his troubles were
ended. "My dear Johnny's illness and death and other things
have *more* than occupied me night and day. . . . He died most
happily and his last words were full of gratitude. . . ." Lily
reported to Annie at the end of November.

The Ritchies spent Christmas at Brandon, but Lily could take
little part in the festivities. She had arrived in Richmond very
nearly exhausted and had come down with a bad cough. Most
of the month of December she was miserable, not only with the
cough but with acute neuralgia for which she took chloroform.

This relieved the pain of the neuralgia but kept her constantly nauseated.

Illness may not have been the only damper on this holiday season for Lily. Was it perhaps during this visit to Brandon that she picked up the first intimation of the sordid business that led to her final rupture with Foushee? Brandon was a large property and Mrs. Harrison had many slaves. Ritchie in his bachelor days had spent much time at the plantation. Was it here that his eye had first lighted on some dusky beauty, perhaps a household servant, whose accessibility made her irresistible? Now, with his wife continuously ill, it may have been all too easy to slip again into old ways. But this is conjecture. The details of the discovery, when and however made, Lily kept carefully to herself. Only the basic fact did she ever reveal. It was through Matilda Wellman that the story was handed down.

Whatever may have been the cause, it is certain that after the winter of 1859 things began to go from bad to worse between Anna Cora and Foushee. The references to her husband in her letters are now hurried and casual, if she speaks of him at all. She was still attempting to preserve the semblance of peace, above all struggling to keep intact the modest home which meant so much to her. The cottage was the first house which she could really call her own since the Melrose days. It was a haven not only for herself but for many others who found rest and loving care within its walls. When Marion Harland once marveled that she should have been so content in this simple dwelling Lily had instantly replied: "Ah, my child, when you have been tossed about as long up and down the world as I have been, you will know something of the blessedness of home and rest when they are given to you."

But as the year 1859 dragged on there was little blessedness and less rest in the cottage for Lily. In addition to the troubles with Foushee there was a shattering experience with Miss Cunningham—whom Lily now looked upon as one of her truest friends. All through the winter, despite her cough and the neuralgia, she had truly slaved for the Mount Vernon project, writing endless letters, articles, solicitations for contributions, and in every way exerting herself to stimulate the flow of money into the Association treasury. Only her zeal for the Cause and her devotion to the heroic invalid who had given her very life, so it seemed, to advance the work kept Lily at her desk. Then in February came a horrifying blow. She received a letter from a Mrs. Eve in Georgia which struck at the root of her faith in the founder of the Mount Vernon Ladies Association. She wasted no time in writing to Miss Cunningham:

Richmond, February 12, 1859

My dearest Pamela:

. . . I enclose scraps and among them a splendid, a sublime letter from Mrs. Eve. She clearly proves, that the first association was started in Georgia and the *credit* should be Georgia's forever! and forever! Do you know that I was not aware of this before and feel strongly inclined to *chide*—nay positively *scold* you for leaving me in ignorance. Here you have allowed me to think and to state *over and over again* that the first association was started in Richmond. In the very first letter that you wrote to me this was the impression that you gave me.—The taking out our charter in Virginia probably *legalized* the first association here—but the movement was actually started in Georgia and under the auspices of Mrs. Eve. . . .

I wish I had time to scold you more. Indeed I am quite vexed with you for not correcting my error. Why, you let me put forth an appeal saying that "the first ladies Mt. Vernon Association of the Union was formed in 1854 in Virginia", and I believed that I was writing the strictest truth. It's too bad. I can't tell you what I feel like doing, for I hold it to be one of the meanest things imaginable to rob any individual of one *particle* of the credit due to them for their exertions. . . . But no more at present. I could not sleep without venting my vexation in these few lines. . . .

How "dearest Pamela" extricated herself from this situation is not revealed by the records. But she was a remarkably clever woman and by July all was well again between the two friends. Edward Everett—now devoted to both ladies—wrote Miss Cunningham on July 12, 1859, that he was "truly gratified to find the former friendly relations restored between you and Cora, if indeed they had been ever for a moment interrupted. The number of congenial spirits in the world is not large enough for those who are so to be chilled toward each other."

The record shows only two outbreaks of real anger in Lily's whole life. One was occasioned by Crisp for a breach of loyalty, the other by Ann Pamela Cunningham for a breach of justice. We can be sure that had Miss Cunningham not produced convincing evidence of her innocent intentions, the break with her would have been as definitive as it had been with Crisp.

The trip north in the summer of 1859 must have been something in the nature of flight. The past winter had been so full of pain and disillusionment that Lily counted the moments until she would be again under Papa's roof and in the shelter of his loving arms. Samuel Ogden was nearly eighty now, but vigorous and clear-minded as ever—still a rock to which Lily could cling when the current was moving too swiftly for her.

More than ever reluctantly, she went back to Richmond at the beginning of the winter. For her father's sake Lily was determined that there should be no break with her husband. She would do nothing to cloud the little time left the old man. But it must have cost something to return to an atmosphere which was now as tense outside "the cottage" as within. For four years Lily had heard nothing but increasingly violent talk about States Rights and northern interference in southern affairs. She was no abolitionist. In fact she seems to have accepted slavery as she did everything else that was characteristic of southern life. But she had a passionate love of freedom, and, believing firmly in the eventual triumph of right, she was convinced that the dreadful institution would pass out of existence. There were southerners who felt the same way, and she had heard it said many times that economic factors, if not moral considerations must put an end to slavery. But she was alarmed now, in the fall of 1859, to find that many of the most enlightened spirits of Richmond were changing their views. The pressure of excited feeling was rising every day, and Lily's position as a northerner added another difficulty to a life that was rapidly becoming intolerable.

The differences in sectional feeling increased the friction

between the Ritchies. But sparks were already flying from other causes. Foushee's antagonism to his wife's religion was one of these. With the passing years and their steady toll of Lily's loved ones—sisters, friends, the two Grey children, beloved nephews and nieces—she could not exist without the comfort of Swedenborgianism. But this was increasingly difficult to have now in Richmond. There is more than an intimation of this in a letter written by Lily to Robert Dale Owen in January, 1860. Lily had just reviewed for *The Enquirer* a book by Owen on spiritualism, in which she found points of correspondence with Swedenborg's doctrines. She wrote the author apologizing for the superficiality of her article, saying that if she had written as she wished "it would not have been admitted into *The Enquirer* any more than a New Church sermon."

The solace of religion was never so needed as in April, 1860, when Samuel Ogden, after a brief illness, quietly died in Lily's arms. She had been summoned in time to spend the last ten days at his bedside. Her father's death was the severest break in the ties of her earthly affections since James had gone. But she was able to accept this break as she had the others, because she knew it was only temporary. She wrote to her old friend Samuel Ruggles that she had had "the sad joy" of nursing her father day and night during his last illness, "of receiving his last breath, his last kiss, of holding him in my arms as the angels took away his happy spirit." She said that his mind was clear to the last, "his affections warmer than ever—his language touchingly elevated—his faith perfect—*his desire* to go strong."

The letter to Ruggles was written from Richmond on June 17. Lily was then preparing to return to Astoria in a fortnight for the wedding of her half-sister Emily Ogden. Her sister Julia Smyth was to return from Europe for the event and would spend the summer with the family. But Lily had barely reached Astoria when news came that Julia was seriously ill and could not make the trip. Lily was frightened. The prospect of losing her darling Julia, so soon after the death of her father, was devastating. She made up her mind quickly. She had come North as usual accompanied by Renshaw and her trunks. Everything else was in

Richmond—all her personal possessions, wedding gifts, souvenirs of the theatre, the framed testimonial from the citizens of New York upon her retirement, all her books and manuscripts. But this did not matter. Julia needed her, and she needed Julia. She also needed to put a great distance between herself and Richmond. This time she did not ask Foushee's permission. She drew all her accumulated royalty money from Ticknor and Fields, and the middle of August, with Renshaw, she sailed for France.

CHAPTER TWENTY-ONE

" . . . *The Sunshine Passes Away*
So Soon"

Whatever Anna Cora may have written Foushee, so far as Richmond was concerned they were still a happily-married couple. Everybody knew of Mrs. Smyth's illness and it was easy to explain Mrs. Ritchie's departure for Europe on that account. Foushee himself did not take seriously Cora's announcement that she was not coming back. He was confident that she would yield to his persuasion, and he let it be known in Richmond that she was expected in the fall. When winter came and she still showed no sign of changing her mind, he made his plans to go after her.

Meanwhile Anna Cora stayed quietly with the Smyths in Paris. Julia was well out of danger, but she still needed her sister's care. Anna Cora had written no one except Foushee that she meant to stay on indefinitely, but her plans for the future were taking shape. The most important thing was to find a livelihood.

Her resources were very limited at the moment. The few hundred dollars which she had collected from Ticknor and Fields were about gone; the money saved from her prosperous days in the theatre had long since vanished. At the time of her marriage to Ritchie she had accumulated something, but the six thousand dollars realized from her last benefit had gone into the wedding, and the rest had been consumed by her ever-increasing charities and other expenses in Richmond. One item for which she had always paid was the annual trip North, involving four or five people, a child or two, Renshaw—and usually Foushee.

So in Paris Lily was once more on her own, repeating the old familiar pattern of turning some talent or other to account in order to survive. But she was undaunted. Three times before she had started from nothing, and she was confident she could do it again. She was so much richer now in experience, so much wiser in the ways of the world, and as a writer so much more accomplished than when she had let Epes Sargent publish *Gulzara* in *The New World* twenty years before. For it was definitely as a writer that she meant now to try her luck. During the previous year she had published in *The New York Ledger* a series of chatty essays ranging over a variety of topics from children's birthday parties to meditations on her first gray hair. Bonner, editor of *The Ledger*, had been very well pleased with them and Lily was encouraged to believe that she might make a living as a newspaper writer.

She may have considered returning to the stage, but not for long. She would have had no trouble securing engagements, for her books and articles had kept her name well before the American public. But she no longer had the strength or the courage for the strenuous life of the theatre. During the last three years she had coughed from the time she left Astoria in the fall until she returned again in the summer. The Richmond climate had been as bad for her as for Margaret Grey whom she had mistakenly thought it would help. Her powers of recuperation had also greatly diminished, so the theatre was really out of the question. But she thought that by living quietly in some mild climate she could manage to eke out an existence with her pen. All she wanted now of life was the freedom to think and to believe as she pleased.

This was what she had well in mind before Foushee reached

Paris, early in March 1861. What happened during the next weeks is not known. Ritchie came abroad with the definite expectation of taking her back with him; otherwise he would not have risked the trip when he did. Lincoln's election had made it obvious that war was on the way. By March 1, it was only a question of where the first gun would be fired. Ritchie, as a journalist and an ardent Southerner, would have an important rôle to play in the moulding of public opinion, and he was not a man to shirk this sort of responsibility. That is why, when his wife made it at last clear that she meant to have nothing more to do with him, and probably told him the real reason, he wasted no time but took the next ship back to America. He reached Richmond just before the attack began on Fort Sumter.

Lily remained in Paris through the winter of 1861 and into the following summer. It was a very quiet time. The war had sent most of the American colony home; the remainder was split into two camps. So Lily stayed close to the Smyths and saw few people. However, two friendships were made during this winter that meant much to her for the rest of her life. One of these was with Douglas Home, the spiritualist, a quite extraordinary man.

Home was a Scot by birth but had spent his youth in America. When he was about twenty he revealed remarkable gifts as a medium. This was during the '40's when spiritualism was beginning to grip the imagination of the country, and mediums were springing up everywhere. But Home from the beginning was different from the ordinary table-rapper. He was a man of some education, breeding, and reticence. He did little to exploit his peculiar endowments; yet these inevitably became known and he was forced willy-nilly to become a professional medium. Samuel Ogden met him at this time and conceived a warm admiration for him. Then Home went abroad and on to a career which placed him at the very top of his profession. The story of his later life forms one of the most fascinating chapters in the history of spiritualism, and if the cult continues to engage the attention of many sober-minded individuals it is in great part because of the record of Douglas Home. The feats performed by or "through" Home sound like the wildest fantasy even to those familiar with the claims of spiritualists, for they can be ex-

plained on none of the usual grounds. He was among other
things a levitationist, and his accomplishments in this highly
specialized field are not easily dismissed. He could, and apparently
did, rise from recumbent, sitting or standing positions and float
for several minutes at a time about a large room, with his hair
just grazing the ceiling. Once, in the presence of unimpeachable
British witnesses—one of them a high lord of the realm—he
ascended from a reclining position on a table, hovered in the
air for a moment or two, then floated easily out of one second-
story window and back into the room through another. With
this sort of performance to his credit it is small wonder that he
should have attracted a distinguished clientele. Among his admirers there was none more devoted than his Imperial Majesty,
Czar Alexander II of Russia.

When Lily came upon Home again in Paris in 1861 he had
just returned from a sojourn of several years in St. Petersburg,
heavily decorated by his imperial patron and married to the
daughter of a Russian nobleman. Long ago Lily had become
interested in spiritualism because it seemed to confirm through
actual demonstration Swedenborg's doctrine of the materiality
of spirits. Perhaps she consulted Home professionally at this
time when she so needed strength for her new start in life and the
two people who had unfailingly given it to her before, James
and her father, were now in the spirit world. In any event
throughout the winter of 1860-61 she was a frequent visitor
at the Home's charming house near the Etoile and became much
attached to Mrs. Home and their little boy, Sacha.

The other friendship which brightened this Paris season was
with a Mrs. Perdicaris and her son Ion, a warm-hearted, brilliant
boy of sixteen whose name was later to be familiar to everyone
who could read a newspaper. In 1904, Ion Perdicaris, then living
in Morocco, was captured by the bandit Raisuli and held for
$50,000 ransom. The abduction made an international incident.
The Sultan of Morocco was held responsible for the crime and
Theodore Roosevelt sent battleships and a contingent of marines
to stimulate the Sultan to action. The phrase contained in Secretary Hay's telegram to the Sultan, "Perdicaris alive or Raisuli
dead!" is well-remembered by our fathers and grandfathers.

No one in Paris in 1861 could have foreseen that young Ion Perdicaris would play a bit, albeit a dramatic one, in American diplomatic history. He was then only a delightful lad, gifted in music and painting, who was spending the winter in Europe with his mother. Ion's father, a Greek, had been at one time a professor at Harvard. The family were old acquaintances of Thomas Ritchie, and it may have been during Foushee's visit in Paris that Anna Cora met them. She and Ion soon became fast friends. The imaginative sixteen-year old boy with his cosmopolitan background and eager curiosity about life appealed to Lily. And Ion found in the beautiful Mrs. Ritchie with her quick sympathy, her understanding of youth, her rich and exciting past, the ideal of his adolescent dreams of womanhood. They spent long hours talking together and exploring odd corners of Paris which Lily made doubly fascinating by her inexhaustible background of information and her appreciation of French life. The disparity of their ages made little difference. Ion's precocious mind and Lily's never-failing sense of the freshness of life made a bridge that easily spanned the years between them.

But for all the happiness brought by new-found friends the winter was a hard one for Lily. The climate of Paris was not much better than that of Richmond, and by spring she was ready to seek a haven farther southward. The place to go, everyone said, was Florence, not only because it was warmer but because it was now the center for the international artistic and literary set. Several people whom Anna Cora knew were there. Among others was Mrs. Horatio Greenough, widow of the famous sculptor and one of the Vice-Regents of the Mount Vernon Ladies Association. There were also the American sculptors Hiram Powers and Joel Hart, and a considerable group of English artists and writers including the aging but still sprightly Mrs. Trollope with her sons Anthony and Thomas Adolphus, Walter Savage Landor, Alfred Austin and a dozen others. In Florence against the rich background of past glory, the mid-century artist was seeking inspiration, away from the soot and grime that was settling over the rest of the world. For Lily, who also needed inspiration, Florence seemed the ideal spot.

She had no reason to regret her decision. She arrived in Florence in June, and within a short time she was on friendly if not intimate terms with most of the literati and many members of the American colony which—considering that the war was now raging—was surprisingly large.

She had begun a novel in Paris but had made little headway. She worked at this all through the Florentine summer. The heat, under which everybody else wilted, she found delicious after the damp, chill months in France, and her imagination, which had but fluttered and drooped in Paris, now took new life and fairly soared.

This book was to be called *Fairy Fingers* in reference to its heroine, an expert needlewoman, who defied the conventions of her milieu and opened a dressmaking shop. It was of course Lily's standard theme. With the exception of Evelyn all her heroines were girls who had to work for a living. This was one subject she could handle with indisputable authority.

By late autumn the novel was half-finished and Lily was seemingly in better health than she had known for years. The climate was partly responsible, but more important were the congenial surroundings and the fact that she was busy. "To be able to work on and on," she had once written Annie Frobisher, "What unalloyed, what unspeakable joy!"

But in November *Fairy Fingers* came to an abrupt halt. Lily had reached the end of her money. Her dream of making her way as a newspaper writer had not materialized. Except for a few letters to *The New York Ledger,* she had had no luck in placing her work. With everything so upset in America it was difficult to establish contacts with editors, and she realized thus late that she would have to go home and make arrangements in person. When that was done she would come back to Florence and really settle down. In December she sent Renshaw back to England for a long-promised visit, and bravely faced the mid-winter Atlantic.

Although the need for money was acute, this was not all that drew Anna Cora back to America. Like so many other expatriates she had come at last to realize the significance of the war. When the fighting first broke out she was too involved in her personal difficulties to understand its seriousness. But now with the battle line stretched clear across the country and with hundreds of thousands of men in uniform, she began to grasp the magnitude of the struggle. At least four of her nephews, Charlotte's sons, were fighting (all four would lose their lives before the war was over), and she felt that she must be on hand to take some share of the burden under which her country and her loved ones were laboring.

Shortly after New Year's, 1862, Anna Cora was in New York, welcomed joyfully by her family and friends who had begun to think she was lost to them forever. And it was almost as a stranger that Lily returned to the city of her childhood. It is true that while she lived in Richmond she had spent her summers on Long Island, but during the warm months most of the people she knew were away. Now everybody was in New York and she was besieged with invitations. She was astonished to find how little the war affected social activities and she noted with distaste the lavish scale on which people were living. The war had produced a whole new crop of millionaires whose extravagances made those of the *nouveau-riches* whom she had satirized in *Fashion*, nearly twenty years before, seem trifling.

New Yorkers rediscovered in Anna Cora a personality made all the more alluring by the years of semi-obscurity in which she had lived away from them. The stories of her romantic past were revived which added color. If anyone now remembered that she had once been ostracized for conduct unbecoming to a lady, it was with a laugh and a shrug at one's own naiveté. Since that far-off day Mrs. Mowatt Ritchie had become an international celebrity, a fact which people had almost forgotten but which, with Lily again vividly present, came suddenly back to mind.

The never-ending marvel was that after so many years her beauty seemed untouched. The little lines about her mouth and eyes were scarcely noticeable and merely added a note of wisdom and experience to the candor of her glance. Though the arch of her high-bridged nose was a little more pronounced, her skin had

retained its youthful purity and creamy pallor, heightened sometimes by a faint flush. Her rich auburn hair, perhaps a shade more
pronounced in color, was still worn low about her shoulders.
She was thinner now, but her figure always attracted attention
and her movements had lost none of their young girl's grace. A
single word of contemporary description sums up Lily's appearance at forty-two. In February, 1862, she went to a dinner-party
at the house of Charles Strong, whose wife was a girlhood friend.
Strong's cousin, George Templeton Strong, son-in-law of Samuel
Ruggles, noted the occasion in his diary and listed among the
guests General Burnside and "gorgeous Mrs. Ritchie."

But dinner-parties were only incidental to Lily's life in war-
time New York. She lived with her sister Louisa, happily sharing
the Turners' family and social life, but she kept faithfully to her
work routine. After many delays *Fairy Fingers* was finished, and
she had also written a number of newspaper articles. Her hope
somehow to aid the Union cause had been rather frustrated;
for outside of nursing, which she was not strong enough to undertake, there seemed little a woman could do. Once in a while
her name appeared in the papers in connection with some bazaar
or benefit where beauty and charm might be expected to stimulate interest. In April, 1864, she was active in the great Sanitary
Fair, the historic display that led to a revolutionized Army Medical Corps; she presided over the Floral Temple. Here George T.
Strong again saw her "in full-blown splendour." Otherwise her
patriotic efforts were confined to picking lint with her sister
Louisa and her friends, and writing letters to her soldier nephews.

She was not anxious to incur publicity. She was still married
to a Southerner and she felt that conspicuous activity in behalf
of the Union would make the separation from her husband seem
more definitive than she wished it to appear.

So far as her friends were concerned there was no question
about Anna Cora's position. The accepted story was that she had
been abroad when war broke out and had been unable to return
to Richmond before communication with the South was closed.
It was also understood that she and her husband held different
views on slavery, but no one considered this cause for a per-

manent breach. When the war was over the slavery question would be settled for the Ritchies as for everybody else, and she would then of course return to her husband. It was a perfectly satisfactory explanation, serving both patriotism and propriety.

This was the way Lily wished it. Her attitude toward her marriage may seem ambiguous, but in the light of her character it was wholly logical. Wild horses could not have dragged her back to Foushee; yet to have this known, more particularly to have the real reason for the separation known, would have been a mortal humiliation.

But her situation was not easy. It was galling to stand somewhat aloof from a cause in which her faith was centered, for the sake of appearances necessary to her pride. As the months passed she found the nervous tension increasing, and this was aggravated by serious illness. After the second winter she found that she could no longer endure the cold of New York. Though in the spring of 1864 she had presented an appearance of "full-blown splendour," actually she was still recovering from the worst in the long series of crises in her illness. But the recovery was slow and neither Lily nor her brother-in-law and physician, Dr. William Turner, had any illusions about her condition. It was obvious that if she wished to live she must find a milder climate. Since for a Northerner in 1864 Italy offered about the most accessible escape from the rigors of winter, it was decided that she should return to Florence.

There had been some changes for the better in her fortunes. Her father's estate had been settled and she was in possession of a few thousand dollars. She continued to receive something in royalties from her books, and she had hopes of more from this source. *Fairy Fingers* had been accepted for publication by Carleton and was now in Epes Sargent's hands for editing. When it was definitely settled that she would return to Europe, she made arrangements with papers in New York, Boston, Baltimore and Philadelphia to write regular reports from Florence. Thus she sailed from America in the summer of 1864 as a full-fledged foreign correspondent, one of the first women in this field.

Back in Florence, Lily was again a leading spirit in the

pleasant group of artists and writers who were devoting their energies to the study of Renaissance masters and the exploration of by-ways of Florentine history. Soon, she too was immersed in the plots of Guelphs and Ghibellines, and her newspaper articles were liberally sprinkled with poisoned cardinals and strangled lovers.

Now that she was actually making some money, she rented a charming house on the Piazza Bellosguardo with a magnificent view of the city. The Villa del Ombrellino, so-named because of an umbrella-shaped summerhouse perched on a high corner of the terrace, once belonged to Galileo, and thus had picturesque associations which Lily turned into copy. From the terrace she watched the great flood of the Arno in November 1864, faithfully reporting the event to her American readers.

In Florence that winter a long-suppressed urge to return to the stage found release. Lily played Lady Teazle in an amateur production of *The School for Scandal*, given for charity. This was a far cry from the Olympic and Niblo's, but it was a taste of the theatre and she felt as she reported to friends, "greater power" than ever before. During the winter she organized a little group called the Dramatic Drawing Room which performed frequently before an appreciative English-speaking audience. Arthur Vansittart acted as impresario for the troupe and Lily directed. In what must have been a truly memorable performance of *The Rivals*, Mrs. Trollope played Mrs. Malaprop to the Bob Acres of her son Thomas Adolphus. To have seen Mrs. Trollope on the stage at any time would have been diverting. But the impression she made on this occasion, when she was seventy-odd, was surely unique. Anna Cora described her at this time, or a little later, as having "entirely lost her memory—not precisely her reason—but certainly her intelligence."

The high point of the Dramatic Drawing Room's season was a production of *Fashion* at the Cocomero Theatre under Lily's direction. It was a gala evening. The house was crowded with a brilliant international audience, and in the royal box sat the Crown Prince of Savoy and his suite.

There were other delights in Florence. After her daily writing stint which nothing was allowed to interrupt, Anna Cora would often join her Bohemian friends for picnics at Fiesole or Poggia. Once with Joel Hart and a party of sculptors and painters she visited the quarries at Saravezza. There in the ateliers she saw scores of artisans at work on the largest order the marble works had ever received, the carved decorations for the new opera house in Paris. Later the excursionists went down to the beach to marvel at the vast array of statues and columns and caryatids lying helter-skelter on the shingle waiting for vessels to take them to France.

Sometimes on warm spring evenings there would be impromptu concerts on the terrace of the Villa del Ombrellino. These were popular gatherings which Lily usually turned to the advantage of some young unknown musician who would be given a chance to perform before a discriminating and influential audience.

Best of all in Florence was the talk. There were so many fascinating personalities with so many things to say! Yet it was not only the flow of wit and ideas from men like Landor and Dobson and Powers that Anna Cora found stimulating. She took pleasure in calling on old Mrs. Trollope with whom it was practically impossible to converse in any normal fashion since that lady now dwelt almost entirely in a world of her own invention. She happily discussed books that had never been written, plays that had never been seen, and even *objets d'art* which presumably decorated her room but were invisible to all eyes save hers. Sometimes she would want to read Lily a passage from a particularly interesting work and would ask to have the book taken from the shelf and handed to her. As both book and shelf were non-existent this was a little disconcerting. Yet Lily admired her always, and though only a shadow of the once sparkling personality still remained she still radiated the kindliness that had won Lily more than twenty-five years before.

Shortly after Anna Cora's return to Florence Mrs. Perdicaris and her son Ion arrived. The boy Lily had grown fond of in Paris was a young man now, good-looking, serious-minded and as devoted as when they had parted five years ago. He was constantly at the Villa where his talents as a pianist were in much demand for the impromptu concerts. He too was interested in Florentine antiquity, and this provided additional ground of common interest to the friendship.

Among the friends Lily had made in Florence there was an American family, a mother and several daughters. Mrs. Matteini had formerly been Madame de Karajan and before that Mrs. Winchester. All three names were current among her children, but it was the oldest girl, Charlotte Winchester, who became Lily's particular pet. For Charlotte she exerted the same kind of spell that had attracted Annie Frobisher to her. Even at forty-five Lily could give herself unreservedly when her sympathies were touched. Her idealism and her still remarkable innocence made her a magnet for younger people. They wrapped her in a warm blanket of affection that tempered the chill of her later days.

Even now the chill was beginning to be felt. It was not only in the sharp winter wind from the Apennines which whistled through the warped window frames of the Villa and kept Lily huddled at the charcoal brazier in her room. Down inside she felt a congealing of her spirits. Except with her young friends, Charlotte and Ion, it was sometimes difficult to keep up the flow of bright talk that people found so enchanting. And the same thing was true when she wrote. It was a struggle to find ideas which once had gushed up in an unmanageable spate.

Despite her varied activities, by the end of the winter of 1864-65 Anna Cora had the sense that she was marking time while life with gathering momentum slipped past. Even Florence for all its beguiling charm seemed a backwash, and she felt a sharp urgency to recover the main stream before it was too late. Too late! That was the refrain that sounded often in the back of her consciousness now. It was most insistent when some slight physical effort sent her into a paroxysm of coughing, or when, for apparently no reason, she began to run a temperature and the doctor ordered her to bed for days. Then she would lie staring at the dim peeling frescoes on the high ceiling and think of how much she must still accomplish, of how much she still had to give —if only she were not so tired and if the pain in her throat, which had been a torment all winter, would cease.

Suddenly when warm weather came it seemed as if her life

might once again take a spectacular upward curve. In the summer of 1865, it was widely reported in the American press that Mrs. Mowatt Ritchie was returning to the stage and would be seen in Boston the following season.

The rumor was not without foundation. The details of what occurred are given by Anna Cora in a letter to Miss Sarah Tracy, secretary of the Mount Vernon Ladies Association. No one greeted the news of Mrs. Ritchie's prospective return to America with greater joy than the Regent of the Association and her faithful assistant, Miss Tracy. The Association had almost disintegrated during the war and Miss Tracy fully appreciated the effect of Mrs. Ritchie in reviving interest, if she were to be available. With difficulty Miss Tracy located Mrs. Ritchie's address (Mr. Ritchie did not seem to have it) and wrote for verification of the newspaper reports. Anna Cora's answer came from London and told the whole story:

> 3 Gloucester Terrace
> Campden Hill
> Bayswater Road—W
> London
> December 18, 1865

Dear Miss Tracy,

I was truly glad a few days ago, to receive your [letter] of November 22 and its valued enclosure from Miss Cunningham.

I will briefly explain the reports which gave rise to the newspaper articles that led you with error concerning my movements. It was well known that my husband lost everything through the war. The manager of the Boston Theatre who was traveling in Europe to secure attractions came to Florence and called on me, and offered me a contract to secure me $25,000 if I would engage with him for eight months and $50,000 if I would engage for sixteen, allowing me the four intervening summer months for rest. Of course the offer was very tempting, and everyone knows I am devoted to my profession. But the state of my health rendered my accepting it impossible. My physician who chanced to be present told the manager so and also that it would be even impossible owing to the nature of my ailments for me to undergo a *sea-voyage*. The manager still urged me—would not take no for an answer—and afterwards wrote to me. The report spread that I had accepted although from the first I had *definitely declined*. I was also in correspondence with other managers, and if my health had permitted I should have been willing to play an engagement in London. But I fell ill, seriously ill as soon as I reached here, and have not left my room for two months, convalescing very, very slowly. The climate is too severe for me—though it is as mild as that of Richmond, and therefore I hoped that I could endure it. I am not even able to endure the fatigue of the journey back to Italy—which is urgently recommended and besides I am engaged as London correspondent for American papers, and am not able to afford giving the employment up. You may imagine that I smiled somewhat in sad surprise when I read your felicitations on my good health. I so long to be well—and have been ill so terribly long—Last winter I was able to play for Charities several times in Florence, but this has been the nearest approach to returning to my profession. . . .

The barrier of the ocean between me and my country is one that there is no hope of my being able to pass until there is a very great physical change in my condition. Virginia ought to have a representative who is on the spot, and I now feel it my duty to make room for her—though with great regret.

My address, Dear Miss Tracy, *is to be for a few months as above*—but care of Baring Brothers London, will always be forwarded to me if I have left London.

Accept my hearty good wishes and sympathy with all your labors. I am writing in a very suffering state—my throat causing me incessant pain.

Yours with true regard
Anna Cora Ritchie

It is not difficult to picture the effect of the offer of $50,000 on Lily in the depressed state of her spirits. It must have given her a sense of exaltation, even though she was made to see at once that the glittering prospect could not be realized. But the idea that she could still command attention and a salary equal to that of any star on the American stage, acted as a powerful stimulus to her will-power. Though she did not dare risk crossing the Atlantic, she determined to go to London to see if she could obtain an engagement there.

In the spring, shortly after the Boston offer had been made and refused, she wrote to her old friend William Chippendale, whom she had not seen or heard from in more than ten years, but who she knew was now stage manager at the Haymarket in London.

> My dear Mr. Chippendale—
>
> I hope the lapse of a few years will not render it difficult for you to call to mind an old friend, and that "Adam Trueman" has not forgotten the author of "Fashion", or "Sir Peter Teazle" the "Lady Teazle" whom he used to astonish in her young days by calling her "a brick". (That being the first time she had ever heard that expressive appellation). . . .

She briefly reviewed the past few years of her life, mentioning the fact that her husband had lost everything and that "this cruel war has separated us for the last four years." (Lily was still anxious to keep up the fiction of a happy marriage.) She told Chippendale all about her acting in the English Dramatic Drawing Room, and then boldly announced her intention of coming to London to seek an engagement. "My experiment here has made me feel that my artistic powers have matured and increased —not diminished, and the Florentine correspondents of the 'Morning Post' and 'Star' give their verdict that *Time* has dealt generously with my physique." She hastened to add, however: "I should hesitate to speak thus frankly were I not writing a letter of business." She begged Chippendale to send his advice at once and mentioned the fact that she "would rather not play juvenile *business.*"

As usual Lily had not only herself on her mind. She also informed Chippendale that there was a beautiful young girl of eighteen whom she had been training and who had acted in Florence. In addition to talent, Lily declared, she had "an exquisite figure" and "a most beautiful voice." Her father was an English writer residing in Florence (the girl was probably the daughter of Thomas Adolphus Trollope), and she really gave great promise. There was also a young gentleman who wished to become a professional actor. He was "exceedingly handsome," fenced and danced to perfection, and had "a superb wardrobe." Chippendale's reply has not come to light, but it may be assumed that he let her down tactfully. After all London was not Boston. When W. C. Jarrett, manager of the Boston Theatre, made his offer in Florence he realized that no foreign star would draw Boston audiences as well as Mrs. Mowatt Ritchie, whose name was legendary in the city where she had appeared so many times and where she had so many connections. But this was not the case in London where Lily had appeared only for three brief, if brilliant, seasons and then completely vanished from the scene. Yet Chippendale did what he could. He discussed the matter of an engagement with Buckstone, manager of the Haymarket, who showed no interest. A memorandum, presumably in Buckstone's handwriting, is sufficiently explicit: "As regards the Haymarket, Mrs. Ritchie would be of no use." But ironically, as the same source indicates, there was a possibility for the young gentleman with the "superb wardrobe", and "if the young lady is all as described I might manage for her".

With no prospect of success Lily nevertheless made up her mind that she would defy the gods once more and come on to London anyway. It was a fatal move. As the letter to Miss Tracy shows she became ill almost as soon as she arrived. Even if she had received an offer from a theatre she could not have accepted it.

The desperate gamble had been taken and lost. But Lily was too proud to admit this. She wrote to her friends that she came to London to be near pubilshers. Perhaps she hoped to write eventually for English newspapers but her work at the moment was appearing only in American publications, including the newly-founded *San Francisco Chronicle*.

She found London terribly expensive after Florence and almost at once began to feel the pinch. Though her newspaper work paid fairly well, she seldom realized the full amounts remitted to her. The absence of a fixed rate of exchange for the dollar often resulted in ruinous loss. One remittance of $400 from *The Philadelphia Home Weekly* netted her less than £50 when it was discounted by the bank.

To increase her earnings she gave elocution lessons. But these soon had to be abandoned. The nervous tension of the effort to teach expression to the stolid daughters of prosperous Kensington tradesmen was too much for her. Besides, the pain in her throat made any attempt to use her own voice a torture. So writing remained the only resource.

But discouragement did not make Anna Cora less productive. During the first weeks in London when she was bed-ridden and suffering excruciating pain she began a novel. Indeed it was the condition of her own throat that set her going. *The Mute Singer*, as the new story was to be called, dealt with the psychological phenomenon of a young girl who had lost the power of speech because of a throat ailment but under certain conditions, obviously highly dramatic, could still sing, and in the end triumphed over her handicap.

Her own wretchedness could not prevent her from helping others. During the latter part of this first London winter Lily shared her little flat on Campden Hill with the young friend of Richmond days, Avonia Jones. The girl had fully justified her expectations and had won success on the stage both in America and in England. In 1863 Avonia had married Gustavus Brooke, the brilliant tragedian with whom Lily and Davenport had starred at the Olympic in 1848. Though the couple were deeply in love, it had been a heart-breaking marriage. Brooke was a heavy drinker and Avonia had had to rescue him from one desperate situation after another. Finally Brooke in an effort to make a new start accepted an engagement in Australia, leaving Avonia in England to join him later. Avonia was at the dock when he sailed from Liverpool in January 1866. That was her last glimpse of him. Four days later the ship, the *City of London*, went down in the Bay of Biscay. There were a few survivors but Brooke was not among them. There had been only two serviceable life-boats and Brooke had given up his place to some one else.

When Lily found Avonia the girl was prostrated with grief. She and Renshaw, who had joined her again, pulled Avonia through the first effects of the shock, but it was only a partial recovery. In the spring Avonia accepted an acting engagement in the provinces, following Lily's advice that only work would help her to endure, but before the year was over she died. Thus another loved one joined the angelic throng of which Lily herself now dreamed so often.

Work on *The Mute Singer* lasted through the summer and fall of 1866, and in January of 1867 the manuscript went off to Carleton in New York. Anna Cora hoped it would do better than *Fairy Fingers* which for all its modern theme of the independent, emancipated woman, had not greatly taken. *The Mute Singer* had been uphill work, not only because her imagination was sluggish but because it was now almost impossible to keep to a fixed routine. Once five hours of steady writing had been a normal assignment; now if she sat at her desk for two hours she was exhausted. On the days that she was forced to keep to her bed she was too weak to write at all.

By spring of 1867 it was evident that even a modest London flat was beyond her means, and that if she was to live without appealing to the charity of her sisters—a thought which had begun to haunt her—she must cut expenses. That summer she and Renshaw moved out to Henley and lived in furnished rooms. Here in the clearer air and almost rural quiet, with the Regatta providing just the right flutter of worldly excitement, Lily got back a little strength.

In the middle of the summer Ion Perdicaris appeared. He would have come sooner, but he had been detained in Florence by the illness of his mother. Mrs. Perdicaris was dead now and Ion was alone in the world with a small independent fortune. The Perdicaris family had many connections in London and the handsome young bachelor with his graceful manners and ready wit was soon immersed in the life of a popular man-about-town. But not wholly immersed. He came regularly three or four times a week to Henley to talk with Lily and give her the latest London gossip and news of the theatre. These reports were a god-send, since Lily's editors in America had informed her some time before that they preferred up-to-date news of London doings rather than Florentine reminiscences. Only rarely could Lily get to town and she was almost wholly dependent on friends for information.

Life was gayer too with Ion on hand, and when he took her

arm and they walked slowly along the river the burden of years, which in these last months had begun to weigh on her, seemed lighter. She never questioned Ion's reasons for coming to England, as she had never questioned any one's feelings for her. It was enough that he cared for her and that he was near at hand.

That summer she experienced a resurgence of optimism. Who knew but what in the proper atmosphere she might not get better after all? At Henley she was able to increase her output of newspaper articles and earn a little more money. On the strength of this she decided to take a house and settle down permanently in the country, somewhere within easy reach of London. Memories of twenty years before drew her towards Richmond. For several afternoons she explored the neighborhood in a carriage with Ion and finally she found exactly what she wanted. The house was a tiny, yellow-brick villa with a little garden. It was located on the Heathcote Road in St. Margaret's Wood, just at the edge of Twickenham. From the river, which was only a few hundred yards from the garden gate, she could see Richmond; and in the other direction, across soft green meadow-land, the view extended clear to Kew. The house was less than a mile from the cottage where she had spent the never-to-be forgotten summer of 1850.

Her favorite spot became the river bank. Here in fine weather she would spend hours writing, or looking out over the water and listening to the happy voices from drifting punts. When Ion came out they sat here together. But often she sat alone for hours, unmindful of the time until Renshaw came hurrying down the path with coats and shawls to scold her for staying so long in the damp air.

She soon became acquainted with her next-door neighbor, Lady Cecil Gordon, an invalid like herself. Before the winter was over the two were firm friends. On Sunday evenings they dined regularly together, the state of their healths permitting, each acting alternately as hostess to the other.

Lily still worked faithfully, but she could no longer push herself. She managed to meet her newspaper commitments, and she had thoughts of another novel. Yet she could not quite make the effort to begin it. During the winter of 1868 she gathered together some of the essays written eight years before for *The New York Ledger*, and these were published by Carleton in 1869 under the title *The Clergyman's Wife and Other Sketches*. Except for a collection of her articles on Italy, published posthumously by her sister May, this was Anna Cora's last book.

A frequent visitor at Twickenham was Douglas Home, who was also living in England now. Home was a lonely man; his wife was dead and his psychic powers had completely gone. There seemed to be nothing he could turn his hand to, although fortunately he had saved some money and was not in want. His little boy, Sacha, was in a boarding-school not far away, and he too came frequently to see Lily. In the autumn of 1869 the child fell seriously ill, and when she heard the news Lily sent Ion to bring him to Twickenham. Under Renshaw's able nursing, with Lily supervising, the boy soon recovered, but he did not return to the school. His presence added such a happy note to the household that Lily could not part with him, and Home agreed to let him stay on the rest of the winter with her. He was a talented youngster with a gift for acting, and Lily planned to train him for a brilliant career on the stage.

She managed at least to maintain the illusion that she was busy, though it was hardly more than that. She could seldom be up for a whole day, and during the last winter she was unable to leave her room for weeks on end. Yet she could not relinquish her hold on life, and her interest in others—Sacha, Ion, Home, Renshaw— was as keen as ever. But her world was rapidly growing smaller.

In December she saw in the London papers that Mrs. Margaret Jean Lander would shortly open a season at the Lyceum. The name brought a flood of memories. Mrs. Lander had been Jean Davenport, the young star whose refusal to accept Mr. Bates's offer in St. Louis back in 1852 had so excited that gentleman's indignation. But Mrs. Lander was remembered in another connection. She was a staunch supporter of the Mount Vernon Ladies Association and had given several benefits for the Cause. Lily had met her in Richmond and had been captivated by her charm and public-spiritedness. At the outbreak of the war she had married General Lander of the Union Army and retired from the stage. Her husband had been killed in action and Mrs. Lander spent the remainder of the war as a nurse, rendering valiant service. When peace came she returned to the stage and was now back in England, her native country, which she had not seen since childhood. She had a solid reputation behind her and had long ago lived down the ignominy of having been the original of Dickens's Ninetta Crummles, the "Infant Phenomenon."

Anna Cora sent a note of eager welcome to Mrs. Lander, wishing her success for her opening at the Lyceum: "How I wish I could be there to cheer you on by hearty applause—and there is nothing like someone to lead the applause."

In the same letter she expressed the hope that Mrs. Lander would come to see her. She explained that she was an invalid and almost never went out, but added quickly, in case Mrs. Lander should think she was lonely, "My friends are good enough to come to see me, so that I see a good deal of society in spite of my invalidism." And as a special lure she threw out—"I am London correspondent of American papers and I shall not fail to make such mention as you could wish of your engagement here."

Lily was stretching a point when she spoke of seeing a good deal of society. Except for Ion, Home, Lady Gordon and two or three old friends who occasionally came out from London, she saw almost no one. She had been content to have it so. For several months now she had known that she was near her last turning and she wished to go quietly, without worldly distractions. Then, learning of Mrs. Lander's presence in London, everything had changed. She felt a wild yearning to reëstablish contact with the world, and the life in which she had once been important. Mrs. Lander provided the first real link with the past, Lily's own great past, since the war, and she grasped eagerly for it.

Mrs. Lander was of course very busy. No one knew better than Mrs. Ritchie how demanding, how time-consuming life in the theatre was. But she would be glad to come to Richmond when she was a little more settled and the weather was better. Her mother was with her, and it would give them both pleasure to see Mrs. Ritchie again. Meanwhile she would be so happy if Mrs. Ritchie would come to see her at the Lyceum.

So Lily, who had not gone out in the evening for months, managed to get into London two or three times to see Mrs. Lander act. She also sent all her friends to the Lyceum, for the truth was that Mrs. Lander's engagement was not going well. This worried Lily and made her indignant, though there was nothing to do about the tastes of the British public. So long as the pantomime was on, the legitimate theatres would remain half empty. But February came and though the pantomime was long past, business at the Lyceum was still not what one had hoped. After witnessing the thin house at one of Mrs. Lander's performances Lily wrote urging her to resort to "papering" (distributing free tickets); one simply could not do one's best to empty seats. "I know this is what your father would have done," she declared, well remembering the promotional devices to which the parent of the Infant Phenomenon had resorted in the first wane of his offspring's popularity.

Late in January she wrote Mrs. Lander: "If you have a box to spare *so near* the stage as to render a floral *toss* possible please send it to me for Saturday next." Mrs. Lander obligingly forwarded the tickets and on Saturday, though she had been very ill all week and scarcely had the strength to stand, she struggled into an evening gown and with Renshaw and Ion took the train into London to see the star perform in *Mary Stuart*. She made Ion purchase a large bouquet at a florist's on the way. It was an excitingly happy evening. In the stage box Lily was just above the footlights, and all through the performance she kept remembering what it meant to have that protective wall of dazzling flame rising between oneself and the strange cold world where other people lived.

When the play ended and it was time for Ion to throw the bouquet it was discovered that the flimsy florist's cord holding it together had disintegrated. Ion was in a panic for fear of strewing the flowers wildly over the stage, but Anna Cora with great presence of mind snatched a long tassel from the draperies of the box and quickly unraveling it produced a piece of solid string.

Afterwards they all went to Mrs. Lander's dressing-room to congratulate her, and again Lily mentioned the long-promised visit. The actress assured her that she would positively come and a time was set for the following week, providing, of course, that the weather was good.

The weather was lovely. Every afternoon the tea-table with Lily's best Florentine cloth was set up in the bay-window overlooking the Heathcote Road, and Lily sat so that she could see when the carriage drove up from Twickenham station. But though the fine weather lasted all week Mrs. Lander did not come. On Saturday Lily sent her a little note. "I looked for you on the sunny days in vain:—I hoped you would come early, the sunshine passes away so soon."

Again Mrs. Lander promised to come, and again the visit was put off. March came and Lily was so ill that she could see no one. By the end of the month she had rallied a little, and then she was frantic for fear that she might not see Mrs. Lander at all since it was announced that the season at the Lyceum was about to end. Once more, this time with a hand that wavered, she wrote:

March 29, 1870

My dear Friend

The days are slipping away—you are going soon—I am still desperately ill, and the doctor declares I *shall not* see visitors until I am much better for it is retarding my recovery—but I must disobey him:—I *must* see you.—and your mother, I hope. You must not mind my cough—sometimes I do not cough for a couple of hours.—then cough for an hour without cessation.— You may fall upon the happy rest. Then come *when you can*, doctors notwithstanding. If you can write and tell me *when* so much the better,—If that is inconvenient take your chance,— I do not care, so that I am secure of seeing you. This month of March always was fatal to me,—April may bring a change. I am so grieved that you must go—I had set my heart upon your having a theatre in London and giving England *legitimate* acting.—Kind regards to your mother—Even the effort to write this note exhausts me.

Affectionately
AC Ritchie

Did Mrs. Lander finally get to St. Margaret's Wood? We have no record of the long-awaited visit. One can only hope that it took place, even though for Mrs. Lander it doubtless represented an ordeal, since there is nothing more wearing for an actor harassed by the problems of the present than to listen to another actor talk about the past. And Anna Cora wanted so much to talk a little about the past. It was what made the future important, and the dead waste of the present bearable.

April did not bring the expected change for the better, nor did May. Lily was too weak now even to come downstairs. The intervals of coughing increased, and the periods of rest became periods of exhaustion. One by one the few remaining ties with the world were severed. Douglas Home left London for the North of England, taking little Sacha with him. The few friends from London who had occasionally dropped in on her, stopped coming since she could so rarely see anyone. The little Sunday dinners with Lady Gordon had long since been abandoned.

Only Renshaw and Ion were still regularly on hand. Early in the summer Ion moved out to Twickenham, and he came to the villa every day. Lily could rarely see him, but that did not stop his visits. He would sit in the garden under her window and read, or if the weather was bad Renshaw would give him a cup of tea by the grate-fire in the drawing-room. Lily always knew when he was there, and she would send messages to him by Renshaw. Sometimes she would ask to have him play for her, and he would sit down at the little cottage piano and improvise on themes from Donizetti's *Lucia* or play some of Moore's songs that Lily had loved when she was a young girl. When Renshaw at last came down to say that Mrs. Ritchie was asleep, he would quietly close the piano and slip out of the house, and walk thoughtfully back to Twickenham.

In June Anna Cora had word from Epes Sargent, who was in Cannes. He too was suffering from a throat ailment. The doctors had diagnosed it as chronic bronchitis (actually it proved to be cancer) and had ordered him to a mild climate. But the stay in Cannes had not helped, and as early as March Sargent had written William Cullen Bryant that he had about decided to return to

America. He was thinking of trying Minnesota the next winter, as Bryant had suggested earlier to him; for perhaps it was, after all, a dry climate that he needed.

But he deferred his departure until warm weather, and when he set out for home in July he passed through London to see Lily.

It was a happy meeting. Lily's bed had been drawn up to the window and the two old friends sat in the long summer twilight with the warm scented air from the garden floating up to them. Lily was propped up in bed with the still bright auburn curls spread over the pillow. She had been easier for several days and was able to talk, though it was obvious to Epes that she was dying.

Their talk ranged over all sorts of topics: the theatre, old friends in America, the young people for whom Lily had such high hopes, and those who had gone ahead into the other world on which the curtain was now rapidly rising. Lily was cheerful, and in her faint smile there was still eagerness. Not once did she speak of herself, for she had neither fears nor worries, and she was beyond pain. There was serene confidence in the clear blue eyes.

There was no sadness in their parting, only a wistful sense that when they next met it would be in different surroundings, and that when they again looked together at trees and flowers and flowing water, it would be with different eyes. But they both knew that they would meet again.

That was on the twenty-seventh of July, 1870. Two days later Anna Cora died. She had made one or two special requests and had arranged for the disposition of her few belongings—some things of value to her faithful Renshaw, remembrances for her sisters, for Epes and one or two friends.

Sargent and Ion Perdicaris carried out her final wish. The grave at Kensal Green was opened and she was buried with James.

There was barely space left on the modest stone slab for her name, and the places and dates of her birth and death. In order to make room for the brief epitaph she wanted it was necessary to remove the scriptural passage after James's name. But this did not matter; the words Lily had selected were for them both:

He Giveth His Beloved Rest

A NOTE ON SOURCES

This narrative is drawn principally from Anna Cora Mowatt's letters, her published works (especially *The Autobiography of an Actress,* Boston, 1854), and contemporary press reports. Other important sources are the memoirs of Anna Cora Mowatt by Mary Howitt (in *Howitt's Journal,* March 4, March 11, March 18,—1848) and Bayle Bernard (in *Tallis's Drawing Room Table Book,* London, 1851). The chief reference for the mesmeric experiences is *The Scientific Basis of Spiritualism,* by Epes Sargent, New York, (1882). Details of Anna Cora Mowatt's life in Richmond have been found in "Recollections of a Christian Actress," by Marion Harland (in *Our Continent,* March 15, 1882) and *Marion Harland's Autobiography,* New York (1910). The work of Dr. Marius Blesi, *The Life and Letters of Anna Cora Mowatt* (University of Virginia, 1938), is the most exhaustive treatment of Mrs. Mowatt's literary career to date. There is also important new matter, particularly on Mrs. Mowatt's Richmond life, in Imogene McCarthy's monograph, *Anna Cora Mowatt and Her American Audience* (University of Maryland, 1952). My indebtedness to both these works is indicated in chapter notes.

Background material has been taken mainly from newspapers of the period. I have also found useful information in *The Diary of Philip Hone,* New York (1936) and *The Diary of George Templeton Strong,* New York (1950), both edited by Allan Nevins. In addition, there was helpful matter in *What I Saw in New York,* by Joel H. Ross, M.D., Auburn, N. Y., (1851), *Queens of American Society,* by Mrs. Ellett, New York (1867), *Sunshine and Shadow in New York,* by Matthew Hale Smith, New York (1868), *Last Days of Knickerbocker Life in New York,* by Abram C. Dayton, New York (1897), *New York Old and New, Its Streets and Landmarks,* by Rufus Rockwell Wilson, Philadelphia (1902).

Details of the theatre of the 1840's and 1850's have been taken prin-

cipally from the following works: *Footlight Flashes,* by William
Davidge, New York, (1867), *Before the Footlights and Behind the
Scenes, by Olive Logan,* Philadelphia (1870), *The Amateur and Guide to
the Stage and Reciter's Own Book, etc.,* by "A Retired Performer," Phila-
delphia, n.d. (1850?), *Crotchets and Quavers,* by Max Maretzek, New
York (1855), *Leaves from an Actor's Notebook,* by George Vandenhoff,
New York (1860); *Theatrical Apprenticeship,* by Sol Smith, Phila-
delphia (1846); *Theatrical Management in the South and West for
Thirty Years,* by Sol Smith, New York (1868); *Dramatic Life As I
Found It,* by Noah Miller Ludlow, St. Louis (1880); *Dramatic Authors
of America,* by James Rees, Philadelphia (1845); *Actors and Actresses
of Great Britain and the United States,* by Brander Matthews and
Laurence Hutton, Vol. IV, New York (1886); *Curiosities of the
American Stage,* by Laurence Hutton, New York (1891); *One Man
in His Time, The Adventures of H. Watkins,* edited by Maud and Otis
Skinner, Philadelphia (1938); *Records of the New York Stage* from
1750 to 1860, by John N. Ireland, New York (1866-67); *A History
of the New York Stage from the First Performance in 1732 to 1901,*
by Thomas A. Brown, New York (1903); *History of the American
Stage,* by Thomas A. Brown, New York (1870); *Before and Behind
the Curtain,* by William K. Northall, New York (1851); *Personal
Recollections of the Stage,* by William B. Wood, Philadelphia (1855);
Twenty-Six Years of the Life of an Actor and Manager, by Francis C.
Weymiss, New York (1857); *A Record of the Boston Stage,* by W. W.
Clapp, Jr., Boston (1853); *The Philadelphia Stage. From the Year 1849
to the Year 1855,* by Charles Durang (published in *The Sunday Des-
patch,* Philadelphia, during the years 1854-1860); *Diaries of William
Charles Macready,* London (1912); *The Autobiography of Joseph
Jefferson,* New York (1897); *Memoirs of John E. Owens,* Baltimore
(1892); *William E. Burton,* by William L. Keese, New York (1885);
Memories of Fifty Years, by Lester Wallack, New York (1889);
Theatrical Anecdotes, by Jacob Larwood, London (1882); *The Life
of Gustavus Vaughn Brooke,* by W. J. Laurence, Belfast (1892);
Edward Loomis Davenport, by E. F. Edgett, Dunlap Soc. Pub. Ser. 2,
vol. 14, New York (1901); *Wags of the Stage,* by Joseph Whitton,
Philadelphia (1902); *The American Stage,* by Oral S. Coad and Ed-
ward Mims, Jr., New Haven (1929); *A History of the Philadelphia
Theatre 1835-1855,* by Arthur Herman Wilson, Philadelphia (1935);
Annals of the New York Stage, by George C. D. Odell, vols. 4 and 5,
New York (1931); *A History of the American Drama from the Be-*

ginning of the Civil War, by Arthur Hobson Quinn, New York (1946).
The most important single source for details of the London theatre
of Mrs. Mowatt's time is *Tallis's Dramatic Magazine,* November 1850-
June 1851. There is also valuable data in *Madame Vestris and Her
Times,* by Charles E. Pearce, New York, n.d. (1926) and *London's
Lost Theatres of the Nineteenth Century,* by Erroll Sherson, London
(1932).

Other bibliographical references will be found in the notes which follow.

NOTES

CHAPTER ONE

1. My information on the Reverend Uzal Ogden is taken from *The Ogden
Family in America,* William Ogden Wheeler, compiler, Philadelphia (1907).
2. The rôle of Samuel Ogden in the Miranda expedition is given in detail in
U.S. Court Records, Second Circuit Court of New York, "Trials of Wm. S.
Smith and S. G. Ogden."

CHAPTER TWO

This chapter is based mainly on the memoir of Anna Cora by Mary Howitt.
Her account of the courtship and marriage, for which James Mowatt supplied
the data is more circumstantial than that of the *Autobiography.*

CHAPTER THREE

The description of Melrose is taken from the *Autobiography* with amplifying
details from *A History of Flatbush,* by Gertrude Vanderbilt, New York (1911).

CHAPTER FIVE

The cast of *Gulzara* is from a printed programme of the original production in
the Theatre Collection, Houghton Library, Harvard University.

CHAPTER SIX

My identification of Mrs. Bates has been a matter of deduction. Anna Cora
refers to her only as Mrs. B——s, in the *Autobiography.* However, she fits in all
respects the description as given. Mrs. Bates was in Paris the winter of 1839-40,
and Anna Cora surely met her then. She was a leader of the fashionable society
frequented by Anna Cora and was a dedicated patroness of the arts (though
Anna Cora apparently did not know this at the time). In earlier years Mrs.
Bates had befriended John Howard Payne in London, and it was for her that
Payne composed the additional stanzas to "Home, Sweet Home." Mrs. Bates is

one of the first of that long line of great Boston ladies who have helped to ease the way for American artists.

CHAPTER SEVEN

For the events of this chapter I have drawn on both the *Autobiography* and Epes Sargent's *The Scientific Basis of Spiritualism*. The two accounts of Lily's experience during the winter of 1841-42 are in remarkably close agreement, though Sargent's is more detailed. Sargent identifies William Francis Channing (whom Anna Cora calls Dr. C——g). The episode of the walk in Hoboken and that of the snake are given by Sargent.

In my attempt to present sympathetically the current attitude toward mesmerism I have utilized *Facts in Mesmerism,* by Chauncey Hare Townsend, New York (1841)—the standard authority of the time.

CHAPTER EIGHT

Anna Cora's memory is at fault when she states that *Etiquette of Matrimony* and *Cookery for the Sick* (main title: *Management of the Sickroom*) were written for Stringer and Burgess. Both volumes were produced for Mowatt and Company, and were advertised on the back cover of *The Drawing Room Library,* a copy of which is in the New York Public Library.

CHAPTER NINE

1. The location of the Mowatts' house on Fourth Avenue is established in the letter to Poe quoted in Chapter Ten. If the house was situated "five doors above Twentieth Street" its back garden must have joined that of Mayor Harper's house on Gramercy Park West, as anyone can verify by walking around the block. My supposition is that James and Lily rented the house, probably at a reasonable price, from Samuel Ruggles who owned almost the whole of their block on Fourth Avenue.

2. My reconstruction of mid-century acting and production methods derives from many sources, principally from dramatic criticism of the time. There is much information in Anna Cora's *Mimic Life,* Boston (1856). Indications of stage movements and business in old prompt books have provided further clues. Some of the details have come from word-of-mouth tradition which I absorbed in my young days through association with old actors who were themselves only a generation removed from the theatre of Anna Cora's time. There is no authoritative work on this subject; in fact almost no research has been done in this department of stage history. However, it is quite safe to say that the so-called "burlesques" of old acting techniques which are occasionally seen in revivals of plays of this period bear no faint resemblance to the actual methods of the time. At the mid-nineteenth century, American acting reached its apogee and was closely allied to that other great art of the time—oratory. In both acting and oratory the human voice was the supreme factor. Beauty of tone, flexibility, and expressiveness gave to the spoken language a charm

unknown to the modern stage. It was in consequence of this great stress on the use of the voice that stage movements were more stylized and less casual than in the theatre of our day. Nothing was allowed to interfere with the music and the meaning of the lines, as in opera, still, nothing must interfere with the singing of an aria. As a matter of fact in the early and mid-nineteenth century the line dividing opera and drama was very slight. Plays always had incidental music, dancing, and usually singing of some sort. Many actors of the time were equally at home in the lyric and the spoken drama, and many straight plays were but thinly revamped operas. Calcraft's *The Bride of Lammermoor,* in which Anna Cora had such great success, is a case in point.

CHAPTER TEN

1. The preliminary notice of *Fashion* in *The Spirit of the Times* is quoted from Blesi, *The Life and Letters of Anna Cora Mowatt.*
2. The "eye-witness" of the première of *Fashion* was A. Oakey Hall, whose account of the occasion (from which I have drawn heavily) was published in *The Dramatic Magazine,* Chicago (March 1898).

CHAPTER TWELVE

1. My account of Lily's first experience with make-up is entirely a reconstruction. The details are taken principally form Olive Logan's *Before the Footlights and Behind the Scenes* and *The Amateur's Guide to the Stage, etc.* (anon.).
2. A. Oakey Hall was also present at Anna Cora's début as an actress. The event is described in the article already referred to. The quoted description of Anna Cora's acting is from the same article.

CHAPTER THIRTEEN

1. Anna Cora does not specifically say that she and Crisp never spoke off-stage after the Philadelphia episode. What she states, in the *Autobiography,* is as follows:

> In the course of one long engagement, I nightly enacted the betrothed— the wife, or the daughter—of a gentleman with whom Mr. Mowatt was at variance and to whom I never spoke.

However, since this remark follows a discussion of off-stage relations of actors, which in turn follows a note about difficulties with Crisp, the association of ideas is obvious. Furthermore there was no other actor with whom Lily played a "long engagement" involving the parts she mentions—except Davenport. Since she and Davenport were never anything but the most loyal and devoted of friends, the actor referred to can only have been Crisp.
2. Poe's criticisms of Anna Cora both as actress and writer are reprinted in the Virginia Edition of his works.

CHAPTER FOURTEEN

1. Data on costuming and production methods of the period are taken from

various sources including Davidge's *Footlight Flashes* and *The Amateur's Guide to the Stage, etc.*

2. Details on the St. Charles Theatre are from *The Golden Age of the New Orleans Theatre,* by John S. Kendall, Baton Rouge (1952).

3. The figures for the receipts of Lily's engagement with Vandenhoff are from a memorandum in James Mowatt's handwriting, in the Harvard Theatre Collection.

4. The quotation at the end of the chapter is from Matthews and Hutton, *Actors and Actresses of Great Britain and the United States.*

CHAPTER FIFTEEN

1. Eliza Logan's sequel to Lily's episode with the slave children at Savannah, is related by Olive Logan in *Before the Footlights and Behind the Scenes.*

2. The excerpt from *The Louisville Courier's* comment on Bates is quoted from Blesi, *The Life and Letters of Anna Cora Mowatt.*

3. The note on Sargent at the end of the chapter is from *The Scientific Basis of Spiritualism.*

CHAPTER SIXTEEN

1. The account of Fanny Kemble's engagement at Manchester is given by Davidge in *Footlight Flashes.*

2. Details of the management of the Princess's Theatre are from *Tallis's Dramatic Magazine* and Sherson's *London's Lost Theatres of the Nineteenth Century.*

3. The list of the Howitts' reform aims is quoted from *Victorian Samplers: William and Mary Howitt,* by Carl Ray Woodring.

CHAPTER SEVENTEEN

1. There are numerous references to Anna Cora's gesture towards abolishing the starring system. W. J. Laurence in *The Life of Gustavus Vaughn Brooke* states categorically that she was the first to do so.

2. Anna Cora's own description of the vase (in the *Autobiography*) omits the words on the presentation inscription "by Walter Watts, Esq., lessee and manager of the Theatre Royal, Marylebone." But this is understandable. At the time of writing *The Autobiography of an Actress* Anna Cora naturally wished to avoid reawakening the echoes of her personal connection with Watts.

CHAPTER EIGHTEEN

1. The account of Watts's arrest and trial is taken from contemporary London newspapers (chiefly *The Times*) with the exception of the information on Watts's acquisition of the two shares of Globe Insurance Company stock and the identification of the portrait. These are from Sherson, *London's Lost Theatres of the Nineteenth Century.*

2. The incident of Dr. Westmacott and the Rembrandt head is from a newspaper interview with Fanny Vining, and is given by Epes Sargent in the appendix

to *The Scientific Basis of Spiritualism.* The little picture was attributed to Rubens, an obvious slip.

CHAPTER NINETEEN

1. The two quotations from *The Spirit of the Times* are given in Blesi, *The Life and Letters of Anna Cora Mowatt.*
2. The excerpt from H. Watkins's diary is quoted from *One Man in His Time,* edited by Maud and Otis Skinner.
3. Badeau's encounter with Samuel Ogden is related in his book *The Vagabond,* New York (188–).
4. The presence of Ritchie at Ravenswood during the writing of the *Autobiography* is established by a letter written by Ritchie to his mother at the time (given in Blesi, *op. cit.*).

CHAPTER TWENTY

1. Anna Cora's remark to Marion Harland revealing her longing for children is from "Personal Recollections of a Christian Actress," by Marion Harland.
2. The item on G. P. R. James is from *Anna Cora Mowatt and Her American Audience,* by Imogene McCarthy.
3. The true causes of Anna Cora's separation from Ritchie are given in an autograph memorandum by the late Professor Samuel Williston of the Harvard Law School. Professor Williston was the husband of May Wellman, Matilda's daughter. The memorandum reads: "The anti-slavery agitation before the Civil war, regarding which Mr. and Mrs. R. took opposite views, and (it is family history) overfamiliarity of Mr. R. with colored ladies, led to a separation." Professor Williston's statement was written June 4, 1948 for Mrs. Marian H. Mowatt who was planning a biography of Anna Cora at the time, so the statement was intended for publication. In view of Professor Williston's reputation, I think the story must be fully credited, though I have come across no corroborating evidence.
4. The letter to Samuel Ruggles is quoted from Blesi, *op. cit.*

CHAPTER TWENTY-ONE

1. My evidence for Ritchie's trip to Paris is a statement in Wheeler, *The Ogden Family in America,* and Ritchie's letter to Miss Tracy, asserting his intention of going.
2. Lily's friendship with Charlotte Winchester is told by the latter's granddaughter, Rose S. Hammer, in *A Daughter of Old Firenze,* New York (1926).
3. The death of Gustavus Brooke is based on details in W. J. Laurence, *The Life of Gustavus Vaughn Brooke.*
4. The epitaphs of James and Lily were transcribed from the tombstone at Kensal Green.
5. The account of Lily's last days is mainly from Sargent, *op. cit.*